Praise for *If Mayors Ruled the World*

"Barber provides a provocative look at how cities can and do lead from the front in addressing the most pressing issues of our time."

—**Michael R. Bloomberg,** 108th Mayor of New York City

"Audacious . . . ambitious. . . . Barber's book should be required reading for New York's new mayor, Bill de Blasio."

—**Sam Roberts,** *New York Times Book Review*

"If you like cities you will love this wide-ranging book that captures the energy, excitement, and importance of what is going on in the world's great urban centers."

—**Fareed Zakaria,** *CNN*

"In an impassioned love letter to cities and their political leaders, Barber (*Jihad vs. McWorld*) celebrates the diversity and ferment that embody urban life."

—*Publishers Weekly*

"A provocative, informative account of a different kind of globalization. Highly recommended reading for policymakers and other readers intrigued by forward-thinking forms of governance."

—*Kirkus Reviews,* Starred Review

"Makes the intriguing, provocative, and counter-intuitive argument the . . . cities and the mayors who run them are the last best hope for a safer, more prosperous, and more just future. *If Mayors Ruled the World* is informative and imaginative."

—**Glenn C. Altschuler,** *Huffington Post*

"If you care about cities, read *If Mayors Ruled the World*. It is the most important book on cities, their leadership and how they can make the world a better place to come along in years. Ben Barber has written a tour de force."

—**Richard Florida,** author of *The Rise of the Creative Class* and *The Great Reset*

"Political theorist Benjamin Barber's latest book is more than just theory. Networked governance by the world's cities is actually happening, and *If Mayors Ruled the World* is the book of the movement. Once again, Barber is ahead of the curve."

—**Colorado Governor John Hickenlooper**

"Benjamin Barber shows us how cities are traversed by networks of all sorts and how inter-city networks traverse the world. Both extremes and all that happens in between are brought to life through empirical details and exciting narratives."

—**Saskia Sassen,** Columbia University and author of *Cities in a World Economy*

"Barber argues . . . persuasively, that city governments are closer to their people than national ones and as such are better at winning the trust of citizens—though the same goes for rural forms of local government."

—**Ben Rogers,** *Financial Times*

IF
MAYORS
RULED
THE WORLD

BENJAMIN R. BARBER

IF MAYORS RULED THE WORLD

Dysfunctional Nations, Rising Cities

With a New Preface and Appendixes

Yale
UNIVERSITY PRESS
NEW HAVEN & LONDON

Yale University Press books may be purchased in quantity for educational,
business, or promotional use. For information, please e-mail sales.press@yale.edu
(U.S. office) or sales@yaleup.co.uk (U.K. office).

Designed by Lindsey Voskowsky.
Set in Adobe Caslon type by Westchester Publishing Services.
Printed in the United States of America.

Library of Congress Control Number: 2014940373

ISBN 978-0-300-20932-7 (pbk.)

A catalogue record for this book is available from the British Library.

10 9 8 7 6 5 4 3 2

To our cosmopolitan mayors everywhere, who take responsibility for a world they have not been given the full power to govern and who—insisting on solving rather than debating problems—have allowed us to step away from the precipice

And in particular to these mayors past and present whom I have been lucky enough to know, a representative few whose glocal leadership in their cities has been my inspiration:

Mayor Paweł Adamowicz of Gdansk

Deputy Mayor Aileen Adams of Los Angeles

Mayor Michael Bloomberg of New York

Mayor Rafał Dutkiewicz of Wrocław

Mayor John Hickenlooper of Denver

Mayor Yury Luzhkov of Moscow

Mayor Antanas Mockus of Bogotá

Mayor Leoluca Orlando of Palermo

Mayor Park Won-soon of Seoul

Mayor Olaf Scholz of Hamburg

Mayor Wolfgang Schuster of Stuttgart

Mayor/President Tony Tan of Singapore

Mayor Walter Veltroni of Rome

Mayor George Kaminis of Athens

The local is the only universal, and as near an absolute as exists.
—John Dewey, *The Public and Its Problems*

The 19th century was a century of empires, the 20th century was a century of nation states. The 21st century will be a century of cities.
—Wellington E. Web, the former mayor of Denver

Look, I'll fix your sewers if you knock off the sermons.
—Jerusalem Mayor Teddy Kollek

CONTENTS

II. HOW IT CAN BE DONE

PREFACE TO THE PAPERBACK EDITION

In 1943 Jean Monnet, the brandy merchant visionary who would make the case for a transnational postwar Europe, spoke prophetic words: "There will be no peace in Europe if the states are reconstituted on the basis of national sovereignty. The countries of Europe are too small to guarantee their peoples the necessary prosperity and social development." Today, in a world where states have grown ever more dysfunctional and the noble European experiment in pooled sovereignty seems at risk, we can say with equal certainty, there will be no peace or prosperity or sustainable economic development on the basis of either national *or* supranational sovereignty. For neither sovereign states nor the international bodies built on their foundation can any longer provide a reliable foundation for human survival.

Under these daunting conditions, this book argues, cities alone offer real hope for democratic governance locally and globally. Only pragmatic problem solving by mayors who are neighbors and homeboys—mayors who are today far more trusted than officials at higher levels of government—promises a sustainable *glocal* future. Cities are our democratic destiny, if we are to have one.

This paradigm-shattering argument on behalf of rising cities and their extraordinarily efficacious but otherwise quite ordinary mayors has provoked worldwide debate since the publication of this book's hardcover edition in late 2013. With foreign-language editions out or forthcoming in the Netherlands, Poland, China, Korea, Germany, France, Italy, and Catalonia, and a ubiquitous TEDGlobal talk that has garnered nearly 700,000 online views, the book has made its mark. But neither the lively debate nor the warm reception among urbanists, sociologists, and other academics has been as surprising as the practical reaction of sitting mayors and leaders of intercity associations and global urban networks to the proposal in Chapter 12 for a global parliament of mayors.

The interest has been city centered, not just mayor centered. This is crucial because mayors come and go, while cities stay. Indeed, in the months since hardcover publication, a number of the leading figures profiled or featured here have rotated out of office.

In New York, the omnipresent urban entrepreneur, media mogul, generous philanthropist, and global opinion leader Michael Bloomberg has been replaced by Bill de Blasio, a hardworking progressive from Brooklyn trying to heal the class rift in New York that rapid growth and new wealth have created—what in his campaign he called a tale of two cities. Committed to universal preschool education for children in all five boroughs, more affordable housing throughout the city, and a New York defined by opportunity for all as the condition of wealth for some, de Blasio has stayed his course despite predictable battles with New York State's governor, the challenge of looming union contracts (a reasonable teachers' union contract has been negotiated), and the usual dip in initially high popularity ratings. But the lessons of pragmatism are quickly assimilated by all successful mayors, and campaign candidate Bill de Blasio quickly yielded to sitting mayor Bill de Blasio with tactical adjustments: modifying a campaign against charter schools that proved imprudent (too many of his supporters viewed the schools as allies rather than enemies in the struggle for public education), softening policies aimed at taxing the rich, and bending tactics to secure alternative forms of funding to realize his universal preschool education plan. Notably, in grappling with a bevy of winter storms, a recalcitrant governor from the same party, and the challenges of big union contracts left unsigned in the previous administration, Mayor de Blasio did not so much as hint at "closing New York." When he ran up against obstacles blocking certain favored strategies aimed at realizing his progressive commitments to justice and equality, he compromised with opponents and explored alternatives, getting much (if not all) of what he wanted precisely by not "standing on principle." And when asked at the hundred-day mark about his achievements, he was proud to announce he had filled 289,000 city street potholes during the tough winter of storms, doing what mayors do, the indispensable "mundane work of government."

In Los Angeles, where a national Democratic Party leader, Antonio Villaraigosa, governed long enough to clean up the port, there is also a new, young mayor—Eric Garcetti—who in his fresh approach to Los Angeles's challenges has made a national impression. Meanwhile, a mayor in Charlotte arrested on corruption charges (Patrick Cannon) has been replaced by city councilor Dwight Clodfleter; a young inventive ex-Marine named Steven Fulop willing to take on Republican Governor Chris Christie has been elected in Jersey City (soon to become New Jersey's largest city); and John Hickenlooper, so independent as Denver's mayor (and former brewery businessman), is now embattled for being insufficiently ideological in the Colorado governor's mansion, even as his successor, Michael Hancock, is sounding more like a conventional Democrat. Up in Boston, the twenty-year veteran Thomas Menino, who is reputed to have met half of Boston's population in person during his long tenure, has turned over the mayor's gavel to Marty Walsh. As mayor emeritus, Menino has joined with a global group of mayors working with me on the global parliament of mayors project.

Fifteen new mayors traveled to Washington in December 2013 to meet President Barack Obama. A few decades earlier, the journey would have been made with mayors holding their caps in hand, looking for federal assistance in executing local programs. Tellingly, this latest trip was defined by a president trapped in Washington gridlock and looking to these fresh mayoral faces for innovation and progress on his own stalled agendas. The nation's new mayors, epitomized perhaps by Rahm Emanuel (featured in the popular CNN series *Chicagoland*), who made a reverse journey from the White House to Chicago City Hall, under-stand very well that in 2014 cities are where the real action is.

It's not just an American story, of course. Wolfgang Schuster, one of Europe's most effective and collaborative mayors, finished his second eight-year term in Stuttgart and now runs his own sustainable cities re-search institute; Moscow's Yury Luzhkov, a true survivor of Soviet autoc-racy over several decades, has not survived Vladimir Putin. And Paris's long-term Socialist mayor Bertrand Delanoë has finally been replaced after thirteen years by Paris's first female mayor (but still a Socialist), Anne Hidalgo, who won her 2014 run-off election (in the first round she came in only second). Women are still rarer in city government than in national government. Recently, however, although women have lost close races in Los Angeles and New York, they have won election not only in Paris but in Warsaw, York, Copenhagen, Omaha, Lodz, New Haven, Montevideo, Albany, Madrid, and Baltimore, among other cities. The glass floor over the foundational and thriving cellar of municipal politics is breaking; there is even a woman today serving as the mayor of Mar-rakesh, Morocco.

The most scintillating story in the past year is perhaps that of London's Boris Johnson, profiled in this book as one of those stellar municipal lead-ers with a global reputation. Despite the argument here that mayors rarely make the journey from city hall to national office (especially in England and the United States), Johnson has been recently preoccupied with the idea that he might have the popularity and political wherewithal to battle David Cameron for the leadership of a listless Tory Party. At least that is what he is being told. This would require that he be elected to Parlia-ment first. Johnson clearly is persuaded that the caveat set forth here about mayors and higher office does not apply to him. It didn't apply to Jacques Chirac (long mayor of Paris) or Jiang Zemin and Zhu Rongji (mayors of Shanghai who became national leaders), so why should it ap-ply to the mayor of what some (though not Michael Bloomberg) think of as the world's greatest city? Meanwhile, a number of Labor candidates are jostling for position in the upcoming elections in what is in principle a Labor city. Showing off the new less-white and less-male face of London, the candidates include David Lammy, an ambitious London MP of color; another Labor MP who is only the second Muslim in Parliament, Sadiq Khan—a former shadow minister under Ed Miliband—who is (he says) "addicted" to marathons; and Tessa Jowell, the former shadow minister for the London Olympic Games. Wags may think Johnson is moving on because ex-Mayor Bloomberg seems intent on taking up residence in London, which, its commodiousness notwithstanding, is too small to hold both of them, unless at least one moves to Number 10 Downing Street.

If Boris goes national, his role as a British star may be taken over by George Ferguson, one of the first directly elected mayors in the country—as an independent! He has made an impression around Europe, has made Bristol the "European green capital 2015," and is active in the global mayors' parliament project as well.

Yet despite these lively shenanigans and the ongoing rotation of women and men in and out of city halls around the urban world, the reality of urban networking and global cooperation among cities depends not on the vicissitudes of mayoral personality but on two blunt realities: the lack of congruence between cities as defined in the old world and their actual domains of activity as defined in the new; and the migration of power to the global level, where cities need to cooperate to have much influence.

Obsolete jurisdictional boundaries are perhaps the most daunting obstacle facing cities aspiring to sustainability and effective cooperation in response to global issues. The challenge here is not their parochialism or their own subsidiarity to national governments (which is a function of the nation-state system and sovereignty and will not change), but the constraints imposed on them by inappropriately narrow borders and the resource limitations that result from them. For the consequence is that they cannot retain for their own uses anything like the roughly 80 percent of GDP they produce. "Failed" cities like Detroit and Stockton are bankrupt because their city limits are drawn on century-old maps that are utterly unrepresentative of their civic, economic, and cultural reach as centers of the modern metroregions to which they have given birth. While old Detroit over the past sixty years went into a deep demographic and industrial decline (from 2 million in 1950—the fourth-largest

American city—to 700,000 today), the ten counties around Detroit went from 3 million to 5 million and today compose one of the nation's most successful and prosperous new economic regions. If in considering taxation, regulation, and jurisdiction, when we say "Detroit," we were denoting the greater Detroit metroregion, the city would not be bankrupt. It would be a postindustrial success story, a poster city for reborn Rust Belt towns everywhere. How many metropolises around the world suffer from such antique mapping unreflective of the new realities? How many are surrounded by "free-riding" suburbs and exurbs peopled with complacent suburbanites who benefit from everything cities offer in culture, jobs, transportation, and diversity, without paying a cent to support them?

The new Italian Prime Minister Matteo Renzi, formerly the mayor of Florence and thus a public figure who retains a deep appreciation of Italy's urban character, is pioneering a fundamental reorganization of his country. He proposes to reduce radically the role of the traditional provinces and in their place recognize the vital role of cities by placing nine metroregions at the center of the constitutional order. An Italy of cities, like a Europe of cities, is a formula for bringing an old governing order rooted in national states and narrowly defined cities into a twenty-first-century, interdependent world of metro-city regions. Renzi offers a model for infrastructural reorganization of relevance just about everywhere. It is not cities per se but metroregions—greater New York, greater Mumbai, greater St. Paul, and greater Lagos—that should and will rule the world.

The second dilemma cities face is that they do not control the origins and causes of many of the forces whose consequence they must address. In an interdependent world, cities must act together in order to assure the efficacy of what they try to do alone. With metroregions dominating, with megacities (and megacity slums) sprouting around the developing world, and with the precipitous and often chaotic growth of cities in China (see Appendix B), cities need each other today more than ever before. Where until recently they were as parochial as they were powerful, today their local and regional potency depends on collaboration. It is these circumstances that have helped generate the surprising practical interest among mayors in the notion of a global parliament of mayors (GPM).

The GPM, which is described in detail in Chapter 12, would act as a keystone in the arch of already extant intercity associations such as Energy Cities, the C40, the ICLEI, and the UCLG (also portrayed below), integrating and catalyzing their separate agendas; it would facilitate global cooperation by bringing democratic legitimacy and policy efficacy to decision making on an ever more interdependent planet; and it would help shape and amplify global public opinion in supporting sustainability, diversity, cultural creativity, and social justice—urban public goods that turn out to be global public goods as well. It would not displace national and international institutions and would obviously have to operate in the shadow of sovereign states; nor would it aspire to become a surrogate top-down "world government" of cities. But by bringing together the world's urban citizens and their public representatives—a majority of the world's population and almost 80 percent of the developed world's people—and focusing on shared best practices and collective purchasing measures that use the market to change or raise standards, such an assembly of cities would amplify the democratic voice of cities around the world—and at the same time enhance governance within cities.

When enough cities raise emissions standards for the automobiles they purchase or regulate, for example, they can not only force the car industry to make cars sold in their states more energy efficient (as California and its cities have) but can leverage wholesale change in automobile technology. If you are upgrading emission standards on the circa 15 percent of your production line that goes to California, why not upgrade the entire fleet? Mayor Steven Fulop of Jersey City has proposed a similar strategy to battle the dangerous guns and ammunition that the National Rifle Association support and Congress lacks the courage to oppose. Mayors have already expressed their dismay through organizations like Mayors Against Handguns, but Fulop wants to give a bite to their bark. Pool the buying power of municipal police departments across the nation (they are the largest single buyers of guns and ammo, responsible for 15 percent of all sales) and purchase only from companies that agree not to sell automatic assault weapons, big-load magazines, and armor-piercing or flesh-rending hollow-tip ("dum-dum") bullets to the general public. The U.S. Defense Department makes up another 25 percent of gun and ammo purchasing, which along with law enforcement constitutes 40 percent of sales. Use the marketplace to challenge the more irrational parts of "don't-mess-with-my-guns" culture. Do through bottom-up systematic intercity cooperation in purchasing, possibly linked to Defense Department spending, what is hard to do through top-down regulation. This is precisely the formula for an effective GPM.

In raising the democratic visibility of the world's cities and metroregions, and addressing the real-world challenges they confront, a GPM would engender optimism and rekindle democratic faith among peoples who have everywhere grown cynical about government and its capacity to deal with pressing issues such as climate change, gun control, and immigration. It would neither displace existing higher jurisdictions (under whose sovereignty and oversight cities operate) nor pretend to represent everyone. But it would lay claim to public goods such as sustainability, justice, and security—call them urban public goods that are also global public goods—and it would give to cities a common forum in which to raise and articulate their cosmopolitan voices and promulgate an urban public agenda that is also a global public agenda.

In concrete and practical terms, a GPM could

- guide global public opinion in appreciating interdependence, recognizing the practical shortcomings of states and state-based international institutions as cross-border problem solvers, and embracing the potential role of cities and networks of cities in achieving global cooperation on crucial challenges such as climate change, illegal immigration, global markets in labor, finance, and commodities, public health pandemics, and non-state-specific terrorism and war;
- create a system of "mentor cities," which would allow successful metropolitan regions to work with and mentor emerging metropolitan regions in the developing world in relationships of healthy competition and compassionate mutual aid;
- establish a secretariat that includes experts and urban generalists who can help originate new ideas and implement those already on the table, and oversee the processes leading up to the actual meetings of the GPM and how delegates are chosen;

- assure that human rights are protected in and nourished by cities and metropolitan regions even where they are slighted or abused at other (higher) levels of government;
- highlight and promote urban *best practices* in a comparative context that recognizes geographical, demographic, and cultural differences that may call for adaptation and modification from one city to another; for example, raised insulation standards for buildings, usage sensors that distribute energy use from high- to low-use time periods, and use of intercity municipal purchasing power to influence private companies through the market;
- highlight and warn against *worst practices:* for example, residential high-rise buildings—so-called "projects"; an automobile-based urban transportation approach; the segregation of work from residential neighborhoods; the neglect of the arts or their subordination to economics and commerce; neglect of the conditions for citizenship and the institutions and processes that nurture citizenship; a naive faith in simplistic technological solutions; and the inclination to construct cities overnight through rapid, unplanned building orgies that allow the physical growth of a new city to outrun its cultural, civic, and democratic development;
- become a "network of networks"—an infrastructural keystone in the growing arch of city networks already working productively in the intercity zone; this networks network could incorporate and align the intercity associations currently operating in silos defined by particular domains (e.g., environmentalism, trade, or security, for example);
- create the conditions for developing a cross-border, intercity *urban party* representing the public interests of cities across the world in influencing their national political regimes to better reflect the interests of cities and city dwellers in national politics (current party alignments, conservative and liberal, market fundamentalist and statist, rarely represent the urban commons or the common interests shared by cities in a globalized world);
- use intercity cultural relations to develop and secure healthy intercity cooperation around other issues in which imagination and creativity play vital roles.

In achieving these important global ends, a GPM would help mayors enhance their efficiency and productivity at home. This is the ultimate test of the value of a GPM for working mayors dedicated to and responsible for the welfare of their own municipalities. For a GPM will have to operate without compromising the ability of mayors to undertake their primary responsibility: governing their own municipalities. With this in mind, a viable GPM might meet regularly via a virtual platform—a kind of Global Google Mayors' Hangout or "glocal cyber commons"—and limit real-world meetings to biennial gatherings. After all, the most serious challenge facing the GPM project in practice is the difficulty of assembling 300–1,000 or more officials on a regular basis in some global city. Spending days away from their home cities and responsibilities, incurring enormous travel costs even as they leave behind scandalous carbon footprints, and courting physical exhaustion at every step, few mayors will be able to sustain such costs long term, even where the value of the summit meetings are recognized.

Current intercity networks have learned that attracting mayors on a regular basis—after an inaugural meeting, or a special anniversary summit with a special agenda—is extremely cumbersome, if not altogether impossible, and this harsh reality has condemned many such networks to relative obscurity. Associations are left with bureaucrat-staffed "global" meetings in which little of consequence can transpire. The UCLG (United Cities and Local Governments), to take a noble example, has been meeting since 1914 with a courageous commitment to intercity cooperation, but despite its many good works, it rarely meets with significant attendance by mayors or exercises a salient influence on global public opinion.

This defect, however, is a function of the imperative to convene *global* meetings physically that are constituted by *local* officials compelled to meet in person on a millennium-old model of physical space, as if the Congress of Vienna (or Westphalia!) were the only template. Such a template is oblivious to our new millennium's technology and steadfastly ignores the innovative possibilities of online gatherings and virtual assemblies. Skype, Facebook, Google Hangouts, online "meetups," and other evolving software platforms that firms such as Cisco and IBM are developing make possible virtual gatherings of dozens or even hundreds of individuals, with many of the features of face-to-face encounters. This should be the real meaning of "smart cities" that overcome time, space, and cost as insuperable barriers to a GPM. Indeed, one of the crucial features distinguishing interdependent cities from independent nations is that while states are by definition sovereign territorial entities, cities are interactive web flows in which interdependence is the key factor driving culture, trade, immigration, transportation, and other intercity activities. It's hard to imagine rival world leaders talking at one another on the web; much easier to think of pragmatic mayors deliberating together on their city hall laptops or even their smart phones. Time for a "networked mayors app."

Moreover, an effective triannual *glocal* cyber commons platform could be complemented by an information and exchange network (perhaps on the model of City Protocol), which would permit regular exchange and interaction between mayors' meetings—both by mayors and by their deputies, as well as by expert staff and policy makers. Citizens too could access both horizontal (citizen-to-citizen) and vertical (citizen-to-mayor) networks, creating a participatory element in the global network. While physical meetings would be absolutely necessary (it is well established that real-world initial meetings make later virtual meetings far more effective), experimenting with large-scale virtual meetings involving mayors themselves (not just their deputies or delegates) opens a path forward in establishing a practical and viable global parliament of mayors. Such an assembly, both local and global, could earn the name "Glocal Parliament of Mayors."

In the technology discussion in Chapter 9, I am rather skeptical about some of the more zealous claims made by fans of "smart cities." But here is an opportunity for truly useful techno-innovation. It would be a genuine breakthrough in adapting technology to the real needs of democracy to create a tech platform on which such assemblies might convene, and which offered a glocal cyber commons—a virtual cosmopolis public square—conducive to debate, deliberation, and decision making by busy mayors. With three virtual assemblies per annum, final decisions might be taken in three "readings" over a year, with the final decision delayed until the third and final annual meeting (which could be a physical meeting) with ample time for fact finding, opinion polling, and deliberation in between. With a six-hour commitment say every four months—eighteen hours per annum—mayors could convene virtually on a regular basis. Well-prepared agendas, predigested proposals, policies already locally deliberated, and carefully crafted policy statements could become the substantive business in executive sessions of mayors fully prepped for the task and not exhausted by travel or distracted by absence from their local obligations. The process would leave the principals free to interact, deliberate, and reach decisions with one another.

Information and communication technology (ICT) companies that have developed social platforms for personal, social, and consumer interaction have not only often expressed an interest in civic and political networking but have organized themselves in ways conducive to bottom-up civic interactivity and networking. The old behemoth top-down IBM (Big Blue) long ago inverted its model and went bottom-up and green, assuring its survival in our web-based ICT era; Cisco Systems has teamed with the city of Barcelona in establishing a platform to share urban best practices virtually (City Protocol); Google has experimented with its Google Hangouts model intended as small-scale virtual public squares in which citizens can meet and talk with one another and interact with political leaders (or celebrities); Mark Zuckerberg has said repeatedly that the principle underlying Facebook and its new iterations is to allow people to *do* and *share* activities *together*—whatever those activities may be—commercial or social, private (friendship) or public (common "liking"); and James Fishkin, a professor at Stanford, has shown that civic interaction on a web platform can transform private opinion into public deliberation and thereby help people become better public citizens. We have already been in fruitful discussion with IBM and Cisco, and a partnership between the GPM and a tech partner seems inevitable.

The proposal for a GPM was offered here as a hypothetical payoff for the book's general argument for global urban governance. I was, in the best sense, just dreaming. But in the year since the book was completed, the idea has gained practical traction among public officials and has led to a focus on virtual platforms that points toward the possibility of realization in the near rather than the distant future. GPM planning meetings have already been held in Seoul, New York, and Amsterdam, and more are planned. The idea has been considered by sitting mayors in Albuquerque, Amsterdam, Barcelona, Belfast, Bratislava, Bristol, Bogotá, Cheyenne, Denver, Dublin, Florence, Gdansk, Hamburg, Jersey City, Las Palmas, London, Los Angeles, Mannheim, Milan, New York City, Paris, Perth, Rotterdam, Santa Monica, Seoul, Singapore, Stuttgart, The Hague, Turin, Vancouver, Warsaw, and Wrocław, and a number of them are participating in the planning process. A provisional plan for a pilot convening of an inaugural parliament in the Millennium Dome (O2 Arena) in early 2016 is in development.

Obviously, an expression of interest in and willingness to deliberate a prospective GPM is not an endorsement of or a commitment to embrace the envisioned parliament. In nearly every instance, mayors have made clear that their support for the idea depends on how well the projected global assembly can serve the interests of their own cities. Only if it does so will they be likely to be able to devote the time and resources a GPM will require, even if most sessions are virtual. For there are already many intercity organizations doing significant networking around global issues. Indeed, an early working subtitle for *If Mayors Ruled the World* read, "Why They Should and How They Already Do." The extant networks, however, tend to be specialized, siloed, and modest and hence little known. They are often more technocratic than political, and have less impact than is deserved. The UCLG is the most important global association nobody has ever heard of. The ICLEI (International Council for Local Environmental Initiatives) is doing truly important work around climate change, and has benefited from the inauguration of newer, more high-profile big-city climate networks such as Energy Cities and the C40 Cities (actually more than sixty-five cities). We must honor these networks and work closely with them and build on their achievements. But a dramatic escalation is needed, a step up in attention and focus and mission that allows mayors to move into the political realm of global governance, where the global problems nations have failed to confront can be addressed.

This escalation will give to intercity association and urban cooperation across borders a genuine *governance* aspect comparable to what the United Nations was intended to establish. It will let the planet's majority of urban citizens be clearly heard and allow them to influence world public opinion with the voice of a global public agenda devoted to sustainability and justice; it will add to best practices and the sharing of ideas a *regulative* element that can address global monopolies and global anarchy; and it will globalize the democracy associated with city governance and hence democratize globalization as it is manifested in a world of brutal but ineluctable interdependence.

Finally, in considering the virtues of the GPM, we must take into account its potential impact on the engagement of citizens, not only in the work of local governance where their presence is natural, but in a global setting remote from their everyday urban lives and their civic experience. The sense of solidarity and communal closeness that defines parochial city government must be reflected in the cosmopolitan arrangements needed to sustain a GPM. This requires what sociologists of social capital call *bridging* capital (which connects us with others beyond our community) as well as *bonding* capital, which binds us together internally. The two need one another but are often at odds. Internal solidarity can raise walls against "outsiders" and "others." Cosmopolitanism can attenuate communal solidarity. This dilemma is a crucial aspect of the opposition between the rural and the urban debated in Chapter 2 and renegotiated in Chapter 11. Global governance that puts cities at the center of interdependence can offer a global platform for citizen-to-citizen communication and collaboration and thus bring citizens and public officials closer, but must do it by building on rather than eclipsing the parochial solidarity of urban communities.

In an era of interdependence, where nation-states have become dysfunctional and cities and metroregions are everywhere rising, it is time to take the visionary leap from effective local governance to true global governance. Until our dangerous market world of disease without borders, climate change without borders, immigration without borders, crime and terrorism and war without borders, can be confronted by a new civic world of citizens without borders represented in a parliament of cities without borders, we will achieve neither sustainability nor justice. In the pages that follow I will aspire to persuade you that it is up to us, cosmopolitan citizens and public officials alike, to cross the old unsustainable borders and constitute a new sustainable world.

ACKNOWLEDGMENTS

This book builds on an encompassing corpus of work undertaken earlier by a host of scholars who, knowing the urban field far better than I ever will, have made the city their subject and sometimes their lifework. Much of what I do here is merely to hold up a megaphone before them so that their measured and persistent voices on behalf of the redemptive potential of the urban can be widely heard. Tom Bender, Manuel Castells, Eric Corijn, Mike Davis, Richard Florida, Edward Glaeser, David Harvey, Peter Marcuse, Saskia Sassen, Richard Sennett, and Ronald van Kempen—and before them Lewis Mumford, Max Weber, Jane Jacobs, and the many others who are cited below—have built a scholarly edifice I feel lucky to have been able to inhabit and explore. My task has been to apply the results of their work to the challenge of establishing a form of constructive interdependence—global democratic governance—in which cities are prime actors.

Like all authors and scholars, I have benefited enormously from myriad others in conceiving and executing this project. Three research associates who worked with me on various stages of the manuscript have made especially important contributions: Patrick Inglis, who helped with research and thinking about the project at the outset, when my focus was just beginning to move from global governance to global cities, and whose own work on India and the urban is so important; Deirdra Stockmann, who was a research associate during the writing of the first half of the book, where her research on networks and inequality proved so valuable; and Daniel London (below). Though not involved directly in research, my former executive assistant and coordinator of programs for CivWorld, Harry Merritt (now returned to graduate school in history to pursue his own scholarly interests), has been a presence throughout the writing of this book, and I owe him much for his curiosity and contributions.

Daniel London, who has worked on research for the manuscript throughout and was a principal creator and overseer of the book's website, has been much more than a research assistant. He has been a careful editor, an exacting compiler of charts and data, and a valuable contributor of ideas. Daniel also spent time as the research coordinator for my CivWorld team at the Graduate Center of the City University of New York. His role in this project has been major.

I have also been the beneficiary of relationships to former students (now colleagues) including SungMoon Kim, with whom I wrote an essay on a new interdependence paradigm for global governance several years ago that was one platform for the ideas here, and whose own work on civil society East and West is so important; and Stuart MacNiven, whose research on Rousseau and love of political theory in combination with his friendship have been a continuing inspiration. Trevor Norris, in his capacity as editor of a forthcoming Festschrift, has also taken a lively and contributory interest in this work.

A number of friends and colleagues, some of them also funders, have offered valuable support for my work leading up to and through this book. That support has helped my NGO CivWorld thrive and allowed me to develop its research side in crucial ways. The friendship and support of Sara McCune, whom I first met in the 1970s when I was editing the journal *Political Theory* at her then young Sage Publications, has been especially vital, along with the corollary support of her CEO, Blaise Simqu, with whom I worked decades ago when we were both young editors.

Heinrich Thyssen has been a friend for many years and has shown repeatedly how business leaders can also be critical thinkers about interdependence. Thyssen's support and that of his Nomis Research Foundation have facilitated my research and my interdependence work. Heine also introduced me to his colleague Jerre Stead, who offered vital support to my work at one key moment. Just recently, Liz Levitt Hirsch (of Levitt Pavilions) has become a friend and supporter of the Interdependence Movement and my own research, for which I am grateful. George Elvin, with his wife, Ginger, has long been a friend and backer of the Interdependence Movement, as well as a lively interlocutor on crucial issues of economics and politics. Finally, I have benefited enormously over the years from my relationship to the Kettering Foundation, whose civic agenda helps define my own. President David Mathews and Vice President and Program Director John Dedrick have offered sustaining support. With Dedrick, this commonality of purpose and generous support have been especially affecting because John was formerly a gifted Ph.D. student who worked with me at Rutgers University.

George Soros and the Open Society Institute are known for their leadership in the field of global civil society and progressive politics. Early in my work on interdependence, Soros offered hospitality to me and my NGO CivWorld at a time when that support counted most. His support was often mediated by Michael Vachon, his assistant, who has offered his own friendship and support over the years. When we left OSI, the think tank Demos offered a home to CivWorld and to me with an appointment as a Distinguished Senior Fellow that allowed me to nurture the ideas leading up to the book. At Demos, former board chair Stephen Heintz—the first president of Demos and a global leader in developing civil society—and Miles Rapoport, Demos's energetic president, embraced the idea and agenda of interdependence and helped make my research on the book possible. Most recently, Professor Kathleen McCarthy has given me a welcome home at the Center on Philanthropy and Civil Society at the Graduate Center of the City University of New York.

My colleagues and friends in the Interdependence Movement Steering Committee have been part of the intellectual climate that made this work possible—especially Bhikhu Parekh, Adam Michnik, Claus Offe,

Guy Gypens, Jakob Köllhofer, Olara Otunnu, Harry Belafonte, Michel Rocard, Luis Ernesto Derbez, and Jacqueline Davis—who has recently become chair of the CivWorld Executive Committee and on whose judgment and warm friendship I have come to depend. David Baile and Rachel Cooper, who serve on that committee, embody the spirit of interdependent cities.

Colleagues who participated over several years in the Global Governance Seminar that convened at Demos were important contributors to the evolution of my thinking on global governance and cities. They include my dear friend and seminar cochair, Professor Seyla Benhabib, a constant prod to creative thinking, without whom the seminar could not have been successful; and Jim Sleeper, Robert Keohane, Nannerl Keohane, Kwame Anthony Appiah, Stephen Bronner, Saskia Sassen, Jonathan Schell, Virginia Held, and David Callhan. Parag Kanna has been a friend and intellectual colleague who has helped me engage globalization, and Hans Joachim Schellnhuber of the Potsdam Climate Institute, a global visionary in combating climate change, has been a source of dialogue and exchange of great value. Jim Anderson and Kate Leonberger at Bloomberg Philanthropies; Wolfgang Schmidt, the foreign minister of Hamburg; and Mayor Wolfgang Schuster of Stuttgart have helped conceptualize a path forward toward a global mayors parliament. Peter Schwartz made possible a trip to Singapore of real value to my research and introduced me to Stewart Brand, the founder of Long Now Seminar, where I presented an early version of my research. Keith Reinhard has been a lively interlocutor on issues from branding and consumerism to cities and interdependence for many years and I continue to benefit from his wisdom.

At Yale University Press, I have been very well served by my editor, William Frucht, and my long-term friend and agent, now an editor at the Press, Steve Wasserman—who was the editor many years ago of my *Jihad vs. McWorld*. Yale and its editors combine the sense of relevance and urgency associated with trade publishers and the careful attention to high standards and scholarly detail that are traditionally the provenance of academic houses. I can't imagine a more productive publishing relationship.

This extraordinary group of friends and contributors to my thinking, research, and writing deserve much of the credit for whatever contribution this book can make to our view of cities in the twenty-first century. The responsibility for its shortcomings and deficiencies is entirely my own.

Leah Kreutzer Barber, the dancer/artist/activist/environmentalist who is my partner and wife and the mother of our gifted daughter, Nellie, knows what she means to this work and my life. There is no idea in the book we have not deliberated across coffee and bagels on Saturday mornings; there is no portion of the manuscript that has not benefited from her editorial acumen, to which she allowed me access long after we both should have been asleep. Her contributions can only be diminished by being encased in words—however apt—like dear, cherished, and adored.

ACKNOWLEDGMENTS

A Country Boy Can Survive
Words and Music by Hank Williams, Jr.
Copyright © 1981 by Bocephus Music, Inc.
All Rights Reserved Used by Permission
Reprinted by Permission of Hal Leonard Corporation

I. WHY CITIES SHOULD GOVERN GLOBALLY

CHAPTER I. IF MAYORS RULED THE WORLD

Why They Should and How They Already Do

> City of ships!
> . . . .
> City of the world! (for all races are here,
> All the lands of the earth make contributions here;)
> . . . .
> City of wharves and stores—city of tall facades of marble and iron!
> Proud and passionate city—mettlesome, mad, extravagant city!
> Spring up O city!
>
> *Walt Whitman, "City of Ships"*

In a teeming world of too much difference and too little solidarity, democracy is in deep crisis. With obstreperous nation-states that once rescued democracy from problems of scale now thwarting democracy's globalization, it is time to ask in earnest, "Can cities save the world?"[1] I believe they can. In this book I will show why they should and how they already do.

We have come full circle in the city's epic history. Humankind began its march to politics and civilization in the polis—the township. It was democracy's original incubator. But for millennia, we relied on monarchy and empire and then on newly invented nation-states to bear the civilizational burden and the democratic load. Today, after a long history of regional success, the nation-state is failing us on the global scale. It was the perfect political recipe for the liberty and independence of autonomous peoples and nations. It is utterly unsuited to interdependence. The city, always the human habitat of first resort, has in today's globalizing world once again become democracy's best hope.

Urbanity may or may not be our nature, but it is our history, and for better or worse, by chance or by design, it defines how we live, work, play, and associate. Whatever large-scale political arrangements we fashion, politics starts in the neighborhood and the town. More than half the world's people now live in cities—more than 78 percent of the developing world. As it was our origin, the city now appears to be our destiny. It is where creativity is unleashed, community solidified, and citizenship realized. If we are to be rescued, the city rather than the nation-state must be the agent of change.

Given the state's resistance to cross-border collaboration, our foremost political challenge today is to discover or establish alternative institutions capable of addressing the multiplying problems of an interdependent world without surrendering the democracy that nation-states traditionally have secured. In order to save ourselves from both anarchic forms of globalization, such as war and terrorism, and monopolistic forms, such as multinational corporations, we need global democratic bodies that work, bodies capable of addressing the global challenges we confront in an ever more interdependent world. In the centuries of conflict that have defined the world from the Congress of Vienna to the defeat of the Axis Powers and the writing of a Universal Declaration of Human Rights, from the Treaty of Versailles to the fall of the Berlin Wall and the end of a bipolar world, nation-states have made little progress toward global governance. Too inclined by their nature to rivalry and mutual exclusion, they seem quintessentially indisposed to cooperation and incapable of establishing global common goods. Moreover, democracy is locked in their tight embrace, and there seems little chance either for democratizing globalization or for globalizing democracy as long as its flourishing depends on rival sovereign nations. What then is to be done?

The solution stands before us, obvious but largely uncharted: let cities, the most networked and interconnected of our political associations, defined above all by collaboration and pragmatism, by creativity and multiculture, do what states cannot. Let mayors rule the world. Since, as Edward Glaeser writes, "the strength that comes from human collaboration is the central truth behind civilization's success and the primary reason why cities exist," then surely cities can and should govern globally.[2]

In fact, it is already happening. Cities are increasingly networked into webs of culture, commerce, and communication that encircle the globe. These networks and the cooperative complexes they embody can be helped to do formally what they now do informally: govern through voluntary cooperation and shared consensus. If mayors ruled the world, the more than 3.5 billion people (over half of the world's population) who are urban dwellers and the many more in the exurban neighborhoods beyond could participate locally and cooperate globally at the same time—a miracle of civic "glocality" promising pragmatism instead of politics, innovation rather than ideology, and solutions in place of sovereignty.[3]

The challenge of democracy in the modern world has been how to join participation, which is local, with power, which is central. The nation-state once did the job, but recently it has become too large to allow meaningful participation even as it remains too small to address centralized global power. Cosmopolitanism responds by imagining citizens—literally city dwellers—who are rooted in urban neighborhoods where participation and community are still possible, reaching across frontiers to confront and contain central power. It imagines them joining one another to oversee and regulate anarchic globalization and the illegitimate forces it unleashes. Eighty-five years ago, John Dewey embarked on a "search for the great community," a community that might tie people together through common activities and powerful symbols into an expansive public organized around communication.[4] In doing so, Dewey delinked democracy from mere government and the state and insisted it be understood as a deep form of association embracing the family, the school, industry, and religion. He was certain that when it is embraced "as a life of free and enriching communion," democracy will come into its own, but only when "free social inquiry is indissolubly wedded to the art of full and moving communication."[5]

A world governed by cities gives democratic form to Dewey's aspirational vision of a great community. It does not require that a new global governing edifice be artificially constructed ex nihilo, and it does not mean that networked cities must be certified by the nation-states they will supersede. It places the emphasis, as the final chapters of this book do, on bottom-up citizenship, civil society, and voluntary community across borders rather than on top-down prescriptions and executive mandates emanating from unitary global rulers. New York's Mayor Michael Bloomberg may seem hubristic, yet his rhetoric—hardly Dewey's, but rooted in realism—resonates with the power of municipal localism played out in an interdependent world: "I have my own army in the NYPD," Bloomberg says; "my own State Department, much to Foggy Bottom's annoyance." New York has "every kind of people from every part of the world and every kind of problem." And if Washington doesn't like it? "Well," Bloomberg allows, "I don't listen to Washington very much."[6]

It is not boasting but both the burdens and the possibilities of the city that give Mayor Bloomberg's claims resonance. For, as he insists, "the difference between my level of government and other levels of government is that action takes place at the city level." While American government right now is "just unable to do anything . . . the mayors of this country still have to deal with the real world." Presidents pontificate principle; mayors pick up the garbage. And campaign for gun control (as with the Bloomberg-inspired NGO Mayors Against Illegal Guns). And work to combat global warming (the C40 Cities). This can-do thinking is echoed in organizations such as ICLEI (Local Governments for Sustainability), whose report following the no-can-do U.N. Climate Summit in Durban at the end of 2011 observed that "local government is where the rubber hits the road when it comes to responding to the human impacts of climate change."[7] The cities' approach to climate change emerged a year earlier, when 207 cities signed the Mexico City Pact at the World Mayors Summit on Climate in Mexico City, even as states were busily doing nothing much at all other than vaguely pledging to honor "strategies and actions aimed at reducing greenhouse gas emissions."

By expanding and diversifying the networks through which they are already cooperating, cities are proving they can do things together that states cannot. What would the parliament of mayors I will advocate in Chapter 12 be but the formalization of voluntary global networks already in existence? The 2010 World Congress of the meta-network called the United Cities and Local Governments, with 3,000 delegates from 100 countries, is already halfway there! What is a prospective global civil religion but the common civic expression of how people actually live in cities? The spirit that enables migrant workers, whether taxi drivers or accountants, to roam from city to city looking for work without ever really leaving town? Cities come in varieties of every kind, but they also resemble one another functionally and infrastructurally. The new City Protocol network suggests best practices that exploit such commonalities by offering a "progressive working framework for cities worldwide to assess and improve performance in environmental sustainability, economic competitiveness, quality of life, and city services, by innovating and demonstrating new leadership models, new ways of engaging society, and by leveraging new information and communication technologies."[8]

How many ways are there to stuff a million people into a radically delimited space? Even in the eighteenth century, Jean-Jacques Rousseau noticed that "all capital cities are just alike. . . . Paris and London seem to me to be the same town."[9] Are São Paulo, Tokyo, and New York that different today? The cross-border civil society we envision is simply the global network of partnerships and associations already sharing common civic values, of communities organized around the struggle for universal human rights, of religious associations with an ecumenical outlook, of international societies of artists and social networks of friends real and virtual alike spiraling outward to encompass strangers. Such a network is not waiting to be born but is already half-grown, waiting rather to be recognized, exploited, and formalized. These synapses that link urban nodes (detailed in Chapter 5) are already marking new pathways to interdependence.

Novel mechanisms of cooperation and common decision making are allowing cities to address, in common, issues of weapons, trade, climate change, cultural exchange, crime, drugs, transportation, public health, immigration, and technology. They need not always be formal: Rey Colón, a Chicago alderman, "first saw how well [bike-share] innovations work on a trip to Seville, Spain."[10] Mayor Rahm Emanuel subsequently made a campaign promise to lay out one hundred miles of "green" protected bike lanes on major Chicago thoroughfares and is currently making good on the promise. New York City's bike-share program opened in mid-2013. Sharing green ideas among cities and cooperating on slowing climate change in city networks like the C40 with bike-share and pedestrian mall programs are not quite the same thing as ruling the world, but they do indicate that cities are far ahead of states in confronting the daunting challenges of interdependence, if only through voluntary and informal cooperation. Networked cities already supplement the brave but endangered experiment of the European Community in pooling sovereignty in vital ways likely to survive a fracturing of the Eurozone.

Long-time (and now former) Mayor Wolfgang Schuster of Stuttgart is a European statesman and civic organizer, but first of all he is a municipal democrat attuned to how local democracy is enhanced by inter-city collaboration. "We are not an island," he insists; "we need a strong lobby for strong local self-government systems. But cities themselves are not islands, so we have to work in networks to make understandable what are our needs, what are our demands [by] . . . learning from each other."[11] It is in this grounded and practical fashion that cities may in time, with their own adroit associations, supplant the awkward dance of European nations in hock to their banks and thus to the machinations of the G-9 or G-20. How? I will propose a parliament of mayors that will need to ask no state's permission to assemble, seek consensual solutions to common problems, and voluntarily comply with common policies of their own choosing.

When mayors like New York's Michael Bloomberg institute measures to end smoking or control childhood obesity by curbing large-container soda sales, Washington can only look on in wonder—deprecating or admiring the initiatives but impotent in the face of mayors elsewhere in the world who might choose to do the same. (Of course, courts can intervene, as they did in overturning Bloomberg's soda ban.) Neither soda nor tobacco companies, influential with national governments through their hubristic lobbies and seductive bank accounts, can do much more than whine in advertising campaigns about the lost freedom to kill yourself (or your children). This is not to say that states are powerless in controlling, even strangling, cities trying to circumvent them. Legislative sovereignty and budget authority give states plenty of ways to block runaway towns. The only global city that coexists friction-free with its state is Singapore, where city and state are one. Yet a surprisingly large arena of municipal activity and cross-border cooperation remains available to determined cities.

The call to let mayors become global governors and enable their urban constituents to reach across frontiers and become citizens without borders does not then reflect a utopian aspiration. It is more than the longing for an impossible regime of global justice. It asks only that we recognize a world already in the making, one coming into being without systematic planning or the blessing of any state-based authority; that we take advantage of the unique urban potential for cooperation and egalitarianism unhindered by those obdurate forces of sovereignty and nationality, of ideology and inequality, that have historically hobbled and isolated nation-states inside fortresses celebrated as being "independent" and "autonomous." Nor need the mayors tie their aspirations to cooperation to the siren song of a putative United Nations that will never be united because it is composed of rival nations whose essence lies in their sovereignty and independence.

If mayors are to rule the world, however, it is clear they will have to pay dues to prime ministers and presidents. Cities may already constitute networks of collaboration that influence the global economy and bypass the rules and regulations of states, but they lie within the jurisdiction and sovereignty of superior political bodies. Mayor Bloomberg may have his own army, but let him try to deploy it in Cuba or Washington, D.C., or Albany—or even across the river in Hoboken or up in Yonkers, a few miles north of Manhattan. He can route bikes through Manhattan, but try doing it on the New York Thruway or elsewhere along President Eisenhower's Interstate Highway System. Governance is about power as well as problems, jurisdiction as well as function, so the relationship of cities to states is of critical concern here. There are two crucial questions: Are the interests of cities and of the states to which cities belong in harmony or in conflict? And can cities do what they do in the face of national governments that are not merely indifferent but hostile to their global aspirations?

The answers to both questions are complex and raise questions of legal and political jurisdiction that are the subject of Chapter 6. But what is clear from the outset is that the interests of cities and of the nations to which they belong (and *belong* is the right word!) are often necessarily in tension. However networked and interdependent cities may become in terms of their economic, technocratic, and cultural functions, they live under the law and in the shadow of the legal jurisdiction and executive and fiscal authority of states that are still very powerful states. States that are not going anywhere. If, as Saskia Sassen has suggested, "what contributes to growth in the network of global cities may well not contribute to growth in nations,"[12] and if the growth of global cities is correlated with deficits for national governments, governments are unlikely to sit back and do nothing while their suzerainty is eroded. In the 1970s, in a funny and futile campaign to become mayor of New York, the author Norman Mailer floated the nutty idea of detaching the city from New York State and perhaps the United States of America, endowing it with independence.[13] Some will see the notion of cities becoming sufficiently independent from states to rule the world as equally nutty. Surely states will fight to regain control of globalizing cities that contemplate cross-border actions, demonstrating forcefully that however collaborative and trans-territorial cities may regard themselves, they remain creatures of state power and subsidiaries of national sovereignty.

Unlike corporations or associations, states are territorial by definition, and cities always sit on land that is part of some nation's territory. New York may not pay much attention to Washington, but Washington will be watching New York. While citizens can dream across borders, they are defined by and owe their fealty neither to the local city alone, nor to some emerging global civic cosmopolis, but to their national flags and patriotic anthems and defining national "missions." For Mayor Bloomberg and his proud New Yorkers—count me among them—this means we must hearken not just to "New York, New York, it's a wonderful town" and the Statue of Liberty, but to "America the Beautiful" and the Lincoln Memorial; to that larger nation that claims to be a "beacon of liberty" to the world. In France, it reminds intellectuals in the 5th Arrondissement that *la mission civilisatrice* is French, not Parisian; and in Germany, it warns that *Deutschland Über Alles* is not just a signifier of vanished imperial hauteur or fascist hubris but also of the sovereignty of Germany over Frankfurt and Berlin. Texas may sometimes imagine itself severing the ties that bind it to the United States, and Austin might imagine itself an independent liberal oasis in the Texas desert, but neither Dallas nor Austin is about to declare independence from Texas or the United States.

The interdependence of cities may erode their ties to nation-states and draw them toward collaboration with one another, but no state worth its salt, as measured by its sovereignty, will stand still and watch cities annul subsidiarity and escape the gravitational pull of their sovereign mother ship. That is true even in Singapore, a city-state where paradoxically a city must coexist with a territorially coterminous state that exercises sovereignty over itself as city and state. Moreover, national communities are important markers of identity and help establish the greater communities rooted in common history, common language, and a common narrative (say a civil religion) that allow urban residents to share citizenship beyond town limits. To suggest a tension between urban identity and national identity is not then to favor one or the other; it is just to state a fact that affects our argument here.

This tension shows that to make the case for cities as building blocks of global governance requires a systematic and sustained argument that takes into account the power and jurisdiction of states and the intractability of territorial frontiers as well as the nature of cities. The task requires that we examine the history and essential nature of cities; that we demonstrate and elaborate their pragmatic, problem-solving character; and that we show how their role as global governance building blocks can be reinforced and solidified in the face of potentially belligerent nation-state opposition by sovereign entities that nonetheless play a vital role in civic and community life. The success of cities must supplement the efforts of states and offset sovereign incapacities without pretending nations away or making them villains in the story of democratic globalization. For as we will see, the dysfunction of nation-states as global cooperators arises at least in part out of their virtues—their independence, sovereignty, and commitments to national equality and liberty.

The argument offered here also requires that we survey, understand, and build upon the successes of lesser known but robust civic entities and networks such as the United Cities and Local Governments, International Union of Local Authorities, Metropolis (the World Association of the Major Metropolises), the American League of Cities, ICLEI, the C40 Cities (focused on addressing climate change), the New Hanseatic League, the European Union's Secretariat of Cities, the U.S. Mayors Climate Protection Agreement, the Association of (U.S.) Mayors Against Illegal Guns, the Megacities Foundation, CityNet, and City Protocol— among many others. These clumsily named and seemingly dull bureaucratic constructions are in fact birthing an exciting new cosmopolis whose activities and ambitions hold the secret to fashioning the global processes and institutions that states have failed to create. Many of these networks were created by or contributed to by a few global leaders such as Stuttgart's Wolfgang Schuster, Barcelona's Xavier Trias, and New York City's hyperactive Michael Bloomberg.

With or without authoritative underwriting, networked cities and megacities are likely to determine whether democracy—perhaps even civilization itself—survives in the coming decades, when the primary challenge will remain how to overcome the violent conflict within and between states, and how to address the cataclysmic economic and ecological anarchy and the inequalities and injustices that the absence of democratic global governance occasions. We are already stumbling into that seductive but deadly anarchy in which pandemics and ecological catastrophes are allowed to flourish in sovereignty's name: "Not at the expense of my sovereignty will you monitor my air quality (or inspect my weapons production or regulate my fracking methods)!" And we are already living in an era of global private monopolies in money and influence that are empowered under the banner of liberty and markets that are anything but free. What is missing is not globalization, but globalization that is public rather than private, democratic not hegemonic, egalitarian rather than monopolistic. In struggling against this global anarchy and the brute force, winner-take-all mentality it facilitates, cities working across borders make a difference. By working voluntarily and cooperatively to pursue sustainability, justice, and democratic equality locally, they can mitigate the depredations of fractious states and temper—even regulate—the global markets that states have been unable or unwilling to control. Cities woven into an informal cosmopolis can become, as the polis once was, new incubators of democracy, this time on a global scale.

While it is true that historically and in most places cities have been subordinated not just to inequality and corruption but to the politics of kingship and empire, their tendencies have generally remained anti-ideological and in a practical sense democratic. Their politics are persuasive rather than peremptory, and their governors are neighbors exercising responsibility rather than remote rulers wielding brute force. Under siege from imperial marauders in an earlier millennium, cities nevertheless had to persist in overseeing the necessities of everyday life. Cities are habitats for common life. They are where people live and hence where they learn and love, work and sleep, pray and play, grow and eat, and finally die. Even with armies at the gates or plagues in the streets, city dwellers occupy themselves with the diurnal—and sometimes also the sublime. Their paramount aims and thus the aims of the mayors they elect to serve them are mundane, even parochial: collecting garbage and collecting art rather than collecting votes or collecting allies; putting up buildings and running buses rather than putting up flags and running political parties; securing the flow of water rather than the flow of arms; fostering education and culture in place of national defense and patriotism. They are at pains to promote collaboration, not exceptionalism; to succor a knowing sense of participation and pride in community rather than to institutionalize blind patriotism.

Cities have little choice: to survive and flourish they must remain hospitable to pragmatism and problem solving, to cooperation and networking, to creativity and innovation. Come hell or high water, war or siege, they have to worry about plowing the streets and providing parking and yes, always and everywhere, picking up the garbage. Indeed, as we will explore in wrestling with the challenge of urban inequality (Chapter 8), in many developing-world megacities, picking up the garbage has become a key to the informal economy and to the employment of the poor. The city's defining association with garbage, as well as with trade, business, transportation, communication, digital technology, and culture—with creativity and imagination—is a natural feature of human proximity and population density. As Richard Florida has written, "the real key to unleashing our creativity lies in humanity's greatest invention—the city. Cities are veritable magnetrons for creativity."[14] Creativity and imagination drive invention, commerce, and culture, but they also are engines of democracy.

To consider the future of the city as a foundation for democratic global governance also means looking to the city's past and its ancient democratic origins. Born in the self-governing and autonomous polis, democracy realizes its global telos in the self-governing and interdependent cosmopolis. The circle completes itself. At the end of the beginning of human civilization the city appears. As men and women produce language, culture, and economy, they gather into communities. As Aristotle once called man a political animal (a *zoon politikon*), Edward Glaeser today speaks of humankind as an "urban species," whose cities are "made of flesh, not concrete."[15] The Greeks gave the name *polis* to their early communities, which in the case of archetypical Athens was a politicized collection of tribes (so-called demes). As in most early towns, the Athenian polis was literally a city of men, though it flaunted its blinkered "egalitarianism." Citizens were native-born males only, while women (and slaves and foreigners) were relegated to subordinate roles and inferior identities. But though the polis began as little more than a village with a yen to sprawl and a site for vibrant but highly restricted civic participation, it still functioned as democracy's local incubator—a first experiment in tribes of men freeing themselves from tribal headmen, monarchs, and emperors to secure a rudimentary form of self-government. These minuscule townships with perhaps 20,000 citizens could, however, hardly be called cities. Moreover, tribalism and strongman governance remained the rule for most other villages and small towns around the ancient world.

Yet the polis was born to grow, and grow it did from polis to town, and town to fortified market; from rural market center to expansive trading crossroads, increasingly outgrowing the walls that protected it against invaders as it reached out to a smaller world ever more connected by highways and rivers, trading routes, and navigable seas. Nearly 90 percent of the world's population lives on or near oceans and seas and the rivers flowing into them—waterways that invite mobility and communication but whose tides, storms, and floods also invite disaster. Even in the West in the pre-Christian era, the Mediterranean had become a watery crossroads around which networked towns and ports constituted themselves as an interdependent regional market. In China's three kingdoms too, and in Japan and on the Indian subcontinent, cities grew along the great rivers and on proto-port coastal towns. The process was unremitting. Over millennia, with pauses and setbacks, cities grew into capital cities and imperial cities, hosting hundreds of thousands and millions rather than thousands of people. The movement was, in Max Weber's early characterization, "from simple to complex, from general to specialized."[16] The world rushed toward what looked like ineluctable urbanity.

This surging history of urbanization and industrialization notwithstanding, however, as recently as 1958 Edward C. Banfield could write with confidence that "most of the people of the world live and die without ever achieving membership in a community larger than the family or a tribe and that outside of Europe and America the concerting of behavior in political associations and corporate organizations is a rare and recent thing."[17] No more. In the half century since the eminent sociologist wrote, the city has taken still another leap forward: capital cities underwritten by megarhetoric have been morphing into networked megacities of tens of millions, intersecting with other cities to comprise today's burgeoning megalopolises and megaregions in which an increasing majority of the earth's population now dwells. Tribes still dominate certain cultures, but even in Africa megacity conurbations have emerged, representing territorially immense urban juggernauts that encompass populations of twenty million or more. Typical is Africa's Lagos-Ibadan-Cotonou region, where Lagos alone is projected to reach twenty-five million by 2025, making it the world's third-largest city after Mumbai and Tokyo, in a Nigeria that has six cities over a million and another dozen with 500,000 to a million—all of them growing rapidly.[18]

Then there is Kinshasa-Brazzaville, two interconnected cities separated by a river in rival "Congo" states. Other megacities have appeared in the Indo-Gangetic Plain, in China's Pearl River Delta, as well as in the Northeast Corridor in the United States, Japan's Taiheiyo Belt,

Europe's Golden Banana (sunbelt) along the western Mediterranean, and the Greater São Paulo metro region in Brazil. China's cities are growing so fast that it is nearly impossible to keep up. A McKinsey study estimates that in the next ten to fifteen years, 136 new cities will join the world's 600 cities with the largest GDPs, all of them from the developing world. By 2025, 100 of the top 600 GDP cities will be Chinese.[19]

The concentration of urban populations into ever more complex systems, at once denser and more expansive, continues to accelerate. Nor is the compass of these conglomerations exclusively territorial. In her study of New York, London, and Tokyo, Saskia Sassen argues that as they become service centers for the new global economy, "in many regards . . . [these three cities] function as one trans-territorial marketplace." They serve not just one by one but "function as a triad," representing a new form of metropolis that is neither territorial nor virtual, but a network composed of the intersecting and overlapping "global city" functions.[20] There are weird new hybrids as well, new corporate "instant cities" like New Songdo City in South Korea, planned to open in 2015 with a population of 250,000, or a proposed city of 500,000 residents to be called Lazika on a wetland site on the Black Sea in Georgia that would become Georgia's second-largest city after its capital, Tbilisi (though notwithstanding construction of its first Public Service Hall, the project is in doubt following the electoral defeat of its advocate, President Mikheil Saakashvili, in 2012). Then there are such random and anarchic counterpoints as the unplanned refugee camps-cum-cities like Dadaab in Kenya, which may have up to 290,000 people jammed into a "temporary encampment" served by mobile courts, traveling counseling services, and sometime youth education centers.

There are also those imagined worlds favored by web-addicted dreamers, "seaworlds" to be set adrift in the ocean. One of these has already been legally founded as Seastead and, according to the Seastead Institute (www.seasteading.org), is to be launched "within the decade" in the Pacific Ocean, off California; and parallel "skyworlds" untethered from the land (and from reason?), conceived as future sanctuaries—urban colonies—for people for whom the planet's continents have grown too small. That such daydreams are more than just fantasy is evident from the plans of futurist entrepreneurs such as Richard Branson of Virgin Air fame, who hopes to service such colonies with novel companies like his Virgin Galactic, which is reportedly preparing to offer space miles benefits to its customers. Even old-line politicians such as Newt Gingrich now talk about colonizing the moon as staples of their political campaign patter.

For some time, idealists and dreamers have looked even further—beyond our known urban behemoths and linked megacities—in search of Marshall McLuhan's global village, a mote in his prescient eye sixty years ago, but today an abstraction being realized not only in digital and virtual forms like the cloud, but in global economic markets and in the complex urban networks that are our focus here. Global village indeed! The urban philosopher Constantinos Doxiadis, pursuing his own science of human development he calls Ekistics, has predicted the emergence of a single planetary city—*Ecumenopolis.*[21] Doxiadis gives a sociological and futurist spin to science fiction writers like Isaac Asimov and William Gibson who for decades have been imagining urban agglomerations on a planetary scale.[22]

Just beyond the global village, pushing out from the imagined Ecumenopolis, one can catch a glimpse of Gaia, that mythic organic entity that, in the hypothesis posited by James Lovelock, is as an evolving and self-regulating system in which biosphere, atmosphere, hydrosphere, and pedosphere all work together on behalf of a sustainable and integral planet, though whether it is urban or not, or even includes humanity, remains a puzzle. In Gaia, Lovelock hypothesizes, "we may find ourselves and all other living things to be parts and partners of a vast being who in her entirety has the power to maintain our planet as a fit and comfortable habitat for life."[23] This is cosmopolitanism on interstellar stilts, hinting at a new phase of interconnectivity mimicking the galactic empires of *Star Trek* and *Star Wars.* Yet there it is in the Mars surface explorer *Curiosity* probing science fiction's favorite planet for signs of life (and finding them!); and in the American government's wackily inspired plan to offer grants to private sector companies hoping to launch manned expeditions to nearby stars like Alpha Centauri. Such hyper-cosmopolitan visions may be pure fantasy, although NASA's "earth system science" takes them seriously, and they are urban only in a vague sense of universal integration. Lovelock credits the novelist William Golding with the term *Gaia*, but the Gaia approach seems to incorporate both the longing for and expectation of an interdependent urbanity as encompassing as humanity's perfervid imagination.

This journey from polis to megalopolis, from parochial pieces to imagined whole, has been a grand voyage from the simple to the complex, the rural to the urban, the local to the global, the mundane to the imaginative and the fantastic. The development, although inspired, has had a feel of pedestrian ineluctability about it, with our real-world population ever more concentrated, commerce ever more global, and complexity continuingly augmented. As if history is shaping a world concretely that we once imagined only in our dreams. For dreams are now being given palpable form by planners and architects. The last several years have witnessed three global architectural contests by the Institute for Advanced Architecture of Catalonia (IAAC), the most recent of which drew over one hundred fantastical but reality-based proposals "envisioning the habitat of the future" under the title Self-Sufficient City.[24] Among the design ideas: the Weightlessness City, Sky-City, Bio-Digital City, Ecotopia, MegaCityBlock, Non-Stop City, Repower City, Hole City, Drift City, Swarm City, and Freedom in Captivity. Inevitable or not, and whether or not we like it (many do not), the developments depicted here, with which the architects of the Self-Sufficient City Contest are grappling, have resulted in and are the products of the forging of civic, cultural, and commercial networks that have made human association in the form of urbanity the touchstone for a sustainable human civilization. Without exceeding the limits of what is actually in process today—leave aside fantasies of Ecumenopolis and Gaia and interstellar migrations of cities— a realistic road to cosmopolis and a world governed by mayors lies before us. It is left to us only to determine whether we wish to take it, and in doing so, take democracy to planetary scale.

For all the contradictions and obstacles presented by cities, they remain a formidable alternative to the conventional nation-state paradigm in which our thinking has been imprisoned for the past three centuries. The very term *inter-national* assumes that nation-states must be the starting place for inter-relational thinking. Global organizations inscribe the prejudice in their defining nomenclature: the old "concert of nations," and of course the League of Nations and the United Nations. This road has led nowhere slowly. Are we any closer today to a semblance of global governance than when Hugo Grotius and Thomas Hobbes tried to imagine a contract among nations or when Immanuel Kant penned his perpetually unrealized *Perpetual Peace*? Closer than we were at the Congress of Vienna or, following the war to end all wars, the Treaty of Versailles? We seek an alternative road forward not for academic reasons (although the teaching of the field atavistically labeled "international affairs" could use a major overhaul starting with its name), but because in this fiercely interdependent world the demand for global governance has become the critical challenge of our times.

The planet itself pleads its case. The seas are rising, the glaciers melting, and the atmosphere warming. But the 193 nations that have gathered annually in Copenhagen, Mexico City, Durban, and Rio remain implacable and immovable. Too busy explaining why their sovereignty and their pursuit of independence for their stubbornly proud peoples justify taking no action, they must make themselves oblivious to imperiled shorelines, to aquifers and watersheds used up, atmospheric CO_2 passing the tipping point of 350 ppm seen by many scientists as an upper limit on carbon emissions and now above 400 ppm, and global temperature already exceeding the rise of two degrees centigrade that scientists only recently set as a limit. Little island nations like the Maldives may vanish and the economies of the great nations may be devastated, but the nation-state seems intent on going down in complacent oblivion with its antique and eroded but ever prized sovereignty intact. "USA! USA!" chant the American crowds at ballgames and political rallies, embracing a proud but lumbering behemoth bereft of capacity to safeguard them from the brutal interdependent world at their doorstep.

Much the same obliviousness affects our attitudes toward poverty. Rich nations find ways to grow richer and the poor grow poorer, but it is as much sovereignty as greed that fuels the dismaying inequalities between North and South and compounds the problems of combating disease, famine, and genocide. The defect is political as well as economic.

The 99 percent watch the one percent dominate the global economy, while the bottom half sinks into abject poverty, wondering why the middle class alone attracts the attention of "democratic" rulers. For not only has the middle class in the developing world watched its status put at risk by a system geared to the wealthiest, but the new emerging middle class in nations like India, Thailand, and Indonesia has seemingly turned its back on the poorer classes from which it only recently managed to detach itself.

The global recession also fails to arouse our attention. Mortgage holders default, businesses go under, secondary markets collapse, and banks fail. Yet the causes are more closely associated with democratic than fiscal defects, above all an absence of global trust and transnational civic capital. Banking depends on trust, and banks are most successful when they are integral to the communities they serve. During the recent meltdown, small community banks and cooperatives were largely immune to the disasters that befell their huge global brethren. The sentimental story told in the classic film *It's a Wonderful Life*, in which the small-time community banker played by Jimmy Stewart prevails over the ambitious big-bank rival who tries to destroy him, contains a nugget of truth about the relationship between banking and a democratic community.

Embedded in these critical economic issues is a tension between old theories and new realities. The new realities are about interdependence. For decades thinkers such as Masao Miyoshi have been announcing the coming of a "borderless world."[25] But the old theory insists on the sovereign independence of bordered states that, lacking a global compass, allow banks and oil cartels (and pandemics and climate change) to dominate the world. The institutions that precipitate today's crises are cross-border, but the states tasked to address the crises remain trapped within their frontiers.

So as futurists and pessimists alike pontificate about a world without borders—a world defined by inventive technologies, unremitting terrorism, liberated markets, uncontrollable labor migration, asymmetrical war, novel diseases, and weapons of mass destruction—complacent sovereigntists and stout "new nationalists," along with their conservative patriot allies, rattle on about the sanctity of frontiers and the autonomy of nation-states. Unwitting idealists all (though they still believe they are realists), they imagine an expiring world in which sovereign states still fashion unilateral solutions to global problems. They fail to notice that traditional democratic politics, caught in the comfortable box of sovereignty, has become irrelevant to new transnational realities that undemocratic bodies like banks and multinational corporations are enthusiastically addressing in their stead. Tethered to independence, and the social contract theory that gave it birth centuries ago, democracy is under duress, challenged once again by the problem of scale that undermined the early polis, but this time on a global scale—unable to rise to the fateful challenges of a world defined by forces of interdependence.

Democracy was born under radically different circumstances. First cultivated in the ancient world in the face-to-face participatory township, it managed when challenged by the growing scale of early modern societies to re-imagine itself successfully as the representative nation-state. But today it must adapt to a global, networked, interdependent world, or likely wither. To survive actually, it must find ways to establish itself virtually. To preserve its local vitality, it must achieve a global compass. It can no longer protect itself inside its borders, or protect the borders that define it, unless it can cross those borders as easily as the stealth insurgent intent on mayhem or the undocumented worker desperate for a job. Democracy must be as infectious as the latest pandemic, as fast moving as the wily currency speculator, and as viral as the World Wide Web.

States will not govern globally. Cities can and will—though not by writing a global charter of cities like the Charter of the United Nations, nor by promulgating a new Declaration of Human Rights. We already understand rights and have codified them in the modern era from sunup to sundown. We understand what rights ask of us. We lack only global democratic mechanisms by which they can be enacted and enforced across borders. Without civic foundations to give mechanisms of enforcement weight, rights are (as James Madison once said of the U.S. Bill of Rights) just paper, parchment barriers offering little real protection against abuse. What we require are ways to act informally and piecemeal across borders that give substance to declarations of human rights, to realize the noble goals about which the Disunited Nations have mostly rhapsodized. States still set the terms, but cities bear the consequences. To take a poignant example, if terrorists manage to detonate a dirty bomb imported on a container ship, it may be nation-states like the "great Satan" United States of America they mean to punish, but it will be cities like Los Angeles and New York that suffer the carnage. Boston is only the latest American city to have experienced the consequences of a terrorist's global rage. Cities cannot wait for states to figure out the meaning of interdependence. As David Wylie has observed, to "redress the disconnect," cities and towns will themselves have to begin to "elect representatives to make common cause with other threatened urban populations."[26]

Yet there is little chance we can jump ahead and constitute a formal world government that like the nation-state is unitary, authoritative, and top-down—and somehow also still remains democratic. Nor is there a need to do so. Wylie wisely notes that "a secure world must be invented piecemeal, in multiple nations. It cannot be imagined or implemented as a unitary, preconceived plan or program."[27] Piecemeal describes what is actually taking place, with results that are real if less than dramatic. Informal governance achieved is better than formal government unrealized. A parliament of mayors (Chapter 12) that deliberates and undertakes to do whatever cities are willing *voluntarily* to do under the purview of states still able to constrain them is better than a world altogether without common aims or shared policies, a world in which international organizations try to represent the interests of a human family that actually is without an effective global advocate.

A global league of cities is, to be sure, not the same thing as a global central government. But this is probably a virtue, since it means that a league of cities will be able to act glocally through persuasion and example, and allow citizens to participate in their neighborhoods and local urban communities even as their mayors engage informally with one another across the globe. Moreover, networked cities already comprise webs of influence and interactivity that are creating new forms of global social capital and global civil society, and are birthing something resembling a global "civil religion" whose reality is interdependence, whose liturgy is rights, whose doctrine is cooperation, and whose practice is democracy. These networks do not extinguish or override the essence of cities but exploit and generalize them. Glocality strengthens local citizenship and then piggybacks global citizenship on it. The hog trained to carry a scrawny lad learns how to bear heavyweights. Cities will not face the impossible task that states face: trying to figure out how to yield their abstract sovereign essence to secure their concrete political survival. Cities have no sovereignty. They will not have to figure out how to overstep the bounds of their jurisdictional authority and cross sacred territorial borders. Borders do not define them.

In the ancient world, cities gave birth to creativity, imagination, and thus civilization; in time they found their way to democracy. Increases of scale broke the spirit of the ancient city and turned it into a parochial enemy of progress. But scale today imperils the states that once saved cities from scale, and the moment has come for cities, now incarnated in the emerging global metropolis, to rescue democracy again. The challenge is practical but also theoretical. The central issue is how the social contract on which modern nation-states depend can be globalized without being de-democratized, and how an institution capable of global governance can be found to succeed the nation-state.

The city is a living organism, but it is also a crucial *construct*, one that permits us to restate the social contract in global terms. For these reasons, I approach the task portrayed here as a political pragmatist but also as a political philosopher. It is only in reading Aristotle, Machiavelli, Hobbes, Rousseau, and Dewey that we can understand the task faced by Athens, Rome, London, Paris, and New York. For these cities must learn to succeed Greece, Italy, England, France, and the United States and a hundred other nations like them in reinventing governance for the twenty-first century.

Full circle then: can cities save the world? That may be too daunting a challenge. But it seems possible that they can rescue democracy from sovereignty and find ways to help us govern our world democratically and bottom-up, if only informally; ways to help us solve problems pragmatically rather than ideologically. Former president Bill Clinton reminded the 2012 Democratic National Convention that "when times are tough and people are frustrated and angry and hurting and uncertain, the politics of constant conflict may be good. But what is good politics does not necessarily work in the real world. What works in the real world is cooperation." Then he looked into the very heart of the city, and to cheers and applause, urged his audience to "ask the mayors who are here. Los Angeles is getting green and Chicago is getting an infrastructure bank because Republicans and Democrats are working together to get it. They didn't check their brains at the door. They didn't stop disagreeing, but their purpose was to get something done."[28]

What I want to do in this book is to get something done. To change the subject: from states to cities, from independence to interdependence, from ideology to problem solving. The city is the right subject today because hope has always been an urban currency and mayors have always in the first instance been optimists hoping to get something done. "The contrast between the optimism of urban commentators and the pessimism of those who focus on nations and multinational institutions," observes urban blogger Matthew Taylor, "is striking."[29]

Yet though a narrative of hope, the story of the city is marked by a dilemma: from the beginning of human communities, we have approached our towns and cities with ambivalence. We fear the urban even as (and perhaps because) it draws us in. The city is both magnet and repellent. Before measuring what we win in the human migration to cities, we must then, borrowing Peter Laslett's somber phrase, take the measure of the world we have lost.[30] And learn how to hold in creative tension the troubling dialectics of the city.

MICHAEL BLOOMBERG
OF NEW YORK

Journalists have already dubbed **MICHAEL BLOOMBERG** "the mayor of the world"—the "mayor of mayors" in the title of a recent magazine article.[1] Some would say that if Bloomberg buys into this, he is dreaming. But as the mayor of one of the world's great metropolises and a billionaire with his own media empire and foundation to underwrite his goals, Bloomberg's dreams track waking reality. A Democrat, then a converted Republican when elected to his first term after 9/11, he is now a declared Independent.

Certainly no mayor has fewer parochial debts and greater global reach. "You look at the way Mike has operated," says a senior adviser, "he's used mayors around the world and his network of philanthropy to produce what I would say are the beginnings of an international infrastructure that can promote a level of change that is hard to fathom." In his third and final term in New York (won after a controversial battle to change the law limiting him to two terms), Bloomberg flirted with running for the American presidency. After all, an insider whispered, he is more qualified to be president than the actual candidates. "He's run a bigger business than Mitt Romney. And he's been a public official longer than Barack Obama." Except, like so many others, what makes him good at being mayor hinders his presidential ambitions. He's too pragmatic, too disdainful of ordinary politics, too focused on solving problems rather than pitching woo; he is too . . . well, mayoral. He's all business and not enough politics.

Business is the right word. For Bloomberg incarnates the idea that mayors are practical rather than ideological, bridging politics and business with a non-politics of practical science and numbers. He made his fortune after being let go by Salomon Brothers when it was sold in 1981, going to work with computer terminals specializing in financial information. Soon after that, he inaugurated the Bloomberg News web portal and media company, situating him for global influence and a run for mayor.

As mayor, he talked like a businessman, and as a businessman today he talks like a mayor: "We don't have the luxury of giving speeches and making promises," he observes. Good as his word, he has focused on problem solving in issue areas that cities around the world share. He was and is about making cities work and fixing the things that get in the way. He raised taxes when he had to, pushed for congestion pricing (blocked by the state), inaugurated bike lanes and a New Housing Marketplace Plan, greened buildings (the source of much of New York carbon pollution), and banned big sugary sodas. And he helped establish the network Mayors Against Illegal Guns in the United States and the C40 Cities to combat climate change worldwide.

The business approach to urban problem solving insulated him from the downside of local democracy: he didn't need to tolerate corruption, please party stalwarts, or take stands for political advantage to advance his agenda. But it also insulated him from some of the virtues of local democracy. He never seemed quite to get the outrage, even among friends, that greeted his Machiavellian move to change the law forbidding a third mayoral term so he could run a third time. His well-intentioned ambitions for school reform were at times tone-deaf, as with his appropriation of the appointment of school heads to himself, or his choice of a quite brilliant businesswoman with no visible pedagogical qualifications as a schools superintendent who failed almost immediately. And that big-cup sugar soda ban seemed conceived without a thought to what beverage companies or kids—or critics of the nanny state—might think.

But Bloomberg trades in successful outcomes rather than in democratic legitimacy, and since democracy requires success some would say it's an acceptable trade-off. He jettisoned the school superintendent the way he jettisoned the Democratic and Republican Parties, and New York City emerged from the global recession ranked number one in the 2011 Cities of Opportunity report, while traditional towns such as London, Paris, and Tokyo dropped out of the top five (replaced by Toronto, San Francisco, Stockholm and Sydney!). The city has become number two in the nation in digital technology and retains a more diversified economy than most American metropolises.

Bloomberg is enough of a conservative to have endorsed losing Massachusetts Republican incumbent Scott Brown over winning challenger Elizabeth Warren in the 2012 Senate race, though he putatively did so less because she was critical of Wall Street than because Brown had abandoned his party to support gun control legislation, a core element in Bloomberg's cities' agenda. For Bloomberg, issues like congestion, climate change, and gun control trump ideology, which is in part why he found a home in neither major party.

Instead, as an independent global mayor, he has become a leading advocate of best practices among cities, using his foundation to catalyze urban innovation and reform both in New York and throughout the United States. He has handed out awards to four hundred American cities and has enticed his City Council into legislating climate change initiatives that are likely to survive his departure from office.

Back in the 1970s, in a nutty campaign for New York mayor he never stood a chance of winning, novelist Norman Mailer floated the idea of severing the Big Apple from the state and maybe the country too, letting it float off like a rogue iceberg, glistening with an alluring autonomy as a world metropolis just offshore from the powerful but parochial nation that did not understand it.

Today, under the guidance of mayors like Ed Koch and Michael Bloomberg (who got a dispensation to allow Koch to be the last man buried in Manhattan), and with some help from the likes of Mayors John Lindsay, David Dinkins, and Rudy Giuliani, without becoming an iceberg at sea, the city has truly become a free-floating world metropolis with global influence. Broadway and the arts, big banking and Wall Street, international deal making and the United Nations, and diversity and immigration are a big part of it. But give credit as well to citizens and mayors alike. Their leadership, made strikingly visible in Mayor Bloomberg's brew of creativity, civic energy, and hubris, has been the difference.

A good friend of the mayor, Carl Pope, who is chairman of the Sierra Club, sums up Bloomberg: He's "almost a Greek city-state guy." Someone who helps "other mayors succeed by giving them a global voice that can compete with heads of state. . . . He believes cities are where you can make the most change. He's really the first urban global diplomat we've had."[2]

CHAPTER 2. THE LAND OF LOST CONTENT

Virtue and Vice in the Life of the City

Into my heart an air that kills
From yon far country blows:
What are those blue remembered hills,
What spires, what farms are those?

That is the land of lost content,
I see it shining plain,
The happy highways where I went
And cannot come again.

A. E. Housman, A Shropshire Lad

The land and its farms were filled with the guilty voices of women mourning for their children and the aimless mutterings of men asking about jobs. State, county and local news consisted of stories of resignation, failure, suicide, madness, and grotesque eccentricity.

Michael Lesy, Wisconsin Death Trip

To comprehend what is won in the long journey of humankind to the city, we begin with what has been lost. It is still there, palpable if not fully recoverable, in the idyll that continues to haunt modern urban memory, a nostalgic naturalist daydream drawn from some farm girl's remembered childhood: family hearth in winter, rustling cornfields on an August afternoon, wide-open skies all year-round. The affecting poetry of loss emanating from A. E. Housman's lament for a "land of lost content" echoes in the anxieties of ambivalent urbanites in cities across the world. It glows on television in the image of a little house on the American prairie or in BBC manor-house comedies celebrating quaint country squires and their seductively simple-minded rural shenanigans. We know, writes Ralph Waldo Emerson, when seen in the streets of cities, how great are the stars above.[1] We know, when imagined from the London underground, how verdant are the Devon hedgerows. And we know too, when imagined from gleaming towers set down in the sands of the bleached Dubai desert, how poignant are the longings of a Bangladeshi migrant worker for the rippling greenery of a faraway riverbank village.

Country reveries dreamt in the dark heart of the city are not the only idylls troubling modern memory. They are mirrored by city reveries dreamt under wide-open skies, visions of a liberating urbanity promising release from the comfortable tyranny of village life. The stars—at least the extraterrestrial ones—may be invisible from the brightly lit canyons of urban thoroughfares, but city lights can be easily seen from orbiting satellites in outer space. Closer in, imagined from the Technicolor prairie, the city is a gray specter that frightens and beckons at the same moment, promising a form of corruption that feels like freedom. Freedom from history, from family, from religion, from gender, it doesn't matter, it is freedom from all the involuntary markers of identity that define and constrain where we come from. For those who prefer to define themselves by where they are going, urbanity is deliverance, the promise of liberation. And the country evinces, as Karl Marx exclaimed, only the "idiocy of rural life"—life incarnated in "stories of resignation, failure, suicide, madness, and grotesque eccentricity."[2] But the rural idyll remains potent, memorialized by a long line of romantic naturalists, many living in the city, for whom the country and virtue have remained synonymous.

For all the lures of urbanity, at least as it is imagined by contented country folk, the city is still a synonym for loss, less a liberation than a prelude to decadence. Nostalgic champions of a vanished rural life include historians like Peter Laslett, who in his *The World We Have Lost* captures Housman's lyric world in prose; and the numberless poets before and after Wordsworth who invoke "The Deserted Village" (Oliver Goldsmith) and *Cider with Rosie* (Laurie Lee) and, like Thomas Hardy, script novels about rural life *Far from the Madding Crowd*.[3] "Oh, happy Eden of those golden years," they exclaim with the poet John Clare, burnishing images of a cherished countryside, nature, and the pastoral. Like the philosopher Jean-Jacques Rousseau, their pastoral nostalgia leads them to curse the wickedness of cities and the temptations of the vicarious and the vapid they have themselves too often lived when they strayed from their roots—temptations endemic to urban theater and the theater of urbanity alike. They are provoked by cosmopolitan seductions in part because they have been unable to resist them. The seeming inescapability of urban life fills them first with dread, and then, when they succumb, regret. For the country is not merely the city's contrary, but in the nostalgic's moral perspective, an Eden from which we all have been cast out and cannot return. The poet Johannes Ewald draws the contrast:

> On softest beds you sleep, and I on softest clay;
> Within grand walls you dwell, in unwalled fields I lay;
> Grand artists paint your portrait, Nature colors me;
> You, sick with satiation, I of every sickness free;
> You pay a Swiss to guard you, my faithful dog guards me;
> You slake your thirst with darkened wine, the clearest springs
> cool me.[4]

Traces of inconsolable yearning for a lost countryside continue to mark our times. In the American setting, Tom Perrotta cites Willa Cather, who "remained stubbornly turned toward the past, nostalgic for her prairie childhood," a presence who is "frumpy and rural" in contrast to dashing, cosmopolitan contemporaries like Hemingway and Fitzgerald.[5] Raymond Williams has tracked a similar path in English literature: "On the country has gathered the idea of a natural way of life: of peace, innocence, and simple virtue. On the city has gathered the idea of an achieved centre: of learning, communication, light. Powerful hostile associations have also developed: on the city as a place of noise, worldliness and ambition; on the country as a place of backwardness, ignorance, limitation."[6] In France the yearning has manifested itself as the persistent sentimentality about *la France profonde*, in India in nostalgia for Gandhi's village communities, in Southeast Asia in memories of waterside shantytowns seen today from comfortable but anonymous subsidized high-rise apartments. In America the nostalgia lives commercially (and ubiquitously) in the country-western music of self-styled urban cowboys. Hank Williams Jr.'s "Country Boys Can Survive" pits country virtue against city villainy with Rousseauist poignancy:[7] Williams's country boy lives "in the back woods, you see, a woman and the kids and the dogs and me." Lives where life is still simple, "a shotgun rifle and a 4 wheel drive" where

> a country boy can survive
> Country folks can survive
>
> I can plow a field all day long
> I can catch catfish from dusk till dawn
> We make our own whiskey and our own smoke too
> Ain't too many things these ole boys can't do
> We grow good ole tomatoes and homemade wine
> And a country boy can survive
> Country folks can survive

Although Hank Williams Jr. and other country singers celebrate the virtues of country life from urban havens like Nashville and Memphis, their songs are weighted by anti-urban animus:

> I had a good friend in New York City
> He never called me by my name, just hillbilly. . . .
>
> But he was killed by a man with a switchblade knife
> For 43 dollars my friend lost his life
> I'd love to spit some beechnut in that dude's eyes
> And shoot him with my old 45
> Cause a country boy can survive
> Country folks can survive.

Not to turn Rousseau into Hank Williams Jr. (or for that matter Hank Williams Jr. into Thomas Hardy or the poet Ewald), Rousseau is nonetheless a prototypical critic of all that country music reviles about the city. "Men are devoured by our towns," Rousseau complains, having been devoured himself during his youth by Paris, where he spent excruciating years as a would-be playwright and composer and an uncomfortable frequenter of the philosophes' *salons*. Men, he writes in explaining his discomfort, "are not made to be crowded together in ant-hills, but scattered over the earth to till it. The more they are massed together, the more corrupt they become. Disease and vice are the sure results of over-crowded cities."[8] Rousseau, a city boy from Geneva, can't survive (and he didn't): not in the capital city of Paris, which he fled; not in his birth city of Geneva, which he tried to celebrate but which in return pro-scribed and burned his books; not in his alpine refuge, the village of Môtiers, whose simple peasants were hardly more sympathetic to him than the Parisians—they stoned him and ran him out of town.[9] He falls into modernity's chasm that stretches out between the Garden to which no one can return and the corrupt capital city from which no one es-capes whole. He opts ultimately for solitude: the loneliness of Robinson Crusoe and the reveries of a solitary walker.

In Rousseau's romantic moral geometry, the city manifests what is wrong with humankind and the civilizational "progress" by which its "development" has been charted. In lunging forward, man finds himself in free fall. It turns out to be no surprise, given Rousseau's lingering Calvinism, that freedom is itself part of the parable about man's fall. Inasmuch as the city portends freedom, our destiny in capital cities (the megacities of the eighteenth century) can only be a descent from grace, however much it feels like progress. To see in the Fall a happy ascent is, insists Rousseau, to throw garlands of flowers over our chains. As Arcadia vanishes and pastoral villages are transformed into commercial towns and then dense capital metropolises that embody the best and worst of the Enlightenment, Rousseau sees faux diamonds encrusted on moderni-ty's fool's-gold diadem. He pillories the city's proud denizens as "scheming, idle people without religion or principle, whose imagination, depraved by sloth, inactivity, the love of pleasure, and great needs, engenders only monsters and inspires only crimes."[10] In the end, the city is but "an abyss in which virtually the whole nation loses its morals, its laws, its courage and its freedom."[11] The very arts—above all theater—celebrated by cos-mopolitan admirers of the city as its salvation, are to Rousseau the cause and manifestation of their downfall.

Yet Rousseau is no ranting iconoclast. Or if he is, he belongs to a vast conspiracy. A late nineteenth-century chairman of the London County Council is scarcely less ferocious about London—a city he helped govern!—than Rousseau was about Paris. Lord Rosebery confides that "he is always haunted by the awfulness of London: by the great appalling fact of these millions cast down, as it would appear by hazard." London is a "tumour, an elaphantiasis sucking into its gorged system half the life and the blood and the bone of the rural districts."[12] Looking across the water from the rural gardens of the new world, Thomas Jefferson too reviles the teeming cities of the old world: because "cultivators of the earth are the most virtuous and independent citizens. . . . I think our governments will remain virtuous for many centuries; as long as they are chiefly agricultural; and this will be as long as there shall be vacant lands in any part of America. When they get piled upon one another in large cities, as in Europe, they will become corrupt as in Europe."[13] Even that epic poet of the urban, Berthold Brecht, takes a deeply cynical tack in his reconstruction of John Gay's *Beggar's Opera*. His *Three Penny Opera* is the culmination of a theater career spent balladeering against urban corruption, beginning with his play *In the Jungle of Cities*: "You are in Chicago in 1912," Brecht writes in *Jungle*; "You are about to witness an inexplicable wrestling match between two men and observe the downfall of a family that has moved from the prairies to the jungle of the big city." The jungle of cities captures in a phrase the indictment of poets and Marxists alike.

Although most European Enlightenment figures were on the other side, discerning in commercial towns paragons of the new commercial virtue that, in the Scottish Enlightenment and Adam Smith, became synonymous with the virtue of cities, in the new United States the biases remained anti-urban. Rousseau's insistence that civic virtue attached to the rural republic alone was actually more in tune with the American than the European view. Thomas Jefferson not only despised Europe's cities but rejoiced in the farmer as the new American man. Not Smith's tradesmen, but the American yeomanry comprised the new republican class. From his own experience, he could write that "those who labor the earth are the chosen people of God" in whom is vested "substantial and genuine virtue."[14] No need—yet—for urban parks or a Garden City in a land that was the biblical Garden incarnate.

Continuing in this republican vein a few generations later, Alexis de Tocqueville undertook a searching tour of the new country, concluding that republican institutions flourished in America precisely because there were no great capital cities of the kind Rousseau reviled. Liberty has a municipal character, but towns, not cities, were its source. The historian Thomas Bender reminds us that less than 200,000 of the 5 million Americans residing in the United States in the Founding era lived in cities. Only eight had more than 10,000 people—all of them seaports on the east coast.[15] Today something like 270 million of America's population of 350 million are urban dwellers. And how could it be otherwise in our era of agribusiness when only 2 to 3 percent of the population is needed on today's farms, as compared to the supermajority of Americans once required in order to ensure the nation was fed before the Civil War? Cities were magnets whose force field grew as the demographic and economic importance of the agricultural countryside declined.

For all this moral commotion, and the early American conception of the yeoman's republic aside, so seemingly inexorable was the rise of cities that in time the only argument against them unfolded within them. Even in the countryside, a faux romanticism turned Enlightenment gardens with their topiaries, pools, terraces, and fountains back into a carefully constructed "raw" nature. In Tom Stoppard's ascerb play *Arcadia*, a character decries "the whole Romantic sham . . . [in which] the sublime geometry was ploughed under . . . [until] the grass went from the doorstep to the horizon and the best box hedge in Derbyshire was dug up for the ha-ha so that fools could pretend they were living in God's countryside."[16] In the city, too, another tribe of pretenders aspired to defend the rural idyll from urban sanctuaries where they had taken up a comfortable residence. So-called decentrist critics, for example, no longer championed naturalist romanticism but pushed for an artificial naturalism that had to be reconstructed inside cities themselves. If, as decentrist pioneer Ebenezer Howard recognized in the nineteenth century, cities were magnets luring people from the country where they were no longer needed, then the country had to reestablish itself downtown. In Howard's own earnest hyperbole, "town and country must be married, and out of this joyous union will spring a new hope, a new life, a new civilization" rooted in the idea of "the Garden City."[17]

Howard, a true dialectician of the urban/rural divide, argued that if garden cities could manage to arrest their development at circa 30,000 citizens, they would be able to preserve the magnetic soul of the country—a "symbol of God's love and care for man"; yet they could do so within towns that, Howard believed, were in their own right symbols of "mutual help and friendly cooperation. . . . of wide relations between man and man, of broad, expanding sympathies, of science, art, culture, religion."[18] Whether Howard's towns would be seen today as anything more than greenbelt suburbs, he strove in his time to combine the virtues of town and country. That was the ideal lurking in the background of "Middletown," that average town in 1929 (based on Muncie, Indiana) that the sociologists Robert and Helen Lynd sought to portray as a transitional American archetype that aspired to conserve the virtue of country with the attractions of city as the nation morphed in the automobile age from a rural republic of towns into an urban republic of cities.[19]

Howard's followers like Lewis Mumford, less dialectical than their muse, fought a losing battle on behalf of human-scale cities, even as they libeled the gargantuan dimensions of the new metropolis with epithets like "Tyrannopolis" and "Nekropolis."[20] Fritz Lang took this nightmarish caricature of the city to the limit in his 1927 silent film classic *Metropolis*, where the city becomes a surrogate for capitalism's netherworld, epitomizing a fierce class struggle between owners living in towers and workers living underground.[21]

This radical moral geometry of the city has been a reciprocal affair. It has generated contrapuntal counterclaims from urbanists no less monomaniacal than those of the naturalists. Cosmopolitan zealots have badmouthed the hinterlands and celebrated rural emigrants fleeing to the city as so many lucky escapees from rural lockdown: women and men who managed to escape the torpid wastelands and their repressively homogenizing culture of redneck hickdom. Here too, compelling archetypes are to be found: an immigrant shoemaker from an East Prussian Staedel abjuring rural catechism and taking up an urban trade on another continent; a Sikh taxi driver as comfortable in London or Chicago as in Mumbai; an artsy cosmopolitan in love with the lonely crowd and the late-night party; brilliant atheists like the late Christopher Hitchins, for whom cosmopolitanism spells the welcome superseding of rigid morals and narrow liturgy; and chic heirs to Fitzgerald such as Jay McInerny, for whom vice is a sign of living fast among the quick and the dead. Such modernist urbanites attribute a terminal ennui to rural life. They insist, with Edward Banfield, on the moral and civic "backwardness" that goes with it.[22] At least some suspicion attaches to the monoculture of country life with its signature antipathy to "others" and sometimes its outright racism or its endemic fascism.

The urban cynic reads into Broadway musicals singing the romance of small towns in Iowa (*The Music Man*) or rural life in the Great Plains (*Oklahoma!*) little more than a cover-up for the stark police-blotter truths of *Wisconsin Death Trip*, Michael Lesy's lurid evocation of small-town crime in rural America a hundred years ago.[23] At sunrise, Oklahomans may croon "Oh, what a beautiful morning!" but by nightfall they face darker thoughts of the kind Norman Mailer explored in his *Executioner's Song*. The Kansas imagined by such cynics is not the dreamy Oz of Dorothy's *Over the Rainbow*, but the hardscrabble land of Truman Capote's *In Cold Blood* and its dead-souled killers, or nowadays perhaps the wrecked towns strewn along Oklahoma's real life tornado alley, where funnel clouds produce only wastelands, not emerald cities. Even celebrants of country culture such as the English poet George Crabbe understood that the rural village was not unblemished: in this classic 1783 work, *The Village*, we find this couplet: "No longer truth, though shown in verse, disdain / But own the Village Life a life of pain."[24]

Carlo Levi brings more balance to country life than Mailer or Capote or Lesy, but his portrait of a forgotten rural village in the south of Italy in his *Christ Stopped at Eboli* is almost more devastating, perhaps because it is unexpectedly sympathetic. He portrays a landscape so primitive and reactionary that it does not even achieve the simplistic Christianity by which rural life in southern Europe is usually defined. Exiled to the remote village of Lucania as a political prisoner of Mussolini in 1935, Levi depicts the region as "this shadowy land that knows neither sin nor redemption from sin, where evil is not moral but is only the pain residing forever in earthly things, Christ did not come. Christ stopped at Eboli," short of Lucania.[25] In that land too remote even for Christ, Levi inhabits an "other world, hedged in by custom and sorrow, cut off from History and the State, eternally patient . . . that land without comfort or solace, where the peasant lives out his motionless civilization on barren ground in remote poverty, and in the presence of death."[26]

Compare Levi's bleak portrait of 1930s southern Italy with Lesy's merciless account of the desolate rural Wisconsin landscape at the end of the nineteenth century, where "country towns had become charnel houses and the counties that surrounded them had become places of dry bones. The land and its farms were filled with the guilty voices of women mourning for their children and the aimless mutterings of men asking about jobs."[27] Wisconsin or southern Italy then, or Somalia today, no matter, rural life unfolds in a moral and civilizational wasteland deemed to be nearly beyond salvation.

Reversing the moral valence of Rousseau, cosmopolitan liberals such as Levi dismiss the reactionary foolishness of the countryside with as much zeal as their romantic counterparts condemn the unnatural vices of the city. They point fingers at the history of *la France profonde* in which is told Vichy's fascist betrayal of the French Republic during World War II; or they redefine the vaunted American Heartland as an incubator of nativist know-nothingism and reactionary Tea Party populism, where ignorance begets bigotry. They trace the origins of country back to some generic rural stupidity rooted in a primitive earth world, the *echt* criminal version of Laslett's "world we have lost." Country boys may survive, they will mock, but at the expense of civilization.

The world they assail is a world of contentious country boys, feuding Hatfields and McCoys, a world in which, as portrayed in Aeschylus's *Eumenides*, human destiny is perforated by cycles of vengeance thrust on women and men by subterranean Furies anticipating the sanguine appetites of the human race and knowing that human vanity married to endemic stupidity will satisfy their lust for blood. Until cosmopolitan reason intervenes. Aeschylus completes his *Orestia* trilogy by recalling how the brave goddess Athena puts an end to the vendettas of the House of Orestes and, suppressing the Furies, banishes vengeance, establishing the first reign of celestial justice over a growing polis. Tiny cosmopolitan Athens, in order to become the first real Western democratic city, must free itself from the cycles of blood. In doing so, it becomes an icon of civilizational urbanity—in the eyes of its own poets as well as of its Enlightenment and industrial age admirers two millennia down the human road.

Told this way, the story of towns carving a place for autonomous citizens from an earth-buried underworld ruled by tyrannical and vengeful gods offers an archetypical if partial tale: a tale of towns rejecting the divine madness of the gods and the human monarchies they prefer in the name of a novel republican democracy; a story of towns morphing into enlightened cities as they secure a home for reason; a story of toiling masses yielding to new "creative classes"[28]—the story told by American partisans today of red state rural Republicans and blue state urban Democrats locked in combat over the future of the American experiment. It is the story, not quite fulfilled, of the human journey from a natural world held uncomfortably between gods and beasts to an artificial world in which human justice is paramount, albeit by no means ubiquitous.

Raymond Williams has observed that "'country' and 'city' are very powerful words," words that stand for ways of experiencing human communities.[29] Opposing narratives about them are correspondingly potent. Narratives portraying the city's journey as an ascent to civility or descent into decrepitude—or both at once, in Rousseau's portrait—offer a striking normative take on the supposed descriptive features associated with the city offered in Chapter 1. Nearly all of these allegedly objective terms appear as mild terms of approbation. But they can easily be restated as pejoratives. Man's civilizing "improvements, so-called," Henry David Thoreau contends, "simply deform the landscape, and make it more and more tame and cheap."[30] What liberates, psychologists warn, can also alienate; mobility is a form of deracination; the lure of proximity can become the call of the mob or the impositions of the crowd—a crowd that, in Thomas Hardy's brutal portrait, as it "grows denser" quickly "loses its character as an aggregate of countless units, and becomes an organic whole, a molluscous black creature having nothing in common with humanity."[31] Hardy called London a "monster whose body had four million heads and eight million eyes," and more recent critics have seen in the verticality of cities and their defining architecture of sky-scrapers a metaphor for uprooting and disembodying. Freedom, per-haps the city's most seductive cry, is just another form of anomie (look at the urban projects); in the lyrics of the pop song, "just another word for nothing left to lose." Emerson associated freedom with nature, while Friedrich Schiller thought its home was in the high mountains, well removed from civilized cities. As for creativity, that super-virtue of cosmopolitanism, it can become an excuse for arrogance and elitism: metropolitan hubris as captured by the Metropolitan Opera and the Metropolitan Museum of Art, if not quite baseball's "wait for next year" Metropolitans.

The same exercise can turn neutral features of the country into a moral indictment of backwardness. Tradition is read as prejudice and superstition; a penchant for natural order is recast as a synonym for ine-quality and hierarchy; conservatism and stability are rendered as aver-sion to change and attachment to immobility; autarky is reformulated as a form of isolation; the natural is made into a euphemism for the jungle, with its Darwinian violence and Malthusian costs. In this normative remake, localism becomes parochialism and neighborliness just a paean to inbred backwardness.

In other words, the idea of the city, while obviously descriptive, is (like almost every other political construct including equality, liberty, justice, the state, democracy, authority, and legitimacy) powerfully normative as well. We cannot describe the city without revealing our assessment of its place in human development and morals, without hinting at likes and dislikes that reflect not the urban community but our views about it. Yes, we regard civilization as an essential and powerfully attractive de-fining characteristic of urban life. Yet when Thoreau espies "civilization" from afar on his walking tour, he sees only a dispiriting picture of "man and his affairs, church and state and school, trade and commerce, and manufactures and agriculture, even politics, the most alarming of them all," and, in his usual understated way, is "pleased to see how little space they occupy in the landscape."[32]

Acknowledging the normative and contestable nature of our subject is not a form of criticism but an invitation to candor and forthrightness in addressing the city. It yields two imperatives for my argument here. First, it demands that we examine the pitfalls of the city, even in its most virtuous and progressive incarnation, taking into account the normative critique of urban injustice, inequality, and corruption. In Chapter 7 ("Planet of Slums"), we will do so, reframing the broad moral critique of the city in terms of concrete challenges, including inequality, corruption, and predatory markets, that stand in the way of the city's prospective role in global governance. Second, it puts a premium on dialectical arguments that accept that city and country each offer virtues and vices, and hence refuses to choose sides—either to celebrate urban virtue and promote an easy trip forward or to excoriate urban vice and embark on an impossible journey to yesterday. Tom Perrotta is careful to qualify his portrait of Cather (above) by noting that the "frumpy" prairie image doesn't do justice to "the magnitude of her achievement. As a pure prose stylist, she ranks with Hemingway; as a self-made American artist and feminist pioneer, she traveled a far greater distance—from tiny Red Cloud to Manhattan—than Fitzgerald did when he made the leap from middle-class St. Paul to Princeton."[33] We should be ready to qualify the dualism between city and country in the same way.

Listen to Raymond Williams, who, about to dichotomize the two at book length, recognizes that the "real history" of city and country has been "astonishingly varied" with a "wide range of settlements between the traditional poles . . . suburb, dormitory town, shanty town, industrial estate."[34] Williams points here to how I will proceed. To choose sides is a hapless and futile strategy. It would be to embrace the ancient drama that has played out between advocates of the city and its riled country critics— a version of what Friedrich Nietzsche saw as the feud between Apollo and Dionysus, sun and moon, reason and feeling—and hence embrace the deep rift in human judgment about modernity itself. This is something no modern can reasonably do, unless she is willing either to deny her identity or to disown her past—thereby forgoing dialectical understanding.

Without dialectics, there is only the game of dueling identities. For women, the old clichéd diptych of goddess and whore; for cities, rival definitions of social man defined alternatively by natural sociability and hence as natural urban being or social man as a veritable product of Sodom and Gomorrah, whose every civilizational virtue is but a rationalization of decadence, corruption, and decay. The same rift is reproduced in sociology in Max Weber's portrait of the bureaucratic, rational city as successor to irrational and traditional kinship communities; or in Ferdinand Tönnies's distinctions between a traditional Gemeinschaft of rural and ascriptive (involuntary) affinities and a modern urban Gesellschaft of chosen civil associations.

The contest offered by this moral struggle over the meaning of the city, even when the absolutes are mediated, is significant because the dilemmas it precipitates are ongoing, and of central importance to the argument I want to make here about cities as possible building blocks of global governance. For if urban culture today has won the struggle with and over the land and has emerged as history's victor, and must consequently be treated as the starting point for networked, democratic governance in a world without borders, then its ancient vices must surely also be addressed. Mike Davis's "planet of slums" is hardly the final word on urban justice, but if slums are not to be taken as synonyms for cities, his argument and related critiques by scholars such as David Harvey (*Social Justice and the City*) must be addressed. If, as I propose, mayors are to rule the world and cities are to become the building blocks of a global democratic architecture, then we must show why their defects and deficiencies will not undermine and bring down the new structure. How are their endemic corruption and inequality as centers of inequality, poverty, and injustice, of crass commercialism and punishing anomie, to be countered as cities become modalities of global governance? Is urban opacity in the face of the need for silence and solitude, for nature and wilderness, endurable on the global scale? Is there a way to overcome the city's tendency to loneliness in the midst of crowds?

We must understand the critique and be able to defend the possibility of moral, egalitarian, and democratic versions of urban living and specify the conditions under which the prospect is realistic. This means we must fathom the dialectic of urbanity and grasp the deeply normative distinctions it generates: distinctions between city and country that turn out to be distinctions between artifice and nature, human association and wilderness, and the economics of trade, manufacturing, and information versus the economics of agriculture and the pastoral. If the reality is both, there is no place for either/or, and we are invited to be dialectical—a prudent option under any circumstances.

We are invited to refuse the simplistic moral geometry of Thomas Jefferson and Benjamin Franklin, who insist "the country possesses all the virtues" and the city none, without yielding to the homilies of zealous urbanists who despise the country as a backward wasteland.[35] One reason America seems to reflect a healthier mindset is that founding poets like Emerson, Melville, and Whitman took a measured and dialectical view of the landscape presented them by the boundless continent. "All science," wrote Emerson, understands America precisely as a delicate balance between civilization and nature, "and has one aim, namely, to find a theory of nature."[36] Whitman was equally at home with the seductions of the city and of the countryside, as evident in the range of his poems from "City of Ships" to "Song of the Open Road"; each in its own way offered the poet and citizen alike a path "leading wherever I choose," a place "loos'd of limits and imaginary lines."[37]

Thomas Bender has offered a meditation on this dialectical wisdom, writing that the leading minds of the American nineteenth century, including J. J. Audubon, F. L. Olmsted, Emerson, the naturalist George Perkins Marsh, Melville, and Whitman all manage, "with a wholeness of response, [to] embrace the scientific and the mechanical and the industrial, and at the same time place these within the ample framework of man's natural and humanistic heritage."[38] Leo Marx's *The Machine in the Garden* pays homage to both Eden and the American capitalist metropolis. There is perhaps no better representation of the wished-for dialectic than in Frederick Law Olmsted's belief that America had "entered upon a stage of progress in which its welfare is to depend on the convenience, safety, order and economy of life in its great cities. It cannot prosper independently of them; cannot gain in virtue, wisdom, comfort, except as they advance."[39]

Egalitarianism might be the city's boast, but it was by importing the country's equal access to bounteousness into the city in the form of parks that the real equality was secured: in Olmsted's parks, bodies of people can come "together, and with an evident glee in the prospect of coming together, all classes largely represented, with a common purpose, not at all intellectual, competitive with none, disposing to jealousy and spiritual or intellectual pride toward none, each individual adding by his mere presence to the pleasure of all others, all helping to the greater happiness of each. You may thus often see vast numbers of persons brought closely together, poor and rich, young and old, Jew and Gentile."[40] Such was Olmsted's vision of an urban equality that depended on the public space made possible by parks.

Olmsted was hardly alone. In 1947, contemplating the expansion of their transit system, planners in Copenhagen devised a "Finger Plan" that allowed the city to grow outward along transit fingers that would be separated by parks, woods, and other green spaces. By planning ahead, Copenhagen avoided the anarchy of urban sprawl and environmentally pernicious brown lands, and it ensured some measure of urban-country reconciliation in a quickly growing capital district. New towns with the luxury of starting fresh on a virgin map labor to integrate Olmsted's and Copenhagen's ideals into their planning. Daniel Kammen, the Nobel laureate energy scientist, recently sketched a vision of his own version of an Ecopolis responding to these ideals on his television series *Ecopolis* (2009).

There are dialecticians on the urban side as well. Even Le Corbusier, the early twentieth-century prophet of verticality, saw his skyscrapers as artificial mountains rising from urban grassland—the whole "radiant city" seen as a vast park.[41] This big-city seer actually assailed New York as too dense, its skyscrapers too ubiquitous, not sufficiently towering to leave large grass plots around their bases. The new urbanists return the favor of advocates who would bring the country to the city by looking to bring some of the city's electricity and buzz to exurban towns and suburban malls. Pursuing architectural and public planning approaches to commerce in the countryside, they incorporate urban edginess into stolid big-box malls and seek design elements that integrate shopping and living in the urban manner. As a park can invite a country commons into the city, a residential development above mall storefronts can bring an urban touch and hint of city risk to soulless suburban malls whose only denizens are otherwise shops and shoppers. When the mall becomes a pedestrian thoroughfare for teens and a plaza for pram-pushing moms and strolling seniors, when nightfall does not mean the vacating of the agora but the lights of a movie multiplex and the sounds of a sports bar, traces of the city's twenty-four-hour liveliness are brought to suburbia and beyond. Urban galleries and theatrical stages can likewise find their counterparts in showcase village storefronts or community dinner theaters, where urban creativity and imagination ride the rural circuit.

Most interesting, and of special relevance to our study, are those reluctant students of the city who yearn for country but have become dialectical urban realists. Focused on the city from its defining sins through palliatives imported from and reflecting the lost Eden of the countryside, they advance a decentrist logic that acknowledges the ineluctability of the center but tries to recreate the ultimate periphery—nature—within it. I have been critical of them, but the decentrists are mediators and have looked to discover elements of the country in the city or put them there—as Olmsted did with his Central Park in the heart of Manhattan.

Olmsted's great park was not part of the urban grid imposed on a yet-unbuilt city in 1811. The Commissioners' Plan of that year, developed when the population of the city was under 100,000 (one-tenth of Peking's or London's at the time) and when most of the land north of today's Houston Street was privately owned or wild, boldly envisioned a population of over 400,000 by 1860 (it was double that when the year arrived!) and a boxy grid of streets extending up into the rocky hills of what would become Harlem, all the way up to 155th Street.[42] While a number of places and squares including Union Place and Washington Square were built into the grid, the absence of breathing space and the dearth of natural sanctuaries in a plan being imposed on pure nature was startling—although an apt tribute to property values, which even then were very high.

A New York visitor to London in 1840 was shocked by New York's seeming obliviousness: "I never enter the London Parks without regretting the folly (call it cupidity) of our people [in New York], who, when they had a whole continent at their disposal, have left such narrow spaces for what has been so well called the lungs of a city."[43] If nature lost its place in city planning in New York in 1811, it won it back in Frederick Law Olmsted and Calvert Vaux's 1853 Greensward Plan for a great central park to occupy the heart of what had been planned as an omnipresent grid already swallowing up the island of Manhattan. Olmsted was as visionary as the 1811 commissioners, for like them he could only imagine what the future metropolis might look like. But in his mind, in the mostly empty fields and ditches around the land staked out for the park, he could envision a dreadful alternative to open space: an "artificial wall, twice as high as the Great Wall of China, composed of urban buildings."[44] Olmsted was hardly a decentrist, yet "the lungs of the city" was no metaphor for him but a necessity that would become urgent as the grid moved north and filled in. Olmsted's park allowed New York finally to compensate for all the missing squares, green spaces, and local commons that made London and Paris livable.[45]

When prudently planned, the city does not obliterate nature or negate open space; it incorporates them into the urban vision—as parks, squares, crossroads, commons, circles, plazas, and zoos as well as in lake- and riverfront developments, ponds, and other public spaces. New York has specialized in transforming "dead" urban places into usable public spaces: a decrepit elevated highway turned into a living park snaking along the West Side, for example, in the Highline project; or the Broadway Mall plan conceived by landscape architect Diana Balmori that would convert one hundred blocks of walled medians separating Broadway's busy vehicle lanes—medians that currently repel human use—into inviting pedestrian islands on the city's iconic boulevard. A belief in nature's power can actually help the urban flourish. Public space is the city's "natural" space, free, open to all, common.

At their best, urban architects dreamed country dreams, imagining edge cities and green spaces—imagining, as Le Corbusier himself did, high-rises nestled in green lands that might decongest dense urban conurbations. Or imagining, as the designer Bruce Mau does, "a city without parks," since the park "functions as an alibi, a moment of goodness in a field of bad." Mau, echoing earlier decentrists, wants to "think about the entire city as a park—a place of beauty and nature and delight."[46] Singapore, a city-state not much larger than Los Angeles and home to over five million people, could, like New York, only maintain open space through careful planning. With its population concentrated into subsidized high-rise apartments, it has cultivated three hundred parks and four nature reserves and fostered extensive tree planting—leaving over 50 percent of its land covered in greenery—and earned itself the title "Garden City."

Parks, squares, and commons are about more than nature, however. They are also emblems of the public character of urban space and represent the deeply democratic meaning of the commons. Think of what the Tuileries meant to the French Revolution, what Hyde Park represents for free speech in London, the role of Tahrir Square in Cairo and Green (Liberty) Square in Tripoli in the Arab Spring, or what Red Square in Moscow and Tiananmen Square have signified both for the Communist revolutions and the revolutions against the Communist revolutions. Would there be an Occupy Wall Street without Zuccotti Park? Surely in closing Zuccotti to protesters, the authorities thought they were closing down the protest? (They failed, but only because protesters found other public places to rally.) Cities collect people into dense communities where street politics and free speech are natural, as long as there is an open-space, an agora, to sustain them. But they do demand public space, as they did in Istanbul in 2013 when citizens stared down their government when it threatened to seize part of Taksim Square for a mall.

The First Amendment to the American Constitution and the rights to free speech and assembly protected by it (and most other constitutions around the world), have little traction in the absence of public spaces where citizens can assemble and listen to one another. One of the most devastating consequences of privatizing space in the suburbs has been the construction of shopping malls that are the only "common" spaces residents have. But they are private property and afford their owners the right to ban political leafleting and speech making, and so are not really public at all. Public and open spaces refresh the soul of the city, but they also empower citizens and facilitate democracy.

So Americans no more need to choose between "blue" and "red" than Singaporeans need to choose between green parklands and gray high-rises. We need neither embrace the virtuous city over the "backward" rural hinterland nor forsake "Sin City" for a virtuous heartland. The heartland can make its pulse felt inside the city: humanize its anonymity, make public its private ambitions, and give room to stroll and breathe and think to what might otherwise become a gasping and strangled mob. Indeed, it is open space that turns a mob or foule into a citizenry, "all classes largely represented, with a common purpose," as Olmsted wrote, "all helping to the greater happiness of each."[47] And as the likes of Teddy Roosevelt and John Muir once helped make the agrarian landscape livable and liberating by preserving the wilderness within that landscape through a system of national parks, so the likes of Frederick Olmsted helped make cities livable and democratic by preserving an element of nature within them through the establishment of parks and commons. John Muir—no taste for dialectics there!—liked to repair to ancient forestland and mountain wilderness to restore his soul to calm. He complained that Emerson was too hasty in telling us that "when Heaven gives the sign, leave the mountains," and made clear he "never for a moment thought of leaving God's big show for a mere profship."[48]

For most of the human race that now make their homes in cities, however, rusticity is not an option. The green lands they have forsaken must follow them to town, or wither and die. If the mountain never actually came to Mohammed, Shakespeare did find a way to bring Birnam Wood to Dunsinane Castle and seal Macbeth's fate. So too, sundry decentrists, architects, and urban planners have figured out how to bring grass to granite: how to deliver to urban dwellers lungs with which to breathe in the stifling urban canyons they inhabit. Lifetimes away from heartland open space where they or their forebears were born, they can still experience its cool winds and enticing scents and make city life sustainable. In the midst of all the private dwellings, private corporations, private businesses and private property, they can join with neighbors and other "republicans" who dwell in free and open public spaces.

If the city is our future, and the future too of global democracy (if democracy is to have a global future), this mediation of city and country, of the urbany and the natural, quite specifically by parks, but generically by enduring dialectic, is a good thing. To reap the rewards, however, we need to make sense of what we mean by the city. Not as moral emblem or repository of virtue (or vice), but as an empirical civic entity. This asks us to make a journey from poetry to prose, from the living practices of urban women and men to the theory and social science through which those practices have been captured.

LEOLUCA ORLANDO
OF PALERMO

LEOLUCA ORLANDO has been thrice elected mayor of Palermo over a period
of twenty-five years and has managed in interims between public service
to make a career as a European statesman, an award-winning actor, and
a warrior against the Mafia. The last is no small thing, since Orlando
has risked his life in living his civic principles.

He was first elected in 1985 with a whopping 75 percent of the vote in
a campaign in which he ran as much against the Mafia as for city hall.
His previous boss, the president of the Sicilian region, Piersanti Mat-
tarella, had been murdered by the Mafia in 1980. At the time, Palermo's
ugly nickname was "Mafiapolis," a title it had held ever since it was
effectively taken over by the Syndicate after World War II. At the time
Orlando first ran, Palermo was still a city in which, the popular saying
had it, "even the lemon and orange blossoms smell of corpses." After his
election, the Italian press referred to the new mayor as a "walking corpse,"
convinced his tenure would be quickly cut short.

Rather than run and hide, however, Orlando, a law-trained crime
fighter, chose to take on the Syndicate and give Palermo a chance to
liberate itself from a pernicious century-old dependency. Moreover, he
did this not only by fighting for an autonomous justice system and un-
corrupt law enforcement—the first "wheel" on what he called the "two-
wheeled cart" of good government—he worked simultaneously on civil

society, the cart's "second wheel," which demanded "a responsive and engaged citizenry and a growing economy."

The ensuing five years of Orlando's mayoralty became known as the Palermo Spring, when the back of the Mafioso economy through which the city had been controlled was broken. During the period, he also labored to transform the cultural climate, working on the civic culture with photographer Letizia Battaglia, who insisted that "common access to beautiful civic spaces—the only places where people were equal despite their wealth—was the first step towards building a culture of respect." A crime fighter who also was an artist and cultural innovator was a novelty in Palermo, but multitasking is typical of mayors around the world.

Orlando was originally a member of the Christian Democratic Party. Like so many mayors, he became disenchanted with ideological politics and in 1991 left the mayor's office to found La Rete, the Network or Movement for Democracy, whose aim was to put moral issues on the Italian multipartisan platform and promote urban democracy. Elected to the national Parliament in 1992, he was reelected in Palermo again in 1993 on the La Rete ticket. In his second term he intensified his effort to cleanse the city of criminal influence, rescinding the many corrupt contracts through which Mafioso firms controlled Palermo.

When La Rete folded, he joined with Romano Prodi in the new Democratic Party and subsequently founded the Daisy Party, which embraced leaders from across the Italian Left. He has continued to serve in the Italian Parliament and has also been a deputy to the European Parliament (with a first term from 1994 to 1999). In the summer of 2012, Orlando won an unprecedented third term as Palermo's mayor.

In the interim he held many regional and European offices, including chair of the Car-Free Cities Network. He quickly achieved a global reputation as a European civic organizer, a writer, and an actor. He has written a dozen books and legal treatises and has won the European Parliament's European Civic Prize (in 2000) for "his struggle against organized crime and his engagement in favor of the civic renewal of his city." The Pushkin Prize followed, "for his outstanding achievements in the promotion of culture." A genuinely global figure, he was subsequently awarded the Bayard Rustin Human Rights Award of the American Federation of Teachers and at the same time was granted honorary citizenship in Los Angeles County, California, in the United States.

Like so many mayors, Orlando is a character—which perhaps is why he can play characters with such aplomb on television and in the movies, and why in 1994 he won an acting prize, the Fernsehen (television) Film Preis of Germany.

Yet all Orlando does globally remains rooted in his love of Sicily and Palermo and his wish to give to his fellow citizens a working and a just city in which crime is merely another urban issue rather than a way of life. He has paid for his civic zeal by having to live under the constant threat of violence from crime-world enemies. One cannot visit with him without being surrounded by bodyguards or travel with him around town (whether in Rome or Palermo) without being shadowed by follow cars from which watchful armed escorts track the mayor's movements.

Orlando responds to the dangers of criminal parochialism by appealing to the aspirations of cultural and civic interdependence. One of the first supporters of the Interdependence Movement, Orlando brought to Mayor Walter Veltroni of Rome and Pope John Paul II the idea of convening the second Interdependence Day Forum and Celebration in Rome in 2004—an event that sealed the role of cities as the primary actors in global interdependence and cooperation.

CHAPTER 3. THE CITY AND DEMOCRACY

From Independent Polis to Interdependent Cosmopolis

> Did you, too, O friend, suppose democracy was only for elections, for politics, and for a party name? I say democracy is only of use there that it may pass on and come to its flower and fruits in manners, in the highest forms of interrelation between men, and their beliefs . . . democracy in all public and private life. . . . It is not yet the fully received, the fervid, the absolute faith. I submit therefore that the fruition of democracy, on aught like a grand scale, resides altogether in the future.
>
> *Walt Whitman*, Democratic Vistas

The story of cities is the story of democracy. To retell the city's history, from polis to megaregion, is also to tell the story of the civic from citizenship to civilization. Urban life entails common living; common living means common willing and common law making, and these define the essence of political democracy. Democracy, however, is more than political. As John Dewey insisted, it is a way of life. In Walt Whitman's provocative challenge, democracy must be made manifest in "the highest forms of interrelation between men, and their beliefs—in literature, colleges and schools—democracy in all public and private life." Democracy's fruition thus "resides altogether in the future."[1]

The democratic way is then more about process than about an end state: it is about the processes by which power is shared, equality secured, and liberty realized—within and not against the community. The institutions embodying the process—polis, nation-state, nongovernmental organization (NGO), international organization, and city—are forever in flux, making their relationship to democracy problematic. The city in particular, our modern habitat, is forever evolving and changing, above all in its relationship to equality and liberty. If democracy is to survive globalization, imagining a global democratic order with the city at its core may be crucial. Envision not states but cities as building blocks for global governance, and global governance has some chance to be democratic.

The key is the city. The argument is about the city. Global governance in which the city predominates is the aim. Yet the city is a generic and catholic construct—that is to say, encompassing, vague, even indeterminate. So what is it exactly? Democracy is but a piece of the puzzle. We have already seen how contentious views about the city's moral valence can be. Early democratic republicans like Jean-Jacques Rousseau, a romantic champion of the rustic, deemed the capital city democracy's nemesis. With other skeptics of modernity, he read progress itself, if not as malign, as dialectical: a deceptive form of evolutionary decline that masquerades as perfectibility. We were also witness to Rousseau's critics—Enlightenment and industrial age moderns and cosmopolitan zealots—who countered rustic nostalgia with a narrative portraying the urban as progress pure and simple.

The generic notion of the urban is then not merely indeterminate but deeply contested in character and purpose (*telos*). In Chapters 7 and 8 we will witness how the critique of the city introduced above plays out as a narrative of inequality and injustice—corruption and cupidity—in the modern metropolis. To make sense of the debate, however, we must also approach the city empirically and historically, drawing from its living experience specific features and teasing out of its disparate practices common meaning. Until we do, the case for global governance by cities will remain an abstraction caught up in a moral controversy. Aside, then, from its promise, aside from whether it possesses sufficient moral capacity and participatory potential to become a building block for global democracy, what is it that we mean when we speak of the city? Or when we describe what is *not* the city? Can what it is not help us discover what it is?

Understanding the City: Some Preliminaries

The city's compass extends from settlements and small towns (if not quite village sized) of several thousand to imposing modern megacities with tens of millions. References to the "urban population" turn out to refer to entities of radically varying size, which is why announcing that more than half the world's population today lives in cities is as problematic as it is dramatic. As I hazard generalizations about "the city" throughout this book and explore the moral debate that surrounds its evolution, there must be some agreement on the meaning of the word. All general claims about cities are compromised to some degree by the reality that, even at the elementary level of size, the city is ill defined. It may be a town of 50,000 such as Pittsfield, Massachusetts, or Tulle in France, or may constitute a megaregion such as Kinshasa in Africa (population 20 million) or Chongqing in China (nearly 30 million). Can we make any convincing generalizations about civic entities so radically incommensurable? How different is OSUM, the association of Ontario Small Urban Municipalities, from the U.S. Conference of Mayors? What do New Tecumseh or Parry Sound in Ontario have in common with Toronto let alone Chicago? They are cities, one and all, but can a town of under 20,000 be compared to a city of two and a half million?

This caveat notwithstanding, the figures that define the urban are shifting in the most startling ways, especially when adjusted to economic indicators. Little towns are morphing nearly overnight into big cities, and people everywhere are migrating into town. McKinsey reports that in 2007, over 1.5 billion people or 22 percent of the world's population lived in the world's 600 largest cities and earned 60 percent of global gross domestic product (GDP), a full 50 percent of global GDP coming from just 380 of the top 600. The top 100 GDP generators produced $21 trillion in GDP or 38 percent of the global total in 2007.[2] Just 380 of the top 600 cities as measured by GDP accounted for 50 percent of 2007 global GDP, and 190 North American cities alone made up 20 percent of global GDP.

McKinsey estimates that by 2025, some 136 new cities will enter the top 600, every one of them from the developing world, "as the center of gravity of the urban world moves south and, even more decisively, east."[3]

Table 1: Top 25 Hotspots by 2025: Cityscope 2025 City Rankings

Rank	GDP	Per Capita GDP	GPD Growth
1	New York	Oslo	**Shanghai**
2	Tokyo	**Doha**	**Beijing**
3	**Shanghai**	Bergen	New York
4	London	**Macau**	**Tianjin**
5	**Beijing**	Trondheim	**Chongqing**
6	Los Angeles	Bridgeport	**Shenzhen**
7	Paris	Hwasŏng	**Guangzhou**
8	Chicago	Asan	**Nanjing**
9	Rhein-Ruhr	San Jose	**Hangzhou**
10	**Shenzhen**	Yŏsu	**Chengdu**
11	**Tianjin**	Calgary	**Wuhan**
12	Dallas	**Al-Ayn**	London
13	Washington, D.C.	Edinburgh	Los Angeles
14	Houston	Charlotte	**Foshan**
15	**São Paulo**	San Francisco	**Taipei**
16	**Moscow**	Durham	**Delhi**
17	**Chongqing**	Ulsan	**Moscow**
18	Randstad	Washington, D.C.	**Singapore**
19	**Guangzhou**	Boston	**São Paulo**
20	**Mexico City**	Belfast	Tokyo
21	Osaka	New York	**Shenyang**
22	Philadelphia	**Grande Vitoria**	**Xi'an**
23	Boston	Canberra	**Dongguan**
24	San Francisco	Seattle	**Mumbai**
25	**Hong Kong**	Zurich	**Hong Kong**

Source: McKinsey Global Institute, *Urban World: Mapping the Economic Power of Cities*, 2011, p. 3.
Bold = From the Developing World. Not Bold = From the Developed World.

Among such cities will be Hyderabad and Surat in India (a country that will add 13 cities to the top 600) and Cancún and Barranquilla in Latin America (which will add 8), while 100 of the top 600 in 2025 will be in China. One might say it is not China, but Chinese *cities* that will dominate the coming decades. Table 1 indicates that in terms of per capita

Total Population	Children	Total Households	Households with Annual Income over $20,000
Tokyo	**Kinshasa**	Tokyo	Tokyo
Mumbai	**Karachi**	**Shanghai**	New York
Shanghai	**Dhaka**	**Beijing**	London
Beijing	**Mumbai**	**São Paulo**	**Shanghai**
Delhi	**Kolkata**	**Chongqing**	**Beijing**
Kolkata	**Lagos**	New York	Paris
Dhaka	**Delhi**	London	Rhein-Ruhr
São Paulo	**Mexico City**	**Mumbai**	Osaka
Mexico City	New York	**Delhi**	**Moscow**
New York	**Manila**	**Mexico City**	**Mexico City**
Chongqing	Tokyo	Rhein-Ruhr	Los Angeles
Karachi	**Cairo**	Paris	**São Paulo**
Kinshasa	**Lahore**	**Kolkata**	Seoul
London	**São Paulo**	**Lagos**	Chicago
Lagos	**Kabul**	Osaka	Milan
Cairo	**Buenos Aires**	**Dhaka**	**Mumbai**
Manila	**Luanda**	**Tianjin**	**Cairo**
Shenzhen	London	**Shenzhen**	**Hong Kong**
Los Angeles	Los Angeles	**Moscow**	**Taipei**
Buenos Aires	**Colombo**	**Chengdu**	Randstad
Rio de Janeiro	**Baghdad**	**Cairo**	**Shenzhen**
Tianjin	**Shanghai**	**Rio de Janeiro**	**Istanbul**
Paris	Paris	**Wuhan**	**Delhi**
Jakarta	**Jakarta**	Los Angeles	**Buenos Aires**
Istanbul	**Istanbul**	**Buenos Aires**	Madrid

GDP, Doha, Macau, and Hwasŏng will rank above Edinburgh, New York, and Zurich, while in terms of households with annual income over $20,000, Beijing will pass Paris, Mexico City will pass Los Angeles, Seoul will pass Chicago, and Delhi will pass Madrid. Yet much of the change is invisible in the West: Chongqing is China's largest metropolitan region, with nearly 30 million people, but it is more or less unknown beyond China's borders. And who outside their host regions has heard of Surat or Barranquilla?

Size and wealth, important as they are, perhaps are not as critical to the meaning of the city as density, however, and there is probably a population/wealth/density threshold under which many of the functions of the city simply cannot be carried out. The ancient village, for example, albeit a commune or community (Gemeinschaft), scarcely exists as a town, let alone a city, and it lacks many key functions and the infrastructure of a city. On the other hand, today's small towns like Parry Sound exercise grown up urban responsibilities and share many of the same functions larger municipalities are burdened with. "Big" cities with populations over a million may not count as global cities or even be particularly well networked with other cities, though functionally they are not that different. Detroit, Leicester, and Sarajevo are large but declining, and they are hardly typical of twenty-first-century networked global metropolises such as Kinshasa or Chongqing—burgeoning metropolises that scarcely existed on such a scale twenty or thirty years ago, and whose names hardly roll off the tongue in the manner of Hong Kong or Paris or Rio.

Even in older cities, new suburban developments quickly become minicities of their own, as imposing as their mother metropolises. Yet some American cities are quintessentially suburban, a collection of suburban mushrooms gathered together into an urban field without a true center (Phoenix or much of Los Angeles, for example).[4] New Yorkers driving down the Westside Highway in Manhattan will blink several times before realizing that the office cityscape growing up just to the right of the new Freedom Tower is actually Jersey City, across the Hudson in New Jersey. Likewise, Parisians looking east along the fabled Champs-Elysées will have to kick themselves to remember that the aging new world architectural wonder of La Défense, with its high-rises and very own arch, lies beyond the Périphérique, outside the limits of low-slung Paris proper. Many older cities in the developed world, locked into a vanished age of urban manufacturing, are insignificant with respect to GDP and have little relevance to the governance issues we address here,

Table 2: Top Cities in Terms of Absolute Household Growth, 2011–2025 (projected in terms of million households)

Megacities		Top-Performing Middleweights		Middleweight's Growth Rate Outperforms (number of megacities)
Beijing	5.5	Lagos	3.2	20
Shanghai	5.2	Chengdu	2.7	19
Tokyo	3.3	Shenzhen	2.6	17
Chongqing	3.1	Tianjin	2.3	15
Mumbai	2.7	Hangzhou	2.1	15
Delhi	2.7	Foshan	2.0	15
São Paulo	2.4	Xi'an	2.0	15
Dhaka	2.4	Guangzhou	2.0	14
Cairo	2.0	Wuhan	1.9	14
Kolkata	1.9	Kinshasa	1.9	14
Mexico City	1.8	Johannesburg	1.9	14
Rio de Janeiro	1.5	Nanjing	1.6	12
Karachi	1.3	Dongguan	1.5	12
London	1.2	Jakarta	1.4	11
Paris	1.2	Bogotá	1.4	11
Manila	1.2	Colombo	1.4	11
Istanbul	1.0	Luanda	1.3	10
Moscow	1.0	Guigang	1.3	9
Osaka	0.9	Hefei	1.2	8
Rhein-Ruhr	0.9	Jinan	1.2	7
New York	0.8	Ningbo	1.2	7
Buenos Aires	0.7	Taipei	1.1	7
Los Angeles	0.5	Taizhou	1.1	7

Source: McKinsey Global Institute, *Urban World: Mapping the Economic Power of Cities*, 2011, p. 15.

while scores of unheralded newer ones are crucial. Cities are in any case undergoing constant change, as Daniel Brook's fascinating "history of future cities" makes evident.[5] Smaller "middleweight" cities are today outperforming many megacities in terms of overall household growth (see Table 2). According to McKinsey, Jakarta does better in this department than London, Jinan better than New York, and Taipei better than Los Angeles. Lagos actually outperforms twenty considerably larger megacities.

Historically, too, the only constant has been change. Even with the later, somewhat larger, medieval walled towns that were beginning to feel like cities at the beginning of the second millennium, conditions still favored a self-sufficiency defined more by exclusion than inclusion— by what sociologists call bonding capital rather than bridging capital. They exhibited fear of the outside world rather than an inclination to communicate and interconnect with it. The early English word *town* derived quite appropriately from the German word *Zaun*, denoting the "wall" that was once the first indication to a traveler that a hamlet lay ahead. What a city wall indicated was not the dwelling place within, but the town's feudal self-isolation from its surroundings. During these dangerous times, the city was designed for insularity and safety rather than mobility and liberty. Yet though walled and built more often on castled hillsides or fortressed islands where water functioned as moat rather than connector, even medieval cities paid tribute to the sociability of the human species. Even in their medieval incarnation, cities remained repositories of knowledge—centers of learning and of cultural and archival activities privileging the new creative classes over others. These features meant persistent change and the transformation of cities in the Renaissance from insulated burgs back to trading towns and global ports of exploration and exchange. It was the rare town built without proximity to water and the flows water entailed.

Despite their importance in the early modern period, the so-called state-of-nature philosophers who rationalized the emergence of new nation-states in the early modern period ignored cities as political precursors to the state. Instead, they looked back to family and tribe and beyond, back to simpler forms of community life of the sort sociologists and anthropologists might recognize, in order to postulate an ur-original human habitat that looked like Eden with people. Theirs was at best an abstraction necessary to making an argument for obeying kings and other sovereigns. By grounding rights in a state of nature or a natural condition, social theorists provided a normative foundation for new political obligations to obey the laws of kings—compliance with laws as a form of self-interest even when the lawmakers were monarchs.

In resorting to (and perhaps fantasizing about) a state of nature as a way to legitimize obedience to authority, an abstract and purely hypothetical condition prior to human association was given a life and a seeming history. No such actual state of nature, however, was identified in anthropology, sociology, or history. The family retained a key role in conservative depictions of the origins of the state, but cities and towns did not. The state of nature was an artificial construct of theorists, but it was the artificial rather than the natural that really defined us: everywhere in social science, human "nature" is social and thus artificial. In Aristotle and Karl Marx, if not in Plato and Rousseau, humans are understood as *zoon politkon* or species-beings—political animals preternaturally drawn to common living and the life of the community, and hence to the artifice of the city. Even anarchists such as Charles Fourier, Pierre-Joseph Proudhon, and Peter Kropotkin have preferred community to isolation and natural cooperation to crude Darwinism in imagining a natural condition. They conceive of an anarchism opposed to central power but inclined to local cooperation and community, more in the manner of American presidential candidate Ron Paul in 2012, for example, than of Ayn Rand or Max Stirner.[6]

Republican founders, aping John Locke, speak about men being "born free," but advocates of individualism always require a theory of individuation to explain how we free ourselves from natural bonds and separate ourselves from the collectivities into which we are actually born. In Rousseau's paradox, though "born free," we are "everywhere in chains." Nation-states were preceded not by the state of nature but by cities and principalities, kingdoms and empires, all of which were well-organized social entities. These realities give the urban its seemingly ineluctable character and allow us to treat cities as potential global democratic building blocks.

There is no need to retrace here the remarkable history of towns and cities that has been narrated by eminent sociologists and historians from

Max Weber, Lewis Mumford, and Jane Jacobs to Peter Marcuse, Ronald van Kempen, Saskia Sassen, and Eric Corijn.[7] Yet we do need to recall that this history, for all its variety, has been marked by a relentlessly progressive development, not just change but seemingly purposeful and "progressive" change: a growth in population density, in diversity, and in specialization of function; and hence in complexity. Like the jungles to which they are sometimes contrasted (or compared), cities grow, often rampantly and anarchically, even when they are hemmed in and hampered in unnatural ways.[8]

Movements that have tried to slow population growth and retain openness and a sense of nature inside the city—the so-called decentrists, for example, who include Ebenezer Howard, Lewis Mumford, and Catherine Bauer—have not been notably successful. It is not surprising that decentrists recoil at the aggressive phallic abstractions of planning zealots such as Le Corbusier, that ideological provocateur of the high-rise.[9] But in setting themselves against growth and concentration, whether via verticality or spread, the dissidents risked setting themselves against the city itself. As Jane Jacobs wrote, "this is the most amazing event in the whole sorry tale: that finally people who sincerely wanted to strengthen great cities should adopt recipes frankly devised for undermining their economies and killing them."[10] To save cities, decentrists almost seemed ready to jettison them, although this was not their intention. Mumford was even more hostile to the car-dependent suburbs than to the urban "Necropolis" he savaged. But sometimes their voices echoed the romantic critics of the urban to whom they presumably meant to respond.

These permutations make clear how difficult it is actually to define the city on whose cross-border potential I put so much store. Yet though definitions of the city are contested, and population thresholds subject to debate, there are measures of the urban widely acknowledged as critical that fortify our argument for networking and cross-border governance. Putting aside the key question of the city's moral valence, there are a number of core elements that, in combination, yield a compelling portrait of the city and its defining urbanity. In some cases, the terms define the city only indirectly, by suggesting what it is not. Indeed, what the city is not is a useful place to begin.

What the City Is Not

As a social and geographical form, the city may be seen as a generic antonym to all that is not urban: to suburbia and exurbia; to the rural, the "country," or even the uninhabited natural wilderness; or to such artificial facsimiles of wilderness as national parks (or urban parks) that are "visited" but not lived in.[11] All such nonurban locales are dispersed and sparsely populated. They may even represent, sometimes deliberately, the absence altogether of the communal and the human, and thus of the "civilized"—the Eden ideal prior to the creation of man and woman.

What communities or individuals in the countryside are tell us what cities are not—and what, instead, they can be. In the countryside, communities are small, sparsely populated, and dispersed, but also "thick" in the sense of being intimate and grounded (Ferdinand Tönnies's notion of Gemeinschaft). In contrast, urban communities are sociologically "thin" (Tönnies's Gesellschaft or "society") but densely populated and encompassing. Where rural villages and towns are often isolated, embedded in domains residents rarely leave, cities are naturally interconnected. The synapses connecting them actually help define the urban nodes they comprise, since mobility within and among cities is inherent in urban living. The economies of the countryside are agricultural or pastoral and are inclined to self-sufficiency or even autarky. They can be as rudimentary as hunting-gathering or even encompass (on the model of the Garden of Eden) a bounteous indolence. Cities are dependent and hence interdependent, tied to food and commodity supplies from outside, and to each other by trade and commerce. The city absolutely needs rural agriculture, but the rural countryside can feed itself and does not need the city to survive (though it may benefit from cities as markets for its goods).

At the same time, cities are workplaces and centers of trade and commerce, and this places them at the center of the capitalist and industrial economy—today, the information and service economy—in ways that bar real autarky or self-sufficiency. The nexus they help establish is endemic to what they are. Neither self-sufficiency nor autarky are long-term options, although there have been times when they were necessitated by siege and the severing of ties to the outside world occasioned by war. Recently, digital communications have allowed a kind of artificial dispersion of information workers to regions beyond the city, but there is little sign that such movements are likely to compromise the urban future, given the city's defining attractions of proximity[12]—attractions that include culture, creativity, exchange, and civic community. Richard Florida confirms that the experiment in a suburbanized or exurban information economy is giving way to a new and youthful emphasis on city-living and city-working.

The many varieties of the nonurban, though sharing a "not the city" essence, have their own distinguishing characteristics. The geography of the plains yields rival economic models in farming and herding, with farmers and cattle ranchers often pitted in battles over land enclosure, for example (ranchers being dependent on open grazing, farmers dependent on fences). Thus does a rural agricultural society founded on cultivated land, isolated villages, and the occasional market center give rise to a set of often quite conservative and rooted norms radically different than those of a pastoral, nomadic economy defined by herding and constant movement, by communal use rather than private ownership, with no permanent centers of population and a penchant for freedom of a kind found in the alpine Swiss and the prairie Sioux alike.

And how different from agricultural and pastoral society is simple wilderness, understood as pure nature without a human presence (other than tourists and voyeurs). Indeed, wilderness living is as distant from farming and herding life as it is from city dwelling. It may contain its singular Robinson Crusoe or its "Solitary Walker" (described in Rousseau's *Reveries*), or, like Eden, may provide an idyllic setting for a solitary couple more natural than civilized, not yet even free in the full human sense. In such settings, women and men are so-to-speak self-conscious participants in a nature defined by the absence of consciousness. Thomas Jefferson included the Native American population as part of the flora and fauna of the New World (a function of racism, to be sure), while

Rousseau understood all humans as originally part of a state of nature in which the absence of humanizing "virtues" was anything but a vice.[13] How different such natural states are from agricultural society.

Where do we then place the sprawling suburbs and exurbs, strange hybrids that appear to be neither city nor country, often possessing the vices of both and the virtues of neither? The complexity and variety of the topology of the nonurban, though useful as a starting point, does less to define some country essence than to delimit the meaning of the urban. Using indirect features of the not-city to help define the city puts us then in the right state of mind but cannot take us very far. It is helpful to recognize that cities, neither dispersed nor isolated, are a not-wilderness (though they may try to import a modicum of wilderness in parks or gardens) as well as a not-agricultural and not-nomadic form of society (urban farms and stockyards aside). But to say what cities are not still cannot fully reveal what cities are.

Competing typologies suggest how vexing the definitional question can be. For example, in his introduction to Max Weber's *The City*, Don Martindale references "the crowding of people into small space" that "bears with it a tremendous increase in specialized demands" for things like "streets, public water supplies, public sewage systems, garbage disposal, police protection, fire protection, parks, playgrounds, civic centers, schools, libraries, [and] transportation systems"—and of course the "more complicated system of administration" needed "to handle the complex problems of engineering, law, finance and social welfare."[14] Such functional features point to a social ecology that can distinguish primary service communities, commercial communities, industrial towns, and special-focus cities like recreational resorts, political and cultural centers, and defense, penal, and charitable colonies from one another.

In the world of economic globalization, cities have also come to be defined by new functions related to markets, especially in what Saskia Sassen denotes as global cities. Jane Jacobs long ago observed that cities rather than nations are the ultimate producers of wealth through innovation and trade activities (a critical factor in the city's current struggle for fiscal sustainability).[15] Sassen elaborates on how global cities have evolved, functioning in four new ways as "highly concentrated command points in the organization of the world economy"; as "key locations for finance and for specialized service firms, which have replaced manufacturing"; as "sites of production [especially] production of innovations"; and finally "as markets for the products and innovations produced."[16] She focuses on how such novel global cities service the changing global economy, but she recognizes that the changes "have had a massive impact upon . . . urban form" to a point where a new type, the global city, has appeared.

Satisfactory as Sassen's analysis is in setting parameters for the global city, the city of functions is at some distance from the lived city. Compare Sassen's corporate MBAs busily accounting for the world's capital flows with Jane Jacobs's neighbors watching the traffic of busy sidewalks from their windows and stoops, seeing their fellow homemakers head to the Laundromat before picking up their toddlers at kindergarten playgrounds. Abstract functions identify the evolving economic regimes that cities serve, but everyday life remains roughly the same whether the economy is rooted in trading, manufacturing, or the information and service economies. Not every human behavior demands urban concentration: obviously a good deal of living and loving and praying and playing unfolds anywhere humans gather. But *how* we live and love and pray and play—and work and deal and trade and compete and create—is influenced by habitat. Of the many habitats our species has fashioned, the city is perhaps the most determinative.

Typology and Defining Features of the City

What then are the commonalities that allow us to talk about the urban and contrast it with the many distinctive varieties of the nonurban? Let me start with a rather standard list of urban features, and then see if some essential characteristics and defining values can be teased out of them. Listed here under the broad archetypes "city" and "country," are the following key characteristics (bold indicates special emphasis, see below):

City	Country
densely populated	sparsely populated
vertical	lateral/horizontal

City	Country
virtual/relational	territorial/grounded
open/public	bordered/private
voluntary identity	ascriptive/given identity
sociologically "thin"	sociologically "thick"
creative	conventional
artificial	natural
cosmopolitan	parochial
mobile	unmoving
changeable	stable
future	past
possibility	necessity
equality	inequality
innovation	repetition
growth	stasis
sophistication	simplicity
secular	religious
progressive	conservative
liberty	tradition
chosen	given
multicultural	monocultural
diverse	homogenous
arts	crafts
proximity	distance
anonymity	intimacy
strangers as neighbors	kinsmen as neighbors
relational/networked	self-sufficient
interdependent	independent
trade	autarky
industry (manufacturing)	agricultural/pastoral
service industry	cottage industry
artificial ecology	natural ecology
immigration	emigration
"civilized"	"backward"

This typology captures generalized features that tend to cluster on one side or the other of the city/country divide, though there are exceptions and contradictions throughout. Surely urban neighborhoods can foster a sense of thick community-based (Gemeinschaft) neighborliness that rural life in isolated farmsteads cannot match, although urban neighbors usually start as strangers whereas country neighbors may be kindred and clan members. And is not equality really a better measure of tribal and clan life in pastoral societies, where all men are brothers, than in mega-cities where inequalities of class and wealth arranged into segregated ghettos live up to Mike Davis's disturbing phrase "planet of slums"? The country is "backward" mainly by the measure of self-styled progressive, cosmopolitan cities. Cities may be first responders to cross-border im-migration, but newcomers then often emigrate outward to suburbs or the countryside in their new host countries. Are there not rural artists as well as city craftspeople who break the stereotypes? Nor do all cities grow: old cities (in the American Rust Belt, for example) can decline, and small towns can burgeon into cities. Cities do not just grow verti-cally, they sprawl like Los Angeles and Mexico City, spawning brown-lands bereft of nature but denuded of urban virtues as well. Meanwhile, skyscrapers can open up land and advantage green zones and parks (as Le Corbusier's modernist "towers in the park" aspired to do), enhancing horizontal features of the urban landscape. The anonymity and anomie of the city finds its counterpart in the rugged individualism and en-forced solitude of country life. Cities may lend themselves to virtual networking, but they occupy territory, have boundaries, and involve ju-risdiction no less than regions and nation-states. Cities produce plenty of private space along with their defining public spaces, while the coun-tryside is "open" geographically if not always psychically. No generaliza-tion holds up to careful sociological scrutiny.

So it is not the individual features of the urban environment taken one by one, but their accumulation and aggregation that capture the city's essential meaning. Together they paint a picture of human society where people live in relative proximity and fashion communities that are naturally connected to other similar communities. The city is, to be sure, a community, but it is not a Gemeinschaft in that nineteenth-century sociological sense of an intimate, involuntary (ascriptive) association forged by time and birth. It is a Gesellschaft association—an impersonal society made up of individuals freely covenanting to live together in ways that allow urban neighbors to remain anonymous and hence free and opportunistic, to live unconstrained by tradition, kinship, or hierarchy even though forced into intense proximity.

There are analogous aberrations in how our typology describes the archetypical countryside, but they do not negate the typology. Telling as Carlo Levi's portrait of rural Italy is, it is exaggerated and time bound. The region today is transformed. The singular features Levi described, drawn from a particularly impoverished part of wartime Italy seemingly excluded from history at that moment, were and are atypical. Those who were left in the villages where he lived under house arrest were "the discarded, who have no talents, the physically deformed, the inept and the lazy; greed and boredom combine to dispose them to evil. Small parcels of farm land do not assure them a living."[17]

Contrast Italy's rural south with the northern countryside captured by Robert Putnam in his study of the birth of social capital in rural villages that supported choral societies, and the differences are apparent.[18] And yet . . . and yet. Nations and cultures everywhere remain sites for a form of rural life that support Levi's harsh portrait when he recalls "the dull, malicious, and greedily self-satisfied faces of my new acquaintances in the square. Their passions, it was plain to see, were not rooted in history; they did not extend beyond the village, encircled by malaria-ridden clay; they were multiplied within the enclosure of half a dozen houses. They had an urgent and miserable character born of the daily need for food and money, and they strove futilely to cloak themselves in the genteel tradition. . . . Penned up in petty souls and desolate surroundings . . ."[19]

We need not, however, insist on these typological distinctions feature for feature. The aim is to focus on those characteristics that point to why the city promises cooperation across borders and global governance in ways that the country, and national governments (as they reflect at least in part the country's disposition), cannot. In depicting that disposition, the city's relational, interdependent character is most important and speaks to the essential (and perhaps necessarily essentialist) features of urban life that serve their global potential. All of the terms in the typology highlighted in bold help shape the city's potential for global outreach. Their openness, for example, is prelude to their potential for networking; in the same fashion, that they are both voluntary and mobile enables their citizens to choose additional identities across borders and to move easily among cities, as do so many of the new service employees of the world economy, whether they are taxi drivers or bankers and lawyers.

Secularism and tolerance mean urban denizens are not divided from others around the world by deeply held religious and cultural principles, which hobble relations among more monocultural nation-states; they also provide a platform for multiculturalism that is linked to immigration and that entails not only the presence of different cultures and traditions but their willingness and ability to live and work together. Trade depends on easy commerce with others beyond the city's borders, but art too, both in its reliance on imagination and in its capacity for cosmopolitan exchange, fosters a defining spirit of interdependence. The city's defining diversity is more than economic. Cities diversify around finance, trade, and manufacturing, but also around innovation, creativity, and entrepreneurship. One-trick behemoths like Los Angeles (movies) or automobiles (Detroit) or trade (Singapore) must work hard to ensure their diversity. New York City is now the second-most tech-oriented city in the United States after Silicon Valley, while Barcelona has transformed itself into a driver in the global pursuit of digital resources. Diversity is quite simply the key today to urban sustainability.

We might add that the seeming indifference of cities to (or incapacity of cities for) power politics and sovereignty—a feature that distinguishes them from states (as we will argue in Chapter 5)—is critical to their inclination to outreach and networking. They prefer problem solving to ideology and party platforms, which is a core strength critical to their networking potential. That they lack an appetite for sovereignty and jurisdictional exclusivity enables them as agents of cross-border collaboration. At the same time, although politically parochial, they are anything but private: they have a penchant for the public. Because they are densely populated, contrived public associations that, unlike businesses and firms, are explicitly incorporated for public purposes, they favor public space and offer a model of what "the public" means. In the framing prose of Sharon Zukin, "Public spaces are the primary site of public culture [and] they are a window into the city's soul."[20]

While traditional pastoral societies may also favor public space and a grazing commons, it is in cities that our strong sense of the public is fashioned. Whether in an agora or souk or marketplace, or in a public square or Hyde Park corner or a pedestrian shopping street, or in the ubiquitous commons that dot the English urban landscape, some idea of a public is captured. The city is in its very essence an integral and coherent commons in a way that an agricultural region or suburban mall never is. That cities are public associations adds to their capacity for interaction with a global public. Distinctive as they are from an economic perspective, both agriculture and capitalism embody private property and private space. The city is a public association that depends on and nourishes a robust conception of public space. This affinity for public space may serve cities in fashioning a global "public" across global networks, although some critics will suggest there is a tension between the privatization that has accompanied the commercialization of cities and their claim to public culture. Yet, even so, Zukin reminds us,

the cultures of cities retain a residual memory of tolerance and freedom. The very diversity of the population and their need for cultural and economic exchanges create unpredictable spaces of freedom: the markets, restaurant kitchens, designated landmarks and parades that become both sites and sights of new collective identities. This is the city that people cherish. It is the transcendent narrative of opportunity and self-respect that lends hope to a common public culture.[21]

Adept as cities are in networking and cooperation for reasons associated with some of their core features qua cities, they also are deficient in some essential ways. The deficiencies are glaring. We do not have to read Marx to grasp that although they may promise a relief from traditional hierarchy and aristocratic pretention, cities generate their own novel forms of inequality born of the forms of capitalism, industrialism, and class intimately associated with the urban. And that these inequalities are hardly less stubborn than the old-fashioned feudal and agrarian inequalities cities leave behind.

Robert Fogel and Stanley Engerman's controversial and troubling book *Time on the Cross* suggested that the inequalities of class that arose in nineteenth-century American cities were actually deeper and more pernicious to freedom than agricultural slavery—which the authors read as a much more efficient (if horrendous) economic institution than it was conventionally given credit for.[22] Many saw their argument as overdrawn, even (and this is unfair) as giving aid and comfort to partisans of the Southern "lost cause" mystique with its myths of the gallant antebellum Confederate South celebrated in films such as *Gone with the Wind*, and more toxically in D. W. Griffith's epic *Birth of a Nation*. Yet however opaque Fogel and Engerman were in fully recognizing how deeply dehumanizing slavery was, they remind us that urban inequality is devastating in its own way.[23] It may not only obstruct democratic networking across cities in ways fatal to the aims of global democrats but may also incapacitate cities from achieving local democracy within the city limits—the argument advanced today by those like Mike Davis, David Harvey, and others who have systematically studied urban inequality.

Add to these powerfully consequential deficiencies the urban disposition to corruption, a disease that often seems endemic to the density and informal relations of city life. Corruption not only poisons local politics and undermines urban democracy, it makes a mockery of the rule of law that must undergird democratic life. If democracy is not simply the government of men but the government of laws made by men and women, it must reflect not human will per se but common or general will enacted in laws whose authors are equally subjects of the law. Corruption is not just a wart on democracy's clean face, but a cancer that can consume it.

Inequality and corruption together are enough to cause cities to lose not only their democratic luster but their potential as global networking nodes.

Were these not enough, there is a final flaw, more likely to be fatal than the others when it comes to the prospect for global democratic governance: the city's unrepresentative character. More than half of the world's population may live in cities, but the slightly less than half who don't will be largely unrepresented in a world dominated by mayors and those who elect them. How are these missing three billion people to find a vote or a voice if, as a consequence of urban virtues, mayors actually do come to rule the world? (I will actually offer some answers to this question in Chapter 12.) The 800 million Chinese still dwelling in villages, and those like them around the world, can only greet the notion of a parliament of mayors as a bad joke—especially because those village Chinese serve by the millions as underpaid and temporary migrant laborers in the cities that otherwise fail to represent them or their interests.

Americans still rightly protest a Senate whose origins in distrust of popular majorities give roughly 20 percent of the electorate (represented by fifty-one senators!) the right to forestall the will of the vast majority (represented by only forty-nine senators) and paralyze government; are we then to seek a global government, formal or informal, that reverses the polarity and sanctifies the dominion of half the world who happen to live in cities over the half who don't? Yes, cities are gaining population every year, and urbanization is the trend for the foreseeable future. Estimates are that by 2030, as many as 70 percent will live in cities. But even if urban dwellers constitute 90 percent of the world's population by century's end, we can hardly omit 10 percent of the planet and still talk with a straight face about democratic governance within or among nations. The obstacles to the city's potential for global governance arising out of inequality, corruption, and representation must then be addressed. This is the task to which Part II of our study will be devoted.

The complete answer to the challenge posed by the deficiencies of the city must also come from addressing the city not only as a complex of intersecting features but by recalling the values common to all urban life that make cities attractive and worthy as a human habitat. Secularism and multiculturalism are descriptive attributes, but the tolerance and variety they breed are values democrats and cosmopolitans can cherish. Mobility is an urban fact, but it facilitates choice and freedom, which are treasured values. Interconnectivity grows out of cities' need to network, but interdependence is a value that trumps both slavish dependency and hubristic and impossible independence. It is a fact but also a virtue. Cities are bound together by common attributes but also united by common values. That so many of these values are liberal and democratic gives cities their promise as building blocks of global democratic governance.

There is then ample support in the character of cities for the argument that mayors can and should rule the world. Further evidence can be found in the failures of their rivals. To some extent, the leading role that cities are playing arises out of a vacuum in international cooperation with a long and telling history. Cities should rule the world for a good reason: nation-states haven't, and can't.

States as Global Actors?

Over the last four hundred years, in the era of nation-states, nations acting in concert have never actually governed the world or shown much capacity to do so. Large empires have ruled regionally both before and during the era of nation-states, while in earlier times, leagues of cities cooperated on an extended regional scale. But nation-states were fashioned to maximize internal unity and jurisdictional sovereignty and hence tended to foster rivalry rather than cooperation among themselves (a point explored in detail in Chapter 6). The social contract helped democratize nations from within but actually impeded the development of democracy *among* nations.

Monarchs appealing to the divine right of kings sought to strengthen their rule at home against usurping pretenders to the throne or aspiring parliaments by relying on their sovereignty. Charles I, at the 1649 trial leading to his execution, could protest that he stands "more for the liberties of his subjects" than his prosecutor, and demands to know by "which particular reasons . . . and by what law, what authority" the court proceeds against him.[24] He seems to be aping the words Shakespeare puts in Richard II's mouth earlier when, confronted by what he regards as "treason," Richard demands of Bolingbroke that he "show me the hand of God that has dismissed me from my position" and protests that "no mortal hand can grab the sacred handle of my sceptre, unless he is blaspheming, stealing or rebelling." But the eloquence of kings was no match for their abuses, and sovereignty was a claim made more successfully by a democratic people defending its liberty and security through a contract. That contract giving a people the right to rule itself, however, did little to justify cooperation among peoples and their sovereign states. On the contrary, with democracy tied to national sovereignty, to yield sovereign and independent jurisdiction was tantamount to forfeiting democracy. The concert of all nations united as one had no more right to rule than the ancient tyrant asserting sovereignty over a nonconsenting people in a single nation.

In some places, a modicum of local control and civic intimacy was maintained through federalism: by decentralizing power into the hands of local duchies or *parlements* (left over from the Middle Ages) or by framing decentralization in constitutional terms through a vertical separation of powers, as in the Articles of Confederation and the American Constitution. But for the most part, governance was at best indirect, via representative institutions, and at worst only hypothetical—with original consent authorizing even the most authoritative forms of monarchical power (as in Thomas Hobbes). The nation-state brought to fruition the idea of consent that had appeared as early as 1215 in Britain's Magna Carta, now celebrating its 800th birthday. But it preserved a semblance of democracy only by reinforcing central state sovereignty and the wall separating one state from another. As the actual walls around towns came down, the symbolic ones around states grew higher and thicker.

The new scale of large territorial states that has seemed to make direct democracy impossible became the new home for large-scale indirect democracies. But at this cost: what held a state together was the unity of a people bound together by the abstract and invented notion of nationality

(Chapter 6)—Benedict Anderson's imagined community bound together by common language, values, and ethnicity; and the imposing unity of force embodied in the idea of indivisible sovereignty, a power to enforce the social contract and the laws arising out of it. This sovereignty was unimpeachable because it derived its authority from those being governed. Whether directly or indirectly, the sovereign embodied a "people": a *Volk* or *gens* or *peuple* with a common history, common religion, common language, and common interests. The vox populi issued not from randomly assembled persons (as the language of social contract theory by itself might suggest) but from a united people organized as a national community.

This new democratic derivation of authority from a people established internal coherence and unity as well as resistance against external interference. But these same features made cooperation among them problematic. It was not an accident that relations among the new nation-states were more often conducted by blackmail and war than by common interest and collaboration. Independence from foreign interference and absolute jurisdiction were defining characteristics of sovereignty. The more popular the base for sovereignty, the more far-reaching its claims. For as Rousseau put it: a people may resist tyrants, but how can it refuse to obey itself?

The sovereign nation-state succeeded in rescuing democracy from its thrall to polis life and a scale so diminutive that it had made democracy in the real historical world impossible. Yet the very features that allowed it to adapt to the scale of the new and invented territorial nation prevented it from making the transition from nation-state to global governance. Although they succeeded for more than four hundred years in securing both liberty and justice from within, democratic nation-states once again today risk the defeat of their aspirations to freedom by the still vaster scale and greater illegitimacy of our new age of globalization. As the town polis once lost its capacity to protect liberty and equality in the face of the scale and complexity of an emerging society that was outrunning the participatory narrowness and insularity of its polis institutions, so today the nation-state is losing its capacity to protect liberty and equality in the face of the scale and complexity of an interdependent world that is outrunning the nationalism and sovereign insularity of its institutions. Participation, the virtue of the ancient town, became the victim of empire and its scale; sovereignty, the virtue of the modern nation-state, is beginning to look like a prospective victim of globalization and its daunting scale.

Nowadays, although it is clear that states can no longer protect their citizens and ought to consider yielding some part of their claim to sovereignty, there is no clear alternative, and so they refuse to do so. For a global government to have legitimacy it would need to be as democratic as the sovereign democratic state, have the capacity to enforce global laws protecting individual and community rights, and rest on forms of common identity as thick and grounded in solidarity as nationality is. There is the conundrum. Nation-states cannot address the cross-border challenges of an interdependent world. But neither can they forge institutions across borders that are capable of doing so. The nation-state, once representative democracy's midwife, is becoming dysfunctional. Its failing sovereignty is increasingly a prison—an obstacle to the globalization that alone can ensure its survival.

The journey from polis to nation-state seems then to have run its course. The journey forward to cosmopolis may demand of us a journey back to the polis, reconceived. To complete the circle in which states trump cities, we need now to encourage cities acting in concert to bypass and supersede states at least in the domains where states have become dysfunctional. It is not the polis today but the metropolis that must become democracy's agent; the aim of the metropolis must be the cosmopolis. The polis proved too parochial and homogenous to allow democracy to expand its compass, enlarge its citizen body, and diversify the community on which it was founded. For democracy to survive required that towns yield to sovereign nation-states. But today it is sovereign nation-states that are parochial and limited, too large to afford that lively neighborliness and local commerce typical of cities, yet too small to contain and regulate the globe's power centers. It is the networked, multicultural metropolis that offers a way forward. If democracy is to have a global future, its chances lie not with the state but with the city. And with the mayors who govern the city.

Mayors are not cities, however, and if our title is to be something more than a provocation, who and what mayors are has a good deal to do with the role of the city as a foundation for global governance. Can *mayors* really rule the world? Who on earth are they?

BORIS JOHNSON OF LONDON

A serious journalist and a slightly less serious mayor (defeating incumbent socialist Ken Livingstone for the first time in 2008 and then again in 2011), **BORIS JOHNSON** makes a joke of everything. When athletes arriving for the 2012 Summer Olympics were lost on wayward buses in London—still a city of almost eight million—for too many hours, he quipped, "They saw more of our fantastic city than they would otherwise have done."[1] And he told Carl Swanson, a *New York Magazine* reporter, that in order to build the new airport London would need to become Europe's gateway, he himself would have to "assume supreme power in England." Pause. "For God's sake, don't quote me saying that." Swanson quoted him, adding by way of explanation that Johnson was "an Oxford-educated classics major playing a buffoonishly triumphant super-twit role he's written for himself."

It seems likely Johnson would take this as a compliment. But he is anything but a joke. The *Financial Times* has called him the most popular politician in England, "blond, absurd, risk-taking, solipsistic, he is in blazing colour while his rivals are in black and white." Serious voices in the Conservative Party are calling for him to rise to the top, if 10 Downing Street is the top. Yet Johnson often appears to be a writer first, and a politician only afterward—if at all, given that mayors are not conventional politicians in the first place.

He was the editor of the *London Spectator*, has written seven books, including the novel *72 Virgins*, and continues to write a column for the *Daily Telegraph*. He has poured his heart into a book about London called *Johnson's Life of London: The People Who Made the City That Made the World*. "It's a concealed manifesto," he says, "a hymn of praise for London" and a nice piece of self-advertising to boot.[2]

One might say to Johnson what Jeremy Clarkson said to him on the TV show *Top Gear*: "Most politicians, as far as I can work out, are pretty incompetent, and then have a veneer of competence, you do seem to do it the other way around." He was pushed almost immediately on becoming mayor to assume that mantle of national leader of the stumbling Tory Party under Prime Minister David Cameron. But the qualities for which he is prized as mayor—biking to work daily, pricking his own balloons, telling it like it is, suffering fools ungladly, taking untoward risks—are unlikely ingredients in cooking up a prime ministerial stew. Gaiety is not much prized on the lugubrious national stage in Britain. He knows as much, recognizing he has "about as much chance of being Prime Minister as being reincarnated as an olive." Given the state of British politics, he may actually have a much better chance of becoming an olive.

Born in New York, and holding dual citizenship, he is fond of Mayor Bloomberg, who is building an outpost of his post-mayoral empire in London. But during his second campaign against "Red" Ken Livingstone, Johnson told Mayor Bloomberg, "I'd prefer if you endorsed my opponent." And he allowed in his repartee with late-night television host David Letterman that he might more easily "be President of the United States . . . technically speaking."

He appreciates the edginess of cities and rarely invokes nanny-state caution in his policy making. He reinstated the hop-on/hop-off buses, loved by Londoners, that were sidelined in the name of safety, and he got rid of the efficient two-car "bendy-buses," hated by Londoners, that were screwing up traffic. At the same time, he has no problem with congestion fees and other interventionist policies when they improve the quality of life in the city. He took 10,000 knives off the street (the equivalent of handguns in other cities), although he did it using controversial stop-and-search tactics. He is expanding rail (firing up the long-stalled Crossrail) and championing both a new sprawl-spewing gateway airport on the lower Thames and new parks and green spaces (more than 450 already established). And he is a fan of local agriculture.

Critics on the left worry about his Tory outlook, but as with so many mayors, fixing things seems more important to Johnson than upholding abstract ideological ideals. He stands ready to try anything, unfazed by party labels. He calls his bike-share program "an entirely Communist scheme put in by a conservative mayor." When asked during a campaign about his drug policy, he replied, "I can't remember what my line on drugs is. What's my line on drugs?" Spoken like the self-described "libertarian Anarcho-Tory" he is. He doesn't really have official "lines." As he says, "The great thing about the mayoralty is that it is independent. I do not have to follow a manifesto dictated by Central Office, even if I knew what it was."

Try to extrapolate an ideology from Johnson's comments about why people flock to big cities like London: "We seek cities because there are a greater range of girls at the bar, of reproductive choice. Number one. Number two is there are better outcomes for health and wealth. And now we care more about the environment, and cities are better for the environment. But above all, talented people seek cities for fame. They can't get famous in the fucking village."[3] It's girls, not geopolitics, it's wealth and choice. Fame.

That's not ideology, it's cosmopolitanism in a Bass Ale mug. Not many climate change deniers among mayors; the consequences are too devastating and their own responsibility to protect the city with floodgates and borrowed Dutch dike technology are too pressing. Just ask Mayor Bloomberg about potential floods in lower Manhattan or Mayor Ed Lee about what rising oceans can do to San Francisco Bay. Or Mayor Johnson about the Lower Thames estuary at floodtide.

Boris Johnson doesn't depend on Richard Florida to tell him about urban creativity or its link to entrepreneurship. "The reason that so many ideas are produced in cities," he says, "is not just that people are cross-fertilizing; it's because they want to beat each other. They want to become more famous than the other person." This isn't neoliberal market philosophy, it's the psychology of ur-capitalism. London is what London is for a thousand reasons from its red double-deckers and movie-set Buckingham Palace to its dual role as financial and political capital of England and a leader of Europe (even though it has spurned the euro).

But it is also what it is because its recent mayors—red Ken and wacky Boris—are true cosmopolitans who love their city more than they love their political parties and are more popular with their constituents than with their party leaders. Mayor Johnson seems a man after Groucho Marx's heart, who can say along with Groucho in *A Night at the Opera*, "Yes, I have principles! And if you don't like them, I have others!" Which may be London's best recipe for survival. It is also why cities are more likely than all those principled sovereign states to figure out how to govern the world together.

CHAPTER 4. MAYORS RULE!
Is This What Democracy Looks Like?

[Being mayor is] like being a bitch in heat. You stand still and you get screwed, you start running and you get bit in the ass.
John Lindsay, The Edge

Welcome to the best job in the world!
Harvard University Institute of Politics, "Transition Manual for Newly Elected Mayors"

Things could be worse, I could be mayor.
Lyndon B. Johnson

I think people desperately want leaders who will make cities work, and they take them in whatever shapes, sizes and colors they come in.
David Axelrod

Mayors rule. Or do they? Neither John Lindsay nor Lyndon Johnson seems to have thought so. Lindsay was actually New York's mayor and got bitten more than most. Mayors may think they have the best job in the world, as Michael Bloomberg of New York likes to say and Mayor Rafał Dutkiewicz of Wrocław, Poland, agrees, and as Harvard with its cheery "welcome to the best job in the world" insists. But in a number of countries, mayors aren't even directly elected by city burghers. Instead, they are appointed by party or state authorities (in many cities in France and China, for example). In others, bureaucratic city managers run the show. This has happened more often than people think in the United States, where less than a hundred years ago, "good government" progressivism tried to confront corruption and de-politicize city government in ways that still affect urban governance today. And as Lindsay's frustration makes clear, no mayor can stand in the way of central government officials determined to impede or deny the will of a city (although Ronald Reagan attributed this frustration to Lindsay's weakness, quipping that being mayor is the second toughest job in America only insofar as "the way he does it, it is").

Even when powerful elected mayors govern their own metropolises forcefully, they can scarcely be said to be ruling the world. The world is not being ruled by anyone, let alone democratically. It is pushed around by warring states and feuding tribes, dominated by rival multinational corporations and banks, and shaped by competing ideologies and religions that often deny each other's core convictions. To the extent urban networks actually comprise some degree of soft and informal global governance, it is cities and their networks, not mayors, that are key. A cynic would say mayors are merely the grandly posturing, anything but sovereign representatives of impotent towns. Cynics are wrong. Cities work and mayors govern.

Cities Work and Mayors Count

Paul Maslin is clear that "cities still by and large work—[the reality is] dysfunction nationally, functionality in cities."[1] Former Stuttgart mayor Wolfgang Schuster has insisted that there can be no "ecological, social, economic or cultural sustainable development without cities," the key agents of change in the twenty-first-century world.[2] This view, Maslin points out, is widely shared by ordinary citizens: "People by and large still think their cities, their mayors, are doing a pretty good job," and mayors such as Bloomberg or Schuster often become the personification of their cities and get much of the credit.

In a world cynical about politics, mayors remain astonishingly popular, winning an approval rating of two to three times that of legislators and chief executives.[3] This can give their role in intercity and transnational cooperation considerable symbolic importance. To citizens, mayors may seem more significant than prime ministers or presidents. Bill Clinton tells the story of a presidential visit to China, where he sat alongside Shanghai's mayor while fielding questions on a local radio station. Two-thirds of the incoming calls were for the mayor. Reporters were surprised, but the former president, no stranger to local politics in Arkansas, got it: "People were more interested in talking to the mayor about potholes and traffic jams," he recalled, laughing at himself.[4] Like potholes seen from the viewpoint of urban drivers, mayors always loom large, personifying the traffic jam or the snowstorm and the imperative to address them.

Mayors count nowadays, even more in the age of globalization than in the past. As recently as 1985, Erik Herzi wrote that the mayoralty was "generally forgotten in the annals of political research."[5] But mayors and the cities they govern are now critical to social research, core subjects in university programming, and very much in the political spotlight.[6] Given that mayors are in a position to help rule the world and are possibly the best hope we have for the survival of democracy across borders, there is every reason to look at them closely. Mayors in many ways incarnate their cities. To think New York has been to think Fiorello La Guardia or Ed Koch or Rudy Giuliani or today Mayor Bloomberg—all huge personalities embodying the city's hubris and "wanna make something out of it!?" efficiency that often masquerades as truculence. Similarly, for better or worse, Richard Daley was Chicago in the 1960s, Frank Rizzo was Philadelphia in the 1980s, and Gavin Newsom has recently been San Francisco—until he disappeared into the black hole of California state government as lieutenant governor without a real portfolio.

Personality outweighs ideology by miles: it's a long ideological journey from "Red" Ken Livingstone to Tory "Mayor Jolly-Good-Fun" Boris Johnson, yet both are characters who stand for aspects of London's urban persona. Livingstone, a radical leftist with "sometimes wacky policies" has nonetheless developed a loyal post-ideological following, and Johnson, despite being a self-described "libertarian anarcho-Tory,"[7] and in the face of "all his maverick bluster" and his status as a "Latin-spouting old Etonian with a quip for every occasion," is in fact a "capable administrator and high profile champion for London," far more popular than Prime Minister David Cameron and, for some Tories, the man who should be Cameron's successor.[8] No wonder that the two rivals again contested the London mayoralty election in 2012 around issues other than ideology, and that despite his Conservative Party's declining poll numbers, Johnson eked out a second victory over Livingstone. A straight ideological party vote would have brought Johnson down.

Mayors are characters who often play roles they invent for themselves. New York's legendary Fiorello La Guardia marked his opposition to a newspaper strike in the 1940s by reading the funny papers to kids over the radio, and he famously took a sledgehammer to the slot machines to signal his disgust with gambling and whoring in the city's tenderloin district (later the subject of Jerry Bock's 1959 Broadway musical *Fiorello!*). More recently, Antanas Mockus's inventive and playful approach to city planning has made Bogotá a city of influence beyond its size and power.[9] Palermo's Leoluca Orlando, noted crime fighter and champion of culture, won the 1994 German Best Actor Award for a television film.

Most notorious of all is Yury Luzhkov, known for his long tenure in Moscow starting in 1977 as a city councillor and then as deputy mayor (1987) and mayor from 1991 to 2010. Luzhkov's urban career reached from Leonid Brezhnev through Mikhail Gorbachev and Boris Yeltsin, all the way to Vladimir Putin and Dmitry Medvedev, making him a Russian legend. Indeed, too legendary for his own good, since his longevity and independence made him such an irksome expression of Moscow's urban autonomy, Medvedev (with Putin possibly calling the shots, and the putative corruption of Luzhkov's wife in the news) felt compelled to oust him in 2010. In Russia, as in France and China, other city officials can play prominent national roles, but it was as mayor that Luzhkov thrived. He was disdainful of national politics and party wrangling, disavowed the United Russia party he helped found, and called the State Duma a "fat bird with one wing, incapable of flight," doing only what the Kremlin tells it to do.[10] Unsurprisingly, the Putin-Medvedev odd couple couldn't wait to get him out. Mayors have also flouted national politics in the Balkans and have become important as symbols of efficiency and continuity—certainly more so than most national leaders, who are mired in divisiveness and incendiary rhetoric. Mayor Edi Rama of Tirana, Albania, for example, an artist and sculptor, was nearly killed several times on the way to turning his office into a counter to the ideological cleavages of his country. In doing so he has become world famous, winning the World Mayor Prize in 2004.

Italians remark that Italy is more impressively a country of cities than it is a country. Mayors have a lot to do with that, ameliorating the burdens of a chaotic and oppressive national political scene often dominated by outsized national bullies like Silvio Berlusconi. Yet local achievement in Italy is no guarantee of national success. Walter Veltroni excelled as mayor of Rome but stumbled badly as the leader of the Left and as prime minister. Leoluca Orlando was not only an extraordinary mayor of Palermo but took on the Mafia in Sicily as no other elected local politician had done before. He gained a European-wide reputation without ever being able to translate his local heroics into national political authority.[11] Although he had a notable national and international career over thirty years, he returned recently to local politics and was reelected mayor of Palermo in 2012. Even as the European Union loses steam as a post-sovereign collective of (dis)integrating nations and lurches back toward monocultural recidivism and southern-tier bankruptcy—reembracing the borders supposedly annulled by the Schengen Agreement—Europe's cities continue to network and collaborate, oblivious to brooding fears of German hegemony and the immigrant Muslim "other." Europe's Cultural Cities project, which nominates an annual "cultural capital," is but one instance of a broader trend signaling urban cooperation in the face of nationalist contestation.

Who Mayors Are

Whether elected or appointed, whether abetted by city managers or left to govern alone, whether operating under democratic or autocratic state regimes, mayors face common challenges that can be addressed only with a set of common skills and competences adapted to the city. These turn out to look quite different from the skills and competences needed by politicians exercising power in sovereign and self-consciously independent central governments driven by national ideologies. Mayor Michael Nutter of Philadelphia puts it this way: "You have to perform, you have to get things done, get things happening. All of us [mayors] sitting around this table see that state governments and Washington . . . We could never get away with some of the stuff that goes on in those other places. You either fill potholes, or don't. The pool is open, or it isn't, someone responded to a 911 call or they didn't."[12] Getting things done demands from mayors unique talents and personality traits not necessarily appropriate to other political offices. Among those that seem to mark successful mayors are (1) a strong personality marked by both hubris and humor, (2) a pragmatic approach to governing, (3) personal engagement in city affairs, and (4) commitment to the city as a unique entity and a possible and even likely career terminus.

A strong persona closely identified with the cities they govern is found in many successful mayors. Think of New York's Mayor Ed Koch, who managed to secure a burial plot for himself in Manhattan's Trinity Cemetery long after Manhattan burials were no longer allowed. Mayor Bloomberg's portrait of Koch as a "quintessential mayor" who was "tough and loud, brash and irreverent, full of humor and chutzpah" in fact describes mayors everywhere.[13] It is not really surprising that Anthony Weiner, ousted from a successful congressional career by a sexting scandal, reappeared two years later (in the spring of 2013) as a candidate to succeed Bloomberg as mayor of New York. Some residents gasped, some shrugged, but in a race with over a half dozen candidates, Weiner entered in the number two spot with 15 percent, behind only Christine Quinn, the frontrunner at the time with 25 percent. If a political rebirth was possible anywhere, it was where "loud, brash and irreverent" draws votes and chutzpah wins elections.

Mayors define cities as much as cities define them, and in ways that national leaders cannot and do not define the nations they lead. An occasional Mandela or de Gaulle or Nehru or Churchill or Mao or Roosevelt come to incarnate a nation at war or otherwise in extremis, but ordinary prime ministers are ordinary politicians, whereas mayors in ordinary times are often extraordinary, bigger than the cities they govern and able to dramatize the city's character and amplify its influence. During the recent Greek austerity crisis, under duress from the banks and Angela Merkel's notion of economic discipline, the national government fell into chaos. But the mayor of Athens, an American-born constitutional lawyer named George Kaminis, took office in 2011 with 27 percent of the population unemployed (59 percent of youth), yet set the city on a correctional path that defied the national crisis. Mayor Kaminis energized the city. Attacked in the street physically by right wing thugs from "Golden Dawn" (a xenophobic movement he had assailed), calling him the "pimp mayor," he faced them down. He has acknowledged the complicity of Greece and its spendthrift habits in the crisis, but insisted at the same time that humiliation is not an effective E.U. strategy and that Athens needs to lead the country out of the crisis.

If a mayor can incarnate the courage of a city, he can also embody its putative sins. Corrupt cities are the creatures of corrupt mayors, but corruption as a vice with special affinities to the city makes mayors especially vulnerable. For every charismatic mayor, there is one in jail (sometimes one of the charismatics!). The mark of urban vice is indelible. For the legendary Boss Tweed of New York, it was a badge of achievement, if not honor. Big Bill Thompson, Chicago's mayor during Prohibition, made no bones about it and hung Al Capone's portrait on his office wall. The first Mayor Daley did not conceal but instead boasted about his undue influence on national elections.

To assail what cities do, critics go after the mayors even when there is no corruption and the issues are not about them. The National Rifle Association focused its critique of the "handgun-ban movement" on mayors, not cities. Even after President Obama came under criticism for making gun control a national priority in the wake of the Newtown children's massacre, mayors like Bloomberg of New York and Rahm Emanuel of Chicago continue to be assailed. Citing mayors allows for a personal critique that merges the alleged personality of a mayor with the putative errors of his or her city. Thus, in the NRA's crisp portrait, Emanuel is "the new boss of Chicago machine politics," willing to pursue "gun bans by any means," who is "unconditionally tied to Obama's reelection agenda" and the man who "launched a vicious attack on law-abiding Illinois gun owners that was stunning even by Chicago standards."[14] Through Emanuel, the NRA tries to personify and libel Chicago's fabled machine politics going back to Thompson, as well as highlight the city's supposed urban tyranny over citizens statewide.

While it is hardly a qualification for the job, mayors are often quite funny in ways related to their vocation. Mayors Ed Koch in New York, Boris Johnson in London, Antanas Mockus in Bogotá, and Klaus

Wowereit in Berlin are just a few of that tribe of local politicians for whom humor can be, as Mockus suggests, an agent of change as well as an instrument of humility and self-mockery. Johnson's wit is notorious—he has about as much chance of replacing David Cameron as prime minister, he quips, as he does of being reincarnated as an olive. Mockus used mimes to embarrass jaywalkers, and upon winning a second term as mayor after his defeat in his first presidential race, arranged to hold a ceremony in a public fountain "to ask forgiveness for leaving the mayor's office in an unsuccessful bid for the presidency." (Rudy Giuliani might have benefited from a similar act of comic contrition.)

Humor can be written off as an accidental character trait unrelated to governing the city. In fact, it gives expression to the strong, sometimes idiosyncratic, personality demanded by the job and points to the role of art, creativity, and satire in urban governance. It is also closely tied to the pragmatism that is a notable feature of successful urban governance. By making fun of himself with greater wit than his critics could muster, Weiner was able to defuse their moralizing anger when he entered the New York City mayoral race in 2013.

A preference for pragmatism and problem solving over ideology and principled grandstanding is a second feature of successful mayors. There is, realists will say, no liberal or conservative way of picking up the garbage. Former president Clinton made this argument forcefully at the Democratic National Convention in September 2012 when he challenged "the politics of constant conflict," which might seem "good" in tough times when people are frustrated, angry, and partisan, but which "does not necessarily work in the real world" where at least among mayors of big cities the aim is "to get something done."[15]

It's mayors who have to get things done. Nowhere is Clinton's point more tellingly illustrated than in Jerusalem, where, after the unification following the '67 war, the city's long-term mayor Teddy Kollek (1965 to 1993), sick of all the religious posturing by rabbis, imams, and prelates, declared: "Look, I'll fix your sewers if you knock off the sermons."[16] Kollek became known as a mediator among Arab, Jewish, and ultra-Orthodox factions of the city as a matter of practical prudence not high moral conscience. What in Jerusalem was a necessity of political survival—

"Jerusalem's people of differing faiths, cultures and aspirations must find peaceful ways to live together other than by drawing a line in the sand," Kollek insisted[17]—is everywhere a token of prudent urban management.

There is a parallel story in Palestine (the West Bank) where the former governor of Jenin (city and province), Qadoura Moussa, became a global symbol of the so-called Jenin model, introduced following the Intifada of 2006. During that troubled time, Jenin had become a center of terrorism and conflict. Moussa's main objective (which came, in time, to be funded by the international community) was "the concentration of effort towards imposing public order by the Palestinian security forces, while simultaneously implementing projects and alleviating measures aimed at fostering trust and enhancing the quality of life in the region."[18]

A similar story unfolded in two other neighboring Israeli-Palestinian towns around sewage and groundwater protection.[19] During the worst of the conflict between the warring nations, the Palestinian town of Tulkarem and the Israeli town of Emek Hefer crossed the infamous green line to forge common solutions to sewage. Despite the Intifada, the pact of cooperation between the two towns survived. Eventually, with the help of EcoPeace/Friends of the Earth Middle East, pretreatment facilities of value to both towns were built. "Spare me your sermons and I will fix your sewers" really is the common mantra of municipalities in distress, and sewers are more than metaphors. They act as digestive tracks to cities, and in the normal course of things are of no significance—until they stop working.

Whether in Jerusalem or Jenin, in Emek Hefer or Tulkarem, governing is local and pragmatism must and can rule—or conflict, division, and urban chaos will prevail. Witness Newark in 1968 or Beirut in 1982 or Sarajevo in 1992. The mayor is hardly everything, but pragmatism and a preoccupation with problem solving rather than posturing can make a crucial difference. Mayor Dutkiewicz of Wrocław (a city once dominated by its German population as "Breslau," now part of Poland) insists, "I work for people and by people, so an ideology in its classic sense is almost irrelevant for me." He does not disavow principle, but insists on a formula that should be a universal mayor's mantra: "I can dream, but pragmatically."[20]

The lesson was well learned in the United States, where a century ago, machine politics and corruption grew sufficiently ugly to put democracy in question and the office of mayor in jeopardy. If elected mayors couldn't deliver efficient governance, then Progressives would replace them with city managers, dispassionate organization-and-management specialists not necessarily even subject to the vote. In reestablishing their legitimacy in subsequent years, mayors had to make themselves over into managers. Since then, the difference between city mayor and city manager has become hard to discern: managing simply is what mayors do when they govern. It cannot be otherwise. However grandiose the personalities of city leaders, to govern the city is an inescapably parochial and pedestrian (literally!) affair: traffic rather than treaties, potholes rather than principles, waste management rather than wars. Fixing stuff and delivering solutions is the politics of urban life. Philadelphia's Michael Nutter says that in the city "things happen on the ground. In Congress it's about philosophy, it's about ideology. . . . We don't have time for those kinds of debates."[21] Solutions to problems are what citizens, living on top of one another, have to care about. Big issues are for big government and unfold at a distance. City politics slides up brownstone stoops and appears just down the street at the bodega (too many robberies?) or barbershop (a hotbed of urban gossip) or boulevard crossing (traffic light or no traffic light?).

Even though he would later unsuccessfully pursue party politics as a national candidate, Rudy Giuliani spoke from his city experience when he said, "it is better to keep your constituents happy than to keep a political party happy."[22] When David Axelrod was an adviser to Dennis Archer's campaign for city hall in Chicago back in 1993, he confirmed this view: "I think people desperately want leaders who will make cities work, and they take them in whatever shapes, sizes and colors they come in." Americans may have to put up with dysfunctional government in remote state and national capitals (as Axelrod learned later as an adviser to President Obama), but they will not tolerate dysfunction close to home.

Similarly, in the Middle East, where decentralization has just begun to allow for local elections, local government candidates representing national political parties tend to be tightly controlled from above, where their activities can undermine national ideology. They are given more latitude locally, however, and have in recent years become more influential. It's not just Mayors Kollek and Moussa who are at once prudent and influential: Hamas in the West Bank and Hezbollah in southern Lebanon, as well as local Shiites in Sunni-controlled Saudi Arabia, have all fielded local government candidates who have won victories that would be unthinkable at the national level—victories secured not because of ideology but because ideology is simply not the core concern of local voters. At least not when it comes to things like jobs, transportation, housing, and education in their neighborhoods.[23] Citizens as patriots must be prepared to sacrifice their children as soldiers in a national army driven by big ideologies, but citizens as urban neighbors and city residents expect local authorities to educate and keep their kids safe. The relevant politics here is about relationships.

The Harvard Kennedy School's Transition Manual for Newly Elected Mayors reminds city government newbies that "mobilizing relationships" must be a key part of an effective governing strategy and requires that they reach out to a remarkably diverse group of actors including their own department heads, city councillors, school system officials, union leaders, business and commercial associations, nonprofits, neighborhood groups, the religious community, media leaders, community-based organizations, and, of course, other elected officials. One might imagine that every elected official at any level of government could benefit from such recommendations, but mayors have no choice. According to an authoritative book called *The European Mayor*, in bigger cities "there is a greater number of medium and large-sized private enterprises and a wide spectrum of public and private actors that are called upon to cooperate" so that the "mayor of a great city has less scope for an authoritarian leadership style" and must work hard to create consensus. The mayoral politics of outsized personalities that we see in global cities is often a compensation for the need to reach out to and compromise with diverse constituencies that cannot be steamrolled. Bloomberg, Johnson, and Luzhkov may at some point have seemed more able as governors than their national counterparts, but their influence depended far more on collaboration and consensus.

On the rare occasions when mayors make it to national office, they are generally distinguished by their pragmatism. Recep Tayyip Erdoğan of Turkey, the former mayor of Istanbul, modulated Islamic political thought and, to the astonishment of many observers, enabled the Muslim AKP party that has dominated the country for the last eight years to be both relatively moderate and stable. How? By taking his city attitudes developed in Istanbul with him to the more ideological and religiously driven capital in Ankara. When in Taksim Square in 2013 he turned authoritarian in trying to replace a park with a mall, he quickly lost his legitimacy and was compelled to back down. In Colorado, John W. Hickenlooper came from a small-business background in homebrews to be elected mayor of Denver with no previous political experience. A Democrat in name only, he solved problems pragmatically in the Mile-High City for over eight years, drawing in allies from both parties. His success got him on *Time Magazine*'s Best Mayors of 2005 list and then helped him win the governorship of Colorado in 2011.[24] Yet his behavior in the statehouse has remained pragmatic, transpartisan, and grounded in getting things done. Explaining his penchant for bipartisan collaboration in his inaugural, he invoked "the best tradition of the West," reminding his fellow citizens that "like every river runner knows, when you get into rough water everybody paddles."[25] The sage speaks the same truth: if you want to go fast, walk alone; if you want to go far, walk together. Mayors need to go far and walk hand in hand with their colleagues and fellow citizens of necessity. Tellingly, both France's new president, François Hollande, and his prime minister, Jean-Marc Ayrault, spent time as mayors—Hollande in Tulle and Ayrault in Nantes. Both cherish their mayoral service, and Ayrault actually transformed Nantes through his innovative cultural policies. Neither has necessarily been able to do at the national level what they did locally.

By the same token, when mayors grow too ambitious too quickly, they court trouble. Bo Xilai, the regional governor of Chongqing, China's largest metropolitan region, displayed an outsized hubris that brought him down in 2012, despite his reputation as one of China's most promising future leaders. It is, of course, a complicated story involving (as with Yury Luzhkov) an out-of-control wife as well as international intrigue, but part of it is explained by Bo's focus on his national ambitions rather than the local welfare of Chongqing. New York City's Rudy Giuliani turned out to be far less formidable as a presidential campaigner than he had been as New York's mayor when he gave up the constituent-pleasing nonideological behaviors he displayed after 9/11. In those grim days, in typical mayoral fashion, he had put the city's fears to rest by putting its hopes on his back and leading it out of shock. As a national candidate, however, he pivoted to an aggressive and polarizing ideological rhetoric that was both charmless and politically ineffective. The politics of fear sometimes succeeds in a polarized national political climate, but it has little effect in governing the city. That's why George Kaminis of Athens was able to neutralize on the city plane a reactionary national movement (Golden Dawn) that had attracted as many as one of four Greeks nationally.

For the few politicians who pinball between statewide and local office, the course can be perilous. Jerry Brown of California had to unlearn the lessons of his first tenure as California's governor during his long and relatively successful tenure as mayor of Oakland. But during his recent second gubernatorial incumbency, one can speculate that he lost the touch for executive leadership at the state level. He was an effective if idiosyncratic governor earlier (like his father before him), but once he had been a mayor, he seemed no longer suited to statewide executive leadership. His lieutenant-governor, Gavin Newsom, also seems less at home in Sacramento than he was in San Francisco's City Hall—though it may be that both Brown and Newsom suffer from the simple reality that the state of California is ungovernable.

Personal engagement in the affairs, crises, and problems of the city seems to come naturally to mayors and is a third feature of what makes cities run. On the way (literally) to their jobs, these neighborhood chieftains pull people from burning buildings (Cory Booker of Newark) and catch muggers (Boris Johnson in London). Chasing police cars and ambulances, acting like urban heroes, and empathizing with urban victims show how deeply personal being a mayor can be. In explaining why the office is "the place to be," Rio de Janeiro's Mayor Eduardo Paes said, "I really do believe that mayors have the political position to really change people's lives."[26] Literally, not figuratively. Directly, not obliquely. Like pulling people from burning buildings. Lives are affected because the turf on which mayors play is relentlessly local—always a neighborhood or a complex of neighborhoods, never a territory or a domain. As Christopher Dickey has written in his book about security in New York, "a city is not an abstraction like 'homeland,' it is home, full stop, to millions of people."[27] Boris Johnson opens his recent book on London's history with a personal anecdote that makes clear London is his heart's home; about the city's diurnal tide of commuters he writes:

> Still they come, surging towards me across [London] Bridge. On they march in sun, wind, rain, snow and sleet. Almost every morning I cycle past them in rank after heaving rank as they emerge from London Bridge Station and tramp tramp tramp up and along the broad 239-metre pavement that leads over the river and towards their places of work. It feels as if I am reviewing an honourable regiment of yomping commuters, and as I pass them down the bus-rutted tarmac there is the occasional eyes-left moment and I will be greeted with a smile or perhaps a cheery four-letter cry.[28]

Could any politician but a mayor paint such a portrait? David Cameron must traverse Whitehall on his way to and from 10 Downing, but can you imagine him noticing the tramp tramp tramp of tourists on their way to take in Big Ben? Would President Obama be able to see, let alone interact with, the anti–Keystone XL Pipeline demonstrators from the armored limo taking him to the Waldorf Astoria in New York for a fundraiser? But mayors ride subways and buses, and miss little of the local flora and fauna. Demonstrators are in their faces, literally. And if they don't take heed, there's hell to pay: to neglect the city as neighborhood can play havoc with a mayor's reputation. Mayor Lindsay of New York learned this the hard way when he allowed snow to lie unplowed on the streets of the outer boroughs in the big storm of 1969.

For all the complaints about government grown too large, Mayor Bill White of Houston notices that "no mayor has ever heard about a citizen grumbling about public employees when a 911 call is answered by an EMS."[29] National politicians can play regional favorites (President Ford didn't have to cater to New York, and Lyndon Johnson could sacrifice his party's fortunes in the South to sign the Civil Rights Bill in 1965), but a mayor ignores Queens in New York or Croydon in London or the hillside ghetto favelas in Rio de Janeiro at his peril. A mayor will often feel compelled to step in even where the responsibility lies elsewhere. When the U.S. Congress failed to provide timely funding for the recent Port of Los Angeles expansion and greening, Mayor Antonio Villaraigosa made a trip to China to secure Chinese funding both for the port and for other infrastructural needs. "Congress," he complained, "has just been indifferent to cities." Taking it personally, the mayor made a difference by crossing borders and oceans and bringing help back home.

Just south of L.A., Mayor Bob Filner of San Diego decided not to leave his city's relationship to Tijuana, a supposed hotbed of illegal immigration just across the porous border, to the vicissitudes of immigration politics in Washington and Mexico City. He established a satellite city office in Tijuana, and invited collaboration. "Dos ciudades, pero una region" he announced: two cities but a single region. The issue is not security, says the mayor, but communication; by making the border "the center" rather than "the end," he hoped to establish a common economic infrastructure of value to both cities.[30]

The personal character of being mayor can add to the tensions between politics and the demands of good government. Personal governance can tip over into corrupt governance, while efficient management may undermine personal engagement. As Richard C. Scragger has suggested, "unlike the presidency or the governorship, the mayoralty has been suspect because it seems to pose the starkest choice between democracy and good government."[31] The Transition Manual, striking a good-government pose, tells new mayors not to be "tempted" into too many public appearances and not to succumb to participation in the "overwhelming number of community meetings and committees and taskforces" to which they will be invited. Good advice for keeping your schedule and sanity intact, but not for keeping your job—which entails cultivating the community at every turn and engaging in every corner of a city's civic network. Local democracy demands commitment. No doubt, Harvard would also advise against having His Honor run into burning buildings or break up muggings, but it's hard imagining a mayor worth his salt who would heed such counsel. As Robert Dahl wrote in his classic study of governance, the success of most mayors is not gained from being "at the peak of a pyramid but rather at the center of intersecting circles."[32]

What we find at the center of intersecting circles in the city is a *homeboy*. Mayors are homeboys—"homies" if you like. "People know who we are, they see us on the street," notes Philadelphia's Mayor Nutter. "I never have to wonder what's on the Philadelphians' mind, because they are going to tell me."[33] Mayors thrive when they are at the center of intersecting circles where they can evince a *commitment to the city as a unique civic entity* that keeps them in town, forever busy, too many commitments, never a vacation. The Harvard Manual says vacations *must* be scheduled and taken: more good advice unlikely to be heeded, unless like New York's Mayor Bloomberg you can fly your own chopper on weekend getaways, though even he seems rarely to have spent serious time in his ten or more homes away from home. Homies stay at home. Their stay-at-home-and-get-the-job-done attitude combined with the it's-not-over-till-it's-over-and-it's-never-over reality of urban politics help explain why City Hall is quite often a terminus rather than a stepping stone for most of its occupants. Except in those countries where mayors are appointed by party chiefs as part of their vocational training, the mayoralty is not often a springboard to a national political career.

In the telling words of an observer of New York City politics, "what [mayors] must do to get elected and re-elected are the very things that prevent them from ever moving on to higher office."[34] Ed Koch of New York grasped that while "congressmen [like Lindsay, he had been one] can pick their fights . . . mayors have to deal with whatever fights are handed to them."[35] Mayors don't much invoke the Almighty and rarely end speeches with God bless Chicago or Viva Ho Chi Minh City. The city is not a divine responsibility or a historical telos but a place where a mayor grows up and gets defined by local circumstances and homegrown fights not of his own choosing. For him, as Christopher Dickey observes, the city is above all a home rather than an abstraction. You can carpetbag a Senate seat in America, but out-of-towners are rarely welcomed in city politics. As a New

Yorker might put it, politically speaking, you gotta come from where you wanna end up. Some of her ardent fans thought Hillary Clinton should run for mayor of New York. The sage of State knew better.

In the United States only two presidents ever served as mayor: Calvin Coolidge as mayor of Northampton, Massachusetts, and Grover Cleveland as mayor of Buffalo, New York, back in 1881. In France, the party system means that national leaders will often serve as mayor as part of their party apprenticeship, President Jacques Chirac was mayor of Paris, for example. But even there the exception can prove the rule: François Hollande, who defeated Nicolas Sarkozy for the French presidency in 2012, began his political career in the small city of Tulle (in Corrèze), where he served as mayor for seven years. Yet though he was a carpetbagger in Tulle (no homeboys in the French system!), having arrived there from Rouen in the north in order to take on Jacques Chirac in Tulle regional legislative elections in 1981, spending time there as mayor had its effect. Outsider though he was, Hollande was a surprisingly effective "local." He ended up, according to the *New York Times*, "helping to modernize area schools, promoting home care for the elderly and cutting costs in a district that is among France's most debt-ridden."[36] Hollande's early constituents gave him over 75 percent of the vote in the 2012 presidential election. The new president returned the favor, giving his victory speech at the Place de la Cathedrale in Tulle, as if it were his true hometown, declaring that it was the region that "gave me the most."

National leaders rule over invented national abstractions—each province to some degree like every other province, each nation a complex of functions and interests, associations, and subsidiary governing units. Yet while cities also resemble one another in function and purpose, they have unique personalities that are rooted less in the cultural particulars of ethnicity or nationality than in geography, local history, and urban character. Never mind one-of-a-kind urban brands like Paris or New York, even "ordinary" cities have distinctive personalities that can be put on a postcard; yes, São Paulo, Shanghai, Venice, Casablanca, and Singapore, but also Louisville, Cano, Metz, Stuttgart, and Yokohama. Chongqing may be China's largest anonymous metropolitan region (almost 30 million residents in the region yet more or less unknown until the recent scandal mentioned above); yet it served as China's besieged and heroic capital during World War II, when Chiang Kai-shek's Nationalist (Kuomintang) army made it a final redoubt against the Japanese invaders. Today it sports the world's large public bathroom, with four stories of toilets—over a thousand of them—with shapes ranging from a crocodile maw to a bare-breasted Virgin Mary. *There's* a postcard! How much harder it is to put on 5×8 photo stock a picture that sums up a nation. It does not come as a surprise that, following the insurgency that overthrew Qaddafi, Libya started vanishing more or less on the very day the colonel was killed, reemerging only as a plurality of clans, tribes, and city militias whose attachment to their hometowns and clan capitals overwhelmed their wan loyalty to the abstract and weak Libyan nation.

How Cities Shape Mayors

Cities and their mayors make for fascinating stories. But are the features explored under our four categories, entertaining as they are, more than journalistic stereotypes or anecdotal quirks defining special cases? Is Mayor Johnson anything more than good copy? Or do his stylish remarks capture a truth about mayoral governance? Is there something unique in the nature of city government that shapes mayors? The diverse understandings of what it means to be a mayor in different cultures and political systems, as well as the distinctive histories and political constitutions that shape the mayoralty in individual cities, certainly make generalizations problematic. Nonetheless, a number of the features highlighted here seem to hold up across political systems, whether mayors are elected or appointed, whether they have ample or limited powers. In comparing the city manager and mayor-council forms of government recently, for example, Kathy Hayes and Semoon Chang found that "there is no apparent difference in the efficiency levels of the two municipal government structures," and that changes in the structure have almost no impact on taxing or spending levels.[37] There was a time, to be sure, when the imposition of a city manager model radically altered corrupt city politics. But the differences have faded. Elisabeth Gerber and Daniel Hopkins report similar findings with respect to party ideology, finding "no differences on tax policy, social policy and other areas that are characterized by significant overlapping authority," suggesting to them that "models of national policymaking are only partially applicable to U.S. cities."[38]

For all their problems, cities retain the confidence of citizens in a way other levels of government do not. Mayors and the urban institutions they lead retain remarkable levels of popular support. While confidence in political institutions has plummeted throughout the Western world, local government is the exception, leaving cities (in the words of Paul Maslin) as "the last remaining redoubt of public confidence." U.S. mayors retain a 64 percent confidence rating, according to a 2011 U.S. Conference of Mayors report, as compared to ratings for the presidency of 47 percent and for Congress of 19 percent.[39]

It also turns out, counterintuitively, that the limited ambitions of mayors with respect to higher office are fairly constant, whether they are elected locally or appointed by party officials higher up. In a provocative recent study of European mayors, researchers found that while the French system (where party politics and appointment is prevalent) nurtured mayors with more salient ambitions for higher office (including Hollande and Chirac), even in France only 39 percent of mayors had such ambitions. And in countries such as England, despite the predominance of appointed mayors, "progressive ambitions" were found among only 11 percent of officeholders, with the great majority having "static" ambitions (to stay put) or "discrete" ambitions (to leave politics after their terms).[40]

The crucial takeaway from these gray but revealing facts is simply this: the local, consensual, problem-solving character of the office of mayor seems to override differences in political landscape, ideological intensity, and the formal method of governing (mayor or city manager). This suggests quite compellingly that cities have essential features that trump the usual political and ideological factors that otherwise shape and constrain politicians. Being mayor is not about being Tory or Socialist, Republican or Democrat, Sunni or Shiite; it is not about being a generic politician who happens to occupy a local urban political office but otherwise acts like any other politician in any other office, local, regional, or national. It is about occupying a special political post that, in Andrew

Cuomo's words, calls for someone uniquely "entrepreneurial, pragmatic, and intelligent."[41] Such characteristics are mandatory if the mayor's "actions are [to be] tangible . . ." in the eyes of "people [who] have a close connection to the mayor" and who believe "the buck stops with the mayor."[42]

In sum, *mayors act as they do because they are governing cities rather than provinces, cantons, or national states.* Mayors are shaped more by what cities are and need than by factors inherent in a constitutional or political system but extraneous to the city, whether it's how they are chosen, what culture they come from, or the ideology they bring to office. Cities make mayors. This truth is closely connected to the claim I will make in Chapter 8, that cities have characteristics that enable them to address inequality in ways nations cannot; and thus to the claim that mayors are in a position to govern globally as no other public officials are—that cities and their networks are ideal cross-border collaborators in achieving global ends by democratic means.

Mayors can rule the world because cities represent a level of governance sufficiently local to demand pragmatism and efficiency in problem solving but sufficiently networked to be able to fashion cooperative solutions to the interdependent challenges they face. It is not just that cities lack that proud sovereignty that cripples nation-states in their efforts at cooperation, but that they are defined by communication, creativity, and connectivity, the foundation for that effective collaboration they need in order to survive. We may pay taxes to, exist as legal subjects of, and even die *for* the state. But we are born, grow up, are educated, get married, have children, work, get old, and die *in* the city—some metropolitan or urban or neighborhood version of the community in the title of Thornton Wilder's timeless drama *Our Town*. The nation-state is an overweening "it." Cities are us. No one wants some monumental "it" to rule the world. The "we" can and must do so. A parliament of mayors is really a parliament of us.

WOLFGANG SCHUSTER OF STUTTGART

Lord mayor of Stuttgart for two eight-year terms that ended at the beginning of 2013, **DR. WOLFGANG SCHUSTER** has been a mayor of European, even global, reach. One references "Dr. Schuster" because, unlike in the United States where "professor" is a political libel, the "Herr Doctor" is actually useful in Germany—perhaps because science is not yet dismissed as opinion, and higher education in political science and law is, remarkably, regarded as relevant to governance.

Schuster was a transformative mayor of Stuttgart but also an ambitious avatar of city networks of the kind that increasingly define Europe's most successful experiments in cooperation. He embodies the inclination of municipal officials today to work together rather than alone to solve their own problems as well as those facing the planet in common. Even as Europe's feuding states deepen the rifts occasioned by their economic differences and worsened by the blackmail of the European Bank and Germany's economic suzerainty, cities are helping hold Europe together. Whatever happens to the Eurozone, it seems likely that Europe's city networks will survive.

Among the networks in which Schuster has been active—the list is stupor-inducing but crucial, so please keep reading—are the German Association of Cities (of which he was vice president), the Council for Sustainable Development, the Congress of Local and Regional Authorities of Europe, the Council of European Municipalities and Regions

(Europe's most important city network, of which Schuster has been president), Cities for Mobility (where he was chairman), Cities for Children (again, chairman) and—this is the kicker—United Cities and Local Governments (UCLG), the most important global association of cities, representing over three billion people.

One might wonder when Schuster found time to govern Stuttgart, which is, after all, the capital of Baden-Württemberg (Schwabia), the sixth-largest city in Germany with over 600,000 residents, a European automotive capital (with Porsche and Mercedes-Benz, as well as the lesser known luxury car manufacturer Maybach), and home to Germany's second-largest stock exchange, such companies as Robert Bosch, Allianz Life Insurance, and Deutsche Bank, as well as more than 150,000 smaller firms. The Stuttgart region is also a leading center of research, technology, and higher education, with world-famous universities like Heidelberg and celebrated research centers like the Fraunhofer Society and the Max-Planck Institutes. In other words, Stuttgart would actually seem to require the attention of a mayor who is not busy founding, chairing, or serving on several dozen demanding intercity organizations.

Mayor Schuster obviously succeeded, because he did not regard his regional and global work as a distraction from his job as mayor. Quite the contrary. "Successful cities, in this century," he remonstrates in an interview, "are cities that are open, international, that really promote tolerance, and intercultural dialogue. Through this they also promote creativity [innovation], promote opportunities to increase their exports, have better chances to understand the culture of customers." For Mayor Schuster, governing in partnership (the name of a concept paper he wrote for Europe) is a necessity mandated by an interdependent world. Cities simply cannot go it alone. That is even more true for midsized cities between a half-million and a million than for larger cities. Stuttgart cannot be called a town, but neither is it a capital city or a megacity. It typifies urban living in an urbanized Europe that is a model for the world.

Economic inequality and unemployment often seem beyond the pale of urban mitigation, but Schuster has made joblessness in Europe—a consequence of Europe's economic travails—a major focus that reflects the need for partnership: "At the moment we are seeing differences between economically strong cities and many cities, even here [in Europe], with terrible problems—in Greece, parts of Spain and Portugal, where 50% of the people are jobless. It's not acceptable to have in the European Union over 5 million young people without jobs."[1] To him it is evident that inequality among cities is no less a challenge than inequality within cities.

Cities like Stuttgart in Germany, Cleveland in the United States, or Lyon in France can make a difference if urban governance is understood as a partnership. Europe will need the young, need them to be educated and trained, but that can't happen in countries in crisis that impede immigration despite their aging population. Since Stuttgart still has a need for qualified workers, it can "help to bridge the gap with some of these cities. They can send their youngsters to us where they stay for some years, become more qualified and then go back."

The many regional, European, and global networks to which Stuttgart belongs and on which Schuster serves are not, then, a distraction. They are tools of governing . . . in partnership. You don't have to be a professor to get that! Herr Doctor Schuster got it way before he left office in 2013 after two terms.

When mayors leave office they often go on doing the things mayors do because, well, they are mayors for life. Thus, Dr. Schuster is now running an Institute for Sustainable City Development in Stuttgart, which will allow him to pursue through civil society the work he did as mayor. In his words in his book on sustainable cities: "In order for our heterogeneous international and multicultural city associations to become sustainable citizen networks, we need to ground all of our work . . . in the culture of sustainability." In or out of office, that's what effective mayors do.[2]

CHAPTER 5. INTERDEPENDENT CITIES
Local Nodes and Global Synapses

The global city is not a place, but a process. A process by which centers of production and consumption of advanced services, and their ancillary local societies, are connected in a global network, while simultaneously downplaying the linkage with their hinterlands, on the basis of information flows.

Manuel Castells

Cities undermine national solidarities and favor glocal growth strategies.

Eric Corijn

The progress of city development, city revitalization, city building, is like the march of a drunkard . . . not a straight line. You go into small alleys, get drunk, throw up over there, cry a little bit when you get up, walk back, you're not sure where you're going. But at the end of the day you wind up in your own bed. You don't know how you got there, but you're there.

Anil Menon, Cisco Systems

Cities once favored walls, but even when under siege, never allowed themselves to be defined by borders. Their natural tendency is to connect, interact, and network. This interdependence is crucial to what makes an urban community a city. The city's interdependence can even undermine national solidarities, as the Belgian sociologist Eric Corijn has emphasized. In the name of cultivating mutual ties, cities are prone to betray the nation-states whose laws and power they normally honor. At times of crisis, they can become literal traitors to their sovereign overseers.

In the financial crisis of the seventies, Washington turned its back on New York City (President Ford's "Drop Dead, New York" scandal). Yet following the terrorist nightmare of 9/11, it was New York City that turned its back on Washington. Following the attack on the city, Mayor Giuliani had dispatched a squad of counterterrorism detectives to Washington in the hope of acquiring global intelligence cooperation, but it was a mistake to look for it there. A frustrating collaboration ensued without producing results, and after a period of futility, Ray Kelly, the new police commissioner, persuaded the new mayor, Michael Bloomberg, to bring the detectives home and redeploy them one by one to sympathetic foreign cities that had robust counterterrorist operations. Bloomberg and Kelly didn't exactly shout at Washington, "Drop dead," but by collecting and coordinating intelligence information with their global peers rather than the central government, where interagency feuding and territorial quarrels had stymied serious cooperation, they won a palpable victory for the city's security. There are many reasons for the city's safety record since then (including good luck), but city-to-city intelligence cooperation is among the most important; and it is a testament to city leaders' preference for working directly with one another rather than funneling their efforts through regional or national political authorities. Mayors still relying on cooperation with federal authorities for intelligence on international terrorism will surely be given pause by what happened in Boston: the FBI failed to share its concerns about the Tsarnaev brothers implicated in the Marathon bombing, despite warnings from Russia and the placing of the two men's names on terrorist watch lists. Had the Boston police had the information, they might have been able to prevent the attacks.

Historically Networked

Cross-border police collaboration is hardly new. Back in 1909, nearly one hundred years before Commissioner Kelly sent his detectives abroad, the NYPD dispatched Guiseppe "Joe" Petrosino to Italy to get information on the Mafia. Unhappily, the syndicate paid a back-handed and brutal tribute to the idea by killing Petrosino before he could uncover much. In fact, information flow and intelligence collection, along with many other goods and services vital to urban life, have run across oceans and through cities but around states and kingdoms for a very long time. Culture, philanthropy, social movements, and NGOs all have urban roots, and all of them nurture global networks and ongoing exchange.

Nearly six hundred years before Petrosino sailed for Italy, seafaring and river cities along the North Sea and the Baltic created the Hanseatic League, conspiring to protect the economic power they acquired when they acted in concert. Although remaining under the exclusive suzerainty of the neofeudal and Renaissance powers in whose jurisdictional hinterlands they had to dwell, the dozens of trading cities that eventually joined the Hansa established a trade corridor that worked its way along the North Sea from London and Brugge (in Belgium), northeast to Cologne on the Rhein and Hamburg and Lübeck (its capital, at the intersection of the North and Baltic Seas) and on up the Baltic to Falsterbo (in Denmark), Visby (in Sweden), and then Danzig (Gdansk), Breslau (Wrocław), and Krakow in today's Poland, all the way to Riga (in Latvia) and Kaliningrad (Königsberg) and Novgorod in Russia— over forty cities in all, along with another dozen *Kontore* or nonmember Hansa trading posts. Not quite a European union, but a remarkable exercise in collaboration before there was a Europe.

Most intriguingly for those seeking innovative modern forms of intercity consultation, the Hansa secured common policies and resolved differences by consensus, even when that meant punting a problem to an appointed group of representatives charged with reaching a consensual agreement for the entire league. Given the vast range of interests among members, and the often violent contestation between the new entities into which the Holy Roman Empire of the German Nation was being carved, the process was remarkably successful for nearly three hundred years. Only in the seventeenth century did the emergence of powerful new nation-states and the dominion of the Swedish Empire over the North and Baltic Seas bring Hansa autonomy to an end. In 1980, a largely but not entirely ceremonial successor association, the New Hanseatic League, was founded, complementing the vast array of intercity organizations established under the European community. For mayors like

Paweł Adamowicz of the old German port of Gdansk (Danzig), the new Hansa is a reminder of the natural community created by free trade and sea travel. Rostock's European League football team thus styles itself F. C. Hansa Rostock.

Three Dutch and ten German cities still identify themselves as Hansa. Tallinn (Estonia) uses its original Hansa membership and inner-city guild architecture as a tourist come-on. In Hamburg, the Hansa link is even more relevant. As Hamburg's Mayor Olaf Scholz told me, his city, along with Lübeck and Bremen, take seriously the traditional label "free Hanseatic city," and literally refuse to bow before kings. When the German emperor Wilhelm II visited Hamburg in 1895 for the opening of the Kiel Canal, the protocol required that the first mayor welcome the emperor as he dismounted the royal steed. The Hamburg Senate, however, argued that a first mayor of a free Hanseatic city should never play stable boy to the emperor. The first mayor met his guest on the landing of the first floor, only after the emperor ascended the staircase—as subsequent mayors have insisted on ever since.[1] Even during the Nazi era the precedent was honored. The league's founding city and capital, Lübeck, became famous for refusing to let Hitler speak during his election campaign, after the Nazis, with the Greater Hamburg Act, had canceled the free city privileges of Lübeck and the other Hansa cities. Hitler was forced to campaign in the suburban village Bad Schwartau nearby. The fascists understood too well that Hansa cities meant free cities resistant to authoritarianism, and hence annulled their historical status, in this case to no avail.

What the Nazis and later tyrants fail to understand is that cities can be occupied and sacked, but their liberties cannot be annulled as long as their citizens breathe. In the eighteenth century, Schiller celebrated Switzerland with the mantra "auf den Bergen, Freiheit!" (in the mountains: freedom!); by the nineteenth century, Tocqueville recognized that in America, liberty was local—municipal. In the twenty-first century, we might say it has become nearly redundant to say cities are free. All cities are now Hansa cities.

It is a very old story. Dial back two millennia before the Hansa, to the epoch preceding the Christian era, and it turns out that in a

Mediterranean world we generally associate with the economic autarky of city-states such as ancient Athens, Sparta, Thebes, Carthage, Rome, and Alexandria, political constitutions and economic life were also shaped by alliances, leagues, and guilds of free polises whose cooperative commercial and trade networks were as critical to the success of the growing web of cities as the proud autonomy of the polis. From the very beginning of urban history, flourishing entailed urban networking. In the face of the imperial power of Macedonia and Persia, both the Ionian League (seventh and sixth centuries B.C.E.) and the Delian League (founded in 477 B.C.E.) became active players in the life of the Mediterranean. After the rise of the Roman Empire, cities maintained some part of their power through the Panhellenion (founded A.D. 132–138). From the end of the Middle Ages into the early modern era, leagues and bunds were widespread, existing somewhat uncomfortably within the burgeoning Holy Roman Empire of the German Nation and the walled burgs it encompassed and ruled. The Hanseatic League, founded in 1157, was only the first of many, including the Lombard League (founded 1167), the Lusatian League, the Dekapole (or *Zehnstaedtebund*) in the Alsace region, and the Swabian League. Best known and most enduring were the leagues of alpine towns and ur-Kantons in inner Switzerland, as well as those in "Alt Frei Raetia" (later Kanton Graubuenden) in eastern Switzerland, which would eventually comprise the Swiss Confederation.[2] The West's first premodern democracy was in fact this feisty little league of Swiss cities and regions, carved out from the French and Austrian empires, whose decentralized participatory government is an anomaly among larger unitary nation-states, but a lesson for cities today seeking collaborative integration. Participation and engagement are the life and promise of the city.

This short list suggests how cities have benefited from cooperating across the territorial borders intended to keep them apart, borders laid down by "superior" authorities with little sympathy for local democracy or global comity. It is not so surprising that when, quite recently, Europe's North Sea coastal cities again reconstituted their ancient league to work to "fulfill their role as homes of living democracy," they had already established a host of other far more active intercity associations.

Or that in 2004, with little fanfare, the largest assembly of mayors and elected city officials ever seen gathered in Paris and formed United Cities and Local Governments. The gathering integrated scores of local government associations, some almost one hundred years old, from all over the world. The UCLG is the world's largest and most influential organization nobody has ever heard of.

The U.N.? WTO? IMF? Any kid poring over middle school homework anywhere in the world knows that these state-based entities, more recognized than successful, have something to do with international relations and the global economy—or maybe with mucking them up. But the UCLG? Yet it represents half the world's population. With 300 delegates from cities in more than 100 countries having participated in its 2010 World Congress, it may be in a better position to nurture global cooperation, and with a far greater claim to represent ordinary citizens, than state-based and money-dominated Bretton Woods institutions such as the World Trade Organization and the International Monetary Fund ever will be.

Recently, led by the city of Barcelona and the tech company Cisco, thirty cities along with allied organizations and universities established City Protocol. City Protocol "aims to define a global, cooperative framework among cities, industries and institutions with the goal to address urban challenges in a systemic way in areas such as sustainability, self-sufficiency, quality of life, competitiveness and citizen participation."[3] It will certify smart cities, create and test urban innovation models "based on standards definition, platform integration and technology and solutions development." It aspires to an efficient use of smart resources as well as economic, social, and environmental sustainability in smart cities.

The natural urban tendency to civic networking around trade, labor, culture, technology, environment, information, and security that this history reflects is endemic to the very meaning of the city. Not many Americans know much about the American association called the National League of Cities or even about the U.S. Conference of Mayors. Yet anyone who works for cities knows they are indispensable to governing. It is this age-old impetus to networking, reinforced by a robust and proven capacity actually to do so in a modern world of global communications, technology, arts, and trade that allows us to ask that cities bear the burdens of global governance—if by informal, persuasive, and consensual rather than centralized and peremptory means.

What makes cities so interactive and interdependent? There are clues in the previous chapter on the character of mayors and the ways in which cities shape that character. Still, it is often hard to see the networks for the cities. City associations function as artificial organisms at a fairly high level, but are less visible than the cities that are their vital organs. Higher organisms have both nodes and synapses, cores and connectors. Cities can and do govern globally because they are organisms in which local urban nodes naturally assimilate and integrate via global synapses into glocal networks defined by their local needs and global interests. The urban synapse is not just a connector; it is an outgrowth of the city node itself. Node and synapse grow together, part of one organism.

This metaphor stretches ordinary understanding, for unlike the individual organisms they emulate, which are integral wholes whose nodes cannot stand alone, social organisms are often visible only as they manifest themselves in their nodes. Their synapses are often out of sight. It is easier to think of cities structurally, in terms of walls and portals, than infrastructurally, in terms of functions and shared interests. We see Gdansk, Hamburg, Kaliningrad, and Copenhagen before we see (if ever we do) the Hanseatic League. We "get" Europe and can't forget its constituent states, but we are less mindful of what might be its most successful and enduring manifestation, its networked cities. Working together in entities such as the European Union's Committee of the Regions, an entity comprising 344 regional and local governments, these networked cities reflect, in Eric Corijn's words, "an important shift of emphasis [in Europe] to regions and metropolitan zones" in which newly "competitive regions and cities undermine national solidarities and favor glocal growth strategies."[4]

An enemy of urban cooperation such as America's National Rifle Association (NRA) may try to prevent cities from thwarting what the NRA falsely claims is a supposed "national will" opposing gun regulation by focusing on the nodes, insisting on seeing in the urban struggle against handguns a one-off triumph of a mayor's ego. The NRA thus advances its assault on gun control by targeting Mayor Bloomberg personally. But in targeting the mayor, the NRA misses the 600-member "Mayors Against Illegal Guns" association Bloomberg helped establish to actually create a political climate favorable to disarming cities, where weapons kill the innocent far more often than they protect them. The intercity organization is the NRA's real adversary, but the NRA obsesses over aggressive mayors like Bloomberg or Chicago's Rahm Emanuel because they are easy to caricature and denigrate.

Naturally Networked

Appearances notwithstanding, however, cities are defined as much by the networks they comprise as by the essential urban characteristics they incarnate. The organism is real. Cities are ineluctably interdependent and naturally relational, not just in the modern context of global interdependence but by virtue of what makes them cities. They define themselves more through "bridging capital," hooking them up with domains outside their boundaries, than through "bonding capital," unifying them internally. The glue that bonds a community makes it sticky with respect to other communities. It is not clear that a community can exist in the absence of other communities: no Robinson Crusoe communities, no unique one-only neighborhoods, no singular social cells not folded into larger social organisms. Isolation is simply not an urban state of being. Because cities are sticky, they do not slide or bounce off one another the way states do.

States collide because their common frontiers define where one ends and another begins. This necessarily turns territorial quarrels into zero-sum games. One state cannot grow without another being diminished. Not so cities, which are separated physically and hence touch only metaphorically and virtually, in ways that do not take up space or put one another at risk. A world of Singapores, in which cities were co-extensive with states, might put cities in the same position as states and compromise their connectivity. Singapore has tensions with Indonesia and Malaysia that Jakarta does not have with Kuala Lumpur. If one city's exterior wall were another city's interior wall, they might also be fated to compete and collide rather than network. To network is to cross nonurban (and hence "uninhabited") spaces, leaving room for virtual ties, synapses, and linking tissue.

We sometimes forget that modern nation-states, seemingly the very nullification of urban autonomy, originated in many cases from the interaction and cooperation of towns and principalities. Eric Corijn recalls that one of the first modern states, Holland, arose out of a federation of cities (*staten generaal*) whose first "president" was the Stadhouder (head, mayor) of Amsterdam. Both Italy and Germany owe at least an aspect of their modern nationality to cooperative agreements among the city-states and principalities into which they were constituted before their integration as states.

Trade is a crucial piece of the puzzle of integration. To speak of "trading cities" is nearly redundant, since trade is at the heart of how cities originate and are constituted. Communities gather so that people can live in proximity and harvest the fruits of commonality, but they gather *where* they do so they can reap the rewards of interdependence with other communities. They may inhabit a protective knoll at the crook of a river to stave off enemies, but they are on the river in order to promote exchange and trade. In mountain regions, cities are built at the intersections of valleys, not on the crags overlooking them (as a monastery or military garrison might be). It is along the natural routes carrying migrating peoples and moving goods that cities spring up, most often on water. Before the Suez Canal was built, Euro-Asian trade followed the Silk Road by land or had to round the Cape of Good Hope and follow southern routes by sea. But with the opening of the canal in 1857, traffic could cross the Indian Ocean and, clinging to the Malaysian coast line, find a fast route to China and Japan. Along this route, the straits on which Sir Stamford Raffles had turned a small village into a modest British colonial port for the East India Company in 1819 burgeoned into a major trading post and in time the global port that is modern Singapore. Trade literally made the city—as it did Amsterdam, Hong Kong, San Diego, Rio de Janeiro, Naples, Istanbul, and Casablanca, to name but a few. Or today, Dubai, which has used international flight routes to capture a position in world trade, commerce, and communication.

Their interdependence gives cities a distinct advantage over nation-states. Too often, internal bonding capital of the kind prized by states is built on exclusion and fear, a national identity, and pride in sovereign independence that can overwhelm bridging capital. Like autonomous individuals, so-called rights-bearing persons (legally and psychologically distinct beings), states do not in theory need one another. That is why, although we might imagine a world state, the actual nation-states of the world seem unlikely ever to be likely to establish one. State-based nationalist patriotism affords integral unity only by diminishing or nullifying the "other" or the "stranger" just the other side of the common border. Consider the United States and Mexico, France and England, Germany and Poland (or Russia and Poland), China and Japan—hostile and anxious because common borders offer neighboring states little in common.

Those who exclaim, "We're Number One!" as fretful Americans often do, are not claiming just an ordinal ranking in which contending number twos and threes are seen as nearly as good. They are promulgating a cardinal ranking in which number one is unique, exceptional, virtuous, and worthy in ways others are not. Nor is it just the Americans who boast of an immodest exceptionalism. Others too have pursued a unique national or civilizational destiny, whether by embracing Sonderfall Schweiz (the Swiss Exception), the *mission civilisatrice* of the French, or the claims to universality of a "co-prosperity sphere" as the Japanese Empire did before World War II; defending a global sphere for an ambitious religion, as the Holy Roman Empire of the German Nation did in the late Middle Ages and the Ottomans did with their expanding empire from the sixteenth century through World War I; or shouldering the "White Man's Burden," as the British did in establishing their global empire. But in cities, where flags and anthems are less useful than tourist promotions and love songs, it is bridging capital, not bonding capital, that is paramount.[5] Cosmopolitanism trumps patriotism.

Paradoxically, urban-sourced bridging capital seems to arise out of the same bonding tendencies that hold the city together. New York certainly sees itself as a world-class city, yet celebrates itself with the slogan "I love New York," not "we're number one." Moreover, "I love New

York" works for inhabitants and visitors alike, promoting solidarity and tourism in the same breath. "We're Number One," on the other hand, hardly signals to French or Egyptian or Japanese tourists that the United States is their country too! The United States is hard to enter; cities welcome visitors and make it easy for them to stay, spend, and enjoy. As a hub of national and global urban networks, and home to the United Nations as well as a capital of global finance and world culture, New York City's essence is cosmopolitan rather than parochial. In America's national politics, cooperation can be libeled as weakness rather than strength.

By the same token, "pandering" to others with the language of interdependence (as President Obama did early in his first term, but prudently, if sadly, stopped doing later) or honoring international law in American courts (as justices of the Supreme Court do at their peril, and Justice Kennedy learned the hard way!) can be politically inexpedient, even fatal. In a fractious and parochial political climate, it becomes indistinguishable from apologizing to foreigners. When Senator John Kerry ran for president he had to conceal his ability to speak French, while President Obama's typically American mixed ancestry has been a political liability for him—"show us the birth certificate!"—rather than the virtue it might be in Brazil or India. In the city, contrarily, cooperation and linguistic facility as well as cosmopolitanism and mobility are virtues that benefit cities as cultural, economic, and trading enterprises.

Trade is paramount and culture primary, but today's myriad city networks encompass a remarkable diversity of functions and purposes. Manuel Castells focuses on information flows,[6] while Saskia Sassen emphasizes "global city functions" centered on the "management and servicing" of the global economy." After specifying her preferred forms of interaction, Sassen is quick to remind us that the functions of intercity associations are wide ranging and include "illegal trafficking networks in people, drugs, stolen goods; immigrant personal and business networks; art biennales; the art market; tourism patterns (for instance, stops for major cruise lines); and activists' networks, from environmentalists and human rights efforts to poor people's advocacy organizations."[7] Occupy Wall Street is scarcely imaginable outside the urban centers where it was born and flourished—Zuccotti Park in the Wall Street district of Manhattan, St. Paul's Square in the City of London, the Tiergarten in Berlin. Barricades are built on urban boulevards where paving stones can be hurled at officials, not country cow paths where there is only mud to throw at trees. Demonstrations take place only when a concentration of people can populate both the protest movement and its indispensable spectators.

Philanthropy too is an urban extension of community building and cooperation, and it is equally at home within and between cities. Kathleen McCarthy points out that the relative underdevelopment of philanthropy in the American South, especially before the Civil War, was closely connected to the South's rural, agricultural, and patriarchal character: "The lack of cities limited the growth of philanthropy in the antebellum South," McCarthy observes.[8] In her history of philanthropy, she shows why: "Southern associations were more dependent on the supervision and control of white male elites, less active in reform, and less likely to play significant economic roles than their counterparts in the North."[9]

Real Networks Today

Urban synapses and the networks they generate, although less visible, are then as much a feature of the new global landscape as the prominence of cities themselves. Such networks are doing real work in the setting of transnational cooperation, work that is too easily overlooked because it is voluntary and cooperative and rarely takes the form of a state treaty or international compact. The list in Table 3 offers a vivid reminder of how important city networks are and how their number has grown.

This list samples only several dozen global networks, out of an expansive and diverse set of intercity associations that number in the hundreds. To be sure, many of the more active and successful groups are regional rather than truly global. Networks tend especially to grow within American borders, representing as they do the cornucopia of American civic associations that impressed Alexis de Tocqueville and define America's rich civil society. The United States includes such stalwarts as the League of Cities and the U.S. Conference of Mayors, as well as organizations opposing handguns, promoting sustainability, and supporting rights

Table 3: Major Urban Networks

Organization Name	Headquarters
C40 Cities http://live.c40cities.org/home/	New York, USA
Cities for Mobility http://www.cities-for-mobility.net/index.php/news	Stuttgart, Germany
City Protocol http://cityprotocol.org/	Barcelona, Spain
CityNet http://www.citynet-ap.org/	Seoul, South Korea
CLAIR—Council of Local Authorities for International Relations http://www.clair.or.jp/e/	Tokyo, Japan
Climate Alliance http://www.klimabuendnis.org/	Frankfurt, Germany
Davos—World Economic Forum http://www.weforum.org/	Geneva, Switzerland
DELGOSEA—Partnership for Democratic Local Governance in Southeast-Asia http://www.delgosea.eu/cms/	Manila, Philippines
ICLEI—International Council for Local Environmental Initiatives http://www.iclei.org/	Bonn, Germany
ICMA—International City/County Management Association http://icma.org/en/icma/home	Washington, D.C., USA
INTA—International Urban Development Association http://www.inta-aivn.org/en/	Paris, France
ISPA—International Society for the Performing Arts http://www.ispa.org/	New York, USA
League of Historical Cities http://www.city.kyoto.jp/somu/kokusai/lhcs/eng/index.htm	Kyoto, Japan
Mayors for Peace http://www.mayorsforpeace.org/english/	Hiroshima, Japan
Metropolis - World Association of the Major Metropolises http://www.metropolis.org/	Barcelona, Spain
Organization of World Heritage Cities (OWHC or OVPM) http://www.ovpm.org/	Quebec, Canada
SCI - Sister Cities International http://www.sister-cities.org/	Washington, D.C., USA
UITP—International Association of Public Transport http://www.uitp.org/	Brussels, Belgium
United Cities and Local Governments (UCLG) http://www.cities-localgovernments.org	Barcelona, Spain

Membership	Year Est.	Primary Issue Area(s)
63 "global cities"	2005	Climate; energy efficiency
550 members from 76 countries	2003	Transportation
41 cities, several universities, companies, and NGOs	2012	Tech cooperation; sustainability
77 full member cities in Asia and the Pacific, 45 associate members, several NGOs	1987	Networking; best practice exchange
Over 900 trainees, offices in 7 cities	1988	International collaboration; development and revitalization
1,600 municipalities in 18 European countries	1990	Climate; energy efficiency
1,000 large companies	1971	Economic development
4 national city associations (UCLG Asia-Pacific)	2010	Democracy
1,012 municipalities and associations from 84 countries	1990	Climate; energy efficiency
9,000 members (city and county managers)	1914	Good government; education
Over 3,000 members (individuals, organizations, governments)	1979	Networking; knowledge exchange
Over 400 from 50 countries	1949	Arts and culture
92 cities	1994	Arts and culture
5,092 cities in 152 countries	1982	Peace, human rights
100+	1985	Networking; environment
238 cities	1993	Arts and culture
2,000 partnerships in 136 countries	1956/ 1967	Cultural exchange; town twinning
3,400 members in 92 countries	1885	Public transit
1,000+ cities (+112 national governments)	2004	Networking

movements for minorities or women or gays (the ACLU), as well as the counterorganizations that grow up to oppose them (the Chamber of Commerce, some might say, or the NRA). Europe's civil society is equally impressive, with its many proliferating city associations often as vibrant and influential as the state network comprising the actual European Union. Cities such as Stuttgart and Barcelona, as well as Hamburg, Vienna, and Amsterdam, have become hubs of urban networking, spawning new associations almost every year. Their ties are not just rooted in currency and administration but reflect culture and civil society (as with the European Cultural Capitals program).

Moreover, among the newer associations are a number in Asia (such as CityNet) and Latin America (such as FLACMA or Federation of Latin American Cities, Municipalities and Associations) that are regional but aspire to being global. Indeed, although the United Nations may be composed of quarreling nation-states, it has nevertheless managed to be an effective promoter of global intercity cooperation. Its Human Habitat program has contributed significantly to interurban development, and core intercity associations such as UCLG and Metropolis—both Barcelona based—are closely tied to the U.N. In 2001, the United Nations Economic and Social Commission for Asia and the Pacific convened an Asia-Pacific Summit of Women Mayors and Councilors focused on the political advancement of women in a part of the world where traditional patriarchy has thrown up formidable barriers. The summit featured U.N.-funded participation by Bangladesh, China, India, Indonesia, Malaysia, Nepal, Pakistan, Philippines, Sri Lanka, Thailand, and Viet Nam, and self-funded collaboration from Japan, Australia, and New Zealand.[10] So while there is a natural tension between the nation-based organization of the U.N. and the impulse to interurban association, the reality has been extensive and productive collaboration. Increasingly, the newer associations are truly global, while the United Nations increasingly cooperates with cities, as with the U.N.-Habitat (Human Settlements) program.

In the interest of our core focus, let me concentrate on two vital categories of global networks that through cross-border cooperation have achieved at least some success in controversial areas where states have failed: security and environment. I will add a few words about a third robust domain, culture and the arts, but leave the lively topic of art and the city to Chapter 10. Further examples of themed networks also abound in transportation, housing, philanthropy, and education. The two primary subjects we will track involve issues of existential survival, however, where there is a critical need for common action but where the sovereignty of nation-states has been a serious impediment to cooperation, and national interests often thwart citizen interests and prevent vital common action. They are thus particularly useful in illustrating the potential of cities where sovereignty-heavy states have failed.

Security

National security has always stirred global anxieties and more or less defines traditional international relations. In contrast, urban security has traditionally been a matter for city police departments addressing conventional local crime. Criminal syndicates and networked criminal activities such as prostitution and drugs have, to be sure, compelled local police departments to cast a national (and at times international) net, and in the United States these problems led to the establishment of the Federal Bureau of Investigation. But when it comes to nuclear proliferation, weapons of mass destruction, and global terrorism—dramatized in the trauma of 9/11 in America, but also a daunting reality in cities from London, Karachi, Cairo, and Berlin to Mumbai, Istanbul, Madrid, and Jakarta—a new imperative for intercity cooperation across borders has emerged unlike anything before. David Wylie has warned with compelling urgency that even in (especially in) the domain of nuclear security, urban citizens can and must play a role.[11] Table 4 lists a few important intercity organizations that address security issues.

The proliferation of such associations suggests that security cooperation among cities is no longer discretionary. As Christopher Dickey has written, "the world no longer stops at the oceans, our world goes every place, and we have to make sure that we get the best information as quickly as we possibly can."[12] In the words of Police Commissioner Kelly: "[Since 9/11] I knew we couldn't rely on the federal government . . . from my own experience. We're doing all the things we're doing because the federal government isn't doing them. It's not enough to say it's their job if the job isn't being done."[13]

Table 4: Urban Security Networks

Organization Name	Headquarters	Membership
European Cities Against Drugs (ECAD) www.ecad.net/	Stockholm, Sweden	262 municipalities in 31 countries
European Forum for Urban Security (EFUS) www.efus.eu	Strasbourg, France	300 local authorities from 17 countries
Global Network on Safer Cities	Undetermined	Undetermined
Mayors Against Illegal Guns www.mayorsagainstillegalguns.org	New York, USA	600 mayors from more than 40 U.S. states
Mayors for Peace (formerly the World Conference of Mayors for Peace through Inter-city Solidarity) www.mayorsforpeace.org/	Hiroshima, Japan	5,664 cities in 157
Women in Cities International (WICI)	Montreal, Canada	Over 300 members

Year Est.	Mission, Purpose, Aims (key issues)
1994	"ECAD is Europe's leading organization promoting a drug free Europe and representing millions of European citizens.... ECAD member cities work to develop initiatives and efforts against drug abuse."
1949	EFUS's mission is "to foster multilateral exchanges throughout Europe, but also with other continents, about locally-developed practices and experiences.... [It] has built a unique body of know-how, competences, and field reports on a wide array of themes linked to crime prevention and urban security." EFUS was created under the auspices of the Council of Europe.
2012	Advisory panel established; constitution still being formulated.
2006	A coalition of mayors working together to: punish offenders; hold irresponsible gun dealers accountable; oppose federal efforts to restrict cities' rights to collect, access, and share data about gun owners; develop technologies to aid detection and tracing; support state and federal legislation that targets illegal guns.
1982	"The Mayors for Peace, through close cooperation among the cities, strives to raise international public awareness regarding the need to abolish nuclear weapons and contributes to the realization of genuine and lasting world peace by working to eliminate starvation and poverty, assist refugees fleeing local conflict, support human rights, protect the environment, and solve the other problems that threaten peaceful coexistence within the human family."
2002	"WICI is a non-profit network organisation, based in Montréal, Canada, that focuses on gender equality and the participation of women and girls in urban development. WICI is dedicated to the identification, study and dissemination of good practices, tools and intervention models. With its partners, WICI facilitates knowledge- and experience-sharing on the improvement of women's and girls' safety and status in cities and communities. WICI specialises in the organisation of networking and training events, the advancement of technical expertise, and the production of research in order to achieve its goals."

Getting that information cannot be left to states. After all, al Qaeda is less a state-based association than a malevolent nongovernmental organization. It knows no national homeland and shifts operations easily, migrating from a training camp in Afghanistan to an ideological ally in the Middle East to a weak state in Asia to a rogue state in North Africa, where it ends up holding hostages in an Algerian oil facility; it can hop from Yemen to Pakistan to Mali without putting down roots or expressing loyalty to anything but the spirit of jihad. Attempts to address terrorist organizations such as al Qaeda and its multiplying offshoots through traditional state-to-state diplomacy or conventional military intervention have been less than successful—as recent incidents in Somalia, Sudan, Libya, and Mali demonstrate. In Boston, two brothers who immigrated from Dagestan bringing Chechnyan sympathies with them turned on the nation that gave them a new homeland with homemade bombs— inadvertent hybrids who emerged violently from a confusing international context that a focus on al Qaeda could hardly be expected to expose.

In New York, Dickey offers the example of a cop who complains bitterly about the ponderous pace of national/international intelligence networks. Agitated over the Madrid bombing of 2007, he says, "Eighteen months later we got a report from the FBI on the Madrid bombing, which was terrific. It was great—it was fucking eighteen months later! They tried the best they could. It's just not their job."[14] The New York Police Department has "fifty thousand employees and a budget of some 3.8 billion" and it was now "going where no local government agency had gone before." Dickey observes that large immigrant populations, an apparent security liability for cities, actually make them safer; immigrants are often hugely patriotic and frequently out the terrorists who choose to hide among them.[15]

The cumbersome nature of national intelligence bureaucracies is frustrating, as the Boston bombers once again made evident, but the asymmetries nations face in trying to go up against local/global interdependent terrorist networks is daunting as well as perilous. A key asymmetry, which unfortunately has defined the Pentagon's war against al Qaeda, involves weaponry and personnel: a B-1 bomber is not really a suitable response to a suicide bomber, while drones cannot be used against resident terrorists waiting to strike Boston from across the Charles river in Watertown, or to hit the new American embassy in Berlin from a fourth-floor apartment up the hill on Prenzlauer Berg.

There is also a deeper asymmetry between the broad counterterrorist goals of nation-states and the narrower concerns of cities. The United States or France will seek an al Qaeda–free Afghanistan or, perhaps more improbably, a Taliban-free Afghanistan. But that is no guarantee that Mumbai or London or New York is safe from al Qaeda's marauding offshoots like those operating in Libya or Mali today. Cities will be less concerned with addressing terrorism at the point of origin (which states focus on), and more interested in preempting its implementation in target cities (the responsibility of municipalities). The FBI and CIA seemed satisfied that, despite President Putin's anxieties, the Tsarnaev brothers did not have formal connections with or emanate from known international terrorist organizations. The Boston police would surely have liked to know that a pair of Chechnyan sympathizers who worried the intelligence-trained president of Russia were living in their city.

Once they have exploited national and international resources such as Scotland Yard and Interpol, or have been disappointed by them, city police departments may well choose to cooperate directly with one another in anticipating terrorism and defending themselves. They are even more likely to do so in light of a recent congressional report on the egregious deficiencies of the regional intelligence-gathering offices called "fusion centers" that are operated by the Department of Homeland Security in the United States. The 2012 report charged that the centers "forwarded intelligence of uneven quality—oft times shoddy, rarely timely, sometimes endangering citizens' civil liberties and Privacy Act protections, occasionally taken from already-published public sources, and more often than not unrelated to terrorism."[16] Mayor Bloomberg and Police Commissioner Ray Kelly of New York grasped early on that developing assets in the city and promoting intercity intelligence gathering and anti-terror planning was a much better bet for urban security than relying exclusively on collaboration with the Department of Homeland Security or the FBI.

Interpol may seem like the exception to the rule, since it involves massive interstate cooperation, but like the United Nations, the international police agency is a cooperative of 180 sovereign states that, though accessible and useful to city departments, channels police cooperation primarily at the nation-state level. Like other international organizations, it risks bringing ideology and corruption with it from its member states. In 2010, its former president, Jackie Selebi from South Africa, was found guilty by the High Court of South Africa on corruption charges related to drug trafficking, which had led in 2008 to his suspension as South Africa's national police commissioner and to his stepping down from the Interpol presidency. Founded in 1923 as the International Criminal Police (the United States quickly became a member), the agency immediately became vulnerable to national ideologies and interests. It fell under the sway of the Nazis after the Austrian *Anschluss* in 1938 and did not reemerge until after World War II with a new name (Interpol) and mission statement.

Since then, Interpol has labored fastidiously to remain politically neutral. Yet it has not always succeeded in avoiding charges of political bias—as when it was accused of complicity in the winter 2012 Malaysian police arrest of Saudi journalist Hamza Kashgari for apostasy (insulting the Prophet Muhammad). Moreover, Interpol's status as a state-based organization like the United Nations (it has a counterpart in *Europol*) means it is more responsive to national and international agendas such as drug trafficking and the apprehension of corrupt national politicians than to urban security concerns; and it is, moreover, hampered by the impediments to cooperation that beset nation-states generally. In the words of a recent scholarly report, that augured badly for what was to transpire in Boston in the spring of 2013, "Police support [for Interpol] at the national level is not self-evident, particularly not when cases involve politically sensitive matters. This was clearly shown in the case of a former Chechen government representative, Akhmed Zakayev, for whom an Interpol warrant on charges of terrorism was distributed on the request of Russian Authorities. The Chechen envoy was freed by Danish authorities."[17] The Danes let Zakayev go, Washington ignored Putin's warnings about the Tsarnaevs. The report also detailed another disturbing instance of lack of cooperation at the national level by police agencies, despite their formal participation in Interpol, in the case of former

Peruvian president Alberto Fujimori. Fujimori, after being charged with corruption in 2000 during his presidency of Peru, fled to Japan where he was able to resist extradition for seven years, and where he remained despite criminal charges against him until 2007.

With or without Interpol, the greatest nightmare cities like Tokyo, Mumbai, New York, São Paulo, and London face in securing themselves against terrorism—with consequences no nation qua nation will directly face—is a downtown bomb strike by a terrorist group. It is too easy to imagine a cell securing a loose nuke or dirty bomb (clad in fissionable radioactive material) and importing it on one of those ubiquitous container ships that enter ports around the world, mostly uninspected. The second half of the twentieth century was marked by the unthinkable peril of nuclear winter, a thermonuclear exchange among state superpowers devoted to "mutual assured destruction"—the so-called MAD strategy of threatening reciprocal annihilation in order to deter conflict altogether. The first half of the twenty-first century will be marked by the "lesser" peril of a singular random act by a terrorist madman, a peril that may however seem even more horrific to urban dwellers. It is more than frightening to witness individual strikes with everyday weaponry— like the one in which two London extremists ran down and then slaughtered a British soldier in mid-afternoon London in May 2013. Imagine what it means to city residents to contemplate a dirty fission device or the unleashing of some novel chemical or biological agent (ricin?) that can kill hundreds or even thousands, weapons of a kind we know (for example) the Syrians actually possess.

The concentration of population that makes cities urban makes them especially vulnerable to attacks in which a minuscule cell of conspirators holding one weapon can eradicate a metropolis of millions and get maximum publicity in doing so. In combating this kind of attack, the first line of defense may be intelligence and counterterrorist cooperation among cities, although in the long term the control of nuclear proliferation and bans on biochemical weapons of mass destruction is of equal importance. In this domain too, cities cannot afford to wait for goodwill treaties to be signed by foot-dragging states more interested in sovereignty and their own arsenals than safety from nuclear annihilation.

Among the more exotic but revelatory intercity networks are those that actually do focus on weapons of mass destruction. Most important among them is the 5,664-city organization Mayors for Peace, founded and headquartered, tellingly, in Hiroshima. Among the scores of brave but politically marginal international peace lobbies including Love-earth, Stop War, Voice4Change, and Coalition for World Peace, Mayors for Peace is the only intercity organization that brings the voice of mayors to the table and puts the municipalities most likely to suffer from global war on the frontline of the peace effort. Grounded in peace declarations issued by Hiroshima and Nagasaki at the Second Special Session on Disarmament at the United Nations in 1982 in New York, Mayors for Peace was established explicitly as an intercity organization. It was not Japan in the abstract, but two very real cities that had borne the cost of the world's only nuclear bomb attacks, and it was the intention of those cities and others joining the new association to focus on cities and give them a voice for global peace.

Since that time, Mayors for Peace, with 5,524 members in 156 countries and regions (as of January 1, 2013), has been calling worldwide for solidarity among cities; conducting a "2020 Vision Campaign" to eliminate nuclear weapons by the year 2020; conducting a petition drive calling for a Nuclear Weapons Convention; and holding a world conference every four years—in Hiroshima in 2013.[18] It may seem hopelessly idealistic in 2013 for cities to be waging a campaign for a "nuclear-weapons free world" by 2020—especially when North Korea has just passed through and Iran is knocking on the door of the fourteen-member nuclear power clubroom,[19] and when the United States still maintains a 20,000-plus nuclear and thermonuclear bomb arsenal designed for the Cold War and more likely today to bankrupt it in peacetime than protect it in war. Yet cities embody a political force few civic NGOs can claim. Were that force to be concentrated in a global mayors parliament and exercised through the democratic majority cities represent in almost all democratic nations, it could conceivably effect real change by the year 2020.

Urban security goals centering on curbing global nuclear weapons are likely to be frustrated for some time to come. But when we move from spectacular threats like those posed by a loose nuke or bio-agent to ordinary realities like controlling handguns, urban action may have a better chance of political realization. This is particularly true for the United States, an outlier among civilized nations in its devotion to the private ownership of guns (rationalized by ahistorical readings of the Second Amendment's constitutional guarantee of the right to "a well regulated militia"). In the aftermath of years of massacres of innocent civilians, college students, and schoolchildren culminating in the Newtown, Connecticut, murder of twenty children and six adults (which tragically but surely will not be the last such outrage), the influence of the 600-member Mayors Against Illegal Guns offers a striking example. Where until 2013 the U.S. national government and individual states had lacked the political will to take on an NRA that deploys an annual budget of $300 million, cities have been under no such constraints. They can be liberated by the potential of intercity cooperation among politicians, police officials, and citizens who can unite around their opposition to guns and take local action to enforce gun control—or at least gun registration and background checks. Analogous massacres in Norway and Australia, and killings in England, Germany, and Switzerland, make it evident that the problem is neither purely American nor a function of the absence of gun control alone—still another reason for expanding the circle of cooperation among cities on curbing gun violence.

It isn't easy. Cities in the United States are constrained to live under state law and are subject to federal law, as the city of Washington, D.C., learned when in 2008 its own bold effort to ban handguns was declared unconstitutional by the federal government to which the city plays host—the Supreme Court in *District of Columbia v. Heller*. The struggle is ongoing. In 2013, New York State's Governor Cuomo fell into line behind Mayor Bloomberg with significant restrictions on assault rifles and magazine size, and President Obama has made gun and ammo regulation a core goal of his second term. But though cities like Chicago (where the lethal combination of guns and gangs remains a leading cause of death) and New York (where deaths are way down) continue to lead the campaign against gun violence, the battle for federal legislation remains deeply problematic. National political leaders seem more moved by lobbyists than by citizens, given that polls show over and over that more than 90 percent of the American public favors forms of gun control their representatives refuse to legislate. When it comes to security, global or local, cities are likely to remain the key players.

Environment

If security is the most acute challenge facing cities, the environmental crisis is the most persistent and potentially catastrophic. In this ecologically challenged era, sustainability is the condition for survival, and ecological interdependence means there will be no survival without cooperation. The proven incapacity of sovereign states to reach environmental accords on such elementary issues as extending and replacing the Kyoto Protocol or signing the Law of the Sea Treaty is likely to be fatal to urban populations first and foremost. Air quality deterioration will eventually affect Aspen, Zurich, and Vancouver no less than it already threatens Beijing, Phoenix, and Mexico City, while the rising oceans that have already flooded Bangladesh's capital city of Dhaka (putting 20 million mostly poor people at risk) and below-sea-level New Orleans are now lapping at middle-class communities in Staten Island (New York) and the New Jersey shore and causing floods in unlikely English villages. With up to 90 percent of the world's cities on water (lakes, rivers, and oceans), urban populations are on the front banks of ecological risk. This is why San Francisco and New York City are already responding to rising waters on the frightening scale of Hurricane Sandy in 2012 with novel "mitigation plans"—a fantasy land of massive sea gates in front of New York Harbor and giant rubber balloons to prevent high tides from flooding Manhattan tunnels, abruptly made real and pertinent. In fact, climate change is quickly morphing into the ultimate security issue, with urban cooperation in addressing the underlying causes of climate change a necessity of survival.

We should not be surprised to discover that among the world's many urban networks, a considerable number are focused on environmental sustainability. Where states can be said to have done the least, cities have done the most. Keeping in mind that many broad-spectrum city networks include environmental and climate change activities as significant parts of their programs (EuroCities, Metropolis, United Cities and Local Governments, and the U.S. Conference of Mayors, to mention just a few), the representative networks in Table 5 (there are many more) focus exclusively on sustainability and environmentalism.

The cooperation these networks reinforce rests on some simple realities. As much as 80 percent of human-generated carbon emissions come from cities and hence can be addressed in cities, whether or not their host states wish to cooperate. Cities that are also ports are where we often find dense concentrations of people, carbon-powered vehicles (trucks, buses, cars, and ships), and energy-consuming habitations (residential and business). Density of population is a boon to conservation, but urban roadways, port facilities, and buildings are invitations to ecological abuse.

Much of Los Angeles' carbon footprint came from its massive port (now revamped); in New York City, buildings are the more obvious culprits (insulation and heating improvements are a key to energy saving there); in Beijing, cars and factories do much of the damage (rapid modernization gets the blame, along with the windless bowl in which the city is set). Given such challenging conditions, cities can wait neither for states to come to terms with climate change nor for city bureaucracies to respond with the appropriate urgency. Political leadership by mayors and city councils, civic and citizen movements taking direct action (on recycling, for example), and voluntary intercity cooperation by members of the networks referenced here are key in confronting both the urban consequences of climate change and the underlying causes. Cities act because they can and they must, and because states often don't and won't.

Among active global networks, the best-known and most effective has been the hard-working, long-enduring 1,200-member International Council for Local Environmental Issues (ICLEI)—a.k.a. Local Governments for Sustainability. Founded in 1990 with 200 members, ICLEI was presided over until recently by a modest but deeply committed civil servant, Otto Zimmerman. ICLEI today calls itself a "powerful organization" boasting membership of "12 mega-cities, 100 super-cities and urban regions, 450 large cities as well as 450 small and medium-sized cities and towns in 84 countries."[20] The association advocates "participatory, long-term, strategic planning processes that address local sustainability while

Table 5: Environmental Intercity Networks

Organization Name	Headquarters	Membership
Alliance in the Alps www.alpenallianz.org	Mäder, Austria	Over 300 in 7 countries
C40 Cities Climate Leadership Group live.c40cities.org/c40cities	New York, USA (current Chair city)	58 "global cities"
Climate Alliance www.klimabuendnis.org	Frankfurt, Germany; Brussels, Belgium	1,600 municipalities in 18 countries
Covenant of Mayors (E.U.) www.covenantofmayors.eu	Brussels, Belgium	3,512 signatories representing over 155 million citizens
Energy Cities/Energie-Cités www.energy-cities.eu	Besançon, France, and Brussels, Belgium	1,000 towns and cities in 30 countries
ICLEI — International Council for Local Environmental Initiatives www.iclei.org	Bonn, Germany	1,200 municipalities and associations from 84 countries
MedCities www.medcities.org	Barcelona, Spain	27 cities in 16 countries
World Mayors Council on Climate Change http://www.worldmayorscouncil.org/home.html	Bonn, Germany	113 member cities in 32 countries

Year Est.	Mission and Activities
1997	"An association of local authorities and regions from seven Alpine states . . . founded in 1997. Its members, together with their citizens, strive to develop their alpine living environment in a sustainable way. 'Exchange— Address— Implement' is the main idea behind the Alliance's activities."
2005	The C40 is "committed to implementing meaningful and sustainable climate-related actions locally that will help address climate change globally." It engages a broad array of environmental and livable city issues, including energy efficiency, emissions, waste reduction, bike infrastructure, public engagement, and urban drainage. C40 Cities partners with the Clinton Climate Initiative (CCI).
1990	"European network of local authorities committed to the protection of the world's climate. The member cities and municipalities aim to reduce greenhouse gas emissions at their source. Their allies in this endeavour are the Indigenous Peoples of the rainforests in the Amazon Basin."
2008	The Covenant of Mayors is a "European movement involving local and regional authorities, voluntarily committing to increasing energy efficiency and use of renewable energy sources on their territories. . . . Covenant signatories aim to meet and exceed the European Union 20% CO_2 reduction objective by 2020." Signatories submit action plans and track their progress publicly on the website.
1990	"Energy Cities is the European Association of local authorities inventing their energy future." It helps cities "strengthen their role and skills in the field of sustainable energy," represents cities on sustainable energy at EU meetings, and develops and promotes initiatives through knowledge and experience exchange.
1990	"ICLEI is an international association of local governments as well as national and regional local government organizations who have made a commitment to sustainable development." ICLEI provides consulting, training, and platforms for information exchange to build capacity and support local initiatives to achieve sustainability objectives.
1991	MedCities works "to strengthen the environmental and sustainable development management capability of local administration . . . and to identify the domains where a common activation could be the most useful means to improve the regional environmental conditions." It aims "to reinforce the awareness of interdependence and common responsibility regarding the policies of urban environmental conservation in the Mediterranean basin."
2005	"The World Mayors Council on Climate Change is an alliance of committed local government leaders concerned about climate change. They advocate for enhanced engagement of local governments as governmental stakeholders in multilateral efforts addressing climate change and related issues of global sustainability."

protecting global common goods" around issues including Rio+20, bio-diversity, climate, eco-mobility, and water, with an emphasis on practical issues of leadership, procurement, and management for resilient and adaptive cities seeking long-term sustainability.[21]

Having grown out of a United Nations Conference in New York, ICLEI also pursues the U.N. agenda focusing on the Rio Conventions on Climate Change, on Biological Diversity and on Desertification (little progress on these), along with the U.N.-Habitat agenda and the Millennium Development Goals. The six Millennium goals established in 2000, listed with a certain obliviousness to consistency, aspired to achieve both "ensuring environmental sustainability" *and* five other development goals including the eradication of poverty and hunger, universal primary education, gender equality and the empowerment of women, reduction of child mortality, and combating of HIV, malaria, and other diseases. Implementing them obviously raises the critical question of whether meaningful development and real sustainability can actually be reconciled or will remain essentially incompatible. Certainly in the absence of North-South exchanges that offset the environmental costs of development on the scale it is being pursued by China, India, and Brazil, for example, there is likely to be little reconciliation. ICLEI's member cities are tasked with trying to ensure such a reconciliation in the urban setting.

Given ICLEI's long-term and impressively encompassing agenda, the establishment in 2005 in London of the C40 Climate Leadership Group suggests both the energizing pluralism of the global environmental movement and the potential for petty political wrangling among rival city associations. It has not escaped supporters of ICLEI that the C40 group was established with considerable publicity in the celebrity setting of the Clinton Climate Initiative under the chairmanship of London's superstar mayor Ken Livingstone. Six years after its founding, the C40 had 58 city members and described itself as a "network of large and engaged cities from around the world committed to implementing meaningful and sustainable climate-related actions locally that will help address climate change globally . . . [working with] city governments, supported by our technical experts across a range of program areas."[22] Most recently, with the cooperation of the Clinton Foundation, it announced a risk assessment program for cities that will enable urban centers to evaluate the environmental and climate change perils they face, perils not necessarily identical from one city to another. These are vital projects, although the not-always-large but very engaged cities of ICLEI might be forgiven for thinking that the size and efficacy of programs rather than the mega-status of city members ought to be the relevant criteria for achieving sustainability.

Yet celebrity leadership can't hurt the campaign for an environmentally stable world. When the C40 was recently chaired by New York's Mayor Bloomberg, his philanthropic arm helped integrate the Clinton Climate Initiative fully into the C40 with the assistance of the World Bank, and everyone who campaigns for a green world applauded. The new risk assessment program will be useful to every city, whether or not it is a member of the C40. Nor has the global prominence of the C40's steering committee member cities that include Berlin, Hong Kong, Jakarta, Johannesburg, Los Angeles, London, New York, São Paulo, Seoul, and Tokyo hurt the campaign for sustainability. Indeed, more than two-thirds of the C40 cities belong to ICLEI and to many other intercity networks to boot (see Figure 1). The plurality of ecological networks is a blessing of civil society. At the same time, pluralism can undermine common policy. An important argument for a global parliament of mayors is the role it can play in adjudicating tensions between and ensuring cooperation among rival intercity groups. The convening of a singular global cities network could be tremendously useful to the environmental movement. A global mayors parliament could help to align and coordinate the plural efforts of urban networks in many different domains (Chapter 12).

In networks like the C40 and the International Council for Local Environmental Issues, we observe formal city networks at work. But in the field of environment and sustainability, as in security and culture, there is a broad spectrum of civic cooperation that defines the real world of informal networking; it would be misleading to think that formal city networks are the whole story. Urban-based NGOs and concerned groups of citizens also network through journals, citizens' collectives, "movements," and online informational websites. City-to-city cooperation takes

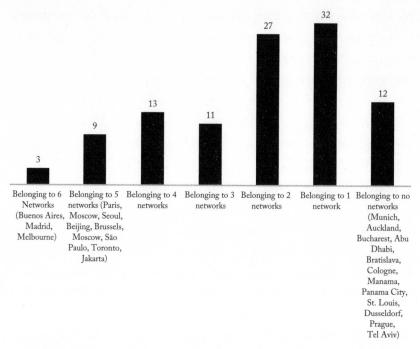

■ Total Alpha and Beta cities (according to GaWC [Globalization and World Cities Research Network] rankings) belonging to six major city-to-city networks (UCLG World Council, C40, ICLEI, Mayors for Peace, Metropolis, City Protocol)

Figure 1: Alpha and Beta city network membership. The intercity association UCLG estimates that "70 percent of the world's cities and their associations participate in city-to-city international programs." At the same time, "less than one percent of global development funding is channeled through local governments." UCLG website at www.uclg.org. GaWC website at http://www .lboro.ac.uk/gawc/world2010t.html.

place not only at the municipal level but at the civil society and citizen level, where borrowing, imitation, and shared experimentation are as important as formal governmental networking. In 1997, with a push from Mayor Leoluca Orlando of Palermo, the European Union founded "The Car-Free Cities Network."

Banning cars from cities is nearly as old as cars themselves. In the early 1920s, the canton of Graubuenden in Switzerland imposed a brief can-tonwide ban on the new-fangled automobile, less to protect large cities (of which it had none) than to protect its narrow-gauge Raetian railways system.[23] Recently it has been citizens and civic NGOs that have taken the lead in the urban battle against the automobile, promoting pedestrian-only zones, encouraging bike-share schemes and bicycle lanes, organizing recycling campaigns, and campaigning for conversion to cleaner energy in public and private buildings.

Cities also work together across borders one on one. When France sends troops to Mali, the whole world knows, but few will be aware that 4,806 French municipalities have been engaged in overseas cooperation in 147 countries over the past several decades; or that more than 500 German municipalities are cooperating with cities in Africa, Latin America, and Asia.[24] Some of this city-to-city cooperation is facilitated by national networks such as VNG International; the International Cooperation Agency of the Association of Netherlands Municipalities; SKL International, a company owned by the Swedish association of local authorities and regions (SALAR); and the federation of Canadian municipalities.

Even when cities act alone, they are often reacting to global trends and intercity viral networks. New York City, an urban sustainability leader, was only the most recent of more than 300 cities worldwide that have introduced bike-share programs (including more than 30 cities in France, 30 in Germany, a dozen in the United States, and at least four in China including Shanghai and Beijing), with cities like Bogotá mandating weekend bikes-only traffic on major thoroughfares—so-called *ciclovias*. Bike-share programs are often associated with other civic issues and movements, which broadens their membership and increases their civic power. Portland, Oregon, was one of the first cities to have one, back in 1965, reflecting its status as a global green leader. In Tucson, Arizona, the bike-share campaign came out of a movement focused on the homeless and reflecting antiwar sentiment; it was launched under the rubric "bikes not bombs." For decades, China's urban transportation was heavily dependent on bicycles (including three-wheeled, one-ton load flatbeds), but today in the new age of automobiles, Chinese cities have come back to bike-share as a way to fight urban congestion and pollution in a newly car-crazed country.

Formal intercity organizations and enlightened urban officials continue, of course, to play a leading role. Leoluca Orlando, recently elected to a third term in Palermo, inaugurated a "car-free cities club" that brings together cities supporting extensive car-free pedestrian zones—of which there are now thousands worldwide. Founded in 1997, his association operated for a decade as the European Union's Car Free Cities Network. Such networks add momentum to civil society programs targeting emissions and congestion, although many, like the Sustainable Cities Collective, are today primarily web based. The Internet allows them to report on and encourage sustainable urban agendas and provide a common virtual space for concerned citizens and groups to meet, communicate, and organize. They put on vivid display the power of voluntary action by individuals and civic organizations that, when taken together, constitute a kind of participatory urban decision making that is as potent in its reach and impact as formal city networks or governmental organizations. Unlike states, cities can act as effectively through pilots, best practices, and informal citizen-based policies as through formal legislation.

The online presence of Carbusters, for example, creates what it describes as the "hub of a world car-free network." Its journal, edited from Prague, offers information on urban sustainability efforts around the world. In this domain, knowing what others are doing and what may be possible elsewhere is the key to taking action locally. Bike-sharing and dedicated above-ground bus lanes are examples of innovation that spreads by common communication rather than common legislation. Such individual actions, taken voluntarily by cities acting in common, are a significant part of how cities may in time "govern the world" without ever possessing top-down executive authority or the ability to legislate for all cities, without even necessarily constituting themselves into formal government-to-government networks.

Toward a Global Mayors Parliament

Networks focused on environmental sustainability are informal as well as formal, rooted in popular initiatives arising out of a common urban culture and the ubiquitous media communications that permit urban residents to be globally informed and take action in common, even when a formal network or urban association is absent. It is crucial to recognize that cross-border cooperation and informal governance are not the products of top imperatives from "superior" authorities. Rather, in large part they grow out of voluntary actions undertaken by individual cities and their citizens in response to common problems. Innovative programs often spread virally rather than legislatively, via civic buy-in, enacted public opinion, and mayoral leadership rather than collective executive fiat. This kind of governance is crucial in changing actual human behavior and reflects the kind of bottom-up urban-based governance likely to make our world modestly less unruly. Cities don't have to wait for states; they can act to achieve a measure of security or a degree of sustainability whether nations are dysfunctional or not. Civil society doesn't have to wait for city government; it can take action of its own even when mayors hesitate. Citizens don't have to wait for civil society; they can work with one another and impel civil society and leaders to act. Moreover, the web stands ready as a newly ubiquitous tool, bypassing traditional forms of political association; it is an informal global network in waiting that can be as formal over time as we choose to make it (Chapter 9).

Cities are obviously not constitutionally authorized to treat with one another as sovereign and independent bodies. Even in federal systems that allow greater local autonomy—and recall that many of the world's most influential cities are essential political units in federal states like the United States, Canada, Mexico, Venezuela, Brazil, Nigeria, Ethiopia, Germany, Russia, Malaysia, Pakistan, India, and Australia—there are a variety of constraints on even the more autonomous cities in these nations. Not least of them is the fiscal noose with which provincial and national governments can strangle urban aspirations. Yet as the examples in the domains of security and environment demonstrate, a great many interactions, if often problematic, remain possible. Voluntary cooperation among cities, civil society organizations, and engaged citizens can achieve outcomes beyond the capacity of powerful nation-states—states that turn out to be crippled by the very power that defines their sovereignty. It is a most remarkable political conundrum that the unique power held by sovereign states actually disempowers them from cross-border cooperation, while the corresponding powerlessness of cities facilitates such cooperation (a puzzle to be explored in Chapter 6). The question becomes how far cities can go together to solve problems that have proved intractable when confronted by individual competing states. Do the myriad networks reviewed here pave a path to a global urban governance? To a Global Parliament of Mayors? They do. For voluntary bottom-up civic cooperation and consensual intercity networking, limited as they may seem legally and institutionally, can lead to quite extraordinary feats of common action, solving real problems urban and global.

The Founder as President and the President as Mayor

LEE KUAN YEW AND TONY TAN OF THE CITY-STATE OF SINGAPORE

LEE KUAN YEW was Singapore's first modern mayor and first president. He was arrogant, inventive, manipulative, and perhaps a living incarnation of that modern political oxymoron—the "democratic authoritarian." There may be less difference than meets the eye, however, between Lee and mayors like Boris Johnson of London, Yury Luzhkov of Moscow, and Michael Bloomberg of New York, all three of whom have enjoyed noteworthy success, not least because they have been unwilling to take local democracy too far or too seriously. In their rather technocratic terms, to do so is to "pander to special interests." Whether such disdain is a good or bad thing (and for me it is mostly bad), it is not a unique problem of Singapore's founder.

In fact, under far more burdensome conditions than most mayors face, Lee was a remarkably successful founder who created a mixed economy in which socialist and market forces combined to lift Singapore out of rural poverty. Lee's fledgling, British Empire–inflected regime took five million people representing rival ethnic backgrounds from waterside hovels and shacks to modern housing, from a poverty-stricken feudal economy to a global trading economy, from massive illiteracy to one of the highest literacy rates in Asia. Along the way, Lee laid the foundations for a democracy that, if rather too ponderously, has emerged with growing confidence as the world's most important free city-state.

Lee Kuan Yew did all of this not as a dictator but under the constraints of a democratic constitution, if sometimes deformed and perforated; and in the setting of a radically multicultural island surrounded by hostile neighbors (Malaysia to the north, Indonesia to the south, China far to the east), whose interests he had to balance and whose nationalist ambitions he had to combat. Hardly an easy task, given the Malay, Indonesian, and Chinese origins of his own citizenry from which he nonetheless managed to forge a novel Singaporean urban identity.

When Lee finally left office in the 1990s after three decades of rule as cofounder and general secretary of the People's Action Party, per capita GDP had risen from 1965 subpoverty levels (comparable to Mexico's at that time) to $14,000 a year. Today, it exceeds the per capita GDP of its erstwhile colonizer, Great Britain. It is the world's third-largest refiner of oil, and its port is the busiest in the world.

DR. TONY TAN is Singapore's current mayor-cum-president. He was a teenager when Lee was founding the new Singapore. As the heir to Lee's extraordinary achievements, he is also the modern bearer of all the burdens and enduring problems of the founding era. In taking on the load, he has surrounded himself with an extraordinary group of leaders. Leadership has always been Singapore's strong point. It is especially crucial in cities, because real problems demand real solutions, which are possible only with the collaboration of a welter of public, civic, and private stakeholders. Not an easy task to bring together such a group.

Tan was once a trusted minister to Lee, who was himself a cautious banker and bureaucrat before he became Singapore's audacious modern founder. Now he has begun to fill the large shoes of the founder, pulling in adept innovators with a democratic temperament, such as the young environmental minister, Vivian Balakrishnan.

Together, Tan and his cabinet are making Singapore a model of adaptive urbanism and environmental sustainability under the most difficult circumstances. They have become models in South Asia (including in China) for economic modernization and social justice. The housing system, combining private and public and allowing home ownership to all, has become a model for Asia and beyond. President (Mayor) Tan himself is a far less dramatic figure than Lee and is viewed as a consolidator following the early years of rapid development. But he has won a reputation for his "particular devotion to science and education," which foundation chair Wolfgang Schuerer says has made Tan a "quiet but tireless force in the rise of the Republic as a global hub of science and education in Asia."

In my interview with Dr. Tan in Singapore in 2012, the mayor was a modest presence who seemed immersed in the responsibilities of governing both as mayor and president and was more than willing to call on advisers and counselors from around the world. Although he refused to see Singapore as a "model" for others, he acknowledged that "the lessons we have learned might be useful for others" in China and India, and even in Europe. Unlike his predecessor, he has no problem with publicizing his city as an Asian entertainment capital with great shopping and fabulous food. (I can endorse the quality of the food and confirm, with regret, the city's success as a new mecca of McWorld-style consumerism.) The old colonial port is a tourist site, while the modern port is a hive of pleasure-palace hotels and workaday tanker and container ships.

This commercialization notwithstanding, Mayor Tan's largest problem remains Singapore's enduring reputation as a sometime authoritarian regime whose one-party government and paternalistic, nanny-state inclinations to regulate private life belie its claim to being a modern democracy. The legacy of Lee's paternalism certainly endures in policies like the ban on chewing gum and the government's aversion to genuine multiparty government (though it is now technically permitted).

Yet this critique seems to reflect an inclination among observers to focus on cosmetics rather than substance, on the lethargic pace of political change rather than the untoward velocity of economic change (including economic and social justice for all). How much is there really to choose between Mayor Bloomberg's big-soda prohibition and Singapore's continuing obsession with a chewing gum ban? How many large American cities have real two-party or multiparty systems? The rush to judge Lee as an authoritarian masquerading as a democrat seems misplaced both in the historical context of the challenges he faced in the 1950s and 1960s—what was amazing back then was that there was even a pretense of democracy!—and in light of Singapore's status today as an economic success story but, under the firm hand of Mayor Tan and his circle, also an ever more genuine democracy.

There is something deeply hypocritical about the Western tendency to judge new democracies by standards no Western democracy can live up to. The United States was a slave republic for the first eighty years of its political life, while Switzerland rejected female suffrage as recently as in a 1959 referendum and finally endorsed it only in 1971—well after Lee Kuan Yew had started down the path to development. We laugh at the corruption of some American cities and the number of local officials in jail in, say, New Jersey, but dismiss cities such as Singapore as hopelessly undemocratic.

City-states have different and perhaps larger problems than cities, though they enjoy real independence. But no reader of Singapore's history, no visitor to Singapore today, no one who talks with Tony Tan, will come away with the impression that Singapore is a ravenous wolf in sheep's clothing. Lee was something of a ram, to be sure, but still a sheep rather than a wolf. Tan is simply the mayor of a great city as free and self-governing as many others today, though with plenty of work to do.

CHAPTER 6. CITIES WITHOUT SOVEREIGNTY

The Uses of Powerlessness

Ford to New York: DROP DEAD!

New York Post *headline, 1976*

I have my own army in the NYPD, which is the seventh biggest army in the world. . . . I don't listen to Washington very much, which is something they're not thrilled about.

Mayor Bloomberg, New York City, 2012

When the governments of nation-states tell their cities to back off— "Ford to New York: DROP DEAD!" screamed the *New York Post* in 1976— you might think the matter would be settled.[1] Not anymore. With his "own army," Mayor Bloomberg of New York declared recently, not only does he not "listen to Washington very much," but he has his own foreign policy and global network through which he can solve problems as he will. After President Obama was thwarted by Congress in his effort to fund a port improvement, Mayor Villaraigosa of Los Angeles in effect began conducting his own foreign policy with China to improve the Los Angeles port installation. Cities around the world are finding ways to do together what nation-states can't.

In the 1976 fiscal crisis, New York City desperately needed Washington, which held out a helping hand only after showing the city its fist. Today, Washington needs New York, while New York often looks to other cities or abroad to find intercity solutions to its pressing problems. On issues from gun control to climate change, the United States is not always the city's ally. That is not to say that states are not capable of playing the sovereign trump card when cities act too autonomously across borders or mayors overplay their hands in trying to thwart national prerogatives. While Mr. Bloomberg was boasting, the feisty long-term mayor of Moscow, Yury Luzhkov, found that when President Medvedev decided Luzhkov was done, he was done. After more than three decades in public office reaching back to Brezhnev's Cold War reign, Luzhkov is no longer mayor of Moscow. It was complicated, involving an allegedly corrupt wife and other more political offenses, but—bottom line—he is gone.

Yet when nation-states stumble, cities are continuing to step in. When the 2011 round of climate negotiations in Durban, South Africa, though slightly more successful than the rounds in Mexico City and Copenhagen, once again failed to achieve a breakthrough, a discerning journalist noted that real progress would not likely "emerge from any global forum but from action at the ground level, by [federated] states and municipalities and private entities, unencumbered by the United Nations climate process and its rules demanding consensus."[2] It was hardly a surprise, he concluded, that California and its politically liberal cities have "arguably . . . done more to reduce carbon pollution in the United States than any other body." Consequently, in Durban, the chairwoman of the California Air Resources Board, Mary D. Nichols, although she had only observer status, was one of the most animated actors. While nation-states are talking and posturing, cities are doing much of the heavy lifting. A New York State court recently upheld a ban on gas drilling by the town of Middlefield in Oswego County.

Relations between big cities and the states under whose sovereign jurisdiction they must live are nonetheless complicated. The technical sovereignty of the state is hardly the only factor. The lack of sovereignty among cities turns out to both disable and enable their engagement in cross-border cooperation. Cities need states, but states also need cities. Cross-border collaboration among cities can be a way for states to elude the limitations of sovereignty. Hong Kong presses its historical advantage as a former British Crown colony with unique privileges under its current status as a Chinese city in ways that can benefit Beijing's purposes, although there are limits Hong Kong dare not overstep under the new arrangements.

There is then a powerful irony in the city's lack of sovereignty and the state's defining sovereign character—in the state's power and the city's relative powerlessness. The very sovereign power on which nation-states rely is precisely what renders them ineffective when they seek to regulate or legislate in common. They may wish to reach a climate agreement but worry that monitoring provisions will encroach on their sovereignty. They may wish to undertake a joint military campaign to protect civilians in some local civil war but will wonder whether one of their soldiers will be required to serve under a foreign officer's command, creating political problems at home. But when New York posts an anti-terrorist detective to London, it raises no such concerns in New York or London (although the Foreign Office and the State Department may grow agitated). No sovereignty, no problem.

In the second decade of the twenty-first century, the old sovereign-state global order (never very orderly) is in jeopardy. Sovereignty is not in decline, but its exercise on the global scene is increasingly counterproductive.[3] States are not necessarily dysfunctional as national political systems (though some are), but they are dysfunctional in their inability to cooperate across borders. The United States is the most powerful sovereign state the world has ever known, but its sovereignty has been the excuse for either not signing or not ratifying a host of international accords embraced by most other states. These treaties, effectively nullified by America's refusal to infringe its sovereign rights, include the Anti-Ballistic Missile (ABM) Treaty; the Kyoto Protocol; the Convention on Discrimination Against Women; the Conventions on the Rights of the Child; the International Covenant on Economic, Social and Cultural Rights; the Chemical Weapons Convention; the Land Mine Ban Treaty; the International Criminal Court; and the Law of the Sea (UNCLOS).

Here then is the paradox: sovereignty, the state's defining essence and greatest virtue, is impressively impervious to encroachment, resistant to pooling, and defiant in the face of the brute facts of our new century's interdependence. Never before has sovereign power been used so effectively to impede and thwart collective action. In the world of independence, sovereignty works; in the world of interdependence, it is dysfunctional. As nations fall prey to rivalry and dysfunction, cities are rising and find themselves in the ironic position of being empowered globally by their lack of sovereignty nationally. Their interdependence makes them likely building blocks for a viable global order.

We know the city as a carnival of interaction, as a thriving seat of networks and economic nexuses, and as a practical way of living. But it is also evolving into a transnational political force: a surrogate for states in forging soft forms of global governance and pushing democratic decision making across borders. There is a problem, however: the ambiguous relationship to power that is the key to the city's cross-border potential can also be an obstacle to its ultimate success. Exercising the cross-border influence that powerlessness affords it also puts the interdependent city on a collision course with the independent nation-state. Although they are not always paying attention and frequently elect not to interfere, states have both the right and the power to do so.

Cities may be acquiring new capacities for soft global governance, but states are hardly disappearing. While the nation-state has not itself been very successful at cooperating across borders, it can and often does try to prevent cities from doing so. Unless this dilemma can be overcome, the question will be whether a natural urban aptitude for piecemeal and episodic collaboration can be translated into a sustained strategy for achieving democratic global cooperation. If not, soft global governance and politically consequential interaction among cities are likely to be regularly obstructed, or simply annulled by sovereign jurisdictions. The District of Columbia's wish to ban handguns, we have seen, has already run afoul of the U.S. Supreme Court, which insisted that Washington's prerogative was preempted by the Second Amendment. Meanwhile, the National Rifle Association launched a campaign assailing "Mayors Against Your Rights" and is sponsoring a "National Right-to-Carry Reciprocity Act" to provide a national framework that would prohibit cities not only from banning guns but from banning the carrying of concealed weapons. Its campaign has been compromised but hardly immobilized by the Newtown, Connecticut, massacre and a renewed American hostility to assault weapons and oversized ammo magazines; for the gun lobby retains extraordinary national clout, and despite President

Obama's second-term commitment to gun control and polls overwhelmingly favoring it, legislative action remains in doubt.[4]

The same dynamic is evident in the carbon industry. When towns such as South Fayette, Pennsylvania, moved to prevent gas companies from fracking on their land (not necessarily for environmental reasons), they discovered they were stymied by state and national authorities, who concur with drilling firms that they shouldn't have "to get a different driver's license in every town."[5] The irony is that cities are effectively seeking a "different license" for each town so they can act in accord with common policies across the globe. Seattle banned plastic grocery bags in 2011 but faces the wrath of the plastics industry, which is trying to bring state and federal authorities into the fray. Mayor Bloomberg used executive authority to ban sugary drinks of over sixteen ounces but must confront not only the soft drink lobby but a majority of voters who see his actions as an undue infringement of their consumer freedom and courts ready to reverse his executive decrees.[6]

These jurisdictional disputes ultimately go to the courts and, in the United States, become ongoing items in the continuing war over American federalism and the appropriate vertical distribution of power. Ironically, in an earlier epoch, the federal government was often the "good" power enforcing rights universally against the parochial efforts of states and localities to thwart them in the name of narrow local standards; but nowadays, when it comes to issues of global cooperation among cities, the federal authorities have sometimes acted to impede universal outcomes, say on climate change, fair trade, and nuclear safety, often as a consequence of the influence of national corporate lobbies on state and national legislatures.[7] Cities seem to speak for the cosmopolitan while nations speak for parochialism and special interests. The irony reminds us that, however weak sovereignty is as a forger of global cooperation, it remains a trump card in regulating the collaborative global strategies that cities are trying to pursue.

Similar jurisdictional battles are being fought around the world, both in federal systems like India, Canada, and Germany, where (as in the United States) localities have significant autonomy, and in centrist and unitary regimes like France, England, and Japan, where there is little vertical separation of powers, and mayors may even be appointed from above—leaving cities with little freedom to act on their own. Either way, and despite the regional differences, cities are where the action is, and clearly where the action will be in coming years, as Bruce Katz and Jennifer Bradley also argue in their new book *The Metropolitan Revolution*.[8] A great deal of informal and uncontested progress toward cross-border cooperation can be made in the shadowed ambiguities of the law and the distractions of national governments too busy to object to or even notice what cities are doing. Still, when nation-states—often driven by lobbies and corporations—say no, cities are compelled to listen.

When states that can't and won't do it themselves can stop cities from acting globally, or impede intercity cooperation even within their own borders, the prospects for urban cooperation across frontiers grow dimmer. Cities face the dilemma that the very factors that facilitate urban cooperation may draw the oversight of the central governments they are hoping to elude. The national authorities in a large state may subject the rural hinterlands to benign neglect, to the unending distress of rural people who will feel at once violated and overlooked, encroached on and forgotten. But this indifference at least protects rural towns and country regions from too much interference. It was no accident that Carlo Levi discerned a telling contradiction in the psychology of the peasantry in prewar southern Italy: "To the peasants, the state is more distant than heaven and far more of a scourge, because it is always against them. Its political tags and platforms and, indeed, the whole structure of it do not matter. The peasants do not understand them because they are couched in a different language from their own, and there is no reason why they should ever care to understand them. Their only defense against the state and the propaganda of the state is resignation, the same gloomy resignation, alleviated by no hope of paradise, that bows their shoulders under the scourges of nature."[9] There is a hint of what agitates the American Tea Party in Levi's portrait. So many populists seem to resent both the federal government and the cities whose cosmopolitan character they associate (not always accurately) with big government. They are angry because big government both bugs them and neglects them.

Yet where rural populists worry that cities and big government may be strategic allies on transportation or education policy, cities notice that too often they pay out more in taxes than they get back, that rural votes against "big government" prevent urban dwellers from getting government services they need, even as farm subsidies or ethanol programs are exempted from the rural diatribe against government. New York's effort to impose a payroll tax on the surrounding counties to support its urban and regional MTA rail service has been challenged in the courts by suburban residents happy to use the MTA's services but unwilling to pay for them. Cities necessarily seek more freedom to pursue their intercity agendas. Hence Mayor Bloomberg's boast about how little he heeds Washington. But though he celebrates his police department, his boast is not about firepower but about capacity, will, and connections. He cannot impose his views on other mayors but can rely on persuasion and the pull of common interests to secure results. It is precisely the absence of power as a dominant construct that compels cities to cooperate in developing common strategies: "Cities and mayors," Bloomberg observes, "are where you deal with crime, you deal with real immigration problems, you deal with health problems, you deal with picking up the garbage."[10] The rhetoric does not, however, help him pay for the MTA.

If dealing with the region is hard for cities, dealing with other cities at a greater distance is easier. In pursuing new methods of garbage collection, engineering limits on emissions, or developing express bus lanes, cities claim no special jurisdiction or independence that might interfere with mutual cooperation. Yet to bring the conundrum full circle, the absence of jurisdictional claims is also the absence of jurisdictional authority and of sovereign power. Because cooperation among cities simply isn't about power per se, because there is no preoccupation with boundaries, no yearning for a monopoly on decision making, no prideful insistence on exclusive jurisdiction, cities can do things together. But the absence of power limits what gets done. It means municipal police forces have limited efficacy, as the drug cartels in Mexico and Colombia have taught us, and as the United States demonstrates in the need to deploy the National Guard in times of crisis. It means that city-supported boycotts of practices cities label "unfair trade" can be vetoed by the World Trade Organization as illegitimate local interference with "free trade." It means that a town's payroll tax on commuters to help pay for the rails that bring them to town might be shot down in higher courts.

In formal terms, the city is an odd foundation for global governance. Cities are naturally inclined to soft power and soft governance. Yet while soft power works well in tandem with hard power, it is not a substitute for hard power. Is this a fatal handicap? Or at least in some respects a virtue? Might cities that cooperate voluntarily and pragmatically across borders achieve victories that executive command and hard power have failed to realize? We need an account of how cities can treat with power without losing that political innocence that protects them from the rivalry, conflict, isolation, and hubris typical of states. How can they come to terms with the state without being lumbered with its vices (such as hard power) that have crippled it as a building block of global governance?

The generic, theoretical question is not easily answered, but it does yield three more concrete questions that can and must be answered if mayors are to forge a passable road across borders and contemplate informal global governance.

The first question is whether states really are existentially incapable of significant cooperation. What obstacles have prevented them from founding and grounding sustainable global governing institutions? Is there something in their nature that prevents them from doing so? Are such essential features insuperable barriers to integration or remediable problems to be overcome through supranational associations like the United Nations or experiments in pooled sovereignty like the European Union? Only if the state's failures are endemic to their nature and irredeemable can the city's potential role as a surrogate be taken seriously.

Second, are cities really free of the encumbrances that shackle states? Can they achieve sufficient autonomy to do what states have not done? If they succeed where nation-states fail, is it that they lack the state's fatal flaws of sovereignty and nationality? If the cooperative inclinations of cities are produced by the absence of sovereign power, do they have to govern without power or can they create a substitute—a participatory politics of consensus that is effective? That is to say, if their cooperative potential lies in soft power, how do cities acquire sufficient influence and force to take on not only the anarchy of global interdependence but the continuing power of independent sovereign states?

Third, if it can be shown that cities can do what states cannot, the paradoxes of power notwithstanding, will states permit cities to act on behalf of a global commons? Or will their sovereign jurisdictional claims be decisive and return what should be global issues to national courts and to the court-empowering sovereignty of the state, where cities are likely to lose the battle? If states prize sovereignty in ways that incapacitate them for cross-border cooperation, why should they permit cities to cooperate in their stead? Or can it be shown that even where states try to stand in their path, cities can find a road around them and manage to achieve a semblance of global governance, either through successful legal strategies, quiet common action, or even a kind of urban insurrection (see Chapter 11 for a discussion of "rebel towns")? In sum: are nation-states really incapable of cross-border governance? Are cities actually capable of doing what stymied nation-states can't? And why would states allow cities to do what they themselves cannot?

Why States Can't Rule the World

The early polis was the perfect home for simple forms of democratic community. But in time it proved too small and parochial for the requirements of expansive popular sovereignty in an early modern sixteenth-century world already divided into vast territorial regions encompassing millions of subjects, whose sense of belonging came increasingly from the novel idea of a "people" or nation. Cities of that era could no longer dominate their regions as they had in the Renaissance, let alone envision autonomous city leagues capable of territorial self-government (not even the Hansa had done this at its height). Empires had become proxies for global governance but left little room for democracy. Yet the early modern nation-state, though it rescued democracy, was from the start too large for the purposes of participation and neighborliness, but too small to address the developing realities of interdependent power that have today become paramount in our own globalized market world. Democratic states rarely make war on one another, but nondemocratic nations facing democratic states do, and war has been a fixture of the state system for four hundred years. The modern metropolis retrieves the capacity to empower neighborhoods and nurture civic engagement, but at the same time holds out the prospect of networked global integration: that is the promise of glocality.

As the scale of national societies once outgrew the polis, today the scale of global problems is outgrowing the nation-state. The state had a good run. It was an adaptive institution that combined a new sense of national identity with a focus on legislative sovereignty that overcame religious divisiveness and imposed secular unity following the Peace of Westphalia (1648). It prospered for centuries afterward. With the help of a social contract theory that presupposed an act of original consent justifying the state's power, it allowed democracy to prosper as well. But the radical interdependence of the globalized twenty-first-century world has now outrun it and pushed cities back into the limelight. Nation-state sovereignty has become an obstacle to solving problems. At the same time, the real victories the democratic nation-state once won for liberty now have calcified into a parochialism that stands in the way of democracy's next stage. Democracy seems trapped within the institutions that first permitted its modern flowering, trapped inside a commodious but parochial nation-state box.

Let me unpack the box: the transition from networked cities to independent nation-states was eventful but successful and did much to conserve democracy (though only by rendering it less participatory). But the challenge of a needed transition from democratic nation-states to some form of supranational democratic governance suitable to the challenges of interdependence has proven much more problematic. The primary obstacles to democratic global governance by sovereign national states turn out, ironically enough, to be nationality and sovereignty themselves.

The Failure of Nationality

Nationality was the artificial creation of early moderns seeking a new home for identity during the period of transition from small city-states and principalities to new and abstract national states in the fifteenth and sixteenth centuries. The novel and largely fictional notion of a *people* (*gens* or *Volk*) made it possible to legitimate new territorial entities that incorporated disparate tribes and clans, cities and regions, counties and duchies—previously often at war—into an artificial and integrated society.[11] Although in time nationality took on the compellingly worn contours of tradition and history (what Eric Hobsbawn would call an invented tradition), it was always a contrived product. Joan of Arc helped invent the France in which the Bourbons would forge a central administration to replace the feudal, quasi-sovereign *parlements* of earlier times. In lieu of England's shires and dukedoms, whose rights are enshrined in Magna Carta, an English nation was born, Henry the Eighth and Elizabeth its first real sovereigns. This nation, as portrayed by Shakespeare's historical melodramas set in the Wars of the Roses, arose out of spectacular hubris, frequent civic miscarriage, and unrelenting carnage.

In swallowing up clan, tribe, principality, and province, the newly invented national identities coalesced around new political associations smaller than empires but much larger than towns and shires—large enough to establish suzerainty across large swathes of land and people. They also provided a new home to a new form of democracy, which had found scant hospitality in the vast medieval empire or in the local feudal duchy. Smaller city-states and principalities such as Renaissance Florence or Amsterdam or Basel, which had been absorbed into regional empires, now reemerged as trading and cultural centers for the new nations. Democracy, which in the era of the polis had presumed communal face-to-face citizenship and common social capital, might easily have vanished. But the new national states, sustained by the emerging theory of social contract, provided a kind of synthetic community and representative citizenship in the name of which a "people" could define and defend its liberty. For it was the idea of a people that allowed social contract theory to envision "popular sovereignty," and to claim that the right to make laws (sovereignty's essence) must be rooted in the consent of those who live under the laws. By thus defining itself as a home to a people freely contracting to obey a sovereign representing it, the new nation-state rescued democracy from the challenge of scale.

Yet while nationality turned out in the early modern era to be viable as a tool for bringing together distinct tribes and parochial towns into sovereign and autonomous states rooted in popular consent, in our own late modern era it has resisted incorporation into or subjugation to supranational entities. Like the term "pooled sovereignty," the notion of supranationality has an oxymoronic aspect to it, reflecting a desperate experiment—or perhaps just wishful thinking. How can we integrate distinctive monocultural "peoples" defined by autonomy into an international, multicultural whole? The very term *multiculturalism* seems self-contradictory.

Centuries ago, the artificial community that emerged from the invented nation had to have felt rather less "thick" than the natural communities typical of ancient city-states or early modern townships, or local provinces such as Cornwall or Languedoc.[12] But over time, the monoculture of nationality became a comfortable identity that could host the kinds of large-scale community on which modern democracy depended for its claims to popular sovereignty. A resident population in the thousands, bound together by common tribal ties—the demes revealed in the word *democracy*'s etymology referred to Athens' tribes—was enough to legitimate polis democracy. But for a people numbering in the millions to be free and self-governing in any meaningful sense required new political ideas associated with the nation-state and its founding theory: the idea of original consent (the social contract) and the notion of representation (even a king, Thomas Hobbes would insist, might be the "people's sovereign representative"). In the last century, we have managed to substitute multicultural for monocultural identity within states in countries such as India, Brazil, Canada, and the United States that are too large and encompassing to be monocultural.

Canada and the United States have achieved success by substituting for monocultural or singular religion a "civil religion" of constitutionalism and civic patriotism. But it has not been easy. How much harder, then, will it be to thin out society's social capital and cultural identity still further by trying to aggregate multicultural national communities into one transnational, cross-border global governing body in which there is on first glance no apparent natural solidarity or civic commons at all? Can liberty be secured in some new and abstract global governing association that is rooted neither in nation (with its solidarity) nor popular sovereignty (with its legitimacy)? To tell Americans or Peruvians or Moroccans that their individual liberty can be better secured through membership in some formal global association than through their identification with the American or Peruvian or Moroccan nation, each one sustained by a unique national narrative, is to court disbelief. Why should the nationals of long-standing states try to wrap their imaginations around such abstract notions as supranationality or a global (multi-) culture? It is hardly an accident, though not a happy one, that the Arab Spring has played out one nation at a time with little common cooperation. Democratic revolutions still depend on commitment by an individual nation to *its* freedom. Revolutions may cross borders virally as they did in 1789 and 1848 in Europe or in 2011 in North Africa and the Middle East, but success is achieved, if at all, one nation at a time.

The transition from networked cities to independent nation-states did much to conserve democracy, rendering it less participatory but giving it a foundation in original consent (social contract) and representation. But the challenge of a needed transition from democratic nation-states to some form of supranational democratic governance suitable to the challenges of interdependence has proven much more problematic. Getting around nationality is no easy task: nations moved by nationalism are hard to unite across their distinctive national cultures, as the United Nations has learned and even the European community is beginning to understand. It's little different with the state's second essential trait, sovereignty.

The Failure of Sovereignty

If nationality is an improbable foundation for securing supranationality, the concept of indivisible sovereignty is even more suspect. It is folly to try to cross borders politically on the backs of associations defined in their philosophical, ideological, and territorial essence by sovereign political frontiers, folly to seek in independence a formula for interdependence. Nonetheless, nearly every attempt to think across borders in the last century, via a concert of nations or a League of Nations or a United Nations, is founded on exactly this folly.

The League of Nations and the United Nations both failed to prevent war and genocide or to generate systematic international cooperation in areas where individual states were unwilling to cooperate. An international system based on nation-states is always subject to the sovereign veto, either implicitly via the noncooperation of powerful states (the League could not even induce the United States, the Soviet Union, or Germany to join) or explicitly as with the U.N. Security Council, where the participation of the big powers was secured by allowing them to paralyze action with vetoes wherever action displeased them. This was not much of a fix, but realism was the only option international idealists had. Beyond the chimera of international law always lurks the reality of sovereign force. The United Nations imposes its will, limited as it is, only when big states or NATO choose to infringe the sovereignty of the weak with the concurrence of the other "bigs."[13] No American president can be too openly sympathetic to the United Nations and expect to elude sharp parochial criticism. President Obama's affinity for the idea of interdependence, made evident in early first-term speeches in Istanbul and Cairo, was met with exactly such broad political hostility at home and was quickly jettisoned. Hardly a trace of the idea was evident in his otherwise idealistic and egalitarian Second Inaugural.

Rather than acknowledging the brute realities of interdependence and grasping how weak the U.N. has been in addressing them, anxious Americans, not all of them conservatives, have managed at once to ignore interdependence and to blame the United Nations for being too domineering in advancing an interdependent (read "foreign") agenda on American soil in violation of American sovereignty. The U.N. has been cast wildly as a foreign conspiracy to coerce the easing of highway congestion and cut carbon emissions at the price of American liberties; and it has been accused of plotting to impose international ("socialist") norms on American cities by taking over local government.

Back in 1992, the United Nations had developed one of its typically hortatory resolutions, a so-called Agenda 21—altogether without teeth—which encouraged nations to use fewer resources and conserve open land. But ever vigilant in the face of "foreign" infringement on American sovereignty, the Republican Party passed a resolution against "the destructive and insidious nature" of Agenda 21. The resolution declared: "The United Nations Agenda 21 plan of radical so-called 'sustainable development' views the American way of life of private property ownership, single family homes, private car ownership and individual travel choices, and privately owned farms all as destructive to the environment."[14] Nor was this just right-wing rhetoric: the cities group Local Governments for Sustainability (ICLEI, described in some detail in Chapter 5) has become a particular target of Americans apprehensive about a loss of sovereignty. Simple conservation tools promoted by ICLEI, "smart meters" for example, have inspired an almost lunatic sense of peril. Such meters help measure electricity in the home and distribute its use to nonpeak hours, saving money and electricity for consumers and city budgets alike. Yet in Roanoke, Virginia, a protester insisted, "the real job of smart meters is to spy on you and control you—when you can and cannot use electrical appliances."[15] The Roanoke Board of Supervisors eventually voted to retain the city's ICLEI funding, but only by a 3–2 vote. Thus does deeply entrenched preoccupation with sovereignty become an instrument of opposition to the most innocent forms of global cooperation.

Indeed, at the end of President Obama's first term, the president, secretary of state, and defense secretary were still pleading thirty years after its introduction under U.N. auspices in 1982 for the adoption by the Congress of the Law of the Sea Treaty. Yet this mild global agreement, allowing nations full control of their coastal waters within a 200-mile exclusive economic zone and imposing a few common rules for shipping, environmental protection, and mining in the international waters beyond, has failed to secure the assent of Republican and Democratic Congresses alike. Treaties protecting women and defending the rights of children have also been rejected as encroachments on sovereignty. Even Interpol's activities on U.S. soil have been assailed by critics as "ceding American sovereignty" and undermining the "U.S. Constitution and American law."[16]

The otherwise promising story of the European Union points to some of the same difficulties. Inaugurated in hopes of fashioning a true European civic identity by visionaries like Jean Monnet, the E.U. actually started life as a Coal and Steel Community. Although it was eventually transformed into a broader economic market (the Common Market) and more recently into a European Union of twenty-seven (slightly less than) sovereign nations, its current plight as a euro-currency zone (including only seventeen of the twenty-seven Union members) points to how hard it is to fashion common citizenship in a world of self-consciously sovereign nations. Much more about economic prudence than civil religion, and preoccupied with currency rather than citizenship, the European Union today seems only as durable as its economic and currency arrangements are useful.

The quest for both liberty and security has also been wrapped in the mantle of sovereignty and tied to the struggle for national self-determination. This was true both in the West, where early modern nation-states were established in the sixteenth through the eighteenth centuries, and in the post–World War II colonial world, where wars of national liberation created autonomous and independent nations through which individual freedom and sovereign self-determination were alone deemed to be achievable. That was the promise of that beacon of hope for the whole human race, the American Declaration of Independence: "To secure these rights," Jefferson had written, "governments are instituted among men." It was as a "free and independent state" alone, he concluded, that the "United Colonies" were to "determine their own affairs" and "do all other acts and things that independent states do." The beacon continues to shine, illuminating a path for liberty-seeking revolutionaries in the Balkans, the Arab Spring, and Iraq. Yet 250 years has made a critical difference, and neither autonomy nor democracy has been the necessary outcome for these emerging nations in the ever more interdependent circumstances of our global world. Declarations of sovereign independence are no longer enough to set nations free, but nations seem unable to conceive of liberty in their absence.

Theorists, lawyers, and practitioners alike wrestled for centuries with this dilemma: can sovereignty be superseded in the name of global peace without robbing us of legitimacy and legislative authority? Traditional social contract theory tried to bridge the difference between independence and interdependence with what has turned out to be a politically debilitating false analogy. It tried to apply to nation-states the same logic of contract applied originally to individuals. At the level of private persons in a hypothetical state of nature, the logic posits quite persuasively that individuals will freely surrender a portion of their abstract "natural" freedom to secure a semblance of real political freedom by subordinating themselves to a common sovereignty. In yielding a theoretical liberty difficult to exercise in the state of nature, where the "war of all against all" imperils every person's life and freedom, they guarantee themselves a practical civic and political freedom they can actually enjoy in a civil state where security is protected. In Jean-Jacques Rousseau's words, "what man loses by the social contract is his natural freedom and an unlimited right to everything that tempts him and he can reach; what he gains is civil freedom and property in everything he possesses." In other words, he gives up an individual freedom rooted in force, but gains "civil freedom" along with "moral freedom, which alone truly makes man truly the master of himself . . . [since] the impulsion of mere appetite is slavery, and obedience to the law one has prescribed to oneself is freedom."[17] It is the independence of the sovereign regime that guarantees the individual liberty of persons otherwise insecure in their freedom in the state of nature.

But when this formula is applied to nation-states, and it is suggested that states too can and should surrender some portion of their national sovereignty and independence in return for global peace, the logic fails. Liberty and sovereignty are not equivalents, and trading independence for interdependence defies the very meaning of independence in a way that trading a natural liberty that is unrealized for a civic liberty that *is* realized does not. It makes sense to yield some part of a private liberty that cannot in practice be secured or enjoyed in the state of nature, where the life of man is "nasty, brutish, and short" (Hobbes again). For yielding natural liberty to an independent and autonomous sovereign capable of enforcing laws makes civil liberty real. But yielding some part of sovereignty to a common international power destroys the very meaning of sovereignty. It appears to impair rather than enhance both security and liberty, whose fate is tied up with the independent sovereign's indivisible power to make and enforce laws in accord with an original contract.

What works to bring individuals out of an anarchic state of nature and into an orderly, independent sovereign state seems altogether implausible as a means to bring self-determining states into an orderly, interdependent collective regime. Liberty is divisible—you can give up some to secure the rest; and it is mutable—it can change from being a natural and limited capacity to do whatever you want into a civic and expansive freedom to do what the laws you make for yourself permit. Liberty secured by laws we make for ourselves defines democracy. Sovereignty, however, is indivisible and immutable. As theorists from Jean Bodin and Thomas Hobbes to modern legal philosophers have argued, its essence resides in its indivisibility, which is intimately associated with the independence of the sovereign state. To ask states to yield sovereignty is to ask them to dissolve themselves. They may on rare occasions do so, as a handful of European nations, tired by two world wars, partially did after 1945, but the task is close to impossible both in theory and (as is now becoming apparent) in practice.

Historical practice clearly tracks theory in this domain and should make believers of those who imagine sovereignty can somehow be divided or pooled without undoing its essential character. For where their vital interests are engaged, states in fact never have surrendered any significant portion of their sovereignty other than under the duress of war. Boundaries may be traded off or "adjusted," but they will not be willingly shrunk or forfeited. Not, at least, as long as a state has the power (which undergirds its sovereignty) to resist. When it lacks such power, it can of course be subjugated, occupied, or destroyed, but these are so many ways to annul sovereignty rather than supersede it. When the Nazis annexed Austria and occupied Poland, one could not speak of the Germans "pooling sovereignty" with the Austrians or the Poles. Democratic nations also annex weaker neighbors (as the United States did in Texas with northern Mexico or in the Philippines). Other than the European experiment, it is hard to think of a nation that voluntarily yielded any part of their sovereignty or territory, although weak and small nations have often been robbed of them by aggressive neighbors or colonizing empires.

Only when nations collapse and their sovereignty evaporates (when they are without the capacity to defend and protect their own people) can they be occupied or "integrated" without compromising their independence—since they no longer are independent. This was the case in Germany and Japan after World War II and has occasionally justified intervention in failed states or under conditions of internal genocide (Rwanda during the liquidation of Tutsis there) or utter lawlessness (Somalia in the 1990s), where sovereignty's first obligations (right to life) have been internally forfeited. Even here, there is the danger that a powerful foreign power will claim internal collapse or putative genocide in order to intervene and infringe another nation's sovereignty.

The quest to build an international order from nation-states is implausible and for the most part futile. Locke's compelling metaphor casting rival individuals as polecats and foxes and sovereign government as a lion makes clear why. Too aggressive and individualistic to temper themselves in the anarchic jungle, polecats and foxes will band together and turn over the policing job to a sovereign lion. But the lion, being a lion whose function resides in its power, is unlikely (unable) to defer to a global elephant even if (especially if!) it finds itself at odds with other lions. Nor will polecats and foxes ask them to. The lion with which polecats and foxes contract for protection is one thing; an elephant with which lions contract is once removed and without obligations to them. An international order resting on cooperation by nation-states is a risky federation of lions putatively dedicated to protecting polecats and foxes who have in fact not been consulted. The logic of social contract intended to protect individuals fails when applied to the lions.

Sovereign states make poor "natural" building blocks for global governance under the best of circumstances. Deploying them as tools for overcoming their defining features, sovereignty and nationality, seems a desperate and futile strategy. Sovereign nation-states can't forge post-sovereign, multicultural global democratic institutions. Can cities?

Why Cities Can Rule the World

To show why and how cities can govern an unruly world that powerful states are impotent to regulate is the aim of this entire project. Here I want only to answer the question of how the city, precisely because it lacks the particular features of states that incapacitate them for governance (sovereignty and monocultural nationality), can succeed as an instrument of global governance; how, moreover, it can do so democratically.

Where the polis once offered democracy a birthplace, the metropolis may today offer it a reprieve. The ancient city yielded to the nation-state because the polis was monocultural, geographically delimited, and often walled against the outside. But the modern metropolis is multicultural, systemically unbordered, and networked into the world in a way that renders inside and outside meaningless. Cities are alike in the creativity, trade, openness, and variety that sustain their interdependence, but unique in the distinctive origins and historical character that define their differences. There is a reason why, with all their cultural differences, New York, Hong Kong, London, Lagos, and Mexico City share a common disposition. Their essence lies in function rather than in identity, in processes of innovation and creativity rather than the substance of their cultural origins. Their citizens are defined not just by who they are or where they come from but what they do and where they are going. They are less likely to be hobbled by the national and cultural distinctions that can make them "monstrous provincial towns" and more likely to unite around their common aims and interests, facilitated by diversity and multiculturalism, that make them cosmopolitan.[18] Bell and de-Shalit argue that it is precisely because cities offer variety, difference, and uniqueness—because they are different—that they are so attractive; but ironically it is these very attractions that make them seductive in common ways.[19]

Embracing a certain prideful autonomy, cities are nonetheless naturally interdependent. They fly signage and advertising rather than flags. Their sacred hymns are songs of love, nostalgia, and place, rather than anthems dedicated to war, heroism, and independence:[20] "I Left My Heart in San Francisco" and "On the Road to Mandalay"; "I Love Paris [in the Springtime]" and "Ich hab' noch einen Koffer in Berlin" (I left a suitcase in Berlin, my heart still in it). The Big Apple hit, "New York, New York, It's a Wonderful Town," is a celebration posing as a geography lesson—"the Bronx is up and the Battery's down, the people ride in a hole in the ground," while "Sweet Home Chicago" indulges an almost boring familiarity: "Oh baba don't you wanna go back to that same old place, sweet home Chicago." Cities inspire neighborly affection and they rely on communication, trade, mobility, and immigration for their vitality and survival. They prize creative classes rooted in imagination and innovation rather than in national origin or regional accent; these creative classes (Richard Florida reminds us) include chefs and designers and new age techies, not just artists.

Cities are defined by connectivity and hence by motion, never by stasis; and they are driven by aspiration, not history. They trade in risk and cultivate danger. They lack that attachment to the earth that gives traditional nations their blood identity, although this opens urbanites to the charge of being airheads, dreamers, and flakes. Mayors don't talk like presidents and prime ministers about autonomy and sovereignty and self-determination. They are compelled to persuade rather than to enact and order, to debate rather than proclaim and pontificate. When they talk, it is about crime, transportation, and jobs; about plowing the snow and picking up the garbage; about common problems rather than distinctive identities, about networking rather than self-determination. Declaring not their independence, but their interdependence, they build not walls but ports and portals, guildhalls and bridges. The absence of sovereignty becomes their special virtue.

The C40 cities, or the older global association ICLEI, for example, can cooperate around controlling climate change because they have no sovereignty that might be infringed by the agreements they make. No wonder they succeed in Copenhagen and Mexico City where states failed. No wonder Hong Kong and New York can cooperate even while China and the United States bicker and quarrel. Dependent rather than independent, they must define success by how well they integrate, communicate, and network with others rather than how well they insulate themselves from and defend themselves against others. The measure of their success is not how well they protect independence in the face of inevitable dependency, but how well they turn inevitable dependency into an egalitarian interdependence that depends on soft governance and forms of efficient reciprocity rather than hard power and executive command.

Yet the fact that neither sovereignty nor independence defines their character also poses a dilemma for cities that can thwart the aspiration to cooperation. Their lack of formal power opens them to networking, but it also incapacitates them in overcoming those who wield power—state and federal authorities in the United States, for example. Cities can cross borders easily, but they exist only within borders as subsidiary civic entities inside of states, subject to statist powers, sovereignty, and jurisdiction. Cities can govern globally where states can't, but only insofar as national states let them or look the other way.

Does this mean cities really cannot realize transnational forms of soft governance? Not necessarily. A survey of thirty-eight members of the CityNet association revealed that a significant majority of cities agreed that city networks facilitated information exchange, international exposure, and technical support; moved relationships with other cities "beyond friendship"; led to better policies and programs and better partnerships with other urban stakeholders; and provided valuable input for policy making and capacity building.[21]

Why States Can't Stop Cities from Ruling the World

There is no question that, from a legal perspective, cities are bound to obey the sovereign laws, the national policy edicts, and the court decisions of the countries to which they belong. These constraints obviously place significant limits on their freedom to act across borders. In practice, however, cities are at liberty to act in cases where superior jurisdictions are indifferent. The greatest freedom, the old adage has it, lies in the domain where the laws are silent. Cities are also free to act where there is no direct conflict between their networking goals and the sovereign interests of the state. Finally, cities can also be protected in their actions by constitutional guarantees securing their autonomy in the face of limited national governments—as they are in most federal constitutions vouchsafing some degree of local autonomy (India, Canada, Brazil, Germany, Switzerland, and the Russian Federation, for example), and as they are in the United States. There, although the Civil War supposedly settled the federalist debate in favor of central government, the relative autonomy of local political authority is still granted by the Ninth

Amendment to the Constitution, stipulating that the enumeration of federal powers does not "deny or disparage others retained by the people," and by the Tenth Amendment, ensuring that powers "not delegated to the United States . . . nor prohibited by it to the states, are reserved to the states respectively, or to the people."

In political practice, the debate continues, especially in light of the three-tier reality of a federal system pitting federal (central), state, and municipal authority against one another. Sometimes cities share in the autonomy of states against central government; at other times, they ally with central government to free themselves from state oversight and coercion. Cities like San Francisco that are supportive of gay marriage may point to and honor federal court decisions upholding the practice against California state laws banning it—as recently happened when the federal Ninth Circuit declared California's Prop 8 (prohibiting gay marriage) unconstitutional. Most such jurisdictional disputes ultimately go to the courts and thus become ongoing items in the contest over American federalism and the appropriate distribution of powers.

Useful as federalism is to cities as a theory, however, it is less useful in practice. As Eric A. Posner and others have noted, the arrogation of power by the executive branch has, to a degree, nullified both the separation of powers and federalist decentralization.[22] Yet even as central state executives grasp at greater authority, the sovereign power they seek to monopolize becomes ever more dubious. The premise that nation-states and their chief executives actually continue to have the power to act as the supreme adjudicators and enforcers of the interests and rights of their people lacks conviction. The noisy media debates about whether America is "Number One," whether decline has set in and the United States is about to yield its place to some other superpower such as China, are moot. They overlook the reality that no nation can be "number one" in a world in which nation-states no longer dictate their own destinies.

Antideclinists such as Robert Kagan argue that American decline is a myth and that by the comparative measures of GDP, military strength, trade, and soft power, the United States is and will remain the first and only reigning superpower.[23] But the real question is not whether the United States remains a sovereign superpower, but whether its sovereignty, however super, can accomplish very much in an interdependent world. Political scientists have typically bestowed on imperial powers a century's reign. The sixteenth century belonged to the Dutch, the seventeenth to Spain, the eighteenth to the French, the nineteenth to Britain, and the twentieth to the United States. In the battle over who will own the twenty-first, Japan was briefly heir apparent in the 1980s (see Paul Kennedy),[24] while today's pessimists put their bets on the Chinese, leaving people like Kagan to insist the United States will retain its title.

Yet the reality is that our century can belong to no one nation; that this will be the world's century in common, or belong to no one people at all. It is not that states are weak but that their strength is without bearing on so many cross-border challenges—problems of immigration, disease, terrorism, climate change, technology, war, and markets. This makes cities relatively functional. Never has a nation—Kagan is correct—possessed the powers that belong today to the United States of America. Never have such powers been so irrelevant to governing an interdependent world. The question is not whether America will retain its superpower status, but whether that status will enable it to solve even its own problems, let alone dominate the destinies of other nations. Or whether the problems will become the provenance of cities, with or without formal jurisdiction to act.

In the space between eroding national power and the growing challenges of an interdependent world, rising cities may find their voice and manage together to leverage change. Lacking sovereignty, cities care little about its attrition. Sovereignty has in any case been passing from the political to the economic sector. As I argued twenty years ago in *Jihad vs. McWorld*:

> Even the most developed, supposedly self-sufficient nations can no longer pretend to genuine sovereignty. . . . When it comes to acid rain or oil spills or depleted fisheries or tainted groundwater or fluorocarbon propellants or radiation leaks or toxic wastes or sexually transmitted diseases, national frontiers are simply irrelevant. Toxins don't stop for customs inspections and microbes don't carry passports. . . . In Europe, Asia, and the Americas . . . markets have

already eroded national sovereignty and given birth to a new class of institutions—international banks, trade associations, transnational lobbies like OPEC, world news services like CNN and the BBC, and multinational corporations—institutions that lack distinctive national identities and neither reflect nor respect nationhood.[25]

Today with nation-states being dominated by forces of terrorism, pandemics, climate change, and predatory markets, and with the power of money over politics officially sanctioned by the U.S. Supreme Court in *Buckley v. Valeo* (money *is* speech!) and *Citizens United* (corporations *are* speaking persons!), it begins to seem that sovereignty is a thing precious only to posturing politicians and paradigm-preoccupied political scientists. Dani Rodrik, for example, continues to insist that it is "one of our era's foundational myths . . . that globalization has condemned the nation-state to irrelevance." He dismisses those who "decry the artificiality of national borders" as "cosmopolitan ethicists" caught up in "wishful thinking."[26] He is of course right to point out that sovereign states are hardly irrelevant and remain powerful actors in global affairs. But it is also true, as K. C. Sivaramakrishnan has written, that "it has long been understood that even the most powerful of the national or state governments is not powerful enough to deal with its cities."[27] This is in part because it is cities to which the most pressing challenges are being passed.

The impact of these lessons on the delicate dance of nation-states and cities is hard to absorb for academics whose curriculum is organized around *national* peoples, sovereign *states*, and inter-*national* relations. Mayors do not have the luxury of this self-serving inattention to reality. To govern their cities they need to be able to participate in governing the interdependent world where most of the city's challenges originate, even as they struggle to accommodate the state governments under whose jurisdiction they live. Former mayor Wolfgang Schuster of Stuttgart thus insists, "we are not an island. We need a strong lobby for strong local self-government systems . . . so we have to work in networks to make understandable what are our needs, what are our demands . . . [and to] learn from each other."[28]

It is the paradox of sovereignty that, when it comes to addressing interdependence, at least with respect to cooperation, it makes strong states weak and weak cities strong. Mayors understand they need one another. Mayor Naheed Nenshi of Calgary notes that "every city in the world has the same issues. We have to take out the trash, we need to make sure the road networks are in good shape, we need police and first responders. . . . So . . . our key is how we share best practices, because we all have to deliver the same services at the end of the day, and we are all looking for better ways of delivering those services."[29] Technically powerless, cities have in fact more than ample room to play in the spaces being vacated by a sovereignty that is disappearing or minimally is being displaced by economic power. Alexis de Tocqueville always believed that at its most compelling, liberty was local and municipal, and this remains true today.

In an earlier epoch, the federal government was more often than not the "good" power enforcing local liberty and civil rights against the secessionist-inflected efforts of parochial states to thwart them. Groups like the Federalist Society (associated with Edwin Meese's influential conservative "limited government" philosophy) campaigned to secure states' rights in order, for example, to safeguard segregated private schools or oppose federal environmental legislation. But nowadays, when it comes to issues of global cooperation among cities, it has been the federal authorities that have often thwarted cosmopolitan outcomes in the name of nationalist parochialism, as in the crucial case of global warming.

Gerald Frug observes that in cities such as Mumbai and São Paulo, "there are a variety of ways to subject city policy—even in countries that have worked to foster decentralized power—to centralized control."[30] But jurisdiction remains a two-way street. Central authorities, whether federal or regional, may discover that if they impose policies and regulations on unwilling cities by force, such *dicta* can lack efficacy or diminish the nation's standing—which is in part dependent on the success and reputation of its great cities. Moreover, laws must be implemented, and, short of federal troops (as happened with the compulsory integration of schools in the South during the Civil Right revolution), state authorities must rely on local enforcement. A national or statewide effort to ban cell phone communication while driving or prohibit the use of recreational marijuana is unlikely to succeed unless local jurisdictions buy in and enforce national standards by arresting and trying those who violate the law. Cities cannot do what nations refuse to let them do, but nations may also be hindered from implementing laws that cities refuse to enforce.

In the end, optimism about the future arises out of the nature of cities themselves. They are already networked and naturally disposed to creative interactivity and innovative cross-border experimentation and collaboration; they are relational, communal, and naturally interdependent. They embody local liberty and promote participatory engagement by citizens. Whether we call it global governance or simply cosmopolitanism as praxis and whether or not it is underwritten by a parliament of mayors or some other global association, cities will play an increasingly crucial role in taking decisions across borders on behalf of humanity. For planet earth, an entity that nation-states always seem to have thought they were obligated to carve up, remains in the eyes of cosmopolitans a global commons that is sustainable only if cities and citizens make it their common cause.

YURY LUZHKOV OF MOSCOW

YURY LUZHKOV was twenty-two in 1968 when he joined the Communist Party of the Soviet Union. He was thirty-one in 1977 when he joined the City Council of Moscow. In the years from 1992, when Boris Yeltsin appointed him mayor of the capital city, to 2010, when he was dismissed by President Dmitry Medvedev (Russian mayors are mostly appointed, not elected locally), he became an exemplary urban leader in ways good and bad, but largely beyond the control of a still-ideological state. Some say he was finally sacked because he was too close to Vladimir Putin (Medvedev's rival, alternating in the presidency), some because the corruption scandals surrounding his wife had grown too public to ignore, and some because, with Putin, he had founded the political party United Russia, suggesting he had national political ambitions.

I suspect he lost his job less for political reasons or corruption (another form of politics in many places) than because he was never political enough. When asked which party platform he ran on, which ideology he favored, he always answered, "the management platform," the party of no ideology (*khozyaistvennik*). You couldn't really be an ideologue and govern Moscow, even before the Soviet Union fell.

When I met Mayor Luzhkov in the early 1990s at an international conference he sponsored, I was struck by how different he seemed from the Soviet political types I had known—including even Georgy Shakhnazarov, the president of the Soviet Political Science Association and eventually a Mikhail Gorbachev adviser. Luzhkov was plainspoken, while Soviet politicians were circumspect and correct in the name of deviousness. He talked about governance as a challenge in solving problems rather than an excuse to argue ideology. He was a powerful personality rather than a prominent politician, a quality closely associated with mayors.

The Kennan Institute's Blair Ruble seems to concur: "It is relatively easy to overstate the impact of a single individual no matter how powerful, especially in a city as large and complex as Moscow," said Ruble, who has written extensively about Moscow. "No one can doubt that Mayor Luzhkov has left the imprint of his personality on Moscow, from his early years when the force of his will made people notice positive changes in the city to more recently, when his preference for large projects has appeared to dominate all opposition."[1] Not to say the corruption charges aren't real.

An old Muscovite in his seventies says, "Everyone knows Luzhkov is a thief." The mayor's wife, Nikolayevna Baturina, worth more than a billion dollars, is the richest woman in Russia, her powerful construction company so important in Moscow that some cynics call the city "Baturinsk." She seems to belong either in a Tolstoy novel or in jail. Nowadays, she is more often found in New York or London than Moscow, and there is little doubt that her excesses and foreign business connections helped bring Luzhkov's long tenure to an end.

Yet for Luzhkov himself, promoting development for Moscow in the rigid, ideological bureaucracy that was the old Soviet Union, and in the new Russian Federation too, required bringing business to the city, one way or the other. The Muscovite who called him a well-known thief qualified his indictment: "but there are thieves who just take everything for themselves, and then there are thieves who put their ill-gotten gains to use."

Whether building a cathedral from corporate contributions more garnished from than contributed by developers, or drawing investors into city development projects with paybacks, Luzhkov did manage to put the gains he won to the uses of Moscow. Russians suspicious of the new post-Soviet plutocrats, so many of whom got rich on wealth in effect stolen from the disintegrating Soviet Union, were glad to see Luzhkov get a fair share for Moscow. One of them allows that "a lot of ordinary people think these new rich, these new Russians should share their wealth with the city, and this is a way to cut, a little bit, their super-profits."

There are many different ways to become mayor—to be elected or to be appointed; to take office as part of a party career or to hold office despite and in the face of a dominant party; to govern under a republican constitution or under a one-party state. What Luzhkov proves is that such categories are not necessarily the most important benchmarks for measuring mayoral success. That to govern as mayor makes demands that push such structural questions into the background. That in the life of cities, pragmatism is not simply an option but a necessity, and corruption can sometimes be a means to cope with a bad system even though it is usually a tool to undermine a good one.

It would be hard to call Luzhkov an interdependent, given his lifelong struggle to find a degree of independence for Moscow from a national political hierarchy that both before and after the fall of the Soviet Union was an encumbrance on local government. Yet he secured a degree of autonomy for Moscow, in no small part by securing its welfare and maintaining its global presence. Nowhere near as cosmopolitan or Europhiliac as St. Petersburg, Moscow under Luzhkov nonetheless managed to find a place as a global city in an interdependent world, and its influence is only likely to grow, whatever the destiny of Luzhkov's wife or of Mother Russia.

II. HOW IT CAN BE DONE

CHAPTER 7. "PLANET OF SLUMS"

The Challenge of Urban Inequality

Instead of cities of light soaring toward heaven much of the twenty-first-century urban world squats in squalor, surrounded by pollution, excrement, and decay. Indeed, the one billion city dwellers who inhabit postmodern slums might well look back with envy at the ruins of the sturdy mud home of Catal Huyuk in Anatolia, erected at the very dawn of city life nine thousand years ago.

Mike Davis, Planet of Slums

Class remains a key feature of American life, shaping everything from our politics to our health and happiness. Overcoming these divides requires nothing less than a new set of institutions and a wholly new social compact.

Richard Florida, The Rise of the Creative Class Revisited

I'm starting to get increasingly concerned about inequality in our city. Great cities have inequality and wealth by definition: the reason they are cities is because people come from different parts of the income scale—but we have to ensure that people at the bottom of the income scale do have the opportunity to succeed.

Mayor Naheed Nenshi, Calgary

No one need tell the billion poor people living in the more than 200,000 urban slums around the world that rapid urbanization has not been an unmitigated good.[1] How are the poor to respond to its supposed democratic and global promise when the city does little more than "incarcerate the underprivileged and further marginalizes them in relation to the broader society," in relation, that is to say, to the middle and upper classes to whom so many of the celebrated advantages of urban life seem to accrue?[2]

The critics of cities featured in Chapter 2 were not nostalgic country boys. They were clear-eyed observers of sins endemic to the city. They greeted with enduring suspicion the city's claim to embody modern virtue, seeing in modernity more bad than good. More tellingly, the critics were convinced that cities exacerbated many of modernity's most troubling features, including consumerism, corruption, bossism, and ghettos; and that they did this in every domain, from education, transportation, and housing to sustainability and access to jobs. We need here to assess the indictment through the lens of modern economics and culture to determine the extent to which the city is crippled by inequality and to measure inequality's effect on the argument for urban global governance. For it looms as the greatest obstacle to successful intercity democracy.

Assessing Urban Inequality

Even its admirers acknowledge that urbanization has entailed a kind of "massification." Critics such as the Marxist urban theorist and activist Mike Davis have observed that, in concert with other forces such as structural adjustment and state retrenchment, urbanization has "been an inevitable recipe for the mass production of slums."[3] Many house more than a million people living under conditions barely captured by Paul Collier's term, *black hole*. As sanguine an observer of cities as Richard Florida recognized recently that the fortunes of the "creative class" he celebrated a decade ago are now imperiled by class divisions. The resulting social divide, he argues, can be remedied only with "a new set of institutions and a wholly new social compact that can leverage the full potential of the new Creative Economy . . . while mitigating the substantial divides and costs it imposes."[4]

I opened this study citing new figures showing that more than half the world's population is urban. Now comes the unsettling news that while only 6 percent of those dwelling in developed cities live in slums, an astonishing 78 percent of city dwellers in the least developed countries inhabit ghettos—about a third of the planet's urban population or one of every six human beings.[5] There is some contestation about what exactly comprises a slum, and close observers have even suggested the term is too pejorative for neighborhoods that are more appropriately viewed as part of the "Kinetic City—a kind of city in motion," constantly being recycled, modified, and reinvented.[6] Suketu Mehta notes that in Mumbai, residents speak of *basti* or "communities" rather than slums, while those who pursue "slum clearance" are often involved in "epic land grabs."[7] Such views are important in making ethical and cultural sense of urban inequality, and I will return to them, but it is also true that poor neighborhoods represent unsavory and dangerous living conditions rooted in a material reality that contributes to fundamental urban inequalities. The United Nations Human Settlements Programme (U.N.-Habitat) focuses on the material, and defines a slum household simply as a "group of individuals living under the same roof in an urban area who lack one or more of the following:" durable housing, sufficient living space (not more than three per room), easy access to safe water, adequate sanitation, and security of tenure (no forced evictions).

By these measures, China has 37.7 percent of its urban population living in slums, India 55.5 percent, and Brazil 36.6 percent. Far worse are Pakistan with 73.6 percent, Nigeria with 79.2 percent, Bangladesh with 84.7 percent, Tanzania with 92.1 percent, and Ethiopia with 99.4 percent. More or less the entire urban population of Ethiopia lives under slum conditions, while sub-Saharan Africa is home to more of the world's worst slums than any other region.[8] While the absence of a baseline until recently makes it difficult to assess trends, U.N.-Habitat suggests there is little evidence that things are improving or that the underlying conditions are being addressed. The *New York Times* reported recently that since Lyndon Johnson's War on Poverty fifty years ago, "despite the expenditure of more than \$16 trillion on means-tested programs . . . the portion of Americans living beneath the poverty line, 15%, is higher than in the Johnson administration."[9]

Depressing as these American statistics are, comparing figures from around the world with those from the United States suggests that there is not one planet of slums, but two. The first is made up of developed countries, where slums account for less than 10 percent of city populations— although in America, rural poverty added to urban poverty leaves one in five living below the poverty line (it's even worse for children), and the disparity between rich and poor in so prosperous a nation makes inequality more egregious. The second slum planet comprises the third world, where the largest and newest megacities, growing at a lightning pace, account for the great preponderance of slum dwellers.[10] As the Kerner Commission in the late 1960s once called America a story of two nations—one rich, one poor, one white, one black—Davis might have spoken of two urban worlds, one middle class, the other impoverished, one defined by glamorous global financial centers, the other by endless slums.[11]

As urban development produces a divided world and the massification of slums, it also generates not just creativity and culture but the routinization of creativity as business and the trivialization of culture as commerce, resulting in a new form of urban living I have elsewhere called McWorld. The inequality confronting cities and societies around the world today is not just a fact of life or a feature of what conservatives have understood as natural human differences in talent, ambition, and goals. These putatively "natural" differences, which social philosophers from John Locke and Edmund Burke to Robert Nozick and Charles Murray have argued are concomitants of what it means to be human and which cannot be altered without radical curtailments of human liberty, may be constants of the human condition. Irving Kristol coolly dismissed the struggle against inequality as a sign of class envy, and his son Bill Kristol editorializes regularly in the *Weekly Standard* about inequality of condition as "a fact of life. Some people will always be poorer than others."[12] I believe these premises about human nature and the supposed order of things are faulty, even obscene, reflecting a complacent rationalization of the status quo by those whom it benefits.

I will not enter the old ideological debate here, however. Even if there were a reasonable case to be made for natural inequality not founded on the interests of the wealthy, it would bear scant relevance to the challenges faced today by Los Angeles or Manila, Cairo or Shanghai. As Joseph Stiglitz and many others have argued, urban inequality and the story of the "one percent" in our global era is not just about inequality but about fairness.[13] The inequality we see around the world is more than a function of difference: it is deeply unjust—irrational and thus inexplicable other than as a function of private interest, along with greed, narcissism, and exploitation. Redressing *inequality* may sometimes compromise liberty, but the redressing of *injustice* is liberty's very condition.

Before any convincing argument can be made on behalf of global governance by cities, we are obliged to ask whether such a development is going to improve or depress the condition of people in either the developing world's "planet of slums" or the first world's planet of radical inequalities. Do we truly wish, with our parliament of mayors, to globalize urban injustice or give corruption a formal role in governance? Does such an innovation merely replicate urban segregation on a planetary scale? Surely we would prefer to believe that, despite the harsh realities of urban life, cities over time can ameliorate the challenges of inequality and poverty and find ways to impact and even transform slums. Yet though as sites of experimentation and progressive innovation, cities continue to contribute new approaches to mitigating and overcoming inequality—some of which we will explore in Chapter 8—the truth is that urban inequality is a persistent and distressing feature of modern cities and the contemporary world, above all in the developing world, where most slums are found, and which have been hardest hit by the global financial crisis and the global economic inequities occasioned by the self-serving "austerity" policies of the wealthy (austerity for you, profits for us).

These are the enduring problems of class, caste, and race associated with—the old-fashioned language remains disappointingly apt—colonialism, imperialism, predatory capitalism, and rapacious financial markets. The old issues appear today in new forms not easily addressed by traditional formulas of the liberal, progressive, or Marxist variety.[14] In India, for example, gender inequality and the systematic abuse of women both economically and physically (rape and the failure by the police and the courts to prosecute is only the leading edge) persist long after there has been systemic change in other domains. Such abuse reflects "a pattern of harassment, assault and ill-treatment that keeps [women] bound to a second-tier citizenship even as many increasingly educated and urbanized women are advancing in the workplace," and at the same time leaves "hundreds of millions of other women . . . still trapped in a web of traditional strictures."[15]

Traditional neocolonial and racist patterns are also visible in many "advanced" societies. In his *Spaces of Hope*, David Harvey reads the contemporary metropolis through the lens of the 1995 French film *Hate* (*le Haine*) as "a place of both artistic and lived impoverishment if not humane impossibility"—a place where "the individuals seem caught, helplessly passive, imprisoned and fragmented within the web of urban life being constructed by agents of power that seem far away."[16] Even without relying on the language of Marxism, it can be argued that the density, multiculturalism, diversity, and immigration patterns usually seen as virtues typical of cities nonetheless exacerbate and deepen inequalities of the kind spawned by state and global capitalism. Mike Davis references Patrick Geddes's grim prophecy that over time the evolution of cities will manifest itself mainly as "slum, semi-slum and superslum."[17] Geddes's fears are vindicated in the poverty and economic divisions that have attended the rapid growth of sprawling conurbations in nations on the Indian subcontinent, where Karachi, Mumbai, Delhi, Kolkata, and Dhaka present themselves as much as megaslums as megacities.[18]

The danger is that in reading Davis and Harvey and the grim prophecies of Jeremy Seabrook in his alarming *Cities of the South*, we become convinced that cities are but a euphemism for slums, and slums are incorrigible features of urban life so profoundly distorting that the city becomes indistinguishable from the latrine, drowning in its own excrement, literally as well as metaphorically.[19] To Davis, "today's poor megacities—Nairobi, Lagos, Bombay, Dhaka . . . are stinking mountains of shit that would appall even the most hardened Victorians."[20] That Davis's stinking mountains of shit is no exercise in hyperbole is evident from this description by Katherine Boo of the new town of Annawadi near the Mumbai airport, a slum in which "almost no one was considered poor by official Indian benchmarks." About this supposedly "most stirring success narrative in the modern history of global market capitalism," Boo writes:

True, only six of the slum's three thousand residents had permanent jobs . . . True, a few residents trapped rats and frogs and fried them for dinner. A few ate the scrub grass at the sewage lake's edge. And these individuals, miserable souls, thereby made an inestimable contribution to their neighbors. They gave those slum dwellers who didn't fry rats and eat weeds . . . a felt sense of their upward mobility.[21]

If this is upward mobility, if the shit cannot be scrubbed from the city, if inequality and injustice cannot be addressed to some significant degree, then to call for global governance by cities is not to ameliorate global market inequality but to take injustice to global scale and authorize not the oversight of mayors but the rule of slumlords.

Faced with so bleak a scenario, I can offer only some partial promise of mitigation. Modest progress has been made in the first decade of the new millennium in meeting the already modest Millennium Goals set by the United Nations in 2000 for 2015 (and described earlier). The percentage of third world peoples living in slums is down from 39 percent in 1990 to 33 percent in 2012, for example, although it is not clear exactly what the benchmark is for this improvement, given the controversy about the definition of a slum. The proportion of people using water drawn from clean sources rose from 76 percent in 1990 to 89 percent in 2010. Yet his own institutional optimism notwithstanding, U.N. Secretary-General Ban Ki-Moon "noted that projections indicate that in 2015 more than 600 million people worldwide will still lack access to safe drinking water, almost one billion will be living on an income of less than $1.25 per day, mothers will continue to die needlessly in childbirth, and children will suffer and die from preventable diseases." His 2012 report ends with the warning that "the 2015 deadline is fast approaching and in order to achieve outstanding goals, governments, the international community, civil society and the private sector need to intensify their contributions."[22]

In the United States, although inequality as a function of both race and the dominion of capital is as old as America itself, there is also improvement. Seventy-five years into the nation's history, President Lincoln issued this sober warning: "I see in the near future a crisis approaching that unnerves me and causes me to tremble for the safety of my country . . . corporations have been enthroned and an era of corruption in high places will follow, and the money power of the country will endeavor to pro-long its reign by working upon the prejudices of the people until all wealth is aggregated in a few hands and the Republic is destroyed."[23] A generation before Lincoln, the *New York Herald* had greeted the financial crisis of 1837 with rhetoric that could have issued from the protesters at Occupy Wall Street: "The present evils which afflict the country have been produced by overbanking, overtrading, overspending, overliving, overdashing, overdriving, overreaching, overcheating, overborrowing, overeating, overdrinking, overpraying, oversinning, overthinking, overplaying, overriding, overstepping, overfiddling, and over acting of every kind and description."[24]

At the beginning of the twentieth century, President Teddy Roosevelt was still exercised about the "malefactors of great wealth." One needn't belong to Occupy Wall Street to think not so much has changed today. In the bounteous nation proud of calling itself the land of opportunity, inequality has been America's other pole, *the* American dilemma from the start—seemingly a product of a devotion to markets more zealous than a commitment to equality; a product of a liberal dichotomy that sees freedom and justice as incompatible goals. Take New York City in 2013, my city—a gilded city "of dazzling resurrection and official neglect, remarkable wealth and even more remarkable inequality. Despite the popular narrative of a city reborn . . . the extraordinary triumph of New York's existence is tempered by the outrage of that inequality."[25] New York's dichotomies are America's contradictions; America's contradictions are the planet's dilemma, especially since inequality also manifests the global economy's structural problems. Mike Davis speaks about slums in a language of universals indifferent to culture, though the global problem can be inflected regionally and locally. Within Latin America, economist James K. Galbraith has argued, "the experience of economic inequality in [Argentina and Brazil] is marked by differences rooted in their divergent social histories and economic structure."[26] China's inequality also seems in some ways to be a special case, tied to the deep urban/rural split that puts a great majority of people in inland villages and a prosperous minority in flourishing cities within 300 miles of the seacoast; and also to the boom economics of the recent period where "the unchecked flow of capital wealth into the leading cities—especially into Beijing—runs counter to the development of a 'harmonious society.'"[27]

Does this mean local cultures of ethnic or racial prejudice need not be seen as part of the challenge of inequality? Certainly not. The American case shows how national and local issues of race and class can shape and deepen inequality that issues from global market forces. In the 1960s, inequality and racism were indistinguishable: in great cities like Newark, Los Angeles, and Detroit, ghetto residents set their neighborhoods ablaze, while middle-class denizens nearby blamed them for violence, urban breakdown, and reverse racism. When in 1968 the Johnson Administration issued the Report of the National Advisory Commission on Civil Disorders (the Kerner Commission Report), it declared, "Our nation is moving toward two societies, one black, one white—separate and unequal."[28] Thirty years later, the underlying divisions had grown worse, the revolutionary fires seemingly extinguished by placidity and hopelessness. In reports commissioned by the Eisenhower Foundation, former Kerner Commission member and presidential candidate Fred R. Harris warned that "Today, thirty years after the Kerner Report, there is more poverty in America, it is deeper, blacker and browner than before, and it is more concentrated in the cities, which have become America's poorhouses."[29] In the fifteen years since Harris wrote—now nearly fifty years after the Kerner Commission—urban inequality has continued to deepen, with race still a key factor. As Figure 2 shows, inequality continues to be heavily skewed along racial lines in American cities.[30]

America's prison population per capita is larger than any country's in the world except South Africa's, and inmates are disproportionally African-American. In Texas and New York, state law prosecutes minors as adults. And in New York City, 50,000 sleep in homeless shelters every night (how many former inmates isn't precisely known), with many more preferring to bunk down on the street or in the parks or under highway bridges. When local cultural issues such as racism are factors, however, there is at least the possibility of local actions to address them. The incarceration of minors with adults is, for example, being contested by the Correctional Association of New York.[31] But the urban dilemma is that even where causes of inequality are local, remedies may not be available to local authorities.

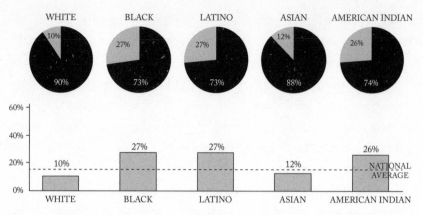

Figure 2: Inequality index by race. From "Poverty by Race: 2010," in *Tracking American Poverty and Policy,* http://www.trackingpovertyandpolicy.org/.

The United States is a federalist decentralized political system, but even here, cities have struggled to control their own destinies. As was apparent in the last chapter's discussion of federalism, cuts in state funding for unemployment or education or the refusal to subsidize deficits in cities with fragile economies can leave a willing city unable to deal with inequalities of opportunity. In the summer of 2012, Stockton, California, a city of over 800,000, led a number of California cities in filing for bankruptcy, in effect declaring its impotence in the face of financial forces it could not control. Detroit is also bankrupt, its local government in receivership. In Baltimore, Maryland, with unemployment climbing and revenues down, the city found itself a victim of the manipulation of a key interest rate (the London Interbank Offered Rate) by global banks such as Barclays, over which it could exert no influence—other than through lawsuits that lead to prolonged and costly court battles.[32] Syracuse, a typical New York State rustbelt city, recently appealed for a state bailout rather than accept Governor Andrew Cuomo's proposal to push its pension costs into the future. The governor's unsentimental response captures the problem cities face: the answer to local fiscal stress cannot be, he said, that "they're going to come to Albany and ask for a check." There would be no more bailouts of "aging cities with aging populations and aging infrastructure that are consuming in greater percentages of their revenues . . . with . . . a declining tax base."[33]

At least as far as aging cities with aging infrastructure are concerned, "city limits" turns out to have a meaning more encompassing than topology or boundaries. To urban populations, the term *stranglehold* may not seem too strong to describe the relationship of region to city, especially for older cities with faltering economies and shrinking populations (not all cities are growing!). At a moment when federalism and states' rights are being revived by conservatives and the Tea Party, municipal power seems to be shrinking rather than expanding. Such realities can only curb our urban optimism and underscore the lingering epithets that have been traditionally deployed by critics of the city whose view of the shimmering towers is blocked by the mountains of shit around them. To them the city still resembles a "tumor," a "jungle," a "necropolis"—what Thomas Hardy in describing London called a "monster whose body has four million heads and eight million eyes." Even the most superficial glance at Kinshasa-Brazzaville or Mumbai or Rio de Janeiro conjures again Hardy's nightmare. Can urban citizens and their mayors then really become the key to global civil society and informal democratic governance? Or are they impotent bystanders in a game of thrones?

If Rousseau's heirs like Thomas Hardy and Berthold Brecht (and modern scholars like Mike Davis and David Harvey) are to be believed, and the city is still Rousseau's "abyss in which virtually the whole nation loses its morals, its laws, its courage and its freedom,"[34] then to argue that mayors should rule the world is to sink the foundation for global democratic governance into the bottom of a deep chasm. In taking the measure of that ravine's depth, segregation turns out to be key.

Segregation as a Tale of Two Cities

Segregation is a common feature of inequality throughout the urban world, yet there is no one global segregation model that can be universally diagnosed and addressed. Mike Davis's "planet of slums," we have seen, is really a tale of two cities, one in the developing and the other in the developed world. Slums in the developed world exist in considerable tension with the putatively democratic character of both city and nation, an affront to achieved civil rights and hence demanding attention. Angela Glover Blackwell, a rights advocate for people in poverty, has acknowledged that "there's no question that we've made progress, that we have done something about the kind of suffering that used to be routine and widespread."[35]

Slums in the developing world, on the other hand, much more encompassing and seemingly endemic to new megacities, often define urban life. Amelioration is hard to effect. Over a dozen years ago, David Harvey warned that the "problems of the advanced capitalist world pale into insignificance compared to the extraordinary dilemmas of developing countries, with the wildly uncontrolled pace of urbanization in Sao Paolo, Mexico City, Cairo, Lagos, Mumbai, Calcutta, Seoul, and now Shanghai and Beijing." These cities are traversing in a generation what "London went through in ten and Chicago in three," with chronic air pollution, gated compounds, and the jobless economy making reform near impossible.[36]

Their urbanization is, moreover, less voluntary than the West's. While historically, the West's big cities *pulled* people off the land and into the city with a siren song of economic opportunity and the seductive excitement of fresh lives of possibility (see Chapter 2), much of the rapid population growth in the developing world's megacities has been the result of people *pushed* off the land by unemployment and the kind of global market competition local agriculture can't combat. It is the negative profile of the rural economy rather than the positive profile of the city that sends people scrambling to the metropolis. Yet jobs are low paying in an unstable and lackluster informal urban economy where poor people's best hope is to find an off-the-grid job and occupy a ghetto squat; and then perhaps one day move from the informal to the formal economy, from squatting to owning a home.

Such a strategy is not simply naiveté. As one of Katherine Boo's subjects tells her, "a decent life was the train that hadn't hit you, the slumlord you hadn't offended, the malaria you hadn't caught."[37] Still, in Mumbai and Lagos and Jakarta, having expectations still makes sense, which is one reason why the poor make war on one another; why in cities like Mumbai, racist Hindu parties such as Shiv Sena campaign to "purge Mumbai of migrants from India's poor northern states," above all, Muslims.[38] There is something to fight over. These pale but seductive opportunities have led to astonishing growth in third-world megacities in the absence of either mobility or genuine hope. In China, for example, construction worker colonies drawn from inland village China (where more than two-thirds of China's population still lives) constitute a new and troubling form of transient urban ghetto, one without roots in any traditional neighborhood and existing only as a temporarily employed male enclave possessing no discernible "rights to the city."

Segregation, whether residential, economic, educational, or natural, must then be appropriately addressed in both worlds of this binary system of urban planets. Formal equality is unlikely to yield equal opportunity unless people can live, ride, work, learn, and play together in cities whose neighborhoods are voluntary communities rather than walled ghettos. Segregation reflects power realities on both planets: "by dividing the city into physically separate racial zones, urban segregationists interpose four things—physical distance, physical obstacles, legal obstacles and people empowered to enforce the legal obstacles."[39] Despite the undeniable impact of forces helpful to integration, including civil rights legislation, the suburbanization of minorities, the complexifying effect of immigration on minority status, and the integrating force of gentrification, segregation persists, if in subtler and less definitive ways. Take for example, newly gated neighborhoods blocked off from major thoroughfares by traffic diversions; or gentrification in the name of integration that actually allows market forces to push poor people out. Thus, we have recently seen what Alan Ehrenhalt has understood as a restratification or "inversion" in which ghettos give way to postindustrial centers of upscale-living downtowns, while suburbs become ghettoized—trends obvious in Paris and Chicago alike.[40]

If the persistence of ghettos is the bad news, the city itself as a form of human community inherently inclined to integration is the good news. Carl H. Nightingale has wisely remarked on the contradiction: "Despite centuries of segregation," he writes, "cities have always been the site for the largest-scale interactions between people from different parts of the world, and they are responsible for most of the mixing of peoples and cultures in world history."[41] Nightingale sees the late nineteenth and early twentieth centuries as the high point of urban segregation everywhere,

remarking on how the neighborhoods around the grand imperial monu-
ments in Delhi and the beaux-arts boulevards in Algiers or Buenos Aires
act as *cordons sanitaires* keeping out the poor. He remarks too on the rapid
expansion of the pattern of segregation in China and around the Pacific
Rim.[42] Since then, segregation in the developed world has declined,
although there are plenty of exceptions in rust-belt cities like Camden,
New Jersey, and Flint, Michigan, in the United States[43]; or Beziers and
Marseille (France's "Detroit") in France, or Hungary's once picturesque
city of Miskolc, in crisis after the closing of the country's oldest steel
plant (18,000 jobs) recently.[44]

In the face of the global recession's impact, it may then seem excessive
to announce "the end of the segregated century" as the Manhattan Institute recently did. Yet as its new study demonstrates, by most standard
segregation measures, American cities are more integrated than at any
time since 1910.[45] The study's authors, Edward Glaeser and Jacob Vigdor,
offer evidence showing that African-American residents today can be
found in 199 of every 200 American neighborhoods, noting that while
fifty or sixty years ago nearly half the African-American population lived
in neighborhoods that were 80 percent or more black, today only 20 percent do. And on the other side of the ghetto wall, they argue, neighborhoods defined as all-white are "effectively extinct." The proof is in census
report numbers: from 1970 to 2010, segregation declined in all 85 of America's largest metro areas. Just in the decade from 2000 to 2010, segregation diminished in 522 out of 658 housing markets. Census figures also
show that in 1960 there were 4,700 all-white neighborhoods in the United
States, whereas today there are 170. These trends inspire the hope that
segregation will continue to wane and turn developed-world cities into
more egalitarian building blocks for global governance.

The same economic trends are everywhere evident in the developing
world, but they too play out in distinctive cultural and religious settings.
In Europe, it is not skin color but Islam, both as religion and culture,
that occasions segregation, bigotry, and inequality. Muslims have not
been as completely ghettoized by geography and polarization as African-
Americans once were in the United States, but the inequalities attending their economic, educational, and residential status have made for

sharp divisions and an insidious reactionary politics of fear that creates ghettos of the mind more perverse than physical ghettos. In what was once East (Communist) Germany, some older citizens still speak with frustration and rage at the "Mauer im Kopf" (wall in the mind) that still divides Germans a quarter of a century after the fall of the physical wall. When it comes to Islam, Europe continues to suffer a regionwide Mind Wall. What David Harvey has called (following Raymond Williams) "militant particularisms" play out on the right not as anticapitalism but as "authoritarian religious, or neo-fascist" movements, as with the National Democratic Party in Germany, Geert Wilders's Party for Freedom (PVV) in Holland, Shiv Sena in Mumbai, or the Lombardy Leagues in Italy.[46]

The greater divide, however, remains the one *between* "the West and the rest," the developed world's modest planet of slums and the developing world's limitless, revolution-inciting megacity megaslums. As segregation fades on the first planet, it explodes on the other. In the developed world, local agricultural markets (green markets) serve the city and even draw urban farmers to the periphery. But here, as in the developing world, local agriculture faces global market forces of bio-engineering and corporate agribusiness with which it cannot possibly compete. We experienced our own rural dislocations here in the United States long ago. Starting after the Civil War, a machine-intensive, labor-sparing new agriculture evolved, which allowed 2 or 3 percent rather than two-thirds of the population to feed the rest (and much of the world beyond). In the developing world, this shock is current. Moreover, the cities to which rural peoples flee do not necessarily offer the possibilities of manufacturing that the developed world's cities once did. The result: massive new megacity slums embodying a new segregation, with nothing like the possibilities of the towns of an earlier era.

James K. Galbraith sees speculative markets as a key cause of the imbalance, with cities where banks are headquartered often less inegalitarian than the cities where their influence is felt.[47] Sako Musterd agrees that "there does not seem to be a strong association between the level of socio-spatial segregation and the attractiveness of a city for business or those who are working in these businesses."[48] There is a dual message in this reality. It means on the one hand that the actual presence of urban banks and financial markets is not per se a cause of a particular city's inequality—though the system it nourishes certainly is. But it also means that the system works across cities, especially third-world megacities, to exacerbate inequality. All politics may be local, but all economics is global, which means as people struggle politically to deal with crisis in stressed first-world capitals such as Athens and Madrid, the real levers of the system are likely to be in Frankfurt or London. Too often the real culprit is absentee power.

The Manifestations of Inequality

Without offering a genealogy of urban injustice or a full discussion of its unfairness, it is apparent that in its more egregious manifestations and compounded by segregation, urban inequality distorts access to housing, transportation, jobs, security (in terms of crime), and education—last on this list but perhaps first in importance. In less obvious ways, it also skews how people enjoy nature and experience sustainability. Each of these forms of inequality is decisively affected by residential, economic, and educational segregation. In its radical manifestation, segregation becomes separation, alienation, and apartheid expressed in those slums that today not only epitomize urban inequality but lead many to despair of a solution. Nonetheless, there are some modest but realistic solutions that suggest themselves when we understand the nature of urban inequality, solutions with which I will grapple in Chapter 8.

Housing

By the measure of urban realism, housing can be more critical than such basics as education. It may be the domain most amenable to redress. *Where* people live and the conditions under which they are housed are clearly critical factors in the quality of their lives, as well as in determining their access to schools, transportation, jobs, and nature (parks, green spaces, waterways).

Housing also is a crucial theater for urban segregation. As the unintended consequences of decisions taken in one domain can often affect others detrimentally, policy decisions made concerning housing turn out to impact each of the other domains under review here. An impressive example of this interdependence is how badly the noble attempt by city planners following Le Corbusier backfired as they essayed to construct low-income housing in high-rise buildings set down in wide-open green park spaces—so-called projects. Their aim was to design housing that was efficient and yet accessible to nature, where kids could play and adults breathe free: their efforts satisfied neither engineers nor naturalists, neither kids nor their parents.

Despite Le Corbusier's dream, the high-rise everywhere became a citadel of anonymity, isolation, and crime. Green and park spaces carved out from the urban streetscape between project high-rises were transformed into desolate backyards where gangs and drug runners could do their business unseen, hidden by insulated high-rise residents from whom architects had stolen the street-level perspective that—as Jane Jacobs in time would teach us—kept city streets safe. You don't have to be a city-dweller to understand why. Any theater spectator watching Elmer Rice's 1929 play *Street Scene* can quickly see how hot and crowded sidewalks that exist as real pedestrian space turn out to be a better bet for the drama of life and love (if not always safety) than the emptied lots around project high-rises, environs that take away security without giving much back in the way of neighborhood or nature.[49] Such projects manage rather to transform public into private, displacing a vibrant public street life to which first-floor brownstone or garden apartment residents can bear witness with a private carnival of criminality. In such infamous housing developments as Chicago's Cabrini-Green (finally razed in 2010) or the Louis Pink projects in Brooklyn (East New York), and in the old proletarian high-rises on the Parisian Périphérique now inhabited by poor immigrants, thugs rule while residents, fearing being thrown off rooftops or caught in gang war cross-fires, huddle inside barricaded apartments, the more isolated for living vertically. Inequalities are augmented rather than diminished by the very public policies and urban housing strategies intended to address them.

For policy makers wedded to ideas of residential stakeholding as an approach to urban stability in poor areas, high-rise apartments actually made it more difficult for residents to embrace their quarters. Low-rise walk-ups allowed individual residents both to feel like proprietors and to stamp properties with their own personalities (a window box, a small garden, a front door decoration or flag, school art in the windows, political signs on the door or stoop or front yard), also giving them direct access to sidewalks that both defined and delimited the permanence of "mine" and extended "mine" into the public thoroughfare, giving residents responsibility over sidewalk and street as urban front yards. No wonder that in Latin American high-rises built in the 1960s and 1970s as alternatives to the ramshackle shantytowns springing up on the periphery of burgeoning metropolises, the same lesson was being learned by unhappy residents of the new "middle-class" housing projects who—mystifying to good-willed city planners—opted to return to their shacks where their neighborhoods and street life gave their existence some meaning. The challenge of equal housing evokes what is almost a cliché: to find clean, affordable, and livable housing that does not extinguish street, neighborhood, and community.

Even under the best of circumstances, residential segregation by race and economic status makes it hard for residents to feel part of a larger metropolis or have access to its goods and services, even when they possess a clear sense of stakeholding and homesteading. The logic of the 1954 *Brown v. Board of Education* decision that, in principle if not in practice, ended the doctrine of separate but equal school segregation, can be applied to housing and other domains. Housing that is separate, however much money is spent on it, and however much "ownership" it entails, is unlikely to feel equal to its residents, or to create a community of equals among residents citywide. Nor will prohibiting segregation by law (more or less achieved in developed societies) end it de facto in housing any more than prohibiting educational segregation will end it de facto in schools.

The challenge for mitigation is clear, then, though anything but simple: equality without deracination, and anonymity without the loss of community: which is to say, community and neighborhood without de facto segregation and without the loss of equal access to all city resources; and desegregation without uniformity and without the loss of diversity and freedom.

Transportation

It might seem that transportation that is public is by definition a universally accessible public good relatively immune to the distortions of wealth or segregation. But what is public in theory can be less than public in practice. There are obviously significant ways in which routes, schedules, and availability of service can adversely impact different peoples and neighborhoods within a city that is residentially segmented if not also segregated. Subways (undergrounds or metros) can be routed (and often have been) to leave ghettos or suburban slums underserved—in order to prevent undergrounds from becoming (in the eyes of the wealthy) feared conduits for criminals or instruments of opportunistic integration. Or they may offer access to and movement around the inner city but prevent residents there from reaching wealthier districts, middle-class malls, or upscale working neighborhoods (big banks, corporate service companies such as law firms and accountants, Saskia Sassen's new economy). Try finding a bus service that runs from an inner-city ghetto to an upscale suburban mall.

Where public transportation is planned to serve poorer neighborhoods, it may eliminate express stops in rich neighborhoods, further "protecting" wealthier residents from "invasion" by the "wrong" persons. Beverly Hills has been engaged in a controversial effort to reroute the expansion of the Los Angeles Metro system westward, some think in order to avoid having a stop in downtown Beverly Hills, say in the vicinity of Rodeo Drive.[50] Or systems built to serve the wealthy may do so at the expense of the poorer neighborhoods. The Washington, D.C., Metro appears to avoid certain neighborhoods and favor others, while the R.E.R. express subway system in Paris seems to advantage wealthier suburbs such as La Défense (a suburban corporate cluster to the east of the Arc de Triomphe). Some may argue these permutations are random or inadvertent. I do not.

Sluggish transportation can also be an issue. In many of Brazil's suburban favelas, there are commuting opportunities so languorous that they require a three-hour round trip to workplaces. A study of commuting times in Rio showed that lower levels of employment and education among *favelados*, when compared to workers living inside

Rio—holding income levels constant—could be attributed to transportation schedules.[51]

The cost of public transportation can obviously also be critical: in Brazil that cost compares unfavorably to average worker salaries and other expenditures they must make. A slum household of four persons in Rio might pay almost as much on transport as it does on rent, and more than twice as much as it pays for food, for example.[52] Such transportation realities make it harder for the poor to go to where the goods are sold, or where the jobs that allow them to buy the goods are found. Even if the West Side spur of the L.A. Metro system eventually comes to Beverly Hills, the residential canyons above it will still remain unserved (unthreatened?) by public transportation at all, leaving the rich in what are for all practical effects gated communities, and complicating the quest of the poor for employment still further.

Wealthy residential neighborhoods also avail themselves of marginally legal practices to wall themselves in or fence others out by petitioning to close their streets to through traffic (with barricades or traffic diversions) and keep the "other" out, if they can, with walls and (as in Manila) with barbed wire and broken glass. Defensive burghers are inventive, and to isolate their neighborhoods from the poor, Carl Nightingale has observed, they have employed

> palisades, battlements, bastions, fences, gates, guard shacks, check-points, booms, railroad tracks, highways, tunnels, rivers, canals, inlets, mountainsides and ridges, buffer zones, free-fire zones, demilitarized zones, *cordon sanitaires*, screens of trees, road blocks, violent mobs, terrorism, the police, armies, curfews, quarantines, pass laws, labor compounds, building clearances, forced removals, restrictive covenants, zoning ordinances, racial steering practices, race-infused economic incentives, segregated private and public housing developments, exclusive residential compounds, gated communities, separate municipal governments and fiscal systems, discriminatory access to land ownership and credit, complementary systems of rural reservations, influx control laws, and restrictions against overseas immigration.[53]

The gated community in effect privatizes public roadways and interdicts public throughways. A simple roadblock at the connection point between a thoroughfare and a local residential street can be erected in the name of curbing commercial traffic and putatively preventing speeding through-vehicles from endangering residents, while actually closing off a neighborhood from unwanted outsiders. Even pedestrian zones, attractive in function and fully public in name, may be perceived differently by the poor and powerless, limiting access to those who cannot get to them by public transportation and cannot afford the steep parking fees. The same is true of "congestion" measures like the one introduced in London in 2003 that charges ten pounds to drive in Central London from 7 A.M. to 6 P.M., a sound idea in terms of reducing traffic and emissions but patently class skewed. The wealthy can afford to pay the fee while the poor cannot, so that a theoretically equitable plan actually becomes a solve-the-congestion-problem-by-keeping-the-poor-from-driving plan.[54]

The takeaway from transportation issues is that there are subtler ways to reinforce or exacerbate inequality, if inadvertently, than residential segregation. What appear initially as "solutions" to problems of sustainability and "public" goods can become impediments. The absence of fast public transportation on the model of Los Angeles or Phoenix is an obvious offense to equal opportunity and access. But there are many other ways in which extant public transportation can impact the poor detrimentally. In Paris, for example, the outer circular road (Périphérique) that affords convenient circumnavigation of the city for the general population has become a kind of vehicular moat separating former working-class suburbs that are now immigrant slums just outside the *Peri* from the prosperous Parisian arrondissements proper. In the United States, the building of highways was also sometimes class insensitive or worse, with new roads cutting through stable working-class neighborhoods or isolating working folks from business and shopping options.

Jobs

Political partisans jaw about unemployment and who is to blame for it, but no one doubts the role of jobs in securing equality. In her final book, a brief and incisive work on citizenship, the political theorist Judith

N. Shklar argued that employment is as crucial to civic status as nearly any other marker, including voting. "Earning," writes Shklar, "is implicit in equal American citizenship." To her this meant quite plainly that there is "a right to remunerated work." Joblessness is tantamount to a "loss of public respect, the reduction of standing and demotion to second-class citizenship."[55] If you work but don't vote, you may feel more embedded in the civic community than if you vote but are jobless. Working is the condition for lived citizenship, conferring dignity, responsibility, and power on the job holder in a fashion that makes voting seem relevant. Given that inequality is in the first instance economic, an urban economy that can provide stable, well-paid jobs with benefits also represents the most obvious and direct route to redress.

Observers as different as William Julius Wilson and Richard Florida have insisted on this point.[56] Although inequality may be caused by and manifests itself as racism or other forms of discrimination, what counts most both for the life of cities overall and for city dwellers themselves are discrimination's economic consequences. Racism per se corrupts racists even as it demeans those they target. Joblessness is a problem for the jobless, who need full economic rights first and liberation from bigoted neighbors only afterward. Racist slurs are demeaning, but redlining neighborhoods of color to exclude residents from receiving bank mortgages or business loans not only offends dignity but cripples economic opportunity. The absence of work prevents the poor from securing the means of their own liberation and increases dependency on so-called big government, public assistance programs, and philanthropy. It deprives them of the first emblem of status and dignity in a market society. President Obama remains a target of millions of blinkered American bigots, but he holds a pretty good job and enjoys the elevated status that goes with it—which is both what insulates him from the stupidity of the bigots and arouses their ire.

It is important to recall that while jobs are vital, their availability will not by itself guarantee greater equality. It is well-paid jobs with some prospect of longevity, that come with health benefits and pensions, that create a sustainable economy and a just urban landscape. The evidence of the last few years in the United States suggests that new jobs are paid less well than old (vanished) jobs and come without pensions or comparable benefits—although the Affordable Care Act (Obamacare), if states allow it to be fully implemented, will help. "Few Cities Have Regained Jobs They Lost," trumpets the *New York Times*, citing a report focused on the absence of any real help from the federal government during the recession years.[57] Worse still, while "a majority of the jobs that were lost" during the recession were middle income, "a majority of those added during the recovery have been low-paying."[58] The result is less a jobs deficit than a "good jobs deficit," which thwarts a long-term full recovery for many cities. Union membership in the United States has declined along with manufacturing jobs and is scarcely more than 11 percent of all workers in the private sector. The decline has many causes, but its impact on job security and benefits is singularly decisive.

Given these discouraging data, the role of public sector jobs looms large in the city, where in both the developed and developing worlds between 15 and 25 percent of urban jobs are public—in New York City, 15 percent; in Johannesburg, 17 percent; in Rio de Janeiro over 18 percent; and in London and New Delhi, nearly 22 percent.[59] The urban reliance on public employment is a strong virtue, but it also makes cities vulnerable both to an economic turndown that depresses public employment and to outside political forces demonizing the public sector and trying to strangle cities. Market fundamentalists attack urban and regional governments for not creating jobs but campaign simultaneously to defund or at least de-unionize all the public jobs that city governments do create.

City jobs are, to be sure, vulnerable to the perils of corruption, one important aspect of which turns patronage and the skewing of hiring into a perverse virtue with respect to public employment. Let me be clear: urban corruption is an unmitigated disaster for democracy in the long term. Payoff in jobs may help the urban economy, often in its most vulnerable sectors, but it undermines urban democracy. Corruption is a universal political affliction, but cities are often especially vulnerable. Just consider the damage former mayors now under indictment have done in the cities that elected them as trustees. Just in the last few years, the corruption hall of urban shame had inducted C. Ray Nagin of New Orleans, Bo Xilai of Dalian in China, Tony F. Mack of Trenton, Vasilis

Papageorgopoulos of Thessaloniki (Greece's second-largest city), Kwame Kilpatrick of Detroit, Loris Cereda of the northern Italian town of Buccinasco (Cereda was also convicted of cheating by the Italian chess federation!), Sharpe James of Newark, Francisco Rodriguez of the Spanish city of Ourense, and Igor Bestuzhy of Stavropol in Russia. (Another Russian mayor—Yevgeny Dushko of Sergiyev Posad—was shot dead for *alleging* corruption by others); and never mind mayoralty corruption in narco-states such as Mexico and Colombia.[60]

Corruption's multiple downsides are obvious. Yet there are many cities where the alternatives to it may seem worse: indigence, poverty, and irrelevance. One still could marvel in the old Soviet Union at how many seemingly marginal jobs (women sitting in front of restrooms or sweeping and resweeping public building hallways) contributed to public employment. When such jobs are called "make-work" (they are that) and cut in the name of efficiency and market capitalism, productivity and profits may increase, but public employment and its many benefits decline.

Like make-work, corruption can effect inequality, though with consequences more ambiguous than generally recognized. Not that there is ever an argument that corruption can seriously mitigate injustice, since by definition it is unjust and usually affects the least advantaged most egregiously. Nonetheless, immigrants and newcomers may be benefited by inefficiency and even by mild workplace corruption, as the waves of immigrants a century ago in New York and Chicago and newcomers flocking to São Paulo and Mumbai today will attest. Corruption (even crime) undermines community and impedes democracy long term, but in the short run it can appear as an equalizer, a kind of crude fast track to proximate equality. This no more justifies corruption than Katherine Boo's vivid portrait of Mumbai children—earning subsistence earnings from sorting and selling the garbage in which, quite literally, they live— justifies child labor. But as Boo writes, "In the West, and among some in the Indian elite, this word, *corruption*, has purely negative connotations: it was seen as blocking India's modern, global ambitions. But for the poor of a country where corruption thieved a great deal of opportunity, corruption was one of the genuine opportunities that remained."[61]

To take equality and justice seriously, then, we must always ask the question: corruption by whom? crime against whom? in whose interests? Crime is in most instances a consequence of greed, selfishness, and psychic disorders; but it can also reflect a twisted society in which criminality appears as the only way out for certain people on the margins. In the setting of a fair, equitable society in which equal opportunity belongs to all, both crime and corruption are unequivocal evils. But in a rigid, hierarchical society in which exploitation and unfairness are built into a system, where upward mobility is a dubious proposition and bigotry and segregation close many of the conventional roads to integration and assimilation, those same behaviors become compensatory opportunities—not "goods" but tolerable tactics in the struggle against systemic injustice.[62]

In Brecht's towering play *Mother Courage*, one of her sons responds to a charge that he is exploiting army corruption by blurting out, "Thank God they're corrupt. Corruption is the equivalent of God's mercy. As long as someone's on the take, you can buy a shorter sentence, so even the innocent have a shot at justice." Katherine Boo merely shows how poor residents of Mumbai live Brecht's cynical idealism—corruption as a last remaining chance to stay alive.[63] In Mexico City or Kabul, Medellín or Bangkok, where police corruption directly endangers local residents, Boo's lessons of Annawadi seem less convincing. Yet even in such cities (and Mumbai also suffers from police corruption in its approach to rape, for example), corruption is more a testament to the failures of democracy in other domains—the persistence of segregation, the ignoring of poverty, the neglect of injustice. Those afflicted by the latter evils might be forgiven for seeing in the former some twisted form of a good, of democracy itself understood as a leveling down that lets them in the game.

Ideally, of course, reforming urban inequality in jobs and other domains calls for systemic if not revolutionary change. Yet as this discussion suggests, partial and contextualized solutions that work under the constrained circumstances of an unfair global society look like a better bet. Most of the solutions put forward in the next chapter are of the second kind—mitigation rather than transformation.

Security and Crime

Crime is not an equal opportunity affliction in the city. An unwritten urban law mandates that the middle class get the subways, the jobs, the pedestrian malls, and the bike lanes and the poor get the gangs, the drugs, and the crime along with the zero-tolerance surveillance and stop-and-frisk tactics conceived as their antidote. For actors ascending the ladder of class, including the poor, crime (at least of the violent kind) may only be a stopping point on the lower rungs; but for those with less mobility, hemmed in by poverty as a state of mind, victimhood and preying on victims become permanent features of economic life. Again, Katherine Boo recognizes that even as India "aggressively addresses" the old problems of poverty, disease, illiteracy, and child labor, it ignores those "other old problems, corruption and exploitation of the weak by the less weak" that are allowed to continue "with minimal interference."[64] For the ambitious poor who lack patience, a nine-millimeter Glock pistol can feel more weighty in pursuing life achievement than a 200-page textbook, and a busy corner location for petty drug trafficking may look more promising for a career than a classroom seat in a community college computer course.

The dialectic of urban life is not equally shared: the poor are victimized by its vices far more than others, while the wealthy are better able to enjoy its virtues. When Chicago's murder rate shot up 38 percent in 2012, there was, as is typical of urban violence, no evidence of a broader crime wave. Yet on the day three people were murdered by terrorists in Boston in the spring of 2013, drawing frenzied media attention, a dozen young black men in Chicago died in gang shootings, with no media attention at all.

Much the same is true in Mexico City or Manila, Kinshasa or Karachi. In Chicago, "the violence has left its largest scars in one of Chicago's most impoverished, strolling neighborhoods . . . places within view of the city's gleaming downtown skyline that feel worlds apart."[65] In Mexico, where criminal syndicates infiltrate and corrupt police and political hierarchies, there is almost the feel of a failed state; once again it is the poor who suffer most from the ensuing mayhem, along with the journalists trying to chronicle the slaughter.[66]

In Afghanistan, where 90 percent of the world's opium is produced, corruption is a way of life from the president on down. It couldn't exist without the markets in which it is sold, where users point to the evils of third-world narco-states with one hand while scoring a bag with the other. It is estimated that 50 percent of revenue raised by the border police in Afghanistan disappears before it reaches the central government treasury. However high up the instigators of crime and corruption, high crime rates everywhere manifest victims victimizing victims: black-on-black crime, poor-on-poor crime, young-poor-on-aging-poor crime, male-poor-on-female-poor crime. Crime tracks poverty, and treating it means addressing injustice. This is not a bleeding-heart-liberal mantra, just a social fact.

As a response to crime, the presence of effective policing (as with other public goods) is sometimes inversely correlated with the crime it is meant to combat. Ghettos may see more of the special units and gang- and drug-busting programs, but less of the ordinary attention and street patrols (whether on foot or in cars) that make neighborhoods safer through preventive policing. Slum residents will be stopped and frisked more often, but have their complaints about crimes perpetrated against them investigated less frequently and effectively than other wealthier denizens of the city. Indeed, crime prevention tactics such as stop and frisk (as in Mayor Bloomberg's New York or Mayor Nutter's Philadelphia) and zero-tolerance may succeed in disarming gun-toting teens and outing big-time criminals by catching them in petty crimes, but they often do so at the expense of holding an entire population hostage to forms of surveillance and oversight that not only infringe rights but reduce dignity and diminish rather than augment the feeling of security.

The problem is sufficiently dire to have drawn the attention of the courts in Philadelphia and New York. The U.S. District Court in Manhattan called out the city's "deeply troubling apathy towards New Yorkers' most fundamental constitutional rights," while the Appellate Division of the State Supreme Court in Manhattan said in a 3–2 decision that a "gradual erosion of this basic liberty can only tatter the constitutional fabric upon which this nation was built."[67] Sadly, however, and attesting to the dilemma, where city officials in Philadelphia have been sensitive to civil rights claims, a slowdown in stop and frisk seems to have been attended by a sharp rise in the murder rate.[68]

As with so many urban strategies, efforts such as stop and frisk intended to make things better do make them better, but by also making them worse. Within the circle of poverty, whether in the domain of transportation or security, solutions make for new problems, while problems resist new solutions; it is in the nature of inequality that it not only generates problems but colonizes solutions. We will look in the next chapter, for example, at corruption as a job creator, yet it exacts a high price in the form of indifference to crime or even (as happens in countries like Mexico, Afghanistan, Colombia, and the Congo) complicity by public officials in criminality. Indian women have learned that reporting rape to the police is more likely to compound than resolve their problems. Of 600 reported rapes (and only a tiny portion are reported), just one perpetrator was actually tried and convicted in New Delhi in 2012. And it took five weeks and an international scandal for the police even to arrest the five men accused of raping and murdering a young woman on a semipublic bus at the end of 2012. Women are more likely to be urged by the police to marry their attackers than they are to witness an arrest, let alone justice.[69] If there are so few cities in the world where policing is color-blind and justice truly even-handed, it is hard to imagine how urban injustice is going to be fully overcome.

Education

The education deficit in the West and around the world is a commonplace of critics reacting to developed-world urban principles and the U.N. Millennium Goals, a policy priority so essential to equality that to mention it is to trivialize it. Andrew Hacker, among many others, has demonstrated decisively that there is no better predictor of economic success or failure or life income or class status than level of education attained. Residential segregation has devastating effects on the economic prospects of the poor, but its impact on class and employment comes first of all through its impact on educational opportunity.

Moreover, democratic citizenship and thus civic empowerment depends on education. We know that political participation correlates directly with years spent in school. Dropouts don't vote, people in prison can't vote, and the poor generally won't vote. Democracy depends on voters being educated in order to be motivated to vote, but it also depends on educated voters capable of deliberation and debate, of assimilating data and making informed judgments, in order to make self-governance a reality. Education understood broadly, not just as training and schooling but as immersion in the arts of liberty that define the real meaning of the liberal arts, is the difference between a self-interested economic actor and a citizen; between the impulsive animal and the deliberative agent. Cities have special obligations to education because in addition to schooling, they are home to museums, libraries, universities, research bodies, and cultural institutions. Their commitment to learning must be broad and deep if they are to retain their character as cosmopolitan capitals (Chapter 10). And if this commitment is to ensure equality, these educational institutions must be public and free, paid from general revenues rather than through private compensation and admission fees. This imperative makes very large demands on cities already financially strapped, making its achievement problematic. Public education and public institutions of science, research, learning, and culture nonetheless remain an indispensable condition of equality, and without them neither democracy nor justice is likely to be achieved.

Nature

Our first five domains of inequality are widely recognized, and my task here has been to comprehend their character in order to point to possible mitigation strategies. I leave till last a feature much less often debated, yet a key to urban injustice. It is not just its novelty that makes it of interest, but its relevance to the great urban dilemma I introduced in the opening chapters: how to reclaim and incorporate into the city that natural bounty of the countryside surrendered by immigrants on their fateful journey from country to town. Since urbanity entails an increase in density and proximity and hence a loss of access to space and solitude, offering equal access to the assets that return these benefits to the city—nature, parks, green spaces, waterfronts—becomes a key tactic in securing true urban equality. Especially when we recall that urban life is largely coastal or water-oriented and that access to water as a feature of nature can be a key factor in achieving equality. When we debate transportation or education or housing, equal access seems an obvious issue, yet it often goes missing in the conversation about nature, water, and sustainability. Access to clean water, safe food, and breathable air is an aspect of the right to life. Moreover, in a world of interdependent water supplies, global agriculture, and cross-border pollution, the impact of cataclysmic climate change falls unevenly on the backs of the poor. The water wars devastate the poor above all. As depicted by Vandana Shiva, they are likely to displace oil wars in future battles for survival. Meanwhile, food is so intimately tied up with climate (and climate change) that the two can no longer be disentangled.[70] These large issues are the backdrop to every discussion of nature and justice in the urban setting. But my focus here is not on the sustaining of nature but access to it.

Parks are the lungs of the city, and hence crucial in establishing a rural presence within the urban—saving urbanity from itself, as it were. This is true literally as well as figuratively. Eric Jaffe suggests urban parks can "enhance your brain" while trees can impact crime rates.[71] More mundanely, Paul Scherer estimates that urban green spaces can provide "substantial urban benefits. . . . Trees in New York City removed an estimated 1,821 metric tons of air pollution in 1994" alone, for example.[72] Yet the poor are often deprived of the right to "breathe freely." A 2008 U.K. study found that "populations that are exposed to the greenest environments also have the lowest levels of health inequality related to income deprivation."[73] Since parks are not equally distributed across city neighborhoods, deprivation patterns are skewed. In Los Angeles, for example, areas with predominantly Latino populations have 0.6 park acres per 1,000 population and areas with predominantly African-American populations have 1.7 park acres per 1,000, while white-dominated areas have 31.8 park acres per 1,000.[74] High-poverty neighborhoods suffer the most: 300,000 young people in tracts with 20 percent or higher poverty have no access at all to parks.

Comparing cities in other parts of the world is equally telling. Hanoi, for example, has only 0.3 percent of its land devoted to parks, while Bangkok has over twice that amount. Cairo opened a 70-acre park (Al-Azhar Park) that is the largest in North Africa.[75] Built on a former field of garbage, it encompassed a twelfth-century Ayyubid wall and rehabilitation of the fourteenth-century Umm Sultan Shaban Mosque and other historic sites. City officials tried to tie the park to economic stimulus, offering microcredits to residents to develop word-carving and other skills in the park. Total acreage, however, is less important than distribution. Washington, D.C., has 12.9 acres per 1,000 residents while New York has just 6 and Chicago 4.2. Washington, nevertheless, is both segregated and rife with poverty, with African-Americans most impacted. Cairo's park served poorer neighborhoods.[76] In Turkey, a threat to a park in Istanbul's Taksim Square nearly brought down the government of Prime Minister Erdogan.

The urban plight of African-Americans with respect to park access has a certain irony, given that they traded in their rural history and access to nature (one of the few advantages of that history) for what was supposed to be urban opportunity. From the late 1930s through the 1970s, in a vast migration portrayed movingly by Nicholas Lemann a generation ago, more than five million African-Americans moved from the rural South to the urban North.[77] They did indeed secure jobs, improved education, and enhanced opportunity, but at the price not just of their historical homeland but of that access to nature that was their rural Southern homeland's lost gift. Middle-class urbanites are potentially hot-weather "summerfolk" (see Maxim Gorky's play of the same name for an early account) with seasonal cottages on the land. They also enjoy the luxury of countryside urban benefits like the parks built specifically for them, the waterfront playgrounds developed for them from old industrial and port sites in cities like Baltimore and Singapore, or new boutique natural preserves like Manhattan's High Line (on a lower Manhattan abandoned elevated rail line) and Chicago's Millennium Park, with its fetching combination of architectural wonders (the Jay Pritzker Pavilion, the Crown Fountain, the Lurie Garden, and the Cloud Gate) and pop carnival entertainment.

In theory, these spaces are public and open to all, but topography, transportation, and cultural use can skew the reality, leaving the poor feeling short-changed in their own residential neighborhoods. Hence the complaint that the charming High Line is more accessible to tourists than many residents of poorer neighborhoods in the distant boroughs of

New York City. On the other hand, the Harlem-adjacent Hudson River Park at 135th Street and the north side gardens and skating rink of Harlem-side Central Park are quite properly celebrated for their proximity to Harlem's now mixed but still predominantly lower-income neighborhoods. Test cases such as the proposed "Grand Park" in Los Angeles (squeezed between City Hall and Disney Hall and meant both to serve nearby poorer neighborhoods and to revitalize the downtown dead district of the city) will turn on how well they actually serve poorer communities and neighborhoods where only a handful of small but precious refurbished parks like MacArthur and Lafayette are currently to be found.[78]

Poverty, injustice, and segregation in every relevant urban sector in both slum "planets," first-world and third-world, remain major obstacles to urban equality and hence the role of cities in nurturing democratic global governance. Too many of the urban advantages we celebrate, from creativity and culture to trade and diversity, have consequences that accrue to the middle and upper classes at the expense of the poor. What should be common city assets become zero-sum games in which one (rich) man's redevelopment plan spells another (poor) man's loss of center-city housing; in which a wealthy woman's riverside playground is housed in former manufacturing warehouses from which poor women's sewing jobs have fled. Too often, city corruption is defined in ways that exempt white-collar criminality (bank redlining to enforce segregation, for example, or bundling and reselling mortgage debt to distant investors insulated from responsibility to borrowers), even as it highlights activities of the poor that, while illegal, might ease their plight, if only temporarily (like the numbers game). Inequality comes in many forms, and—appropriately in this era of interdependence—these forms are intimately linked. Attack educational discrimination, and it reappears as housing discrimination. Increase the number of working-class jobs, and inadequate transportation blocks the poor from getting to them.

With the problems so ingrained and their origin at least in part associated with national and global forces outside the city, remediation is extraordinarily difficult. Only with innovation and imagination is inequality likely to be touched. Only if we are willing to look at the informal as well as the formal economy, and ignore the common wisdom about corruption and squatting and hidden capital, are we likely to find some partial answers to the burdens under which the most progressive and prosperous cities labor. Only if the underlying and intransigent realities of urban segregation in all its forms can be addressed are we likely to instigate mitigation successfully.

AYODELE ADEWALE OF LAGOS

Being mayor anywhere is a tough job. Running the show in an African megacity with burgeoning megaslums in what is nonetheless a relatively wealthy city in a mineral- and oil-rich country is a mega headache. **AYODELE ADEBOWALE ADEWALE**, still in his late thirties and not so long ago a chemistry major at Lagos State University, is technically the executive chairman of the Amuwo Odofin Local Government Area of Lagos State since 2008. But his constituents call him the mayor of Lagos, and in his second term he understands the burdens the title carries—whether mayor or executive chairman.

Born only in 1975, Adewale is a new breed of African mayor with roots in civic activism and political protest rather than military service or tribal politics. To him, "activism is just a medium of expressing yourself particularly if you have a government that is not pro-active or a government that does not obey the rule of law. Then you have the right to civil disobedience. Activism does not mean that you're not part of the society and does not make you an angel."[1]

Adewale would not endear himself to America's conservative legislators, since he has put local government to big purposes: to address unemployment and redirect urban policy toward public sanitation, sustainability, safety, and youth education. He has imposed road use fees to fund new road and sewer projects that employ 6,000 young men, and he is unapologetic. "I am a social critic who advocates for positive change," he says. "The most excellent way to convince people that this change is feasible is to contest for an elective position in government where you will have the authority to effect the changes you consider appropriate that would make a difference." He seems to think, against the cynicism of our times, that this is the meaning of democracy.

Neither angel nor political hack, Adewale is clearly his own man. He sometimes refers to Marx in ways that will seem atavistic: "Marx said man is a political animal, but I say man is a political being." And he is sometimes called "comrade" by his, well, comrades. But his achievements are pragmatic and have come in a hurry. In his first year in office he is credited with

- creating hundreds of new jobs in important public sectors from education and health to drainage and road work—6,000 aimed at young people;
- a program of free pharmaceuticals for children under sixteen and seniors above sixty, with 10 percent reduction in prices for all others. Nearly 20,000 residents have benefited as a result of these changes, and improvements in postnatal service and upgrades of primary health centers;
- in education, promoting a new online schooling project, distributing nearly a half million school exercise books and 7,000 school bags, replacing chalk with markers and marker boards, and providing new schools (and life jackets!) for children in underserved river-area slums;
- offering a city-sponsored microcredit program at near-zero interest rate for applicants who can secure a reputable sponsor; hundreds have applied, and many have been approved;
- environmentally, furthering the work on drainage (above), which has cleared drains of silt and reduced flooding risk; planting 4,500 trees as part of a greening project;
- starting a community newspaper (*Amuwo Odofin Prism*) as a community platform, and engaging residents in town hall meetings;
- developing a public-private partnership with the private security firm Blue Waters Security to enhance public safety using new tech security equipment and new security posts;
- expanding public transportation through a contract with Ashok-Leyland Motors (India) to build one hundred buses at a nearby plant

in Ojo; the buses will seat fifty-seven passengers and be equipped with cash-free electronic fare gear; and

- planning recycling plants capable of yielding bio-fuels as part of an environmental greening program.

Lists like this are not necessarily very compelling and can represent little more than official propaganda. After all, Adewale is known as a publicity hound and campaigned to win the 2012 World Mayor award. (He did not succeed.) Cynics will thus be tempted to see many of these programs as traditional patronage aimed at securing constituents and building a public reputation. But all of Adewale's reforms reflect a focus on real urban problems from unemployment and poor transportation to pollution and alternative energy, and the results to date represent genuine improvements achieved in a very difficult setting.

In the words of a supporter, Adewale is "the youngest elected Chairman [ever, who has made] his local community which used to be slum . . . into a cosmopolitan city within the fastest growing megacity in Africa. He has created an economic growth hub for the state. He has brought free healthcare, good roads, fuller citizen participation, security to the area and has increased the value of his local government. He measures himself by the standards of global leadership and democratic practices, and has diplomatic relations with mayors of Mexico and South Africa."[2] More than anything else, Adewale looks and acts like a mayor: a pragmatist operating locally while engaging globally to solve real problems with real fixes. That would be a boon to any global metropolis. In a developing world megacity in Africa like Lagos, it is—let's not be patronizing and call it a miracle—a genuine blessing.

CHAPTER 8. CITY, CURE THYSELF!

Mitigating Inequality

> Lively, diverse, intense cities contain the seeds of their own regeneration.
>
> *Jane Jacobs,* The Death and Life of Great American Cities

> We need to make sure that we're building . . . neighborhoods that are mixed, where people from different backgrounds, ethnicities, and particularly income levels can live in the same neighborhoods. . . . Social inclusion . . . can go a long way in reducing inequality.
>
> *Mayor Naheed Nenshi, Calgary*

> If you fix cities, you kind of fix the world.
>
> *Tony Hsieh, CEO of Zappos*

> Youth unemployment is an incredible problem in Europe, [where] we have 5.5 million youngsters without jobs, without hope. . . . I think it's awful for me, it's an awful situation. [To deal with it] we will need different levels of responsibility and competence, but it will only happen if we have different ways of cooperation. Not hierarchical.
>
> *Mayor Wolfgang Schuster, Stuttgart*

Inequality and injustice appear as intractable features of the city because they are endemic to its urban character—its density, its topographical and demographic inclination to segregation, its "natural" ghettos, its susceptibility to economic stratification. This is cause for deep pessimism. But the sources of mitigation and amelioration, I will argue here, are also endemic to the city, and this offers grounds for hope. As Jane Jacobs says, "cities contain the seeds of their own regeneration." Inequality can be addressed by such urban characteristics as mobility, creativity, and innovation. Richard Florida has been arguing for some time that "urban centers have long been crucibles for innovation and creativity." Now, he notes, "they are coming back. Their turnaround is driven in large measure by the attitudes and location choices of the Creative Class."[1]

Those features that contribute to urban inequality can be the consequence of particular cultures and histories as they shape the development of different metropolises.[2] But they need not be specifically urban and often are the product of a global market society that affects cities and nations alike in both their rural and urban regions. When Michael Harrington published his groundbreaking *The Other America* in 1962, he did not so much describe as discover American poverty, and it was not at America's cities that he was looking back then. Inequality at that time was construed as something foreign by a nation unwilling to look inward; it was regarded as the problem of starving children in India to whom Americans might send their scraps. Harrington startled the country by showing just how *American* poverty could be, with 22 percent of the population under the poverty level. But in Harrington's America, inequality was still predominantly white (if a rising issue for minorities) and largely rural in its character. Appalachia rather than Harlem was its signature venue. Harrington brought the reality of the emerging global economy home by referring to the "underdeveloped nation in our midst."[3]

Yet whatever poverty's sources—local or universal—in the last half century inequality has urbanized right along with the world. Today, it threatens to leave the majority world population that lives in cities in destitution, and to obstruct and undermine the city's prospective role as a facilitator of cross-border civic cooperation and informal global governance. Skeptics may even suggest that this stark reality puts the fundamental objective of the argument here in doubt: if the "other America's" inequality today is city centered and if the "second planet of slums" is predominantly urban, how can global democracy be advanced by globalizing the city? Mitigation is the more challenging because, we have seen, cities often cannot control their own destinies. They are too dependent on the sovereignty and fiscal dominion of central governments. Patrick Sharkey has argued that the United States needs to make a "sustained commitment" to urban neighborhoods, yet acknowledges the reality that "cities are entering a new era of neglect by the federal government," despite (failed) programs from the Obama administration's White House Office of Urban Policy such as the "Promise Neighborhoods" project.[4]

This leaves cities reliant on solutions to their problems that can at best only be partial and hence never altogether satisfying. Nonetheless, diminished power has its advantages, inasmuch as it leads to greater pragmatism and a makeshift but effective focus on getting done whatever can be done within prevailing limits. Driven by universal ideologies and empowered by sovereignty and central government, nations too often imagine they can *cure* maladies, eradicate problems completely. They end up incapacitated by their power and hubris. Cities offer a stark contrast: pragmatic in approach, close to real people and their problems, and without sufficient autonomous power to cure anything independently, they must be satisfied with mitigation. They operate interdependently both with the governmental regimes to which they belong and among one another, to ameliorate conditions beyond their solitary power to solve. They do what can be done rather than all that should be done. Ironically, their dependency drives cities to interdependence.

When nations face up to limits on their power, their obsession with their sovereignty tends to make them peevish rather than humble. Unable to do everything, they too often stubbornly do nothing, as has happened with climate change and weapons proliferation. Striving only to mitigate, seeking small and partial successes measured by what is possible, cities achieve real if modest progress, often through compromise and cooperation. Several hundred mayors went to Copenhagen and then Mexico City and Rio and did what nations had failed to do: signed on to carbon reduction protocols. As a tactic of the relatively powerless, mitigation gets things done, permitting progress toward networking and informal cross-border governance to continue.

If a degree of greater fairness and increased opportunity can be achieved in the short run through piecemeal tactical approaches rooted in core urban traits such as creativity and the informal economy, and if we can find in democracy itself a key to addressing the defects of democracy, we may be able to legitimize our quest to give cities and their mayors global influence. If revolution is undesirable or impossible and if cities are to act democratically in seeking solutions to inequality from within, then there are two realistic urban strategies: make the city's core urban traits sources for addressing its inequalities; and ask democracy to overcome its deficiencies democratically. To the city and democracy alike, the demand must be cure thyself! But how to do that?

Ameliorating Poverty: City, Cure Thyself!

The editor of the *New Republic*, Tim Noah, acknowledges that his remedies for correcting inequalities in wealth are unlikely to be "enacted anytime soon," but in his book *The Great Divergence* he still is anxious to try "soaking the rich," "fattening government payrolls," importing more skilled labor, universalizing preschool, imposing price controls on colleges and universities, and regulating Wall Street. Oh yes, and reviving the labor movement (about 11 percent of the workforce in the United States today and not a factor in much of the developing world).[5] If we were able to do all that, the problems we would then be positioned to address would no longer exist. So let me put aside universal measures addressed to global market forces and consider instead what I have called the self-correcting features of urban life. The inequality debate raises important issues of capitalism and socialism, yet in ways too ideological to yield practical solutions, especially in the city, where pragmatism is a virtue and a short time span the counsel of urgency.

I will not try to convince fans of Charles Murray he is mistaken in insisting that the word *capitalist* "has become an accusation" or that too many capitalists are themselves left-wingers who "appear to accept the mind-set that kept the world in poverty for millennia."[6] Miring ourselves in a fundamentalist critique of capitalism or the big-government/small-government quandary makes little sense. Instead of wrestling in the political mud, I want to explore pragmatic best practices that can affect segregation and inequality, and perhaps even ameliorate market fundamentalism down the line. I will be satisfied if we can achieve an outcome less inegalitarian and more democratic than any alternatives, and hence ensure that mayors do not in the first instance become planetary slumlords.

Mayor Nenshi of Calgary worries that "great cities have inequality and wealth by definition: the reason they are cities is because people come from different parts of the income scale." Yet there is a corollary: great cities also have characteristics that permit them to combat and overcome inequality. Despite the crucial difference between inequality in the developed and developing worlds, these characteristics suggest common (glocal) approaches to the problems of inequality and injustice available to cities everywhere. The abstract idea of "glocality" (a paradoxical fusion of the global and the local) takes on concrete meaning in the city, where government is local, about neighbors and neighborhood democracy, but also about universal urban issues and global intercity networks. Alexis de Tocqueville insisted that liberty is always municipal, yet we know today it cannot survive without exercising a global reach.

The mobility, innovation, entrepreneurship, and creativity typical of cities allows them to experiment and reform themselves, and borrow and adapt best practices from others. The differences people bring with them to the city generate the inequality that worries Mayor Nenshi, but their very diversity becomes an element in the city's variety and mobility. Nations are, to be sure, different from one another: Switzerland as a landlocked alpine nation cannot borrow Holland's sea-based trade policies. But Zurich and Amsterdam can exchange drug policy information and borrow bike-share and anticongestion programs. Inequality in Nigeria is of a different order than inequality in France, but rapid-transit, limited-access bus lanes can ease traffic and ameliorate the plight of poor people trying to get to jobs in both Lagos and Paris.

The city has in the past always been a magnet to rural dwellers because it promised creativity and mobility—an arena of change in a world of stasis. Although no longer true in every case, especially in the developing world, as compared to the countryside the city today remains what historically America was to Europe: a bounteous arena of possibility where the past can be left behind and the future made present—where the gaze shifts from the ground upward and tracks towers and skyscrapers; where self is less rooted in an essentialist nature and more susceptible to plasticity and self-invention; where inequality is a challenge but not a destiny.

Creativity and plasticity, like innovation and mobility, are twins in the city. Future-thinking is a critical draw to immigrants who leave "old" countries for the "new world," leave the land to embrace the urban. "I am an American," exclaimed Mitt Romney in the speech in which he accepted the 2012 presidential nomination, "I make my own destiny." Romney was hoping to seduce country folk, but his was the cry of city dwellers over the millennia and is what draws country folk imprinted in the old ways to the liberating tabula rasa of the metropolis.

In Boswell's *London Journal*, the young scribe reported in 1763 on how in London he had "discovered that we may be in some degree whatever character we choose."[7] In the same era in Paris, in his *Rameau's Nephew*, the philosophe Diderot depicted a character so plastic as to become a literary sensation. Yet Diderot was doing little more than parodying an anomic and scattered new urban man:

> Nothing is more unlike him than himself. Sometimes he is thin and haggard, like an invalid in the final stages of consumption. You could count his teeth through his cheeks. . . . The next month, he's sleek and plump, as if he had been eating steadily at a banker's table or had been shut up inside a Bernadine convent. Today, in dirty linen and torn trousers, dressed in rags, almost barefoot, he slinks along with his head down. One is tempted to call to him to give him a hand out. Tomorrow, he marches along with his head high, powdered, his hair curled, well dressed, with fine shoes. . . .
> He lives from day to day, sad or happy, according to circumstances.

Of himself, the young Rameau says in Diderot's words, "The Devil take me if I have any idea what I am deep down. In general, my mind is as round as a ball and my character as open as a wicker chair—I'm never false if I have any interest in being truthful and never truthful if I have any interest in being dishonest."[8] Rameau, proudly plastic and inauthentic, is the new man Rousseau despises. The Tartuffes and Rameaus embody the creative (read immoral) city Rousseau censors, because it turns inauthenticity into a virtue and treats deformity as self-invention.

Yet to modern celebrants of the city, self-invention and creativity are leading urban virtues. Diderot's essay is part of the empiricist's modern metaphysics. We are blank tablets (tabula rasa) on which environment and circumstances inscribe character. The city helps wipe away any essential features supposedly placed there by God or deep human "nature." The consequences of this empiricist turn, for our purposes, are momentous: inequality is evidently acquired, not natural, and hence subject to correction. The city may be a seat of injustice, but it also contains the tools and points of view that allow us to secure justice. Self-invention may be a perversion of nature, but it allows an escape from the natural past and thus from that weighed history that Voltaire construed as little other than superstition and error.

The metaphysics are mostly gone today, but current admirers of the city share the Enlightenment preoccupation with mobility, creativity, and innovation; they agree that inequality is amenable to mitigation and that cities can self-improve even where nations cannot and do not. In her *Cities and the Wealth of Nations,* Jane Jacobs observed that just because they are salient political and military entities, nations are not necessarily "the basic, salient entities of economic life."[9] It is rather the city and its capacity for innovation that grow urban economies. "Cities do not depend on the entire nation state for their growth" although "neither do they exist on their own here—they depend on surrounding regions."[10]

No one since Jane Jacobs has made the argument for creative invention as an engine of urban growth and reform as compellingly (and controversially) as Richard Florida, with his focus on the captivating notion of the creative class. "Urban centers," he writes, "have long been crucibles for innovation and creativity. Now they are coming back. Their turnaround is driven in large measure by the attitudes and location choices of the Creative Class."[11] Citing George Gilder, Florida recognizes that traditional big cities may reflect "leftover baggage from the industrial era." They create conditions of stagnation and economic suburbanization (sprawl), and they encourage the development of so-called edge cities that actually undermine urbanity. Yet he sees too that neither size nor density is a crucial measure of what energizes the city or allows it to recover from downturns. Stubbornly hopeful in the way of urban optimists from time immemorial, Florida insists, "it turns out that what matters most for a city's metabolism—and ultimately for its economic growth—isn't density itself but how much people mix with each other."[12] Productivity and economic growth cannot in themselves guarantee equality, which depends more on patterns of distribution and government policies of redistribution. Without growth, however, jobs cannot be created and poverty cannot be addressed.

The good news when it comes to jobs and their relationship to inequality is that the underlying fundamentals of the city, such as its diversity, afford more economic opportunity than other venues. After all, urbanization is driven and thus defined in part by the concentration of resources and such economic forces as immigration, mobility, proximity, and creativity, all features that give cities their entrepreneurial attractions and draw in people both from the countryside and from the larger world beyond. Cities are gateways for immigrants seeking jobs in an open and mobile environment; they are magnets for the ambitious and adventuresome everywhere. Despite its technological feasibility in the age of digital media, the experiment with economic decentralization and business suburbanization as practiced in the final decades of the last century has been largely abandoned. New information-economy efficiencies may lend themselves to home offices and suburban corporate parks, but the underlying attraction of dense populations, social proximity, cultural friction, and urban creativity—the seductive edginess of city life—make cities a natural habitat for business, bosses and employees alike. It wasn't a surprise to students of the city when Marissa Mayer, Yahoo! Inc. CEO, ended Yahoo's experiment with work-at-home employees, specifically citing the need for creative workers to be engaged in "communication and collaboration" that comes only when people are "working side-by-side. . . . That is why it is critical that we are all present in our offices."[13]

As Richard Florida has shown, it is a "people climate," not tax breaks and government handouts, that draws business to cities; it is the "frills and frivolities," as Florida's critics describe them, the creative pleasures of urban life that *spur* economic development, rather than being their consequence.[14] We see Florida's argument vindicated in urban homesteading by artists in neighborhoods without economic promise and how it can transform those neighborhoods, drawing in business and other entrepreneurs and integrating them into a once-segregated city (riverfront St. Louis, for example, or Soho and Brooklyn). Today even the prideful suburban denizens of Silicon Valley are looking to relocate to New York and San Francisco for reasons that—though of great significance to the economy—are driven less by economic than civic and social logic. William Julius Wilson and his colleagues have made a powerful argument, suggesting that until African-American and Latino minorities are educated for and find jobs in the new economy, they will continue to be the first victims of the old economy. Their best hope lies in joint training programs that firms like IBM and Caterpillar Inc. are "partnering with area community colleges, vocational schools and the Department of Labor."[15] Such programs are ideally instruments of a national economic policy to combat inequality, but they are also available to cities. There they can have an impact augmented by their collateral urban virtues.

In other words, cities make economic sense and can be reformed through economic policy, but in no small part because they make civic, social, cultural and political sense. Cities create jobs, but jobholders like cities. The poor need new economy jobs (and training for them), but cities (Detroit, for example) are where new economy jobs are being created. Not everyone gets it: in New York, the financial industry has once again begun to flirt with decentralizing its workers to promote economic efficiency; but financial workers are once again defecting from their employers' plans, refusing to go along with the diktat of efficiency. The attractiveness of cities and their compelling civic logic of creativity and innovation make the challenge of distributing work equally in the city easier to address. The jobs are there, the job seekers are there, economic modernization is there: the question is how to ensure they find each other, and do so equitably and justly across class, race, and segregated neighborhoods.

Florida also emphasizes the city's natural capacity for recovery, showing how cities like Louisville, Portland, and Indianapolis turn new jobs in the creative employment sector into a recipe for lower levels of inequality (as compared, say, to Los Angles, Boston, or Houston).[16] Florida values the service economy as crucial to the success of the creative economy but concludes that just as the Industrial Revolution did not deal with nineteenth-century urban inequality until jobs were unionized, well paid, and pensioned, the creative economy will not serve equality fully until service work today is well compensated. Here Florida makes the necessary transition from theory to practice, demonstrating how "failing" cities, caught up in powerful economic transitions, nonetheless find roads to recovery.

Nations appear and fall, but cities endure and rediscover how to succeed. Their longevity gives them time to develop free institutions and a loyal citizenry. Beijing, Athens, Damascus, Philadelphia, Cairo, Delhi, and Rome, to name just a few, have seen empires come and go while they remain.[17] The fall of the Roman Empire never entailed the fall of Rome. The Prussian Empire and then the Third Reich were vanquished, but Berlin, though bombed into rubble, survived and reasserted the cosmopolitan reputation it had won in the Weimar Republic. Nations and empires are how humans organize themselves on a large scale and are subject to all the forces of fraud, erosion, dysfunction, and collapse that beset vast organizations. We read about the "Decline of the West" (Oswald Spengler) and the "Rise and Fall of Nations" (Paul Kennedy) and most recently "Why Nations Fail" (Daron Acemonglu and James Robertson), but not about "The Fall of Cities" or "Failed Towns." We are taught how to "see like a state" (James O. Scott), but what we really need to learn is how to "see like a city." For cities are where people live and renew themselves under ever-changing circumstances and even under changing sovereignties, and they have a better chance to sustain local liberty and endure over centuries, even millenia. Wrocław (Breslau) persists even as its national identity is ruptured. Singapore and Hong Kong are anomalies in an age of nation-states whose political circumstances keep evolving, but to their inhabitants they remain fixed living habitats. Cities can also be reinvented, as Singapore was in 1821 (when through British intervention it was transformed in a few short decades from a seaside village to an imperial port), and again in 1961 when it hived off from Malaysia and established a new identity as a sovereign city-state. Dubai has been newly invented by Emirs in the United Arab Emirates hoping to construct a new global city that will both harbor their ancient culture and liberate their global ambitions.

In the United States, traditional industrial cities like San Francisco and New York have become magnets to venture capital and the new tech firms they capitalize, attracting them away from Silicon Valley. Even American rustbelt dinosaurs like Pittsburgh and Detroit are drawing the business of new high-tech and financial service industries to their rehabilitated downtowns, buying a new chance to combat crime and decay and create a foundation for new jobs and wealth. São Paulo and Mexico City are doing the same. It is not Detroit or São Paulo or Bangalore or Barcelona in their distinctive personalities, but the city qua city in its defining creativity and plasticity that makes such renewal possible. This is how urban virtues can be turned to the mitigation of inequality and the ameliorations of problems caused by the market economy. David Harvey argues that it is but one of the many "myths" of urban life that solving urban problems "depends on the prior solution of economic development and population growth problems." Cities are all about wealth creation. The myth that "the problems posed by urbanization are essentially a consequence of deeper rooted social processes that need to be addressed independently" needs to give way to the truth that "urban forms might be redefined and factored in as moments of transformation."[18]

This is not to say that cities can simply will themselves immune to corruption and class division, or that the absence of educational opportunity, adequate housing, efficient job training, and accessible transportation will not continue to seriously curb development and place limits on opportunity for urban dwellers. Richard Florida accepts that those not recognized as belonging to the creative class (even when broadly defined as including managers and businesspeople as well as designers, entertainers, inventors, artists, and other cultural workers) and those not paid as the creative class is paid will not be positioned to enjoy the benefits of the city or exploit its possibilities. He argues (in the more controversial part of his thesis) that service employees working in hair salons or landscaping or health spas are potentially members of the creative class —but need to be recognized, respected and well paid for cities to benefit. In the age of Wal-mart, McDonald's, and private hospitals, such recognition will not be easy. Artists have to stretch canvas on frames, which is drudge work, but if stretching canvas is all artists do, creativity dies. Nor is it clear how much creativity there really is in the fields steeped in drudgery that Florida wants to redefine. Perhaps drudge work is not recognized or paid in the way skilled creative work in, say, architecture or digital technology is because it really is drudge work.

Pure artists are, in any case, today everywhere subordinated to the market and its pursuit of private profits. Today's creativity crisis is unfolding in the shadow of the financial meltdown and an economic climate where public jobs are being cut from Athens and São Paulo to Chicago and Stockton, where persistent recession undercuts private job growth and rationalizes minimum wage jobs, and where unpaid internships and other inequities hostile to the development of a creative class proliferate. The persistence of economic segregation walls off too many from the advantages of urban generativity. Cities are not merely creative but capable of generating and nurturing hope, innovation, and a sense of possibility and hence of breaking the vicious circle in which segregation, poverty, and inequality feed off one another.

In pursuing practical and particular remedies associated with the city's core virtues, it is easier to break the vicious circle in the city than anywhere else. These remedies include recognizing and restoring a public sector that is less likely to be demonized locally than nationally; recognizing and formalizing an informal economy that, above all in cities, is ripe with unexploited opportunity; making urban education, civic education, and job training (Wilson's preoccupation) a foundation for equal opportunity in the city; exploring best practices in housing, transportation, and cultural affairs that rest on public-private ventures and have been shown to work in more than one city; and finally, using new technology to spur "smart cities" that through cooperation and technology can mitigate if not overcome inequality (Chapter 9).

Addressing Injustice: Democracy, Cure Thyself!

The remedy for the ills of democracy, Jefferson quipped, is more democracy. Citizen reformers have not waited for the collapse of capitalism or constitutional revisions to engage in direct action on behalf of social justice. Social movements, nonviolent actions, and civic protest are not just efforts at reforming democracy, they are democracy in action. A half century ago, Michael Harrington appealed for "a vast social movement, a new period of political creativity" to alleviate the poverty he had chronicled.[19] In the same spirit, David Harvey writes today that "it will take imagination and political guts, a surge of revolutionary fervor and revolutionary change to construct a requisite poetics of understanding for our urbanized world, a charter for civilization, a trajectory for our species-being."[20] The poetics of understanding, however, risk pushing real change into a remote future and leaving behind all those who are paying the costs of inequality today, above all (always) poorer women and children. It is the virtue of social movements, however, that they favor mitigation now over revolutionary change in some remote future.[21] By "pushing turbulence to its outer limits," Frances Fox Piven reminds us, they can leave behind a "residue of reform" that helps catalyze real if modest change.[22]

Occupy Wall Street was another kind of social movement geared to the age of big money and big media; it too responded to a structural crisis (the global financial meltdown) but aimed at raising media and public consciousness of radical inequalities in countries of great wealth. With its mostly middle-class, youth-led protest gatherings, it initially seemed to aspire to engage in participatory democratic processes that demonstrated "what democracy looks like." Yet it also engaged with unions and created encampments open to the homeless and unemployed, effectively trying to do in practice what it preached in theory. Although it eschewed conventional politics, it was overtaken by the 2012 American elections. Nonetheless, it too has left behind a residue of reform and a fresh understanding of democracy as more than just voting. This is not the place to render judgment on Occupy Wall Street.[23] But it does have lessons for urban democratic activists, reminding them that social movements are important democratic tools and can affect both the media and the political system and also transform participants in the process.

Even normal democratic politics in the city helps to combat the bias against government and the public sector that has gripped national politics in the United States and the West. The three-decades-old assault on the public sector that has accompanied market fundamentalism has made the battle against inequality and injustice at every level of government more difficult.[24] In the city, taking on the privatization ideology is both less practical (its causes lie well beyond the city in national political ideologies and divisive party principles) and yet also more doable because slurs against "big government" have less traction in municipal politics. The corrosive de-democratization in the political sphere that attends market fundamentalism nationally makes much less sense where government is neither big nor bureaucratic and where mayors are seen as fellow citizens struggling to address common problems. Built on civility, cooperation, and common work, on traits that depend on a sense of affinity between individuals and neighbors and between citizens and their elected representatives, the city feels more like a genuine commons than its regional and national counterparts.

When Speaker Tip O'Neill famously quipped "all politics is local," he reinforced Tocqueville's conviction that all liberty is in the first instance municipal. The halo effect that protects individual politicians from being despised by their own constituents, even where those constituents are cynical about politics in general, does double duty in the city, where trust levels for mayors are much higher than for governors, legislative representatives, or presidents. While overall trust in government has declined to historical lows in 2010, trust in Congress falling to under 20 percent in 2012, the figures for trust in local government remain far higher.[25] The closer citizens are to their government, the harder it is to cast elected officials as aliens or enemies. Borough presidents, city councillors, and education and zoning board officials have a kind of parochial, face-to-face credibility national politicians can no longer achieve.[26] Hence, when asked specifically about whether they trust government to "do what is right," only 15 percent harbor such hopes for the federal government while 70 percent do so for local government.

When Americans talk derisively about big government, they are actually indicting themselves as failed citizens caught up in large-scale bureaucracies with which they feel little affinity. When citizens assail taxation, they deny their common citizens' right to pool resources to do things together that cannot be done alone. Because the common achievements of national government are distant, national citizens fail to see the connection between their local interests and a war thousands of miles away, a farm subsidy in a distant part of the country, or the mitigation of global warming measured by vanishing polar bears that nobody can see anyway or remote floods in Bangladesh covered only by the BBC. When the floods are in New York City and the blizzards in London, however, they take notice. A feeling of powerlessness fuels the assault on power; engaged citizenship assuages it. Citizens deride a theoretical "it"—an abstract sovereign "we" from which they have allowed themselves to become distanced. Not so the concrete municipal "we."

In the end, then, the antidote to market fundamentalism and political alienation is not less government but more transparency, more accountability, more public oversight and regulation; also more public interaction and consultation. In a word, more democracy. Strengthen the bonds with city government so that civic alienation is not an option. After all, it is not markets themselves but market fundamentalism with its animus to all public goods and government regulation that is the problem. Joseph E. Stiglitz has noted that a "more efficient economy and fairer society will also come from making markets work like markets—more competitive, less exploitative—and tempering their excesses."[27]

Given the city's scale, its immediacy, and the local character of city politics, cities have a better chance to do this temperately than any other level of government, both through intervention and public employment, and through public-private partnerships and collaboration with the business and NGO sectors. Detaching a citizen from her city councillor or a businessman from the mayor is hard work. Persuading neighbors to regard their block associations or school boards as vast and punitive bureaucracies is even harder. So while cities must inevitably suffer to some degree from privatization ideology, and business-oriented mayors like Michael Bloomberg and Boris Johnson sometimes focus too much on efficiency and private sector solutions, they also have the option to enlist citizens in ameliorating neoliberalism's consequences. Cities are theaters of strong democracy and civic and entrepreneurial creativity, and as such the last, best hope for real civic empowerment. Participation on behalf of equality is always locked in a struggle with power in defense of privilege.

But as experiments in participatory design, participatory decision making, and participatory budgeting make clear (Chapter 11), participation is always in the mix, and democracy is still the best bet for remedying the ills of democracy.

Making Capitalism Work: Formalizing the Informal Economy

The renewal of the alliance between citizens and their local government, rooted in the government's capacity to provide jobs, regulations, and private-public cooperation and in the citizen's inclination to participate in local decision making and neighborhood affairs, is the urban key to ameliorating inequality. Social observers and civic advocates like Hernando de Soto, the director of the Institute for Liberty and Democracy in Peru, have long recognized, however, that urban economics is as much about informal power as about city government, as much about the invisible economy as about public jobs or formal corporate institutions. As Katherine Boo poignantly shows, the reality in third-world megacities in Africa, Latin America, and Asia is an informal economy that offers employment to the technically "jobless," lodging to the technically "homeless," and hope, however wan and perverse, to the actually "hopeless." The question is how to unlock the informal economy and liberate the "dead capital" trapped inside.

De Soto has observed wryly that if the formal Egyptian economy was really the only recourse for twenty million educated young men without jobs, the country would have been swallowed up in permanent revolutionary struggle decades prior to the Arab Spring or suffered mass starvation on a Malthusian scale. As things stand, the informal economy prevents the poor from falling into the abyss without necessarily lifting them out of poverty. Advocates of microfinance, of legalizing squatters' rights, of giving title to property users who are not owners, and of other policies aimed at formalizing the informal economy and bringing practices outside the law within the circle of legitimacy, have placed a bet, however. It is the informal economy that minimally keeps the poor from expiring, and if elaborated, formalized, and made legitimate, it can help overcome radical inequality and foster mobility—in time, greater civic integration as well. "The problem with poor countries," de Soto writes, "is not that they lack savings, but that they lack the system of property that identifies legal ownership and therefore they cannot borrow."[28] Their capital is "locked up" and cannot be deployed until it can be "revealed and transformed into active capital." Capital, that is, that can be represented "in writing—in a title, a security, a contract," which is what makes capital actually useful.[29]

De Soto's theory, which he has applied in practice in many parts of the developing world, has shown some significant results, although it is flawed by its treatment of the "legal" economy as a wholly neutral marketplace. For in the absence of real civic and political equality, legalizing invisible capital can subject it to exploitation and expropriation of a kind not possible when it remains "dead."[30] In settings of relative civic equality, unlocking dead capital can succeed, but this involves breaking the circle from inside the circle. It means overcoming political inequality through exploiting an invisible economy, which can happen only in the context of relative political equality. It thus is likely to work best when coupled with political and democratic reform.

C. K. Prahalad also advocates exploiting what he deems an "inclusive capitalism" to treat third-world poverty. Rejecting the idea that they are mere victims and wards of the states, he seeks to enlist the poor in the "growth opportunities" that become possible when one applies the "resources, scale, and scope of large firms to co-create solutions to the problems at the bottom of the pyramid, those billions of people who live on less than $2 a day"—a great many of whom live in cities.[31] The idea is to convert "poverty into an opportunity for all concerned," which requires public-private collaborative activity. Prahalad seeks to turn what may seem an offensive idea—profiting from poverty—into an opportunity for the poor themselves to overcome it, and he captures in more formal terms the processes Boo describes. To be successful as a mitigation tactic, however, it must clearly do more than relabel poverty as "opportunity."

Microfinance, a strategy pioneered by Muhammad Yunus, the founder of the Grameen Bank in Bangladesh, also seeks to bootstrap women out of poverty by recognizing their economic potential when catalyzed by small loans that allow them to turn creativity into new local business ventures.[32] In what can be seen as a kind of ingenious amalgam of

Richard Florida and Hernando de Soto, Yunus effectively recognizes the human capital represented by women's creative entrepreneurial energy and releases it with the help of microfinance. Originally aimed primarily at village women, the approach has also been used in cities, including New York, Los Angeles, and San Francisco. By acknowledging and facilitating the special role women play in family and neighborhood in stabilizing society, microfinance becomes a fiscal strategy for urban integration. As with de Soto and Prahalad, Yunus has courted controversy and been visited with more than his share of it; recent critiques of microfinance have certainly tarnished its luster. But the unsubstantiated attack by Bangladesh Prime Minister Sheikh Hasina on Yunus, a Nobel Prize winner, suggests a personal vendetta rather than a judicious inquiry.[33] My own view is that innovative ideas, especially those impacting "normal market capitalism," almost always come under assault from those representing the standard capitalist paradigm, often through personal libels against the authors of such ideas. Global finance has yet to receive anything like the scrutiny unleashed on Yunus, and it does not pretend to serve the poor.

An Example of Mitigation from Los Angeles: Pro and Con

On the West Coast of the United States, to take one instance, microfinance, "illegal" jobs, and invisible economy street vending activities have impacted inequality significantly. The Los Angeles Microfinance Network (LAMN) is an example of an effective microloan strategy allowing both small businesses without access to commercial banks and individual entrepreneurs to get their start. In San Francisco, a small company called Gentle Parking was founded with $10,000 from a Bay Area microlender called the Opportunity Fund. With six lots and twenty-five employees, founder William Ortiz-Cartagena has become a self-styled David up against the Goliath of big banks and insurance companies, which have done little to help. But the Opportunity Fund became his life-saving "slingshot."[34]

Jobs also grow out of the informal economy in ways that indicate how it is already linked to the formal economy through practices in which the wealthy and the poor are complicit, often outside the law, but softening the impact of segregation. As undocumented Mexican workers pursue nationally the low-paying jobs offered by American corporations more interested in cheap labor than documentation, so seemingly divided neighborhoods in cities like Phoenix, San Diego, and Los Angeles also engage in reciprocal exploitation around jobs. We have already pointed to an innovative partnership between San Diego and Tijuana that turns a contested and violent border into a zone of potential collaboration. Up in L.A., despite egregious residential segregation, a large population of L.A. County workers from Southside neighborhoods move freely in and out of the quasi-gated communities of Brentwood, Beverly Hills, and the canyons above them, watering lawns, cleaning pools, and keeping houses tidy and children well attended. The gates separating communities come down every morning and every evening to let the two classes collaborate and deliver a working if minimum wage to the people who most need it.

Those who work in larger cities, whether legal or undocumented, actually get a better wage. When government steps in to provide health, education, and good transport, or offer "urban visas" (see Chapter 11), these integrating synergies actually make a difference. They do not have to be legislated into existence but do need to be legislatively protected and legally secured. Jobs are not enough. The problem with the informal economy is that wages are very low and work itself uncertain, while benefits and pensions are nonexistent and upward mobility circumscribed. In Rio and other Latin American cities, as well as in Mumbai and Manila, invisible economy scavengers, often children, pick through urban dumps in search of usable or sellable items that support their street-vending entrepreneurship. Even in first-world American cities, bottle and can collectors make a sparse living sorting recyclables. The developing-world scavengers in effect sell the by-product of the (literal) shit in which they live in order to survive. Nevertheless, what is exploitation to privileged onlookers may feel like opportunity to the underclass in these global undercities.

Perhaps the most important but also troubling element in the informal economy in both the developed and developing worlds is street vending—sometimes legal, mostly illegal but overlooked, always in the shadows of the real economy, invariably critical to survival for the poor.[35] Whether they are selling commodities scavenged from dumps, imported from local agriculture, bought at tag sales, or filched from Goodwill, or vending hot dogs or falafel, street vendors must combine ingenuity, street smarts about policing, and long hours outdoors marketing their "merch." All this to secure an all-too-modest living that nonetheless is their security against deep poverty and dependency. It is thus one of city government's most urgent tasks to find ways to legitimate and underwrite street vending, to turn careers of desperation in tension with licensed businesses and conventional practices into legitimate occupations that can support whole families.

Just how difficult this can be is shown by the good-willed attempts of the City of Los Angeles—where 35 percent of the population is foreign born and up to 750,000 of 9.8 million people are illegal—to deal with "a vast parallel society lured by the promise of work yet barred from the formal workforce."[36] Since for many Latino immigrants "the ban on street vending represents the criminalization of their most entrepreneurial instincts," grappling with the vending issue has become a priority for which the thriving street-vending culture in the multicultural and poor MacArthur Park neighborhood has become an alternately fascinating and dismaying case study. The dramatic story related by Jesse Katz of trying to sanction and support street vending by establishing an "ArtGricultural Open Air Market" on Little Street cannot be retold here, but the effort nearly destroyed the neighborhood's traditional unlicensed but thriving vending economy, which, Katz writes, was a "hodgepodge that sustained an ecosystem, an entry-level marketplace in which anyone could afford to participate, as buyer or seller."[37] This is the very definition of the informal economy's potential for creative entrepreneurship, which, if harnessed, can impact inequality significantly. But in Los Angeles, Katz shows, city efforts echoed other well-intended urban policies like those that lead to the construction of dysfunctional high-rise projects.

Formalizing what had been working informally can then undercut the informal economy's core spirit without facilitating its incorporation into conventional business practices. Trying to order and legalize what vendors on their own were doing, creating a system for "allocating space and resolving disputes" that duplicated the informal system was simply not a recipe for success. Yet endorsing the existing conventions, in which neighbors who looked after one another enjoyed only the sorts of "durable property rights" that are possible when "possessing no property rights at all," was also unsatisfactory. The L.A. neighborhood of MacArthur Park began with what was the informal economy at its best and worst, where "to vend is, indeed, to rise in status . . . [where] so many desperate people—the drugged, the ill—lug their lives around the streets that someone who actually has a fungible product to offer from a wheeled conveyance is less an outlaw than an impresario: the shopping cart a symbol of upward mobility." On the way to trying to formalize it, the city nearly lost the "best" without overcoming the "worst."

This example from Los Angeles, described with such nuance and sensitivity by Jesse Katz, embodies both the bold promise of the informal economy and the extraordinary difficulty of transforming it through political policies without destroying its vitality. This is a puzzle I cannot begin to solve. I can only point again to how the promise of the informal economy can pay off when formalized effectively and how it makes more sense to allow capitalism to work for the poor rather than trying by some miracle of ahistoricity to abolish it. This is what de Soto, Prahalad, Yunus, and the civic leaders of cities like Los Angeles have tried to do. It is also the task capitalism itself needs to undertake in order to prove it can work with rather than defeat government. The idea, in Stiglitz's crucial phrase, is to make capitalism work; to assist squatters in becoming tenants, tenants in becoming owners (see Singapore!), owners in keeping their homes, entrepreneurs in getting finance, undocumented workers in securing visas, and illegal vendors in securing licenses; to turn victims into agents and subjects of exploitation into citizens by effecting collaboration between city government, civil society organizations, and private firms.

A Best-Practices Approach to Mitigation

In Chapter 7 we reviewed the ways in which inequality and injustice manifested themselves in each sector of the city—transportation, housing, jobs, education, parks; and we pointed to some possible practices that could ameliorate conditions in each domain. We have just seen how ambiguous is the success of a potential Los Angeles best practice. It would require an encyclopedia to enumerate the experiments and policies developed around the world to address urban inequality in each of these domains and in different cities on different continents. I hope instead to recommend continuous urban experimentation with new and shared practices of the kind regularly reported on the City Protocol or C40 or Sustainable Cities Collective websites, practices that may be specific to distinct sectors and sensitive to cultural and historical differences among cities but that can nevertheless be accommodated to cities everywhere.

Singapore offers an example of a pragmatic mixed economy approach to best practices that might be imitated more often if not for critics on the right who think a nod toward socialism is a call for totalitarianism and critics on the left who pay more attention to a ban on chewing gum as a sign of paternalistic authoritarianism or on resistance to multiparty election campaigns than to Singapore's democratic record in fair housing, a green environment, and education for all. Lee Kuan Yew, Singapore's modern founder and long-time leader, has certainly governed paternalistically, but he has also eschewed ideology. "We believe in socialism, in fair shares for all," he acknowledges. But he also recognizes the market: "Later we learnt that personal motivation and personal rewards were essential for a productive economy." So he approached and "decided each matter in a pragmatic way," the aim, which was difficult, being "to strike the right balance."[38] In cities like Singapore, leaders facing the challenge of bootstrapping an entire urban population just recently in wholesale destitution and burdened with a feudal economy, are often blamed for not stepping smartly into a comfortable liberal democracy and critical pedagogy that took centuries to cultivate in the West.

In both the developing and developed world, education is an ideal arena in which to experiment and explore new best practices. There is little disagreement about its importance in the struggle against inequality. The road to freedom has always passed through pedagogy and schooling, what were once called the "arts of liberty" and later became the liberal arts. The American Constitution, brilliant as its design was, could be "kept" only by citizens educated and competent enough to keep it—averred James Madison. Thomas Jefferson prized his founding of the University of Virginia above his presidency. Tocqueville spoke of an "apprenticeship of liberty" by which Americans would learn the meaning and acquire the competences of citizens. Schooling has long been the immigrant's ticket to assimilation and citizenship.

Today education remains the key lever of power and opportunity in modern cities. Education entails general and liberal education, civic education for citizenship, and job training too (in which the first two play a role). Yet if there is no dispute about education's role in political and economic empowerment, its practices remain contested. It is well known that it costs much more to keep a man in prison than a boy in school, or keep a girl in servitude than a woman in business. No one doubts that planting apple trees is better than giving away apples. Even gang members know they can do more with books than with guns in the long term—if only they could believe they had a long term. But how to do it?

The debate is not about the goal but the means.[39] How to educate the young in tolerance, critical thinking, and civic skepticism *and* educate them in values, tradition, and civic patriotism? And to prepare them for thinking, for life, and for jobs? Through public or private school, or some mix? With big schools or small schools? By teaching to tests or by testing true teaching? Through focusing on neighborhood and community schools, even though they can reinforce segregation? Or going citywide and ensuring common standards at the cost of community? Should schools indulge in the particular and the parochial or foster cosmopolitanism? Should they be geared to the mean or geared to excellence? Is choice for some at the price of loss for others who are left behind the only response to the equalities fostered by an unfair and not very public "public" education system? Even the question of how much to spend on school is contested, since more money doesn't always translate into improved performance (although broken windows, leaky roofs, overcrowded classrooms, and insufficient playground space almost always translate into declining performance). The bottom line is that if educational opportunity is the first and most important strategy in the struggle against unequal economic opportunity, economic inequality is the first and most important determinant of the education deficit—which seems to close a vicious circle and leave little room for improvement.

Vicious circles are broken one at a time. The strength of cities is their variety and their capacity to experiment. Best practices are likely to be situational and parochial, geared to the needs of particular places and cultures. Parochial (religious) schools are not public in the traditional sense, but neither are they private. Catholic schools and Muslim madrassas have alike contributed to equal opportunity and upward mobility in cities where public schools have proven inadequate; yet they can also offend the separation of church and state and pit religious values against science and secularism. Vouchers sometimes empower hopeless families or jumpstart a neighborhood, but they can also undermine a common curriculum and make integration difficult in immigrant neighborhoods, where public schools are the first step to community and citizenship. Charter schools can improve public schools generally, except when they undermine them.

In education, then, as in the other sectors, we need to seek partial solutions, relevant remedies, and best practices that are best because they are salient and pertinent to the specific challenges being addressed. That is in fact what cities do. Washington, D.C., New York City, and Chicago have all faced crises in public education, all confronted militant unions that may or may not be supporting the interests of parents and children. Mayors try, sometimes taking on the unions as Rahm Emanuel did in the fall of 2012 in Chicago, sometimes promoting charter experiments as New York City did under Mayor Bloomberg, and sometimes throwing out a schools superintendent too out of tune with teachers (as Washington did with its celebrated but controversial superintendent, Michelle Rhee).

We need not enumerate or mandate best practices here. They arise out of experiment and action, which is to say they are practices, not theories. Those are "best" that work, at least in some city at some critical moment. The virtue of practices is precisely that they are experimental and plastic, ever changing. Which means they can be compared and shared, especially in a new virtual world in which smart cities defy the walls, maps, and time zones in which they were once trapped and can coexist and cooperate in a "cloud" of commonality that is no longer a metaphor for their imaginative capabilities but the reality of a digital planet.

SHEILA DIKSHIT OF DELHI

Women are only infrequently found in city halls around the world—a seeming oddity in light of the link between urban governance and local democracy. Even in the West, there are fewer female mayors than there are female legislators or chief executives. Women have served as president or prime minister of the United Kingdom, Ireland, Germany, and even Switzerland (where women didn't even vote until the second half of the twentieth century), for example, but no woman has served as mayor of London, Dublin, Munich, or Basel. Women have served in the U.S. Senate from California and New York but have never served as mayor of Los Angeles or New York City (both cities had women running in their last elections, but neither won).

These startling (or perhaps all too predictable) realities make the three-term tenure of **SHEILA DIKSHIT** as chief minister of Delhi a felicitous surprise—all the more so in a nation whose treatment of women, wives, and girls is egregious. In fact, women have served as mayor in a number of Indian cities, including most recently Mumbai, where Shraddha Jadhav of the Shiv Sena Party served in 2010. Born in 1938 and educated at the Convent of Jesus and Mary School, Sheila Dikshit joined the dominant National Congress Party and served in the 1980s as the minister of state for parliamentary affairs and as a minister of state in the prime minister's office.

Though she has won several national prizes—best chief minister of the year in 2008, best politician of the year, 2009—Dikshit has not avoided controversial women's issues. She not only has served her party on commissions focused on women, but was also a member of the Indian delegation to the United Nations Commission on the Status of Women. She went to jail for her commitments for twenty-three days in 1990 when demonstrating against the atrocities committed against women in the state of Uttar Pradesh. In that period, hundreds of thousands of women followed her lead in civil disobedience. Dikshit also helped establish two of the most successful hostels operating in Delhi to house working women.

Dikshit brings to Delhi a sense of possibility that India's largest cities desperately need (see Katherine Boo's dispiriting study of a Mumbai slum): in an interview, although she lists the physical and infrastructural improvements won under her mayoralty with pride, Dikshit seems most gratified by how "Delhi has changed from a cynical city to a city of hope."[1] Like Mayor Johnson of London, she believes culture attracts people to the city no less than jobs, and that hope is driven by culture as well as economics.

The mayor grew up in Delhi and considers herself what could be called a homegirl—like most mayors, a homie, someone who, as she says, is "a citizen before a chief minister." She adds, "I'm going to remain a citizen." Like mayors everywhere, Dikshit understands the constraints under which she functions in a municipality that is part of a province (state) and is subordinated to the financial and legal sovereignty of a national government. To respond to the global challenges they face from within their delimited municipal jurisdictions, she suggests treating big Indian cities like Delhi, Mumbai, Kolkata, and Chennai as "city-states."

Dikshit can turn subversive, assuming the mantle of the radical that mayors need at times to be in order to get urban business done: "I am sure politically no one would agree with this," she counsels, anticipating the opposition, "but I think administratively it would be good for the country's development (to) create city-states and give them the power to undertake development. *They should not be under the state governments but rather under their own chief minister or chief administrator or whatever you want to call the position.*" Talk about "rebel towns" (Chapter 11), Dikshit seems to be imagining an "insurgent city."

Mayors are radicals by necessity, not choice; they understand that to pursue very conventional ends like eradicating slums and promoting sustainable environments and diverting national resources focused on, say, national defense to local education, they may need unconventional methods, above all a single-minded obsession with cities and their citizens, and what they can do together. So Dikshit reaches an obvious conclusion: "You just can't do it with the same old administration where you're dependent on various constituents for every penny."

Even without securing infrastructural change, Dikshit has accomplished a great deal. According to a report by McKinsey, she completed the first phase of the Delhi Metro on budget and on schedule, privatized power distribution, reduced pollution, improved school performance by students, and expanded green areas within the city. Still more impressively, in a city and nation known for bureaucracy, inefficiency, and unresponsiveness, she established a strong democratic initiative brokering regular interaction between city bureaucrats and citizens. This program of town halls *(Bhagidari)* has become a global model of good governance and is part of the new democratic agenda that includes town meetings, participatory budgeting, and urban interactivity that is changing the face of urban democracy globally.

It should come as no surprise, given her role as a leading voice in the Indian community of women, that along with her radical notions of municipal autonomy and practical achievements in municipal governance, Dikshit has launched a new program—*Stree Shakti*—aimed at empowering women through employment training, financial aid, and access to health care and medicine.

Katherine Boo has written movingly in her *Beyond the Beautiful Forevers* about poverty-strapped boys and girls in a Mumbai slum whose only path upward seems to be through grueling labor in the garbage dumps, whose only hope for redemption in a corrupt, inegalitarian metropolis is corruption itself. Sheila Dikshit offers a different and more sustaining version of hope: a promise that urban governance and mayoral leadership can alter the corrupt system and turn cities into genuine arenas of possibility for the poor no less than the wealthy.

CHAPTER 9. SMART CITIES IN A VIRTUAL WORLD

Linking Cities with Digital Technology

> For the first time cities have their own voice on the internet world.
> *Artur Serra, Research Director, Citilab in Catalonia (Spain)*
>
> The future is already here, it's just not evenly distributed.
> *William Gibson*

A host of enthusiasts, from the early pioneers of *Wired Magazine* and the Electronic Frontier Foundation to the newest innovators of City Protocol (the new web-based global cities network in Barcelona), are persuaded that digitally linked, so-called smart cities are on the cutting edge of urban innovation. In keeping with the soft technological determinism of Google founder Eric Schmidt and his ideas director Jared Cohen (a political scientist), many observers are sure that "the new digital age" is "reshaping the future of people, nations and business."[1] Integral to this idea of a digital world is the notion of smart cities, which are presumed to have the potential to give new meaning to the idea of digital rights and to promote intercity cooperation. Do they?

Let me pose the question this way: Can the ubiquitous technology that everywhere promises digital Nirvana actually further the goal of global networking and the governance of mayors? Or is it burdened by too many of the weaknesses that have stymied technocrats, too many of the failed promises that have repeatedly disappointed the techno-zealots yearning for transfiguration by engineering? As democrats and advocates of global urban governance, we need to have convincing answers to such questions in order to assess the possibilities of smart cities. Should we heed the giddy champions of technology and raise our expectations, or allow a prudent cyber skepticism to dampen them?

To start with, we need to understand the phrase "smart cities." It may reference little more than novel gadgetry and the impulse to try to conduct conventional business unconventionally—electronically, digitally, and hence virtually. This understanding, though important, is trivial. It dates back to the fashionable nineties notion of "e-government," which was born with the early Internet. For nearly a quarter of a century it has been a focus of cities interested in electronic voting, electronic administration, electronic records (patient health records, for example), as well as electronic communication within city administrations and between administrators and citizens.[2] There is more to it than doing virtually on computers what has previously been done live in print and broadcasting. Raising money on the web as MoveOn.org and the Howard Dean and Barack Obama presidential campaigns have done may be efficient and tap new resources, but it does little to reduce the pernicious impact of money on politics or to transform campaigning into something genuinely interactive. As Joe Trippi, Dean's 2004 web guru qua campaign manager, pointed out, on the "day the [Dean] campaign ended, there were 1.4 million blogs in the world. On the day Obama announced there were 77 million blogs."[3] Back in 2004, Facebook was still a Harvard undergraduate's experiment in girl-watching, it now has a half billion or more subscribers throughout the world. Yet even today, Trippi writes, "government seems to be the last place that's taking advantage of it." Except in cities. New, cutting edge smart cities.

Smart cities are in the first instance simply tech-savvy towns that utilize digital innovation to do their business. But smart cities are also self-consciously interdependent cities that use technology to enhance communication, hoping to make smart cities wireless nodes in a global network and reinforce their natural inclination to connectivity and collaboration. For civic entities defined as much by interaction, creativity, and innovation as by place, maps, and topographical boundaries, the cloud isn't a bad place to be. By digitally escaping the limits of space and time, cities embrace and realize—they literally *virtualize*—the metaphors and constructs that define them. The great interdependent thinker Manuel Castells has captured this paradigm-shifting evolution in his term *the networked society*:

> The communication revolution has fundamentally changed the relationship between time and space. In previous societies social organization was largely facilitated by a spatial organization that enabled simultaneity . . . (e.g., the weekly market place). Recent developments . . . have enabled simultaneity to be virtually created worldwide without people having to physically come together. This is a new form of society: network society. A new global space of flows is replacing an old national space of places.[4]

The new global space of flows is profoundly urban. Increasingly, cities are depending on technology as the key to sustainability, economic vitality, and commercial and cultural exchange. They hope to be able to turn the abstract notion of flows into concrete interconnectivity. To be sure, cities know technology per se is only a means, and as such, carries its own baggage (which we will unpack below). Yet cyber-zealotry is infectious. As one proponent of smart cities has noted, "we can collect and access data now from an astonishing variety of sources: there are 30 billion RFID tags [the new tech barcodes] embedded into our world . . . we have 1 billion cell phones with cameras able to capture and share images and events; and everything from domestic appliances to vehicles to buildings is increasingly able to monitor its location, condition and performance and communicate that information to the outside world."[5] Cities have always been interdependent: the digital revolution has simply rendered that interdependence palpable—putatively both efficient and concrete. Maybe.

A recent example of how seductively the web and the innovative companies attending its evolution can claim to facilitate urban connectivity is City Protocol, a new website project and cities association promising a new set of virally shared best practices for its members. Fashioned initially through a partnership between the city of Barcelona and Cisco Systems (whose chief globalization officer, Wim Elfrink, is an urban governance innovator), it currently includes thirty cities working with key universities, tech companies, and civic organizations.[6] Its aim is "to define a global, cooperative framework among cities, industries and institutions with the goal to address urban challenges in a systemic way in areas such as sustainability, self-sufficiency, quality of life, competitiveness and citizen participation."[7] It focuses on the role of technology in urban innovation and aspires to "platform integration and technology and solutions development."

At present, City Protocol is in the early stage of development, but though it offers proof that technology is no longer just a mote in the eye of urban innovators or the subject of speculative reflection and research at think tanks like the Intelligent Community Forum, it has yet to prove whether it actually can produce results for cities aspiring to work together.[8] In the organization's vision, "City Protocol will be a new differentiated and meaningful program that will enable better understanding and cooperation among the different actors (city councils, academia, institutions, companies, and society) involved in the development of a more sustainable, efficient, cohesive, innovative and smart city. It will deliver benefits within and between cities, by addressing cities in an integrated systemic way."[9] Working with multinationals such as Cisco, Telefónica, and Schneider, and a new "Smart City Campus," the project hopes to develop best practices and technological solutions that can be used by cities around the world.

Putting the enticing verbiage aside, however, the question is whether putting best practices and innovative policy initiatives on a web feed that goes directly to member cities actually alters the urban landscape. Will ideas spread more quickly? The bike-share program so popular in cities today actually caught fire initially, at least in part, through tourism and travel, with a Chicago city councilman seeing something exciting in a Latin American city he was visiting. Tradesmen and commercial travelers have always been "viral" carriers of ideas, even when they traveled by camel. The question we need to ask today is whether efficiency in communication and information access will improve urban services (that is the promise of digital health care record-keeping and metro schedule screens) or merely centralize surveillance and control and infringe privacy. Thousands of urban video cams centrally monitored (of the kind London now deploys) will no doubt be regarded by police officials as a boon to crime prevention, and London is being imitated in many other cities today, including New York. In Boston, it was these street cams that helped identify the Marathon bombers. But will citizens concerned with rights see the London practice more as something resembling Foucault's Panopticon, sweeping away the last vestiges of privacy with ubiquitous surveillance? Or will the yearning for absolute security bury even modest notions of rights?

I will not track here the new literature that toys with distinctions between smart cities and so-called cyber cities or digital or intelligent cities, though it must be noted that the plethora of hip brand names suggests that the many new public-private partnerships that are emerging around technology and the city are being rather heavily hyped. The reality is more ambiguous and complex. The digital world encompasses thousands of cable and satellite broadcast channels, 600 million Internet sites, almost a billion Facebook users, and perhaps 70 million bloggers (with more than 50,000 new ones appearing every day), along with storage for all photos, files, programs and all that "big data" in a virtual cloud no longer safely inscribed on our own hard drives. Almost all of these public technologies are privately owned by quasi monopolies. Because the federal Telecommunications Act of 1996 passed in the Clinton years allowed the privatization of all such new media (spectrum abundance supposedly eliminating monopoly and thus the need to regulate media), cities cannot become smart without forging public-private partnerships.

Many of the technologies were developed for commercial (for-profit) purposes: multiplying applications can locate pizza parlors and runaway pets or find open parking spaces and pay parking fines. But when the chips and GPS applications are adopted by the state, they let every cop and every political snoop know exactly where dissidents and "subversives" are—and permit the location and rounding up of lawful demonstrators an oppressive regime may wish to shut down. So-called Big Data inundates us with information more useful to marketers or security officials than to policy makers trying to make prudent judgments and looking for knowledge and wisdom. Knowing where available parking places are via sensors is useful to urban drivers, but may increase automobile use when the better part of environmental wisdom is to limit driving altogether.

I will argue, then, that technology can both facilitate and compromise what cities are doing to enhance their interdependence, but way too often, those employing it don't know the difference.[10] Nor do they necessarily grasp what it means to partner with powerful private-sector corporations. Corporations have a fiscal obligation to their shareholders to make money off their urban technology, but cities need to be aware that the smart-city portion of the business sector was estimated to have earned as much as $34 billion in 2012 and has been projected to be able to earn $57 billion by 2015. Tech companies do not embrace smart-city initiatives disinterestedly in the name of public goods, though that certainly does not mean their partnerships cannot also serve such goals.[11]

A cursory hunt on any search engine under "smart cities" turns up multiple listings that mirror City Protocol's Barcelona-Cisco partnership. IBM Smarter Cities, for example, is working with IBM in Birmingham, England, on mapping inputs and outputs on policy decisions. Then there is Siemens Smart Cities, along with dozens of other companies putting commercial applications to apparent political purposes, including Schneider Electric, the Thales Group, Oracle Corporation, and Wonderware. Many cities are developing planning programs, tech parks, and research centers that allow them to throw around heated if somewhat opaque self-descriptions like Smart City Málaga, Dubai Internet City, or Yokohama Smart City. Such handles often seem like little more than advertising slogans akin to The Big Apple (New York) or The Eternal City (Rome) or City of Sails (Auckland, New Zealand). Even private programs such as Open Trip Planner (Portland, Oregon) and Moovel, which use technology to help cyclists and hikers plan energy-efficient trips, are trying to make green profitable and contribute to urban sustainability. Smart water meters in Dubuque, Iowa, help citizens monitor and control water use.[12] In Birmingham, England, an app has appeared that can help catering services direct their excess food to charities that distribute to the hungry, addressing poverty directly. Brave new frontiers indeed, blurring private and public; an example is The Smart Cities Council, a self-styled for-profit with paying partners to whom it promises "business success" through advocacy and action by acting as "an advisor and market accelerator for jobs and revenue."[13]

The partnership of tech firms and cities on which the new urban "smart" is predicated is quite real but needs to be scrutinized as well as celebrated. Real change is taking place. Digital technology is minimally making cities more efficient, communicative, sustainable, and livable, qualifying them as smart. But it aspires to do more than just that. According to former San Francisco mayor Gavin Newsom or Nigel Jacobs, cochair of the Mayor's Office of New Urban Mechanics in Boston, far from being just about efficiency, ITC (information and communication technology) can be "a gateway drug for civic engagement."[14] Elaine Weidman, the vice president for sustainable and corporate responsibility at Ericsson Broadband, agrees: "When combined with different types of social media, [technology] is creating radically new ways of engagement. Before, you could communicate one to one with another person or maybe cast your vote with the government. But today you get a much more global conversation, whether it's climate change or an issue within your local city government. Today you have the possibility not to just tell the government what you think but to get others involved in your cause and to share your views."[15]

Boyd Cohen, the urbanist and self-described climate strategist, offers a more modest and straightforward description, calling those cities smart that use "information and communication technologies (ICT) to be more intelligent and efficient in the use of resources, resulting in cost and energy savings, improved service delivery and quality of life, and reduced environmental footprint—all supporting innovation and the low-carbon economy." He proposes as "Top Ten" smart cities a list including (not very surprisingly) mostly developed Western cities—Vienna, Toronto, Paris, New York, London, Berlin, Copenhagen, and, last on Cohen's list but first on mine, Barcelona.[16] Two developed non-Western cities, Tokyo and Hong Kong, complete his list. It is not necessarily the case, however, that cities that are smart in how they are governed internally are smart in their relations with other cities. Vienna and Copenhagen are a far cry from Saskia Sassen's trilogy of high-tech powerhouses, New York, London, and Tokyo—where financial connectivity invites technical networking and drives interdependence.

Maybe the web can be a gateway drug to civic engagement, but drugs often make us less rather than more social and interactive. After all, technological innovation in the age of the Internet is little different in its impact from innovation in earlier tech revolutions, promising more radical change than the culture in which it is produced can deliver. Digital technology and its most significant social product, the World Wide Web, have unquestionably revolutionized communication and how we live socially but have also produced effects that distort human relations, undermine deliberative democracy, enhance aggressive commerce, and trivialize and privatize our life-worlds. Among reasonable skeptics open to change but suspicious of uncritical ardor, there are significant questions to be raised before we embrace the promise of smart cities as a path to constructive interdependence.

Smart Cities: Dumb and Dumber or Better than Ever?

The high expectations for a technology that will smarten up cities are belied by its failure historically to live up to its promise. Technology is a tool, and whatever its potential, it reflects the values and aspirations of the society that produces it. It always threatens, in Thoreau's phrase, to turn the toolmakers into tools of their tools. The appearance of new digital electronic technologies in a largely commercial, privatized consumer society were thought to promise a new arena for improved civic and social relations and suggested to zealots a new electronic frontier for direct deliberative democracy. Yet not very surprisingly, these technologies have, to date, produced mainly commercial, private, and trivial outcomes, for cities no less than for society at large. The web's creative democratic architecture notwithstanding, it seems more in tune with the commercial character and aspirations of those who developed the new applications than with the ideals of those responsible for the original innovations.

In theory, the Internet (though originally a product of the Defense Department) offered a remarkable new social and civic as well as pedagogical and cultural interface. It proffered a horizontal rather than a vertical technology, connecting people directly with one another. It disintermediated authority and gave birth to a crowdsourcing wiki-logic in which knowledge would be subjected to democratic (critics would say anarchic) processes. Yet in application, the technological dreams were diminished. Social media as imagined by a college sophomore named Mark Zuckerberg (obsessed with rating girls and sharing gossip rather than generating a new mode of uplifting civic and social interaction of value to educators, deliberative democrats, or creative artists) instead produced the popular blockbuster Facebook—a product in which, though it defined *social* media, neither civic culture nor the culture of cities was visible. We can hardly be surprised that the new digital technology pushes partisanship more diligently than it catalyzes civility. It sells goods more effectively than it cultivates citizenship, though, ironically, the puzzle of how to monetize the Internet has yet to be solved.[17]

As the technology is today applied to urban interaction, questions remain about whether the consequences will be wholly constructive. When commerce and markets overshadow technological architecture, the results are not inspiring. In the words of one web commentator: "There's been a distinct change recently in how we describe what a 'Smarter City' is. Whereas in the past we've focused on the capabilities of technology to make city systems more intelligent, we're now looking to marketplace economics to describe the defining characteristics of Smarter City behaviour."[18] Are smart cities really civically smarter? Or dumb and dumber?

These critical questions are asked only occasionally in the cyber arena and rarely posed by advocates of smart cities and technologically augmented urban development. The seductions of cyber zealotry among advocates of participatory democracy are not easy to resist. I myself was fascinated when, nearly thirty years ago, I enthused about emerging interactive technologies and the impact they might have on citizenship and "strong democracy":

The wiring of homes for cable television across America . . . the availability of low frequency and satellite transmissions in areas beyond regular transmission or cable and the interactive possibilities of video, computers, and information retrieval systems open up a new mode of human communication that can be used either in civic and constructive ways or in manipulative and destructive ways.[19]

Mine was one of the earliest instances of anticipatory enthusiasm (though laced with skepticism), but a decade later with the web actually in development, cyber zealots were everywhere predicting a new electronic frontier for civic interactivity. Recently, experienced and able mayors like Gavin Newsom have embraced the participatory potential of what they call Web 2.0. Yet technology had rarely been unambiguously transformative, and in the new epoch of electronic communications, it was anything but. The effects of evolving technologies have been both constructive (movable type democratized literacy and facilitated the Protestant Reformation) and destructive (it also catalyzed propaganda and put an end to illuminated manuscripts); gunpowder enabled construction and mining but also democratized warfare and facilitated mass killing. The Enlightenment ushered in the age of the machine and nonstop technological innovation, speeding up history and, in Marx's poignant portrait, breaking asunder the feudal bonds that for millennia had tied us together. Capital manifested itself first of all as machines that amplified labor's productivity, transforming the creation of both wealth and exploitation and producing both vast wealth and class war, productivity, and revolution.

In the twentieth century, a radical transformation in communications technology (radio and then television broadcasting) significantly affected political and social institutions, augmenting the reach of both civic knowledge and propaganda, both democracy and demagoguery. By the end of the century, all eyes were on the portals through which the Internet first entered our consciousness. The first revolution was as radical as the second. These words, for example, might have been spoken about the Internet: "Let us not forget that the value of this great new system does not lie primarily in its extent or its efficiency but for the first time in human history we have available to us the ability to communicate simultaneously with millions of our fellow men, to furnish entertainment, instruction, widening vision of national problems, national events, and democracy."[20] These words were spoken by Herbert Hoover, commenting on the advent of radio broadcasting nearly a century ago.

Every technological innovation in history has elicited caveats and warnings. Zealots today dismiss the critics as Luddites, but skeptics recognize the ambivalence that the idea of "progress" has engendered since the time of the Greeks. The ancient poets warned against the hubris of prideful innovators like Prometheus (punished for stealing the dangerous secret of fire from the gods) and Icarus (whose quest for flight occasioned the first iconic crash and burn). Communication at the speed of light brings its own dangers. With digital technology, we encounter both utopian hopefulness about its transformative power—how it will democratize us on the way to creating a new human consciousness—and dire predictions about its capacity to undermine literacy, corrupt democracy, and trivialize experience, destroying everything human about us. The antinomies that divide zealots and cynics overwhelm the moderate middle where most of us experience the digital every day.

On the one side of the divide stand the digital evangelicals, noisy in their technological righteousness and certain of their convictions— cyber fundamentalists who see in the new technology a deliverance from all that ails us, a new electronic frontier for freedom and democracy, new liberating forms of social organization and interaction. If democracy is about horizontal communication among peers, then the new technology surely can expand democracy's compass in remarkable ways, among individuals and cities alike. Aristotle thought democracy was limited by the size of a territory that could be traversed by a man on foot in a day (so he could get to the assembly). The new technology allows us to assemble en masse anywhere and at the speed of light, but the billion on the Internet gather only as individuals in small coteries of friends and family; others, aliens, and enemies are not welcome. The web removes all physical limits from deliberation and common decision making but seems to reinforce social ghettoization and groupthink, as Eli Pariser shows in *The Filter Bubble*, his book on Google and search engines.[21]

Enthusiasts cite the Arab Spring and Occupy Wall Street as exemplars of how technology can catalyze democracy. The culture of the web, they say, is embedded in the genes of contemporary rebels, defining not just how dissidents organize as free agents but how they think, how they understand their freedom. The promise of cyberspace surely can incite cyber rebellion, nurture cyber deliberation, promote cyber democracy. For cities that once pushed across the waters on the sails of trading ships and mingled across the continents on the wings of airliners, this means that, all at once today, they can interact and cooperate across the planet at the speed of light.

Yet the speed that accelerates global democratic interaction overruns democratic deliberation, obliterates democratic judgment, and undermines the slow pace of democratic decision making. Participation is encouraged but participants, inundated by big data and enamored of and encouraged in their own private judgments by wiki-process crowd-sourcing software, are ever less public and civic in their inclinations. Perhaps rather than accelerators, democratic traffic on the electronic highway needs speed bumps. Parliaments (including the one recommended at the end of this book) quite properly seek to slow rather than quicken the pace of decision making. They employ multiple "readings" of bills over a period of time where reflection, reconsideration, and regret are factors; or require supermajorities to ensure there is no rush to judgment; or even deploy the filibuster so that a single skeptic can slow the pace of legislative business. (The abuse of the filibuster by modern political parties bent on thwarting the will of elected majorities does not invalidate the argument for a deliberate approach to legislation, or the prudent and selective use of delay tactics.) The promise of the digital is also the peril: a world of on/off circuits operating at the speed of light in ways that can outrun human judgment with its defining "slowness" that is the virtue of taste, culture, lovemaking, judgment, and prudent democratic deliberation. The "Slow Food" movement is but the iceberg lettuce tip of a set of features that, neglected by the web, suggest that what it regards as its greatest virtues—speed, quantity, volume—are actually addictive vices.

The new technology is then bound to arouse cynics, quietly confirmed in their skepticism by enthusiasms that deny or obscure the web's deficiencies. These doubters track not just what the web promises in its democratic architecture or what it offers in its applications, but who owns it. Who owns the new media and for which ends, and in whose interests they employ their innovative technologies, is no less important than its architecture. Critics remain disquieted by the web's capacity for surveillance, its indifference to privacy, its mirroring of the manipulative commercial society. They worry that its inclination to "push" (to tell us what we want) will overwhelm its capacity for "pull" (to ask us what we want); or that "pull" will be subjected to endless marketing and manipulation and become another form of "push." They worry that calculating how to control and monetize the web may overshadow efforts to open it to all and put it to public and civic uses. They observe that the profit motive shows little interest in net neutrality (an open web in which all information is equal and those controlling the networks may not favor any particular content or consumer group).

Google advertises that it opens the world of information access to all, but in practice it has occasionally allowed tyrants to manipulate the search engine and censor its content. Twitter is the new glamour communication medium, yet it recently began blocking access in Germany by the neo-Nazi group *Besseres Hannover*, an outfit banned by the government. One may applaud censoring neo-Nazis, and appreciate the *Sonderfall* (special case) of Germany in this domain, but the precedent is troubling.[22] What if Twitter folk decide the Tea Party or the American Socialist Party present an analogous clear and present danger to American democracy and need to be blocked? The privatization of formerly public media means that what should be public decisions about free speech are now in private hands. "Trust us" is a poor recipe for preserving rights.

Apple also promotes a transparent and open world of egalitarian geeks but outsources manufacturing to outfits like Foxconn in China that operate oppressive labor camps to get parts (glass screens, for example) built in a hurry and on the cheap. Will the mayors who are beginning to network and collaborate and informally engage in cross-border governance use the new technology to elicit civic interactivity and enhance participation, or to suppress opposition and perhaps bypass constituents unfriendly to their goals? Will they try to enhance deliberation and facilitate the engagement in legislation of those they represent (as with participatory budgeting?). Or will they favor a rush to judgment in which the positions of corporate partners are favored and citizens have no chance to engage ideas but can only push electronic buttons and vote without thinking? Facebook allows friends to gather and prosper but may deepen the alienation of those left out of closed social circles defined by the ubiquitous "like" icon.[23] Why is there no civic Facebook; no social medium for citizens in a deliberative electronic space where those who disagree with others with whom they are bound to live together seek common solutions (the chief challenge of citizenship)? Google has introduced an intriguing new offering promising participation and exchange ("Hangouts") but so far it has mainly been an instrument of celebrity interviews. A true digital commons prompting interaction among citizens of different backgrounds and conflicting ideals seems a long ways off.

The ideology of market privatization was certified for new media by the Clinton administration with its shocking Telecommunications Act of 1996 (which set aside the 1934 Federal Communications Act that made broadcast media a public utility). The new law declared that spectrum abundance (the seemingly endless availability of bandwidth to everyone and anyone) had made the doctrine of mass communications as a public utility obsolete. Radio and broadcast television might have been scarce resources requiring that their public uses be protected. New media demanded no such protection. Yet this decision, perhaps the most ill-conceived in the history of public regulation, ignored the reality of global new media monopolies and reaped disastrous consequences. It turned out that theoretical diversity and plurality notwithstanding, cell phones and the web, hardware and software programs, pipes and content, are all owned by a handful of global monopoly corporations without the slightest interest in democracy, fairness, or civic education.

Along with still-powerful also-rans like IBM, AT&T, and Microsoft, four commercial megacompanies—Google, Amazon, Facebook, and Apple—between them today embody and represent everything that digital technology is about in the second decade of the third millennium. Whether you are shopping, researching, chatting with friends, looking for partners, watching a movie, listening to music, searching for porn, calculating figures, seeking information, or trying to play or learn or even vote remotely, you are probably doing it on, with, or through products of one of these companies (or one or two of their fading merge-prone competitors). These content providers and hardware and software producers, along with their archive in the "cloud" (*their* servers) are all you need to live, think, and breathe digitally.[24] The fraught ideals of net neutrality and privacy do not stand much of a chance against the realities of monopoly power in the hands of a few global corporations.

Yet everyday consumers and enthusiastic urbanists alike shower applause on these companies and the innovators who founded and run them, teaming up with them without subjecting them to scrutiny or questioning. The era is long gone in which an outfit like the Benton Foundation maintained a "Digital Divide Network" focused on unequal access to the web, which is monitored with monthly reports from "The Bridge." The Benton Foundation and newer initiatives like Common Cause's Media and Democracy program under the leadership of former FCC board member Michael Copps continue the battle for public media, old and new, but have a hard time being heard in all the white noise generated by the companies they try to scrutinize and report on.

These companies are abetted by the enormous publicity campaigns they run to market their brands, advertising the consumer virtues of pads, pods, and play-stations and boasting about the democratic architecture of their wizardry. Billionaires like Bill Gates (Microsoft), the late Steve Jobs (Apple), Mark Zuckerberg (Facebook), and Jeff Bezos (Amazon) are pop celebrities and media heroes. As such, though they regularly swallow up their rivals (critics talk about "Facebookistan"), they are rarely subjected to the harsh spotlight once shone on earlier tycoons such as John D. Rockefeller or Andrew Carnegie.[25] The term *plutocrat* is widely used today to disparage Wall Street and big finance, and is occasionally employed to batter traditional media bosses like Rupert Murdoch or Silvio Berlusconi. But it is hardly ever applied to new media moguls, who are treated more like the angels of a prospective media heaven—the true cloud?—than the founders and CEOs of immensely powerful tech firms that are first of all profit-seeking, market-monopolizing, consumer-craving commercial entities no more virtuous (or less virtuous) than oil or tobacco or weapons manufacturing firms. It should not really be a surprise that Apple will exploit cheap labor at its Foxconn subsidiary glass manufacturer in China or that Google will steer to the wind, allowing states like China to dictate the terms of "information retrieval" in their own domains. Or that the World Wide Web is being called the "walled-wide-web" by defenders of an open network who fear they are losing the battle.

Dictators, nowadays mostly faltering or gone, are no longer the most potent threat to democracy: robust corporations are, not because they are enemies of popular sovereignty but because court decisions like *Buckley v. Valeo* and *Citizens United* have allowed them to shape and control popular sovereignty to advance their own interests. Thus Jason Lanier (a digital insider and veteran of Atari and video games and an adviser to *Second Life*) has raised the alarm about the "fake friendship" that underlies social networks: such friendship is "just bait," he says, "laid by the lords of the clouds to lure hypothetical advertisers."[26] Lanier also worries about the "digital Maoism" implicit in Internet groupthink.

Lanier's voice echoes Foucault's and reminds us that what frees us from the old order may imprison us in the new. As the second great French critic of the Enlightenment argued (Rousseau was the first), the moral geometry that justified the rational orderliness of a new Age of Reason penology, substituting rehabilitative imprisonment for bodily punishment, was itself fraught. The hoped-for liberation from justice as vengeance (an eye for an eye and limbs pulled apart by the rack) actually birthed new forms of domination unforeseen by the Enlightenment. In place of torture of the body: a permanent surveillance over the soul—inspiring Jeremy Bentham's bleak vision of an all-seeing prison Panopticon that in Foucault's imagination became an emblem of the new and subtle tyranny of modern rationality.[27]

How Foucaultian, then, are the new media to which we look with such hope for social and civic progress, even as they look back at us, watching us 24/7 with electronic "cookies" and taste assessments and information collection and "push commerce"? Can mayors and urban citizens afford to welcome the digital age uncritically? Or fail to feel anxious about the implications of the late Steve Jobs's chillingly cheery Apple mantra, "It's not the consumers' job to know what they want"? Apply this formula to democracy—"it is not the citizens' job to know what they want"—and the result is demagoguery skidding down a steep path to tyranny.

The new technology is, among other things, truly a "push" technology that delivers its values and wares whether or not they are sought. Democracy and civic cooperation require "pull technology" in which the autonomous will and values of the user drive the machine. Or do we want a civic web that might one day tell an individual: "You voted for Obama but you oppose immigration and reproductive choice; here's the candidate for you!" Maybe even "and by the way, we voted for her in your name, OK?" (You can always "opt out" if you don't like the choices made for you.) Or should we be seeking forms of tech deliberation that help us to align our values and opinions when they are inconsistent and work to develop more coherent political principles? That such a media-based deliberative practice (initially via television) is possible has already been demonstrated by James Fishkin and his pioneering deliberative polling project, which has had a successful run of applied test cases in more than a dozen countries including the United States, China, Brazil, Bulgaria, Argentina, Japan, Korea, Poland, and the United Kingdom. Fishkin's technique "combines deliberation in small group discussions with scientific random sampling to provide public consultation for public policy and for electoral issues."[28]

We must then be both enthusiastic and wary of digital progress—and for the very same reasons. In his skepticist tract *The Shallows*, Nicholas Carr focuses on the costs of technological innovation. Written text, he notes, sidelines oral literary traditions; movable type pushes aside illuminated manuscripts; television puts an end to radio plays.[29] Carr's complaint about the web is that its incessant noise makes reading books difficult (though Kindle and Nook readers might disagree). But more pointedly, in the civic realm, the interactivity that could enable us to control new media and communicate with one another actually ends up (for the same reason) allowing the new media to watch and control us; allowing us to influence each other, sometimes in ways we don't even notice. While the web hosts a plethora of independent sites and critical blogs of real value to public debate, they are often overshadowed or simply buried by a cacophony of digital noise and the din of big companies.[30] Sharing is a great virtue of new media and has become Mark Zuckerberg's defining ideal: he wishes to help us do together just about anything that can be done. Except, unfortunately, politics and civics, which are activities that *must* be done together. Yet in a world of polarized ideology and divisive rhetoric, they rarely are.

Jeff Jarvis has celebrated at book length how the "publicness" of sharing compensates any loss of privacy.[31] Lori Anderson writes about the flip side of Internet sharing, that it is not always voluntary.[32] Collecting and sharing information on consumers and citizens alike is a multibillion-dollar business whose primary object is the commercial exploitation of consumers. It has a potential to become the political manipulation of citizens. As the pugnacious but prescient Evgeny Morozov puts it, the NGO called Privacy International, with a full-time staff of three, isn't exactly a "terrifying behemoth" when seen next to Google (lobbying expenses in 2010 of $5.2 million), however intimidating Jeff Jarvis and other Google fans might think it is.[33] The web that knows what books you might like to read and which sites you like to visit, knows how you think politically. With such empowering knowledge it can put appropriate books in your hands but also find reasons to put your hands in manacles. It can help you think through for whom you should vote, or help those who want your vote to get it regardless of what you think. Big data is big business and, as Tom Friedman never tires of telling us, is a boon to globalization; but it also has affinities to Big Brother, against whom big cities need to be constantly on guard.[34]

There are obstacles aplenty on the electronic highway and enough curves in the road ahead for smart cities hoping to get even smarter to proceed with caution. Caveat emptor.[35] But proceed they should and proceed they will. There is no way back after tech revolutions have occurred. What is needed now is a careful examination of the forms of cooperation technical innovation tries to promote, a systematic look at best practices. Knowing the pitfalls, the aim must be to do not merely what technology allows but what we choose and want to do with technology's help. What cities want to do is secure technology's assistance in augmenting interdependence and promoting intercity cooperation. But first a word about how technology is changing the way cities do their *own* business.

Smart Uses of Smart Technologies Inside Cities

The most important, as well as (literally) revolutionary, entailment of new technology is to enable opposition and dissidence in corrupt or illegitimate regimes. Chinese dissident Liu Xiaobo proclaimed the Internet "truly God's gift to China," while the Arab Spring was promoted as "Revolution 2.0"—a product of nerdy organizers moving protest crowds around by cell phone and promoting a secular ideology of protest on Twitter and in the blogosphere. As the mimeograph and later the Xerox machine once enabled organizers in the Soviet bloc to amplify and spread their voices, and helped promote early green efforts like Earth Day, the web today is everyone's megaphone. In the era of digital revolution, every blogger is a potential Gandhi (or Lenin!).

In Africa, where it has been far too expensive to wire a whole continent that missed the wired revolution, or in ex-Soviet countries like Estonia that were never wired, cell phone technology has leapfrogged the cabled world and become the instrument of choice for economic and civic as well as social and private communications. And in self-advertised open societies not altogether friendly to full transparency, dissidents like Julian Assange and Edward Snowden continue to leak and hackers (such as those in the "Anonymous Movement" and "The Chaos Computer Club") continue to hack digital information in a fashion intended to compromise elites (along with, some claim, national security) and to render opaque intelligence networks transparent.[36] Democratic technology has also been a friend to democratic protest and democratic rebellion in fully democratic nations, having, for example, played a key role in Occupy Wall Street.

Digital technology's role in already-democratic societies has been less confrontational and more conventionally instrumental—an aid to efficiency and clear communication and an invitation to greater participation. From the early days of "e-government" more than two decades ago, when European nations turned to technology to enhance their interior communication and their record keeping as well as their relationship with citizens, right down to the role of new media in enhancing traditional campaigning in recent years—Howard Dean's Meetups, MoveOn's rapid-fire progressive propaganda, and President Obama's vaunted but mostly one-way use of the web to jump-start his campaign and fundraising in 2008—technology has essayed to transform politics. Gavin Newsom exclaims a little too breathlessly that "technology has rendered our current system of government irrelevant, so now government must turn to technology to fix itself."[37] But that's not happening. Following the contested 2000 presidential election in the United States, the Help America Vote Act pointed the nation toward online voting. But digital divide issues of access aside, it eventually became clear that security questions made the option less desirable than many hoped it would be. A few states, such as Arizona and Michigan, experimented with online primary voting, but within a few months a review undertaken by the Internet Policy Institute issued a judgment devastating to fans of politics on the web: "Remote Internet voting systems," the report concluded, "pose significant risk to the integrity of the voting process and should not be fielded for use in public elections until substantial technical and social science issues are addressed."[38] Little progress has been made in the decade following.

The result has been a pretense of participation that has spread thinly across what is little more than a participatory gloss on traditional top-down, one-way politics. President Obama's White House website has hardly been any more interactive than anyone else's, the spirited efforts in his administration of digital advocates like Cass Sunstein and Beth Noveck notwithstanding. And try to communicate with one of those election-year fund-raising websites with more than a "Contribute Now!" link, or write back to a politician asking for your support (and dollars) to explain why you don't like her pitch . . . well, you can't. It is once again clear that new technology is used first of all to conduct old business. Shopping is still the web's main activity today, and about one-third of net traffic follows the road to porn. No surprise then that the promised interactivity of the web too often turns out to be a cynical cover for promoting unilateral top-down politics or that the promised speed of digital technology turns out simply to do more quickly what has long been done slowly by traditional means.

Yet these realities should not obscure the genuinely new uses of digital tech that make cities more energy efficient, more citizen friendly, and more participatory. Electronic (principally wireless) sensors are, for example, introducing a valuable new layer of automation to city sustainability and efficiency in transportation and energy. Sensors that facilitate the "platooning" (efficient spacing) of vehicles and the democratization of parking information and other measures that reduce engine idling are surely useful innovations. A number of American states, including California and Nevada, are experimenting with "self-driving cars" that are far more energy efficient than traditional vehicles and are intended primarily for cities. Smart thermostats save electricity and make heating and air-conditioning more efficient. Smart sensors of every kind are being used in cities across the world, including Cairo, Dubai, Kochi, Málaga, Malta, Yokohama, Songdo, and Southampton. Santander, Spain, may have the world's most extensive sensor network, with the company Libelium having installed 400 devices to locate parking spots and 700 more to measure and control ambient parameters for noise and carbon monoxide as well as temperature and sunlight.

Remote health exams via the web can offer improvements in urban (and rural) health care, especially for those without regular access to doctors. And electronic record keeping is a money-saving boon to public health that improves patient care and helps cities deal with new global pandemics. Even video games, going all the way back to *SimCity* (which was issued in a new version in 2013) and *Second Life*, allow experimentation with modes of urban design and cosmopolitan living. *Second Life*, like most web-based innovation, may be exploited mainly for entertainment (virtual sex and shopping and partying), but it also includes rules for living, principles of design, and a virtual currency with some real-world value. It also is host to a "democracy island" for democratic innovators created by the same Beth Noveck who worked with the administrations of Barack Obama and David Cameron to sustain civic uses of the web. *Second Life* even boasts a number of virtual embassies, representing such real world countries as Denmark, the Maldives, and Estonia, suggesting that virtual play is capable of doing real-world work and that virtual experimentation can impact actual best practices.[39]

There is, in short, a great deal to be said about what cities are doing currently to employ technology as a creative means to improve efficiency, sustainability, governance, and citizen outreach. For our purposes, however, the most crucial aspects of smart-city programs are those involving the role of technology in affording enhanced citizenship and civic exchange *among* cities and across national borders. Unfortunately, in this domain there is less innovation, and the way forward is genuinely hard. The British new-media observer Rick Robinson suggests that although cities "need to work together to create and deliver Smarter City visions," precisely because they are "complex ecosystems of people and organizations . . . bringing them together to act in that way is difficult and time-consuming." He concludes:

> Even where a city community has the time and willingness to do that, the fragmented nature of city systems makes it hard to agree to a joint approach. Particularly in Europe and the UK, budgets and responsibilities are split between agencies; and services such as utilities and transport are contracted out and subject to performance measures that cannot easily be changed. Agreeing [on] the objectives and priorities for a Smarter City vision in this context is hard enough; agreeing [on] the financing mechanisms to fund programmes to deliver them is even more difficult.[40]

Really Smart Cities: Connecting City Networks Electronically

The difficulties notwithstanding, proponents of intercity cooperation and cross-border participatory democracy continue to innovate. Over a dozen years ago the still-robust British charity Citizens Online proposed a "Civic Commons in Cyberspace" intended to realize democracy online. The aim was ambitious and nontraditional, "not about e-mailing the Prime Minister or watching a video stream of the Budget" but about "creating a new and innovative component for representative government in the 21st century."[41] Yet a decade later there is no civic commons. We might want to consider how such an online commons, were it established, could enhance democracy and even facilitate the development of a parliament of mayors or assembly of cities (Chapter 12). What can be found in the United Kingdom today are programs run by Citizens Online in Bristol, Leeds, Barnsley, London, and other cities focused on civic outreach. These programs involve citizens in city affairs and teach them how the Internet can inform and augment their citizenship— microsteps in a long journey to greater urban democracy.[42] Another British charity, UK Citizens Online Democracy (UKCOD), does similar work. Its poster project is mySociety, which aspires to "build websites which give people simple, tangible benefits in the civic and community aspects of their lives" as well as tutor the public and voluntary sector in how to use the Internet efficiently. Modest as its goals were, the UKCOD, founded in 1996, was dormant for a number of years and, however admirable in its aspirations, has been marginal in British democratic life.

In France, Le World e.gov Forum (with a mirror English edition) is dedicated to providing a web space for public debates among decision makers, elected officials, private actors, and members of civil society across the world, who can access the space via teleconferenced mobile phones. The project is fully in the spirit of informal cross-border governance and, almost alone in the field, tries to provide cross-border communications to public and private civic communities alike. As such, it offers a useful digital prototype for a parliament of mayors hoping to connect virtually to cities around the world.[43]

In the United States, the Benton Foundation's Digital Divide project has mainly played defense, trying to overcome the impact of digital inequality by working to redress the continuing gap that keeps the poor and destitute in both the developed and developing worlds from enjoying whatever civic and economic benefits the web may offer. As sci-fi prophet Bill Gibson has said, the future is already here, it's just not evenly distributed. The Foundation's Digital Divide Network and Digital Opportunity Channel continue to press the case for fair distribution, for a more egalitarian and civically accessible-to-all web, but the firms that control the technologies evince little interest in a domain so bereft of profit. Many of the city networks portrayed in Chapter 5 hope to use the web for communication and interaction, and as I suggested in opening this chapter, the new Barcelona-based City Protocol hopes to give it a more central and productive role in sharing best urban practices and expanding the compass of technology in intercity relations. In Germany, the Pirate Party has delighted cyber enthusiasts with its commingling of anarchism, tech zeal, and political innocence (or perhaps it is naiveté or simple irrelevance), and the Party has succeeded in Berlin and elsewhere well beyond its own modest expectations. A German site called parliament-watch.org (abgeordnetenwatch.de), dedicated to "creating trust through transparency," allows German citizens to put questions publicly to elected officials and track whether they answer and how. Politicians ignoring the questions have discovered they pay a price for their refusal to respond to constituents. This is a truly interactive use of the Internet.

The web has achieved the greatest success in linking cities around common action through its role in virally sharing city indicators and disseminating important urban initiatives in sustainability and democracy. Through the City Indicators project, for example, U.N.-Habitat, ICLEI, the World Bank, and other global partners are helping cities to share data about key performance figures with one another, a first step to more effective collaboration.[44] Among those innovative participatory experiments unfolding within cities and being shared through the Internet and other means, participatory budgeting (which we will look at in Chapter 11) is perhaps most notable. The evolving practice has spread from Latin America to North America, Europe, and the world primarily through the web, although it is important to note once again that its initial momentum came from the real-world site of Porto Alegre, Brazil, the town that was one of its birthplaces and that hosted antiglobalization conferences for many years.

There can be little doubt that cities are getting smarter and finding ways to use digital technology for outreach, information, and education and for involving citizens in neighborhood business, mainly within but also among towns. The possibilities (and perils) of crowdsourced knowledge—call it Wiki-logic—developed on the horizontal and disintermediated terrain of the Internet has powerful democratic implications. The assault on authority can liberate common women and men and invite them into deliberation, policy making (participatory budgeting), and a greater sense of ownership over government. Or it can unleash prejudice and the shameless promotion of straight-out lies. Epistemological anarchy. In other words, as Lee Siegel has argued, democratizing information can mean empowering disinformation.[45] The web is a powerful tool, but it is not hard to believe with Siegel that "with the rise of participatory culture, pop culture has entirely merged into commercial culture." And that "enchantment of the imagination has given way to gratification of the ego . . . welcome to the Youniverse," Siegel's version of a narcissistic Internet world.[46]

Critics such as Siegel are vindicated not only by the undeniable narcissism and commercialism of so much of what the new technology has yielded but by the fact that, for all the promise and all the promising, there is as yet no cyber commons, no digital public square, Google's experiment in Hangouts notwithstanding. Innovations like participatory budgeting, though spread by the web, are rooted not in high tech but in traditional citizens' assemblies and boards or participatory councils exercising meaningful budget control through co-planning processes. Such experiments may have resulted in an "empowerment of civil society and, most notably, of the working class," but these results are unrelated to technology.[47]

Technological implementation of participatory ideals among cities remains aspiration. And for good reason. It is generally acknowledged that online communities are rarely invented on line but are initiated in the real world and then pursued and sustained virtually. James Crabtree, an editor at openDemocracy.net, has prudently noted that "if we are not interested in politics, electronic politics will not help."[48] And if politicians remain cynical about democracy, we might add, they will use new technology only to get elected. Even a techno-zealot like Gavin Newsom admits politicians "love to use social media—but only for getting people involved in campaigns or getting into their wallets." Yes, he confesses, "we build fancy Web sites; we ramp up our tweeting and texting and engaging and mashing up; we host online town halls. And then, once we get elected, we just shut all that off and go away—until the next campaign season rolls around. No wonder people feel disconnected."[49]

Crabtree still would like to see the music file-sharing techniques (peer-to-peer or P2P technology) behind Napster applied to politics, and he asks the question: "Napster is to music as what is to politics?" By analogy there should be a "Citizster, or Polster." Yet it is not so much the application that is missing as the civic desire to develop and support it. If we are not interested in politics, e-politics won't help. It is for this reason that a true intercity civic commons online—a "citizster" civic file-sharing program—will likely have to follow rather than precede a civic campaign to establish intercity governance and the establishment of a parliament of mayors. Indeed, the fashioning of such a digital commons might even become a high purpose of a global cities secretariat.

With respect to the democratic uses of the new technology, I remain today what I was twenty-five years ago, not a skeptic, certainly not a technophobic, but a realist. The promise of the web's democratic architecture remains. E-participation and computer-supported cooperative work (CSCW) are now as current as e-government once was.[50] Online civic practitioners like Beth Noveck are not only wedded in theory to "wiki-government" and the proposition (in her book's subtitle) that "technology can make government better, democracy stronger and citizens more powerful" but are developing real-world practices to prove their point.[51] Noveck cites the chief architect of IBM's Internet strategy as saying that while "a participatory governance model would have been very difficult to implement only a short time ago. . . . The Internet and the World Wide Web have changed all that. They have enabled the more distributed, collaborative governance style being embraced by leading-edge organizations."[52] Moreover, while much of the technological innovation has occurred within cities and national systems, organizations like City Protocol and OneWorld (online) and e-gov Forum have begun to point the way to intercity collaboration via the web, even if they are unlikely to be able to *lead* the way.

The virtual always mimics the real. Citizens do not need a gateway drug for civic engagement, they need to take their citizenship cold-sober seriously. If they do so, technology can certainly help them engage across time and space, and companies like Cisco and Ericsson can then become their (our) allies. Google might even be able to turn its Hangouts into a true digital commons. Where cities go and citizens lead, there technology can follow, reinforcing and augmenting their progress in significant ways. But as in the past, truly smart cities will rely first not on instrumental technology but on the primary intelligence of citizens and the judgment of mayors in solving the (not just urban) problems of an interdependent world.

TEDDY KOLLEK OF JERUSALEM AND QADOURA MOUSSA OF JENIN

If rabid ideologues make for deficient problem solvers and hence ineffective mayors, cities defined from the top all the way down by ideology and political zealotry face unique leadership problems. Moscow's mayor Luzhkov ultimately succumbed to the presidential ideologues he could not please, and Chinese mayor Bo Xilai (Dalian) stumbled when he allowed ambition and corruption to overwhelm his competence. It seems, then, that there is nowhere in the world where urban pragmatism is more likely to be defeated than in Israel and the West Bank, where local politics is mired in an ideological struggle for national identity and religion that infects national and local politics alike.

For this reason, it is a tribute to their remarkable personalities and capacity for leadership that two recent mayors (both now deceased)—the celebrated **TEDDY KOLLEK** of Jerusalem, and the more controversial but equally unusual **QADOURA MOUSSA** (Kadura Musa) of Jenin—managed to pursue a politics of peace, reconciliation, and pragmatism in the face of bitter conflict. Once again, under the most difficult circumstances, we see the potential of local politics to elude ideology even when it seems omnipresent.

Theodor Kollek, born in Hungary in 1911 and with his childhood spent in Vienna, emigrated to Palestine and became a founding member of Kibbutz Ein Gev in 1937. Sustaining the kibbutz meant cultivating relationships with the British and the Arabs, and honing pragmatic skills that served him in his intelligence work in the United States for the Haganah during World War II. These skills proved decisive when, following service in the Foreign Office and Prime Minister's Office, he became the mayor of Jerusalem in 1965—a post he retained until 1993, when at eighty-two he was defeated by future prime minister Ehud Olmert.

Governing Jerusalem certainly meant picking up the garbage and "fixing the sewers," but as his biographers Roger Friedland and Richard Hecht have written, "the decision to build a road, hire a worker . . . or live in a neighborhood can be absorbed into, or come to express, struggles between opposing social movements, between nations, between states far from Jerusalem." Even as Kollek went about his quotidian activities, he faced conflicts that could quickly "form the basis for communal warfare and government crisis."[1]

Shortly after his election, the freshman mayor found himself having to deal with the consequences of the '67 war and the occupation of East Jerusalem. Kollek pledged full equality of services and parity of religions and oversaw what some called an "enlightened occupation" that included a memorial to those Israel had just defeated in battle—an unprecedented exercise in tolerance, unfortunately not imitated in later years by Israel's national leaders.

Kollek's global efforts brought considerable outside funding to the city, up to 15 percent of revenue, and facilitated the establishment of the Jerusalem Museum and Jerusalem Theater. Yet the historian Tom Segev, who ran Kollek's city office for two years in the 1970s, challenges the notion that this was all a kind of "miracle" that redeemed Jerusalem. Yes, Kollek was "considered pro-Arab" but the reality was "he was simply pragmatic." He liked to say being mayor of Jerusalem isn't the "most important job, but it is harder than being prime minister." Why? Because (as philosopher and rabbi David Harman wrote), "Jerusalem is a city that aspires to fanaticism. This city is messianism, it's revenge, it's the music of eternity, it's the city of pilgrims and dreams. You get away from reality and come here, you get away from reality and walk where Jesus walked, or King David. And then along comes Teddy, who says 'Look, I'll fix your sewers if you knock off the sermons.' He is the epitome of Machiavellian reality in a city which denies the whole notion of reality."[2]

Not so different from Qadoura Moussa (Kadura Musa) of Jenin. Although Moussa was on the "other side," and spent twelve years in Israeli prisons, his tenure as Jenin's governor and mayor was equally pragmatic—and effective. When it come to cities, to Jerusalem and Jenin, which side is the other side is hard to figure. A city is a city. As governor in Jenin, though a founder of Fatah and active in the first Intifada against Israel, Moussa was seen as pro-Israel in the same way Kollek was seen as pro-Arab. Problem solvers make poor ideologues and are always being seen as too tolerant, on some "other side" than "our" side.

His work involved building roads where there had been no roads (Jenin to Bilboa, for example)—"a living road," he said, is the key to bustling civic life—and focusing on industry and water resources when others were focusing on outmaneuvering a wily and adversarial Israel. He hoped his pragmatic urban projects might be "one step amongst many toward peace" between all Israelis and Palestinians.

Less free to travel than most mayors, he still looked abroad for alliances and networks. He had visited Cologne and observed how it had been rebuilt after World War II. His Valley of Peace Initiative promoted economic cooperation between Israel, Jordan, and the West Bank and stressed common industrial and economic projects and new canals and waterways. His successes were palpable in a climate of bitter discord. There is probably no more enduring if heartrending tribute to his life than how it ended: following an attempted assassination by vigilantes seeking revenge, Moussa died of a heart attack at sixty the very next day, in May 2000.

Some might see in Kollek and Moussa two sides of what is one side, comprising together a Möbius strip, that symbol of interdependence former mayor Antanus Mockus wears as a finger ring. Each was determined to govern cities not defined by sides. To me, this makes them less urban heroes than outstanding neighbors. What they did is remarkable but not exceptional. It is simply what mayors do.

CHAPTER 10. CULTURAL CITIES IN A MULTICULTURAL WORLD
The Arts of Interdependence

> More than ever before the city will be culture. A space of freedom and contact, a space for creation and exchange. . . . A quality public space, at the human scale, with efficient energy-sustainable systems of mobility where people are the essential core in what today defines the value of a city.
>
> *Javier Nieto, president, Institute for Advanced Architecture, Catalonia*

> UNESCO works to "highlight the role of cities, museums and tourism as vectors for the rapprochement of cultures, peace and sustainable economic and cultural growth."
>
> *UNESCO mission statement*

Culture defines the city and is critical to urban interdependence and to the democratic imagination. Some even insist that to speak of art *and* the city is redundant. Quite simply, art *is* the city. The city is culture and, as the architect Javier Nieto has declared, "will be culture." Urban space is free public space that facilitates public communication, civic imagination, and intercity cultural exchange. Creativity, imagination, collaboration, communication, and interdependence are essential constituents of what we mean when we speak of both the urban and the cultural, of both democracy and the arts.

Inasmuch as we can speak of the "us" of art, of what can be called the creative commons, the arts point to the idea of the public and the kinds of communication, community, audience, common space, and shared ground urban life affords. Inasmuch as we conjure with Walt Whitman a "democratic imagination," art also points to the ideals of equality, participation, and justice that emerge from empathy and common ground and are equally the terrain of the democratic city and the artistic spirit. Inasmuch as the city is borderless and interdependent, it mimics art in its aspiration to the cosmopolitan and the universal—to a world without boundaries in which what binds people together outweighs what keeps them apart. "The whole world," says cellist Yo-Yo Ma, "is in our neighborhood."[1]

I want here to advance this argument both conceptually, through an exploration of art and imagination, and concretely, through a survey of cultural networks. In the process, it should become apparent that the very notions of the "urbane" and "urbanity" we use to capture the disposition of the city also evoke the civilized and cosmopolitan—what I understand as the interdependent creative commons. Art is certainly grounded, even rooted, but it is rarely parochial; it speaks from the particular and is influenced by time and place, but it challenges limits and invokes the universal. The German composer Bach is defined but in no way constrained by the unmistakably German aspects of his music. To what country does Stravinsky or Picasso belong? Robert Wilson is from Texas, but the opera he created with Philip Glass, *Einstein on the Beach*, carries no passport and discloses no country of origin.

In associating urbanity with culture, I do not mean to suggest an instrumental, let alone commercial, relationship in which the arts are subordinated to other purposes of the city. Culture certainly generates economic benefits in the neighborhoods and towns in which it flourishes, and it more than "earns" what it costs city government and taxpayers.[2] Yet it should not have to justify itself by economic payoffs. If one must choose, it is more appropriate to treat the city as the instrument of the arts rather than the other way round, for it exists in a certain sense for art.

No need to pontificate, however. George Bernard Shaw famously dismissed such high-minded talk when, visiting Hollywood to find out whether Sam Goldwyn might be willing to make a movie of Shaw's play *Pygmalion*, he interrupted Goldwyn's reflections on culture, remarking, "the trouble is, Mr. Goldwyn, you want to talk about art whilst I have come to talk about money." Money is not my subject (though it is relevant), but considering art concretely, as a practice or a set of practices, makes good sense. Art is what artists do or produce rather than something they (or we) talk about, but this does not mean it can be reduced to entertainment, sex, politics, recreation, consumerism, or celebrity.

I want to consider three specific contexts for urbanity that help mediate art and the city: the idea of the public, the idea of democracy, and the idea of interdependence. These mediating ideas provide a context that helps render the abstract practical, the invisible transparent. In the words of Peter Brook, these contexts give to the "holy" in art an invigorating dose of the profane.

The three contextualizing ideas, briefly elaborated, are these:

The Idea of the Public, which points to the "us" of art—to communication, community, common space, and shared ground, and hence to a richer conception of audience;

The Idea of Democracy, which points to the ideals of equality, participation, and justice, and identifies in imagination a fundamental affinity between the arts and democratic life;

The Idea of Interdependence, which points to the cosmopolitan and the universal, a world without boundaries or border that demands to be recognized but has been largely neglected, even denied, by the parochial and insular for whom walls are a form of security.

In mediating the city and the arts, these three notions suggest how culture can advance the civic and collaborative interests of the city without reducing the arts to mere instruments in service to the urban. Not that such mediation is easy. Our times are hostile to the idea of a "public"—to community and common goods. They are equally hostile, for some of the same reasons, to democracy and equality. And they resist the looming idea of interdependence with a stubborn parochialism that prefers competition to cooperation and takes comfort in the shadows of once-mighty urban walls rather than the hope of much-needed urban bridges—above all in the United States, but increasingly in other parts of the world that ape American market practices.

American audiences are not themselves enemies of the arts. On the contrary. But the forces dominating American society, because they are hostile to community and democracy as well as to interdependence, are inhospitable to art. Trends inaugurated in the United States are evident today in Europe and elsewhere. A recent article on megamergers in the book business carried the overheated but descriptive title "How Raw Capitalism Is Devouring American Culture."[3] Art's continuing hold on its urban audience as an essential aspect of urbanity and civility is everywhere contested.

Artists have responded by trying in their practices and performances to reinforce the affinities of culture for the ideas of the public, the egalitarian, and the interdependent. As it makes its case for public life, democratic citizenship, and constructive interdependence, art practice makes a case for itself and its indispensability to the life of free democratic societies. But it is a hard slog, with big money and corporate organization too often on the other side. Nonetheless, in essaying to *create* a public, to *imagine* equality by accessing and sublimating otherness, and to *subvert* boundaries and build bridges among generations, traditions, and nations, art forges the conditions it needs in order to flourish.

The City as Public Space and the Perils of Privatization

Of the three contextualizing ideas, the idea of the public is perhaps the most at risk, above all in those cities in the developed world where the arts have traditionally flourished. Sharon Zukin has warned about commercialization and privatization as potent threats to the "mystique of public culture." In *The Culture of Cities*, she writes, "If entire cities, led by their downtowns, continue to be ghettoized by public rhetoric and private investment, the dream of a common public culture will fall victim to an empty vision."[4] Nonetheless, culture and commercial exchange are rooted in a common urban connectivity. Art is endemically communicative and depends on commonalities and shared ground that artists, with audiences, manage together to create. The idea of a "cultural community" is in a sense redundant, since culture always presupposes and fosters community. A culture is by its very nature collective, common, and public in character. In offering a creative vision, art invites spectators and listeners to join a community. Cities flourish where art thrives because the arts help create the public space cities need.

Yet the very notion of community as it is associated with public goods has been under siege for some time. The neoliberal ideology, though kept at bay more in the city than in the suburbs and less threatened on the local than the national plane, has made urban inroads in film, theater, publishing, and even the fine arts, where celebrity exhibitions increasingly overpower representation of a wide spectrum of artists. The neoliberal skirmish against bloat and inefficiency quickly becomes a battle against "big government," which becomes in turn a veritable war on the very idea of what a public is, even in cities defined by their public character. The arts can be compromised in a privatized arena because, when construed as a commodity in a commercial market, like education, religion, and recreation when they are reduced to commerce, they need to make a profit to survive. Commodification poses a puzzle to artists: art, even when it is critical of commerce, is often driven by it. To make, present, or perform art is also to sell tickets, seduce audiences, compete for limited media space. In an essay pertinently titled "Rude Ludicrous Lucrative Rap," Dan Chiasson captures the contradiction in the domain of rap music: "Even as rap undermines its whole demented code of money, cars, ho's, and hustlers, it markets it, markets itself." Jay-Z may be a critic, but "the critique doesn't undermine the business: it is the business."[5]

The historical priority of public over private space, of the nonprofit civil sector over the private market sector, was evident in the traditional architecture of our towns and cities but is today endangered. In traditional townships, centered around a commons or public square were once found the nonprofit symbols of the *res publica* and a robust and pluralistic civil society: an art gallery, town offices, a community theater, and a church or synagogue or mosque (this isn't political correctness; all three can be found on one square in today's Istanbul); and of course those emblems definitive of our public lives—a public school, a public library, a public town hall, a public post office, and, in England once upon a time, the public drinking establishment known as a public house or pub, which like the American barbershop or general store or neighborhood bar served as a public clearinghouse, not just for gossip and social life but for public talk and civic interaction. This varied cityscape embodied an architectural ensemble inflected by design that was defined by Main Street and the roadways around a public square, streets whose business was to cater to the public souls of commoners and citizens.

In town today, however, public architecture is being overtaken and displaced by private buildings: corporate towers and bank-sponsored skyscrapers, high-rise cooperative residences, hotels, and urban malls (consider Dubai) that are to the commercial essence of cities what cathedrals and massive public buildings once were to their religious and civic essence. Surrounding the city, suburbia swallows ups villages and townships, leaving behind diversified but decayed downtowns that are eclipsed by monomaniacal retail malls demarcated by big-box chain stores and private-use commercial space. The vanishing minicenters that once defined the township are hardly visible. In the new suburban mall spaces, defined often as private rather than public, political leafleting, playing, praying, and even people-watching are discouraged if not outlawed (no benches in most malls; keep the customers shopping). No art galleries or theaters or museums. Only the multiplex with its brand-permeated commercial movies. Not even a public post office. No leisurely restaurants, only fast-food courts that are nutrition pit stops to fuel up tired shoppers for the next round of consumerism.[6]

In destroying public space, privatization undercuts the conditions that nourish culture. With the corporatization of cities and the malling of towns, we can hardly be outraged or even surprised when art both mimics and mocks the commercial culture on which it depends by making its price tag the measure of its worth. The art game is shaped today by megastar concerts and celebrity exhibitions such as the one a few years ago at the Tate Modern in London. The Tate's aptly named *Pop Life: Art in a Material World* celebrated Andy Warhol, Jeff Koons, Keith Haring, and other creators who had figured out how to cash in without (they hoped) abandoning their aesthetic. A performance art piece by Andrea Fraser involved a video installation in which she beds and fucks an art collector on camera, who pays $20,000 for her and the video she makes of their activity. The price presumably represents about $1,000 (by current British standards) for the sex and about $19,000 for the resulting video "art work," which in keeping with contemporary narcissism features . . . the buyer in action!

Modern artists, from rappers to painters, work hard to rationalize their sellout to commerce (who can blame them?) as a form of subversion. Subversion and cashing in turn out quite conveniently to be more or less the same thing. So Damien Hirst, no second fiddle to Jay-Z, can stud a skull with diamonds and sell it for tens of millions, far more even than the in-your-face gems are worth, construing it as scabrous commentary on a commerce-mad modern society. Yet is it really anything more than a backhanded tribute to the triumph of that society not only over art but over the artist?[7] Selling out has always been profitable; that's its point.

The artist's temptation to buy in by selling out is the danger associated with very persuasive arguments about the economic benefits of what are today (regrettably) called cultural workers. The arts are forced into playing the privatized commercial game favored by management consultants and politicians worried about reelection, a game aimed at proving their worth not in terms of intrinsic value and inherent meaning but in terms of how much they pay back financially to the communities that deign to support them. Moreover, if they take even a few dollars from government or charity, arts institutions are subjected to an oversight that corporate firms with far more public influence never endure. It is perfectly true and more than important to recognize that the arts help create and sustain communities, and they pay back to cities far more than cities pay to support them. While cities should be transparent, they should perhaps only be subject to standards applying to all corporations.

At the international conference Florens 2010, a featured study showed that for every $100 invested in arts and culture, $249 was added to GDP; that every three jobs created in the arts sector yielded two more in the private sector. Statistics from *Americans for the Arts* show that "nonprofit arts organizations and their audiences generate $166 billion in economic activity every year and support almost 6 million jobs."[8] They return

$30 billion in government revenue every year as well. In New York, in the new downtown ground zero neighborhood, the arts have helped repopulate residences and revitalize retail stores and hotels in depressed areas. The Brooklyn Academy of Music, under Harvey Lichtenstein and then Joe Melillo, has not only become the most vital presenter of the international performing arts in the United States but has been a pioneer in the borough's cultural and commercial rebirth.[9] Long after the Brooklyn Academy paid its dues to the development of Brooklyn, big capital is cashing in, as evidenced by the opening in 2012 just a few blocks from BAM of a new sports and performance arena (the Barclay Center) that rivals Madison Square Garden in Manhattan and whose opening night featured (who else?) Jay-Z.

Yet focusing on the economic arguments for supporting civic art shifts the ground from culture to commerce. As Carey Perloff, the artistic director of the American Conservatory Theater in San Francisco, has observed, "we have come to rely on metrics that measure success according to the cost per person of producing a given play or mounting a given art exhibition" rather than trying to "nurture and cultivate that which may have lasting value."[10] For the long-term good of the city, the commercial ground is not where the arts should be. Too often it leads to treating arts institutions as urban homesteading pioneers in the world's cities, where the arts fail to benefit even as cities they help to sustain flourish. Decades before 9/11, the lower Manhattan neighborhood "south of Houston Street" (SOHO), left in economic purgatory by the death of local manufacturing, was turned into a viable living and working neighborhood by pioneering artists and art galleries. They too were forced to move out as their success produced an economic upswing and boutiquing beyond their means. Later, in DUMBO, the riverside industrial wasteland "down under the Manhattan Bridge overpass" into which some of SOHO's erstwhile pioneers had moved, a similar development is nearly complete, and the artists are again vagabonds compelled to move on to Queens or to New Jersey's Hoboken, across the Hudson River.

In Berlin, a similar story emerges from the experience of the community arts complex Radialsystem. After the fall of the Wall, Jochen Sandig and others helped create first the art commune and sculpture park on Oranienstrasse called Tachelas and then the theater and com-munity complex Radialsystem in an old Berlin pumping station on the Spree Kanal, turning an East Berlin industrial zone near the Ostbahn-hof into a neighborhood both fashionable and attractive to corporate business.[11] Yet in doing so, it hastened its own sustainability crisis by making its once-critical cultural presence superfluous in the face of the influx of grasping developers and corporations enticed into the neigh-borhood by the theater's artistic and community success.

Artists and arts producers represent the soul of the city yet are too often driven by scarce resources to become reluctant urban pioneers in developing or restoring unprofitable neighborhoods abandoned or neglected by commercial interests. All too often, the instigators and cultural catalysts become the homeless detritus of newly chic new neigh-borhoods where they can no longer afford the exorbitant rents they have made feasible. Harry Belafonte, who in an exemplary career of more than sixty years as an artist and advocate for social justice refuses to go away, just recently forged an alliance with the Service Employees Union 1199 to revivify Bread & Roses, the union's decades-old cultural arm, a few blocks from Times Square. More than the Broadway theaters pre-senting megahit musical revivals up the block, Belafonte's theater in the union's headquarters invokes the cultural core of the city. But Belafonte's story is a rare and precarious success and, unfortunately, probably turns more on his commercial celebrity than his deep commitment to social and racial justice.

The arts are surely viable sources of economic productivity for cities. But neither artists nor politicians should be forced to offer only these instrumental arguments in campaigning for culture. Russell Bishop poses a question intended to be rhetorical but that is quite real in an essay showing how economically valuable culture actually is. "Are We Wasting Money on the Arts?" he asks. The prudent answer is "no, we are not!" but the better answer is "I certainly hope so!" Because if we are actually earning money off the arts and regarding that as its raison d'etre, it may not be art that is purveyed or culture that is served. What we value, we spend money on; what we cherish, we must be willing to "waste" money on, since money will never be its measure.

So the arts benefit the urban economy, because to benefit the commons, to enhance the community, to help create common goods and public space, *is* economically beneficial. Demanding that artists "prove" their value to the city in commercial terms can only be counterproductive. It means treating the public space that culture sustains as private commercial space, which corrupts art and robs the city of its defining commons. Art loses, but we lose more. In proving how well it helps pays the bills, we forget what art is for—and what we as an urban audience need from it: in Perloff's account of theater, "juicy literature performed by great actors, rather than . . . desperately chasing every passing trend."[12]

The City as Democracy and the Power of Imagination

Democracy, our second crucial cultural construct, is closely related to the idea of the public and equally vital to the arts. It invokes equality and participation, but it begins with a deep regard for the human rights that generate the egalitarian ideal. The equality of all is the premise of the individuality of each. Liu Xiaobo, China's persecuted Nobel Prize winner who has been censored and shuttered by the country's frightened party hacks, has written, "freedom of expression is the foundation of human rights, the source of humanity, the mother of courage and truth." Such human rights, in theory the human birthright, are in fact a product of human association and democratic citizenship. Equality of rights is an artificial construct that depends on recognition and reciprocity. We are "born equal" in theory but must become equal through civic activities and constitutional faith in practice. That is why Tocqueville spoke of the "apprenticeship of liberty," which he called the "most arduous of all apprenticeships." To put it another way, equality is neither natural nor discovered but invented: it is the product of civic aspiration and an empathetic imagination.

The faculty that ties art to democracy and democracy to art is imagination. Citizens (real citizens, not consumers or clients of government services) have in common with artists a capacity to envision: to look beyond apparent borders, to see beneath appearances, to apprehend commonality where others perceive only difference. They are seers of the common, adept at finding what humans share. Individual women and men are defined in the first instance by their distinct private interests: citizens, like artists, use imagination to discover common ground and shared values sufficient to adjudicate private differences and achieve high common purposes. Democracy's paramount norm is equality. Equality is above all a product of imagination. Immediate perception and blunt reality reveal only the distinctions of race, gender, accent, class, religion, and ethnicity that divide us and turn us into potentially hostile "others," dividing the world into warring tribes. Equality demands an imaginative faculty that sees through walls and beyond otherness to underlying human sameness—to a cosmopolitan core reflecting what imagination alone can conceive as our "humanity." Lionel Trilling captured the intimacy of imagination and liberalism when he argued that the job of criticism would seem to be "to recall liberalism to its first essential imagination"—in Trilling's vision, the imagining of "variousness and possibility, which implies the awareness of complexity and difficulty."[13]

Turning Trilling around, we ask a simple question: what is a bigot but a man without imagination, a woman blind to the variousness of the human tribe? It is a backward tribute to our imagination that we must first dehumanize those we would kill. The demeaning terms we unload on our enemies are so many attempts to eradicate the human essence that stands in the way of homicide. Training warriors requires first of all the erasure of imagination—that spring of empathy that sees in supposed enemies not "others" but beings like ourselves and so insists on a reciprocity of treatment that impedes killing. Imagination is the end of enmity and the beginning of justice.

The democracy I am invoking here is not democracy as a formal governing system but, in John Dewey's phrase, democracy as a way of life. It is the plural democracy Walt Whitman limns in poetry in his *City of Ships* (see Chapter 1) and in prose in his *Democratic Vistas*; it is the democratic America he celebrates in "By Blue Ontario's Shore" (in *Leaves of Grass*)—a democracy as rich and multitudinous, as various and multivalent and paradoxical as Whitman himself:

O I see flashing that this America is only you and me,
Its power, weapons, testimony, are you and me,

Its crimes, lies, thefts, defections, are you and me,

Its Congress is you and me. . . .

The war (that war so bloody and grim . . .) was you and me,

Freedom, language, poems, employments, are you and me,

Past, present, future, are you and me.

I dare not shirk any part of myself, nor any part of America good
or bad.[14]

In this notion of democracy, Walt Whitman's and John Dewey's, it is not just talk but silence that defines democratic life. For imagination's most precious tool is listening, apprehending what can be gleaned from stillness. In elections, we seek out electrifying talkers, the garrulous lawyers and noisy politicians to whom silence is an affront. Once elected, they sit and gab in our "parliaments" (talk-aments) around the world. Would that we elected listeners who took their place in "audiments." (*Audioment* would be the clumsy but apt name I would give the parliament of mayors, if I had Adam's power.)

Listening has sometimes been deemed a feminine virtue—and not to praise it. The so-called ethics of care that Carol Gilligan or Virginia Held embrace is hence construed as soft, an unmanly take on morals.[15] Perhaps this is why women, trained (compelled?) to listen and acculturated to empathetic imagination (not necessarily for the "right" reasons but out of necessity in the male's hormonal world), are natural democrats and peaceful problem solvers. As Gilligan has said, "There's a patriarchic so-called notion of care, which is care as self-sacrifice and selflessness. And there's a democratic notion of care, which is: To care is to be present, it's to have a voice, it's to be in relationship."[16] The city's affinity for democracy grows in part out of this notion of care, this disposition for relationship, for voice as listening no less than speaking. To become neighbors, individuals living in proximity must listen intently to one another and envision what they may share; voice must be reciprocal, otherwise they remain strangers—rights-bearing individuals, self-interested consumers, special-interest vendors. Likewise, city council members and mayors are more disposed than officials at higher levels of government to use their ears as well as their lips as instruments of governance.

In art and democracy alike, imagination is the supreme virtue. Art thus nurtures democracy, and democracy embraces art. Civic education is as much arts education as social science. Before imagination, bigotry withers, "others" melt away, and obstacles to community both within and among cities fall.

Urban Interdependence and Cosmopolitan Culture

Like art, democracy enlists imagination to cross boundaries, allowing individuals to become citizens and letting citizens forge common ground with others despite alien identities and origins. Yet also like democracy, art is necessarily rooted, embedded in culture and nationality, to a degree even imprisoned in the independent nation-states that contain it. Folk music, for example, an element in all music, is literally the cultural inflected music of a Volk or people. In the eighteenth century, Rousseau and the composer Jean-Philippe Rameau (along with others) engaged in a famous quarrel about whether French or Italian music was more melodious and pleasing, with Rousseau insisting that Italians were superior because their music was so much more reflective of cultural inflections than the abstract French school.

Yet the more cultural inflection, the less universality (Rousseau was targeting Rameau's abstract and formal understanding of musical pitch). Anthems and songs of battle and conquest reflect and celebrate a particular history that can exclude, diminish, or deny the history and cultures of others and turn the "other" into an enemy. Democracy's capacity for empathy and taste for equality has often evaporated at the democratic nation's frontiers. Although the old cliché insists that democracies never make war on one another, the democratic community, so free from boundaries within, can nurture hostility to "foreign" cultures. For too many Americans, an exceptionalist America is righteously superior to other nations.

The Europeans worked miracles after the Second World War to eradicate the old borders across which they had been slaughtering one another for centuries but managed to rebuild a wall around the new Europe as impermeable as the old national frontiers. Cultural triumphalism (in which many nations including the Germans, the French, the Russians, the Japanese, the Persians, the Turks, and the Chinese have all indulged) can, just like exceptionalism, become a heavy club with which to hammer cosmopolitanism. In the shadow of national parochialism, cosmopolitanism is easily demeaned as an insidious form of cultural deracination.

I do not wish to suggest that the art of a nation's cultural roots and urban art are wholly contrary, but interconnected cities laced with multiculturalism are less constrained in their cultural self-definitions and democratic outreach than nation-states. Their virtue is to cross borders rather than secure and fortify them, to define themselves in cosmopolitan rather than parochial language. Cities comprise both walls and bridges, but it is the bridges that stand out when we speak about urban art or urban democracy. Built on water (nearly nine of ten are), cities flow. They too seek local identity in rooted art forms, but theirs is a dialectic of art in which both a rooted culture and a multicultural commons stand in healthy tension. Art both creates and subverts identity and is probably most successful when it is doing both. It succeeds in being cosmopolitan only inasmuch as it grows out of a particular place, a parochial *politeia*.

The Chinese dissident and artist Liu Xiaobo, like his colleague Ai Weiwei, is a case in point: he is a natural interdependent and yet wholly a product of Chinese culture and civilization. In embracing human rights, he has necessarily abjured walls. "I have no enemies," he says, "no hatred." For him, as for so many artists, "otherness" is a phantom construct of narrow minds, although he is no less Chinese for that. His cosmopolitanism is merely a concomitant of what it means to be an artist, the logic that leads from his creative individuality to human equality founded on common human creativity and hence to human rights—the right to equal treatment. Rights are both the beginning of interdependence—no rights for one or some without rights for all—and the reason artists are the vanguard of an interdependence movement: no art without imagination and the constant quest to overcome otherness.

I can think of no artist who puts the unique gifts of his native culture to more cosmopolitan and democratic purposes than Walt Whitman, a man for whom poetry and democracy are twins. Whitman was no lazy idealist, blind to democracy's faults. From him we learn that ambivalence is democratic art's calling card. As self-described in his *Song of Myself*, Whitman was "an American, one of the roughs"; he was "a kosmos, of Manhattan the son, / turbulent, fleshy, sensual, eating drinking and breeding, / No sentimentalist . . . . Unscrew the locks from the doors! / Unscrew the doors themselves from their jams!" Surely that's the ticket for art today! "Unscrew the locks from the doors!"—that's Tony Kushner or Ai Weiwei or Belgian choreographer Anne Teresa De Keersmaeker. That's Robert Wilson reinventing Einstein on a metaphysical beach for which no stage is large enough! "Unscrew the doors themselves from their jams!" —that's Anna Deavere Smith in her stunning monologues or Ivo van Hove in his startling direction of *Hedda Gabler* or his participatory staging (with the audience mingling with the actors) of *The Roman Tragedies*; the old, unbowdlerized Mark Twain; the playwright Athol Fugard in a not-yet-free South Africa; the novelist Chinua Achebe taking the measure of Africa; or the new New York musical reassessing the first president from outside the thirteen colonies, *Bloody Bloody Andrew Jackson*!

Whitman's democracy was no Jeffersonian aristocracy of landed yeoman but a congeries of everyman and everywoman unbounded: "I acknowledge the duplicates of myself, the weakest and shallowest deathless with me, / What I do and say the same waits for them, / Every thought that flounders in me the same flounders in them." Whitman's equality feels real and palpable and speaks still today to the endless variety of America, to its now-global cities, to cities everywhere teeming as ever with immigrants who are the hardy new specimens of an emerging global civil society. Whitman celebrates not government but society, and a pretty rough society at that. But like Tocqueville and Dewey, he understands, from the depth of his poetic imagination, that formal democracy depends on informal democracy, that voters must first be citizens. To be more than mere commands inscribed on paper, the rights that Liu Xiaobo prizes must be embedded in the habits and mores of a free people. In this sense it may be that Walt Whitman's rough brief for civil society with all its abrasive edges, his equality of grittiness and sweat and sex and blood, is a firmer foundation for democracy than any written constitution. We need citizens to animate constitutions, we need poets to animate citizens.

Whitman's democracy, like the city's, is finally a democracy of hope, a democracy that looks forward because its history "remains unwritten . . . [and] has yet to be enacted." It is a democracy that responds to terror fearlessly by refusing to yield its liberties to security or sacrifice equality in the name of surveillance and profiling. To the degree democracy overseen by anxious nation-states is at risk today (and democracy is always at risk), it may be because we have neglected the spirit of poetry and have turned imagination into a guardian of our fear and a prognosticator of catastrophe. Whitman knows the tasks of democracy are more than governmental and greater than the vouchsafing of security. In *Democratic Vistas*, he writes:

> Did you, too, O friend, suppose democracy was only for elections, for politics, and for a party name? I say democracy is only of use there that it may pass on and come to its flower and fruits in manners, in the highest forms of interaction between men, and their beliefs—in religion, literature, colleges, and schools—democracy is all public and private life.

Like John Dewey, who insisted democracy was not a form of government but a way of life, Whitman embraced a democracy that could contain multitudes. This was the special gift of the city: its pluralism. Yet it is today imperiled by the spirit of our age: the shrunken, greedy animus of the imperious corporate banker or the grasping consumer with whom the citizen is too often confounded. If ever a market-obsessed world needed democratic voices, ardent dreamers, and lawless artists, it needs them today. In chaotic times, fresh from a terrible civil war and the assassination of a president, on the eve of a gilded age of robber barons, Whitman taught America to hear and to sing the song of democracy. Artists today, reaching out across frontiers that states have drawn but neither cities nor the culture they instigate need recognize, teach the world the song of democracy. To sing the poet's old song of democracy is to chant a melody rich in the new promise of interdependence.

Art and the City: Institutions and Networks

The arts manifest the city in all of its public, democratic, and interdependent aspects. They do so by embodying and embracing imagination and creativity; but also through cultural institutions and networks that tie cities together and contribute to a common sense of purpose and mission. Production and performance institutions within cities often become nodes for cultural exchange and networking, exploiting the global character of theater, opera, music, and dance in today's world. A mere listing does not do justice to the role these institutions play in introducing artists cross-culturally, in linking cities, and in helping to establish an interdependent global culture. But the myriad organizations linked together in the International Society of Performing Arts (below), including the Brooklyn Academy of Music in New York, the Theatre de Paris in Paris, the Kaaitheater in Brussels, and Radialsystem in Berlin, are examples of producing and presenting organizations that ensure culture also means multiculture in global cities everywhere and that cultural relations also entail personal relations among artists. Typical of such organizations is the Brooklyn Academy of Music, over 150 years old but aspiring to engage "both global and local communities" through the "programming of both emerging artists and innovative modern masters." Artistic director Joseph Melillo has said his job is akin to being a kind of "mayor for the arts" with responsibilities to artists and audiences everywhere. Such a view is common to arts producers and artists alike.

It is hardly an accident that so many artists today see themselves as nodes in global networks. Musical director Kurt Masur, when he conducted the Dresden Symphony, played a crucial role in engineering the link between Hamburg and Dresden as sister cities in the shadow of Cold War barriers. Daniel Barenboim's leadership in establishing an Israeli-Palestinian orchestra is no less formidable than theater director Juliano Mer-Khamis's leadership of a West Bank theater that crossed an even more riled and violent territory (Mer-Khamis was murdered for his multicultural aspirations in April 2011). Individual performers have not merely exploited global interdependence for commercial benefits but used their global presence to nurture cultural interdependence. The cellist Yo-Yo Ma, for example, a global performer renowned for his mastery of the classical repertoire, has pioneered creative collaborations that bridge the classics and music from countries on the Silk Road from Europe to Asia or tap the roots of Appalachian folk music as a source for performance collaborations that cross the classical/popular divide. Yo-Yo Ma has spoken explicitly about the power of interdependence musically and civically. He insists that, first of all, "Music is one of the best ways human beings have invented to code their lives, and one of the values musicians practice is that we are always working toward something bigger than ourselves."[17] "This connectivity of the intimate and the worldly goes to the heart of culture, helping to give Yo-Yo Ma his universal appeal.

Performers such as Ma and the civil rights activist Harry Belafonte, choreographers like Pina Bausch, directors and designers with the gifts of Robert Wilson are what make the arts sticky, connecting people around the world in ways culture may not always contemplate. In Kinshasa, a megacity in the sometimes anarchic Republic of the Congo, a symphony orchestra was conceived and made real as a musical rebuke to third-world stereotypes.[18] That is not to say, however, that there are not also networks and associations in the domain of culture that do for the arts what the organizations we examined in Chapter 5 do for the environment and security. There are scores of networks that formalize arts entrepreneurship and give shape to their natural interdependence, acting as synapses between city nodes in which art is a vital marker of community and commonality.

Typical of such unheralded but influential organizations is the International Society for the Performing Arts (ISPA), a "global network of more than 400 leaders in the performing arts with representation from more than 50 countries and all regions of the globe," whose members include "facilities, performing arts organizations, artist managers, competitions, funders, consultants and other professionals."[19] The organization, which was founded after World War II, describes itself as a meeting place (two world congresses per annum) and professional network; it makes a number of prestigious awards, including a Distinguished Artist Award, but is particularly concerned with facilitating emerging leaders.[20] It embodies in a practical professional manner the spirit of interdependence that makes the urban arts natural connectors among cultures and people. In the words of David Baile, ISPA's executive director (CEO), cities are "hubs of cultural activity" so that art is "urban-centric."

Nonetheless, Baile notes, cities are set in regions and neighborhoods that, while not always well served by the arts, need to be understood as "underserved areas" requiring attention. Inequality turns out to be an affliction of culture as well as economics. Big cities with culture over-shadow small cities without. The cult of the professional demeans the practices of the amateur, and in the city's own version of elitism, provin-cialism comes to refer to taste as well as geography. As a consequence, the differences that divide cities are too often mirrored in access to cul-tural and artistic funding. Associations like ISPA manage to offer some common ground but can hardly overcome the divide on their own. To fill the gap, public funding of the arts is essential. Its role is to equalize where the market excludes and segregates; to distribute urban culture across urban maps no less subject to redlining than ghetto neighbor-hoods. City funding needs to flow to small theaters like (in New York) Three Legged Dog and the National Black Theater no less than to Lin-coln Center and the Public Theater; state and national funding in France needs to be funneled to Metz and Clermont-Ferrand as well as Paris and Lyon. Or better yet, to the working-class banlieues populated in recent decades by North African immigrants.

Baile points to two other organizations that share ISPA's values and have resources of the kind that can address inequality and foster new art in new venues: the International Federation of Arts Councils and Cul-tural Agencies (IFACCA), based in Sydney, which is a government coun-terpart of ISPA just twelve years old; and the Eurocentric web portal IETM (Interactive Electronic Technical Manual), based in Brussels. IFACCA has a very diverse representation including both countries and regions and, Baile suggests, "would not view themselves as an intercity network," since members tend to be national funding agencies.[21] Its mis-sion statement offers a vision of a "world in which the arts are valued in themselves and for their contribution to strengthening communities and enriching lives."[22] As IFACCA's precious but revealing logo says, "the arts mean the world to us." Like other global arts associations, IFACCA offers vital regional and global resources to its members that encourage cross-border collaboration.[23] Other global arts organizations that are more marketplace oriented include WOMEX (WOrld Music EXpo), IAMA (Intermountain Acoustic Music Association), and to a lesser degree APAP, the Association of Performing Arts Presenters, that tries to broker artists and production organizations on a global plane.

The arts also are the subject of policy in a number of international organizations, though in contrast to culture within and among cities, there is a pronounced instrumentalism in their approach. The best known United Nations agency, UNESCO, promises in its cultural mission statement (culture is one of five areas) to develop "operational activities that demonstrate the power of culture for sustainable development and dialogue." It also aspires to "promote the diversity of cultural expressions and the dialogue of cultures with a view to fostering a culture of peace." Cultural justice, like diversity and peace, when it is not merely a shibboleth, can be a by-product of culture but also its object. To be sure, as the arts become instrumental, political values can be sucked in. No telling where this can lead: it could be to the American defunding of UNESCO by a parochial Congress; or on the other side, an "anticolonial" campaign for a new world cultural and information order not dominated by the West—but one that ends up being as antiprovincial as its adversary and antiartistic to boot. The virtue of cities, as creators and consumers of culture, is that they are less driven by explicit political agendas and are more interested in demonstrating culture's self-referential attributes that mirror what is best about the city.

Artists and cultural organizations can nevertheless hardly afford to turn away from institutions that are, of necessity, bureaucratic and utilitarian. International institutions like UNESCO may treat art primarily as a vehicle for achieving other goals that, while laudable (diversity, nonviolence, even the achievement of the Millennium Development goals), presume and exploit rather than foster culture and its creation. In the language of the Millennium Declaration (2000), the U.N. "emphasizes the important contribution of culture for sustainable development and the achievement of national development objectives and internationally agreed development goals, including the Millennium Development

Goals"; it "invites all Member States, intergovernmental bodies, organizations of the United Nations system and relevant non-governmental organizations . . . to ensure a more visible and effective integration and mainstreaming of culture in development policies and strategies at all levels." The aim is to focus on "the role of culture in promoting economic equity, social cohesion, reconciliation, peace and non-violence." No program is too remote from culture to be excluded from UNESCO's purview: thus, "initiatives begun in the last millennium to highlight the role of cities, museums and tourism as vectors for the rapprochement of cultures, peace and sustainable economic and cultural growth will be scaled up," while "efforts to mainstream culture into national poverty reduction strategies" will continue.[24]

Cities have little choice but to walk the line separating art for its own sake from art as a vehicle of related urban and democratic goals. Thus, UNESCO takes a lively interest in cultural programs that manifest both cultural identity and artistic expression, both of value to the arts community (the arts *and* the community). Its current works include efforts "to promote dialogue among cultures and increase awareness of cultural interactions, through flagship projects." These projects make clear that underlying UNESCO's work is an awareness of the key relationship between art and democracy.[25]

If UNESCO necessarily presumes that the arts have uses justifying their underwriting by nation-states but not necessarily concerned with art per se, and promotes uses as remote from culture as poverty reduction and peace-keeping, then national cultural diplomacy programs can be even more explicitly instrumental. Cultural diplomacy is an important aspect of global arts networking though its focus is on national cultures—urban arts that are grounded in nation-states. Many countries push their own national cultures as instruments of national marketing and branding—an approach typical of U.S. programs dating from the Voice of America and America House programs of the Cold War era.

A few programs, including Germany's Goethe Haus, the Austrian cultural office in New York, and most notably the British Council, promote cultural creation and exchange not just on behalf of the cultures of Germany, Austria, or the United Kingdom but in the name of global art networking, art diversity, and more generally the interdependence of the urban arts. They prove that underwriting arts at home and abroad is a good in itself that can also address inequality and be of some value to democracy. The Austrian cultural office hangs exhibitions in its unique mini-skyscraper in New York that feature work from many places: typical is the showing of art portraying the intersection of essential urban work (garbage collection) and essential urban art (photography) as depicted by Mierle Laderman Ukeles, whose 1977–1980 *Touch Sanitation Performance* features the artist in encounters (shaking hands) with all 3,000 members of the New York City Sanitation Department "on location" in venues like the Fresh Kills Landfill. Nothing Austrian about it, yet profoundly urban in ways citizens of Vienna and New York alike can appreciate.

In the Muslim world, collaborative efforts around culture have also appeared, well before the Arab Awakening that began in 2011. In 1978, at a meeting of foreign ministers in Dakar, Senegal, focused on "the awakening of Muslim Community [Ummah]," a plan was introduced to establish an Islamic International Educational, Cultural and Scientific Organization (ISECO), to be based in Morocco, that would "undertake the task of coordination between Islamic universities and educational and scientific institutions and supervising Islamic educational policies."[26] Cultural in the generic sense, and less concerned with the arts than with "establishing an educational system inspired by the Holy Quran and the Sunnah and also in tune with modern educational developments and concepts," ISECO nonetheless demonstrates that cultural networks are a universal aspiration of peoples across the world and that culture can be a tool of integration no less than segregation. Thus, the declaration founding ISECO affirms not only "the need to emphasize the traits of Islamic culture and education promoting them in the Islamic world as well as throughout the world," but also "establishing understanding and cooperation among institutions and eminent figures in the field of Islamic culture, on the one hand and other cultures, on the other hand, for the benefit of humanity and world peace." Today, ISECO members include fifty of the fifty-seven countries composing the Organization of the Islamic Conference (OIC).

Table 6: Global Cultural Organizations

Organization Name	Head-quarters	Membership	Year Est.
Association of Performing Arts Presenters (APAP)	Washington, D.C., USA	1,400 members worldwide	1957
Creative City Network of Canada www.creativecity.ca/	Vancouver, Canada	Over 100 cities	2002
European Capitals of Culture http://ec.europa.eu/culture	Brussels, Belgium	All E.U. states	1985
International Delphic Council — Delphic Games www.delphic-games.com	Berlin, Germany	Members from 20 countries	1994
International Federation of Arts Councils and Culture Agencies www.ifacca.org	Sydney, Australia	69 national members, 50 subnational or NGO affiliates	2000
International Society for the Performing Arts (ISPA) www.ispa.org/	New York, USA	Over 400 from 50 countries	1949
League of Historical Cities www.city.kyoto.jp/somu/kokusai/lhcs/eng/index.htm	Kyoto, Japan	92 cities	1994
Organization of World Heritage Cities www.ovpm.org/	Quebec, Canada	238 cities	1993
U.S. Urban Arts Federation (Americans for the Arts) www.americansforthearts.org/networks/usuaf/	Washington, D.C., USA	60 (large cities)	1960

Table 6 is a list of global cultural organizations with an urban-centric character. Lists like this can evoke listlessness, miring art in the mud of descriptive prose; at the same time, aesthetic theory can float away on clouds of superheated poetry. In the case of the arts, both prose and poetry are needed. Prose, especially, because it is crucial to recognize and describe the many largely invisible city and intercity arts organizations that are actively making the case for the role of art in urban democracy and global governance while acting as conservators of culture. In solidifying the sublime ephemera that compose creation, a list of associations expresses a core meaning of urban life absent at other levels. It is one of the attractions of putting cities at the center of global governance that to do so puts art and culture there too. City authorities often worry about whether art is for the city or just "out for itself," a burden the city must carry or a resource it can exploit. But this question turns out to be reflexive and unproductive. For in truth, art and the city, if not exactly synonyms, reflect a common creativity, a shared attachment to openness and transparency and a core commitment to play and playfulness—in short, reflect the creative commons that is the fruit of their collaboration and intersection. As all cities are Hansa cities, incarnating liberty, all cities are Renaissance cities, incarnating generativity and art.

ANTANAS MOCKUS OF BOGOTÁ

Mayor **ANTANAS MOCKUS**, a mathematician and philosopher who is the son of Lithuanian immigrants, ran Bogotá for two nonconsecutive terms with such an inventive imagination and comic wit that (unfortunately) he convinced himself he should be Colombia's president. He is now a senator and a scholar (working on issues of corruption), but the presidency has eluded him, as it has such ambitious mayors as Luzhkov in Moscow and Bloomberg in New York.

Becoming rector at Bogotá's Universidad Nacional not long after studying for his master's there, Mockus quickly was recognized as a reformer with ambitions beyond academia. As his deputy mayor would later remark, Mockus soon saw the whole city as his classroom. His mantra throughout his career has been "Con educación todo se puede"—with education, everything is possible.

He was first elected to Bogotá's city hall in 1995 at forty-three years old, just two years after he had dropped his pants (literally) to moon a crowd of students—an example of "the resources an artist can use," he explained. He spent only $10,000 and otherwise relied on the comic and histrionic resources he had shown as an educational reformer. It was a surprise only to those not paying attention that he won by nearly 65 percent of the vote.

After a whirlwind but productive stewardship in Bogotá, he resigned in 1997 to run in the 1998 presidential elections. And lost. So he got himself reelected in Bogotá in 2001, where he continued to promote political change through satire, art, and comedy. Want to get city residents to conserve water? Appear on television in the shower. (Water usage dropped 40 percent!) Want to curb traffic violators? Hire mimes to poke fun at them. (Traffic deaths went down!) Want to impact crime? Close the bars early (1 A.M.) and encourage women to take to the streets—his Noche de las Mujeres, a day on which 700,000 women came out. (Crime reportedly went down 40 percent!)

Colombians are more afraid of ridicule than fines, Mockus reasoned. Making them look foolish beats putting them in jail. To energize his fellow citizens, he sported spandex and a cape and toured the city as "Super-citizen." He actually prompted 63,000 Bogotá citizens to pay an extra 10 percent on their tax bills voluntarily—try that, President Obama or Prime Minister Cameron! The comic cosmopolitan's antics amused the middle class and catalyzed some real reforms, including an abstract but popular war on civic incivility and a quite concrete reform of transportation (that led in time to a limited-access express surface bus system that was imitated in many other cites). But they did little for his presidential ambitions, where comedy looks frivolous.

In 2006 he ran again nationally, coming in only fourth and being soundly defeated not just by elites who refused to take him seriously but also by elements of the working class that deemed his comedic self-promotion itself to be elitist and unproductive of real economic change. Inequality and poverty, they complained, were not much impacted by his three terms in office—though one might ask "as compared to what?" His 2010 run as Green Party head also failed, though his numbers improved. In the end, however, he was routed by Juan Manuel Santos. Despite a surge in Mockus's national popularity, Santos was seen as the more "serious" candidate by Colombians concerned with security.

Given that most mayors realize governing cities is a poor stepping-stone to governing states, the educator Mockus has been a remarkably slow learner on this score. Despite the penance represented by the ceremony he held in a public fountain when running for mayor again in 2001 (to "ask forgiveness for leaving the mayor's office in my unsuccessful bid for the Presidency"), he went on to run again in 2010.

Throughout his career, Mockus has pursued a political platform grounded on "Citizens in Formation," aiming to "transform political and citizen culture through pedagogic, communicative and symbolic endeavors." He wears a ring forged into a Möbius strip, a single side weaving around itself in an endless band that has no "other" side—a tribute to the power of art and mind as tributaries of interconnectedness and interdependence in all things. When Mayor Mockus spoke at the Interdependence Movement's Berlin conference in 2010, he made being mayor seem like an occupation fit only for philosophers who can laugh at themselves, for comedians with deadly serious civic goals, for artists who want to move mountains. Perhaps it is just that. Johnson of London and Park of Seoul give that impression.

One can't forget that, like Orlando in Palermo, Mockus's stewardship in Bogotá unfolded in a country wracked by crime and drug trafficking, one sometimes described as a narco-state—a fact that makes his accomplishments the more remarkable. During his second term, Bogotá suffered through numerous attacks from the terrorist group FARC that has held Colombia in fear for decades. Although President Uribe urged counterattacks and arrests, Mockus, who not unexpectedly was a pacifist, responded by wearing a jacket with a heart-shaped hole cut out over his breast. Shoot me if you will, I will not mimic your violence. If Boris Johnson is a mayor who has fun, Antanas Mockus is a mayor who—however much fun he is for others—is in dead civic earnest. His comedic gestures are proffered at the risk of his very life.

His gesture was not a signal of softness. As a presidential candidate, Mockus always refused negotiations with FARC. But he also insisted "it is impossible for the state to compete with the funds of these armed groups and drug traffickers. They can always offer more. The state must compete with and for its legitimacy." Law first, always. Yet not law alone. That is what he had learned as mayor.

"At first, I had the illusion that if I wrote new laws, those words would become reality. But it soon became clear that if you want to change society's habits, law is only one of the means. Most people prefer internal mechanisms for determining for themselves what is right and what is wrong, but perceive other people as needing to be regulated by laws. The question I asked was how to reduce the difference between the laws and cultural and moral means of self-regulation."[1]

This seems deeply compelling, undeniably true, but it isn't very funny. Humor, like art and creativity, are for Mockus indispensable agents of change in the civic arena—an insight every mayor usually comes to appreciate, but wisdom Mockus brought with him to the urban table from the very start.

It remains to be seen whether Bogotá's latest mayor, Gustavo Petro, who is a former guerilla fighter in the disbanded M-19 group, will learn the lesson. But he has made a good Mockus-style start, a guerilla from the seventies banning weapons from Bogotá's streets in 2012.

CHAPTER II. CITIZENS WITHOUT BORDERS
Glocal Civil Society and Confederalism

> The spirit of democracy cannot be imposed from without. It has to come from within.
>
> *Mohandas K. Gandhi*

> Houses make a town, citizens make a city.
>
> *Jean-Jacques Rousseau,* The Social Contract

> Where there is an absence of international political leadership, civil society should step in to fill the gap, providing the energy and vision needed to move the world in a new and better direction.
>
> *Daisaku Ikeda*

Our aim has been to show why mayors can and should rule the world, if ever so softly. To speak of "rule" or "governance" (a soft synonym for government) is to focus on the mechanics and institutions of the political order. Hence, in the next and final chapter, I will offer a political argument for a global parliament of mayors and lay out some guidelines for how it might be organized and what it might do. I have always believed, however, that the political is grounded in the civic, that democratic governance whether local or global must first find its corresponding spirit and character in democratic civil society. The failure of political constitution-making often originates in a failure to recognize this bottom-up character of democracy. Because working top-down is so much easier and quicker, the lessons of centuries of political sociology from Rousseau and J. S. Mill to Tocqueville and Dewey are pushed aside by democracy builders in a hurry, whether in Moscow in 1917, Teheran in 1979, or Cairo in 2011.

Yet top-down revolutions have inevitably bred anarchy rather than order, factionalism rather than unity, demagoguery rather than democracy.

Why then should we think a global parliament of mayors can breed global democratic governance unless it develops civic and cultural conditions conducive to participation and fairness? We conceive of citizens as building blocks for and agents of government and politics. They are actually products of civic education, of engagement in civil society, of those free civic (but not yet political) spaces in schools, churches, union halls, and workplaces that democratic theorists Sara Evans and Harry Boyte long ago showed us were prerequisite to establishing both competent citizens and a living civic commonwealth.[1] First civil society and citizens, then politics and government: there is no other path to democracy.

To say mayors should rule the world is really to say that citizens should rule the world, which requires first that citizens are nurtured and shaped by (and help shape and nurture) local and global civic institutions that give their liberty and equality meaning and substance. In cities such as Seoul, Mannheim, and Bogotá, mayors like Park Wan-soon, Dr. Peter Kurz, and Antanas Mockus have thus devoted considerable time and budget to nurturing civil society and engaging citizens in governance. In Delhi, mayor Dikshit has initiated a system of town meetings (*Bhagidari*) to promote what she calls "interactive governance." These bottom-up civic commitments give expression to Rousseau's etymological insight that to speak of the city is to speak of citizens. Without citizens there can be no democracy—not locally, not nationally, and certainly not globally. Pursuing the etymology linking *city* and *citizen*, Jean-Jacques Rousseau was already focused in the eighteenth century on the city as the home citizens build for themselves and the community that defines their primary civic life. Here we build on the fact that the city accommodates participation and civic engagement in a way other levels of government cannot.

Before I endeavor to imagine the convening of a parliament of mayors as a step toward global democratic governance, then, I need to fix the civic context within which such a body alone can succeed: democracy and civil society within and among cities. To advance the linked notions of cities without walls and democratic governance without borders, there must be a viable notion of citizens without frontiers, which alone gives the civic potential of cities a reach that is global and democratic. To be democratic, global governance by cities must be complemented by global relations among citizens and their civic associations that reflect some measure of participation, transparency, accountability, and equality. A global infrastructure unmediated by civic, cultural, technological, and social institutions in which citizens play a significant role will only be another variety of political hierarchy. It will be dominated by vertical power, where political officials and bureaucrats are at best elected dictators, leaving citizens as little more than occasional voters and consumers of intercity services. A parliament of mayors so conceived fails the test of democracy. As political theorist Seyla Benhabib has wisely noted, "the neglect of social movements as actors of social transformation . . . has led to a naive faith in legal experts, international lawyers and judges as agents of democratic change. . . . But surely democratization without political actors who seek to empower themselves by creating new subjectivities in the public sphere, new vocabularies of claim making, and new forms of togetherness is neither conceivable nor desirable."[2]

To honor Benhabib's insight and move far enough away from legal architecture to establish a civic context for the parliament of mayors proposed here, we need to answer three pointed questions: First, how can the relationship between city officials and citizens be strengthened *within* the city in ways that legitimize the role of mayors and help engage citizens in the intercity civic arena, where their influence is inevitably going to be diluted? Second, what does the global civic infrastructure look like? What are the vehicles of cross-border cooperation—the organizations, structures, and social movements—that engage citizens with one another across cities and across the planet? And third, how can this infrastructure realistically accommodate both the promise of intercity governance and the reality of sovereign national power as it is presently constituted in provincial, national, and international institutions? The answer to the first question is "participatory governance"; to the second, "intercity networks"; and to the third, "confederalism." In fleshing out these responses, I will offer selected practical examples and best practices that help illuminate the larger civic context in concrete ways. For citizen engagement within cities, the example is participatory budgeting; for citizen engagement across borders, it is sustainability as reflected in the distinctive practices of such cross-border intercity associations and civic movements as ICLEI, UCLG, Metropolis, CIVICUS, Occupy Wall Street, and the Interdependence Movement; and for global infrastructure, it is the architecture of confederalism and experiments such as the novel practice of urban visas that empowers cities in a confederal setting to act glocally in a domain normally reserved to states. The aim throughout is to consider innovative developments that empower citizens within and across cities and to put on display the salient role civil society and social movements can play in both grounding and jump-starting cooperation among cities in the stalled and stale world of dysfunctional bordered states.

My goals here are not derived from a wish list. A decentralized planet of networked cities, provinces, and regions, while obviously still dominated by traditional nation-states, already exists. It encompasses a wide variety of substate and nonstate actors, from multinational corporations and global financial institutions to civic NGOs and global social movements. Each of these bodies addresses in its own manner such critical topics as rights, climate change, social justice, genocide, public health, child labor, and immigration, topics traditionally the provenance of sovereign states. Each such issue will naturally attract the attention of a parliament of mayors and those they represent. Meanwhile, however, *the intercity civic infrastructure already in place comprises in its present form an informal approximation of the kinds of collaboration and confederal partnership that a prospective mayors parliament will represent.* We need only strengthen and formalize this infrastructure in order to make soft global democratic governance a reality. In other words, even short of a mayors parliament, in the words of British political theorist David Held, "the prospects for 'civilizing' and 'democratizing' contemporary globalization are . . . not as bleak as some suggest."[3] In sum, I am urging only that we work hard to secure ends that, careful observers of civil society and the city acknowledge, are already well on the way to being realized. Even as we embark on what seems a daunting journey, we are arriving without fanfare at the destination.

Strong Democracy in the City: Participatory Budgeting

The neighborhood, the town, and the city and thus the cosmopolis they compose all share the potential for strong democratic participation. Because they can engage citizens locally and directly in deliberation and governance, and because they play out in a pluralistic but dense civic domain where participatory citizenship can dynamically complement representative institutions, they endow the networks to which they belong with a potent participatory spirit that can help keep the global governance of cities democratic.[4] At the same time, however, we face a dilemma: strong democracy, a principal virtue of local government at the municipal level, is also associated with a principal vice of local government: NIMBY. Cities consist of neighborhoods, and neighborhoods foster participation. But they also encourage a competitive impulse to treat public goods as semiprivate neighborhood interests and reject paying the costs of larger community goods: "put your drug treatment center (prison, half-way house, sanitation truck storage facility) anywhere you want, but Not In My Back Yard." Such thinking is pre-civic, a sign that private-interest consumerist considerations are trumping deliberative public thinking. It signals not selfishness per se but the absence of civic processes that extend the compass of "me" thinking to "we" thinking and allow neighbors to calculate their interests in terms of citywide (or still broader) concerns. If NIMBY is the neighborhood's vice (if sometimes a vice in service to important private and personal virtues), civic participation and deliberation are its countervailing public virtues—another key reason why it is so crucial to ensure that city government reflects not just top-down leadership by mayors and city councilpersons but bottom-up participation and civic deliberation by citizens who understand the difference between private and public thinking, between "me" and "we."

Cities are natural venues for citizen participation. But citizens are made rather than born, and cultivating civic virtue requires ongoing education, innovation, and experimentation, what Tocqueville called an "apprenticeship of liberty," the most "arduous of all apprenticeships," he averred. There are many ways to train citizens, and formal civic education is only one of them. The American community service movement of the 1980s (when the focus was on voluntarism in the Thousand Points of Light program) and the 1990s (when service learning or service plus education culminated in President Clinton's Corporation for National and Community Service), taught an important lesson. It offered a testament to the potential of learned citizenship.[5] More recently, in the experiment I will describe here, the practices associated with participatory budgeting have presented themselves as allies in the struggle for civic learning and strong democracy.

The experiment in popular decision making around municipal budgets began in the 1980s and continued into the 1990s, initially in Latin America when the continent was experiencing painful birth pangs on a new road to both democratization and decentralization. It was a period in which anarchic, market-driven globalization had aroused the fears of progressive forces and had turned the Brazilian town of Porto Alegre into the home of an annual "antiglobalization" conference focused on economic and social justice.[6] Since those combative years, participatory budgeting has spread across Latin America from Brazil to Bolivia, Guatemala, Nicaragua, and Peru, and then around the world, an attractive option now in Europe and the United States, where in cities as large as Chicago and Los Angeles it has been incorporated into practices of popular engagement of a distinctively nontraditional nature.

Although novel, participatory budgeting is not a complicated idea. Like the complementary notion of participatory design developed in Scandinavia in the 1970s,[7] it engages an urban citizenry in allocating city revenues in accord with priorities determined by popular vote, albeit usually only in specific districts where participating citizens dispose of only modest funds that are but a small part of a far larger metropolitan budget. Its aim is both to enhance participation in and hence augment the legitimacy of the municipal budget allocation process and to advance policies such as the mitigation of poverty that might not otherwise be met by representative government hierarchies. Benjamin Goldfrank has drawn this useful portrait: "What was once an obscure process of popular participation championed by a few partners on the left in South America as a step towards reviving socialism has become a 'best practice' in the mainstream international development community's toolkit for reducing poverty and practicing good governance."[8] According to other observers, as an exercise in "grassroots democracy," it has "led to a real empowerment of civil society and, most notably, of the working class."[9]

By engaging citizens directly in one of the most mundane but significant functions of urban governance in a part of the world long accustomed to authoritarian politics and the rule of economic elites, participatory budgeting has become a notable urban instrument of both democratization and social justice in Latin America and other developing regions. Refusing to "speak the language of hegemonic globalization," its advocates have instead tried to "counteract social exclusion, open up spaces for democratic participation, for community building, for alternatives to dominant forms of development and knowledge."[10]

The process has hardly been straightforward, however, and because it has generally been applied only to some limited part of municipal budgets, it has produced ever more diverse outcomes, not always in accord with the original campaign for social justice that generated the idea. Still, in Goldfrank's view, although the experiments lasted in many cases only a year or two and did not create "widespread local success in encouraging citizens participation, fiscal transparency and effective municipal government," they nevertheless did achieve a degree of success "in some remarkably diverse locales, from small, poverty-stricken, indigenous rural villages to major cities."[11] The decisive factors in Latin America have been support by local mayors, the absence of opposition from political elites, and project funding and technical assistance provided by national or international aid organizations. Even at its most successful, participatory budgeting in Latin America has been most productive when supported by movements pursuing social justice, and most impeded where blocked by or skewed toward market ideology, obstructive elites, and international institutions out of tune with civic participation. In other words, participatory budgeting as a democratic process has at times been thwarted not because it was democratic but because it put democracy in service to social justice ends opposed by ruling elites. An unconventional process is one thing, a radical outcome is another.

In Porto Alegre, where it unfolded in what was at the time the "anti-globalization capital," with its annual "world social forums," the process was open in theory to all citizens and involved deliberation and decision rather than just consultation.[12] The explicit aim was to redistribute funds in ways that favored the poor, who were generally without advocates in traditional representative politics. More generally, the process can expand to involve public hearings, lobbying, and town-hall meetings as well as popular referenda and voting (these elements often appear in the soft practices adopted by cities such as Los Angeles). The original Porto Alegre experiment ended up as one of the forty urban experiments worldwide presented at the United Nations Second Conference on Human Settlements (Habitat II) in 1996. Being thus featured at the United Nations gave it a global boost so that a dozen years later participatory budgeting had spread to Europe and Asia and was being used in more than 3,000 cities globally.

In the United States, progress has been slower, but in 2012, following an experiment in Chicago's 49th ward, New York City's City Council offered $6 million in capital discretionary funds to residents in six districts where projects chosen by residents would be approved by the council.[13] Los Angeles has been even more aggressive in pursuing the idea, with nearly one hundred local councils receiving $35,000 a year to be disposed of by citizens in 2012.[14] While the several million dollars devoted to local council participatory budgeting is but a tiny fraction of the city's more than $4 billion general fund, it incarnates a commitment to direct civic engagement rare in American cities but essential if the slogan "let mayors rule the world" is to also mean citizens are to have a voice. Using town halls, online consultation, hearings, surveys, and direct engagement with small business, Los Angeles tries to honor a commitment to "deep and broad consultation," which is reflected not only locally but in the allocation of the general fund budget.[15]

The process has been criticized as window dressing (such a small part of a city's budget is dedicated to it, and it sometimes amounts to little more than glorified consultation). Nevertheless, in many of the cities in which it has been introduced, it has been retained by successive administrations unsympathetic to its egalitarianism but unwilling to challenge its popularity—including in Porto Alegre itself. Like all such participatory practices, participatory budgeting makes serious time demands on its participants, demands that can turn beneficiaries into detractors. Oscar Wilde once quipped that the trouble with socialism was "it takes up too many free evenings." Democracy takes up whole weekends and participatory democracy can occupy the rest of the week as well. Moreover, the process can be manipulated or co-opted by elites (a complaint from Porto Alegre), or simply bypassed by city officials who write off the small sums as public relations and spend the larger portion of their revenues in domains more subject to cronyism and in accord with the interests of the powerful and wealthy. As with so much that happens in cities, participatory budgeting draws snickers from the cynical.

Yet the experiments suggest that, at the municipal level, citizen participation is feasible even in decisions where the questions are fairly technical and citizen competence and expert knowledge are required, and where the commitment of time is a prerequisite of success. It also offers evidence for the claim by James Fishkin and other deliberative democrats that debate among citizens can affect value rigidity and open the way to common ground.[16] It seems obvious that such a process by itself, when pursued in an environment that is otherwise closed to participation and uninterested in social justice, can have only limited success. But it also seems likely that the practice can produce enhanced citizen participation and enhanced trust between citizens and local governors in ways that not only improve local democracy but create a hospitable context for greater intercity cooperation involving both citizens and their elected representatives. This is certainly the way it has worked on cooperative and condo boards in cities like New York, where indifferent residents can turn into engaged stakeholders. Mayors wishing to endow their global leadership in a prospective parliament of mayors and in other theaters of intercity cooperation with greater legitimacy and efficacy could do worse than embrace these participatory budgeting practices.[17] This may also offer a lesson to virtuous mayors hoping to change behavior—as was the case with Mayor Bloomberg in his court-blocked effort to legislate sugary soda portions. Engaging citizens in that decision-making process—parents and teachers and doctors, for example—might have helped secure the outcome he was hoping to produce and which the big cola corporations thwarted in court.

Given our discussion of smart cities, it is worth noting that technology can play a salient role in participatory budgeting and in civic consultation more generally (James Fishkin's work in deliberative polling uses both real-life and virtual techniques). Although most towns utilize a real- time process, combining online and off-line practices can offer significant advantages. In the words of an enthusiast, "the two key aspects of Participatory Budgeting that create concern in relation to electronic Participatory Budgeting (e-PB) are transparency and community cohesion. Both of these issues can be mitigated by joining up online and offline PB activity."[18] As the size of cities and the scale of participation increase, technology becomes more crucial. In Brazil's Belo Horizonte, with more than 1.5 million inhabitants, many of them poor, the role of technology has become paramount and has made citizen democracy "one of the most significant initiatives in the world in the domain of eDemocracy and eParticipation."[19] In Ipatinga, using the Internet to draw in younger and less educated citizens to register their priorities increased participation in the city participatory budgeting process significantly. In Lichtenberg, Germany (a district of East Berlin), where officials have a €31 million discretionary fund for citizen spending, the process allows postal and web voting as well as a citizens' forum in allocating the five votes per citizen made available for prioritizing policy goals. It turns out that the medium actually affects the message here, as Table 7 (which offers a useful portrait of the kinds of policy options citizens are allowed to address) makes clear.[20]

The 600 citizens voting in forums around the Lichtenberg district put the upkeep of the music school first and the cycle path sixth; 2,500 e-voters put the cycle paths first and the music school fifth. They agreed, however, in placing "economic promotion" last. Participatory budgeting is, of course, only one experiment in urban democracy and cannot by itself either make the case for participation or prove that urban governance is capable of more effective, strong democracy than other levels of government. But as a spreading best practice that has persisted in the face of critics, it offers hope for those who believe there may be a little less distance between mayors and citizens than between voters and state authorities. And it sustains those who argue that as mayors come to rule the world, if only informally, they are likely to bring citizens with them.

Table 7: Citizen Priorities of Lichtenberg, Germany, By Input Mechanism

Priority Rank	Postal Voters	%	Online Voters	%	Citizen's Forum Voters	%
1.	Equipment for youth clubs	11.4	Cycle path plan	16.7	Upkeep of music schools	11.1
2.	Upkeep of senior citizens' social clubs	9.2	Children's and youth work activities	12.4	Upkeep/ development of sports centres	8.3
3.	Cycle path plan	8.1	Dog station	8.7	Upkeep of grammar school	7.8
4.	Library media work	5.1	Upkeep of grammar school	6.5	Library media work	6.8
5.	Upkeep/ development of sports centres	4.2	Upkeep of music schools	6.2	Repair/ development of skating facilities	5.5
6.	Upkeep of music schools	4	Library media work	5.1	Cycle path plan	5.5
7.	Projects for all ages	3.8	Projects for all ages	3.3	Upkeep of senior citizens' social clubs	4.9
8.	Children's and youth work activities	3.7	Equipment for youth clubs	2.9	Equipment for youth clubs	3.7
9.	Dog station	3.6	Upkeep of arts and leisure centre	2.9	Projects for all ages	3.1
10.	Upkeep of arts and leisure centre	3.4	Continuation of economic promotion	2.9	Continuation of economic promotion	1.5

Source: Yves Sintomer, Carsten Herzberg, and Giovanni Allegretti, "Learning from the South: Participatory Budgeting Worldwide—an Invitation to Global Cooperation," Dialog Global, no. 25, Berlin: Capacity Building International, 2010, p. 38; http://www.buergerhaushalt.org/sites/default/files/downloads/LearningfromtheSouth-Participatory BudgetingWorldwide-Study_0.pdf.

Cross-Border Strong Democracy:
Global Civil Society—NGOs and MNCs

Municipal democratic practices contribute importantly but only indirectly to global civil society because they unfold *inside* cities; the practices of networks *among and between* cities contribute directly, and they are our focus below. There are, however, other organizations and institutions that play a role in global civic relations and deserve brief scrutiny. Chief among them are nongovernmental organizations (NGOs) and multinational corporations (MNCs) along with traditional international organizations such as the international financial institutions born of the Bretton Woods conference or those associated with the United Nations. There are also cross-border religious associations such as the Quaker American Friends Service Committee and the interfaith Catholic association Focolare, both of which are global civic associations with big-hearted civic purposes including tolerance and world peace.[21]

Such nonstate actors are patently significant despite the fact that academic political science and the media have focused almost obsessively on states and state-based international relations. There is an extensive literature already devoted to these nonstate players, so I will simply note their relevance to fostering a robust cross-border civil society that can undergird the proposed mayors parliament.[22] Their chief defect compared to intercity networks is that they are notably undemocratic in their structure and organization. Multinational firms gain a certain legitimacy from their shareholding nature, while nongovernmental organizations draw moral status from their often admirable, even noble, values and goals. Yet although NGOs are frequently viewed through a democratic lens because they pursue universal interests such as combating climate change (the Sierra Club or Greenpeace), pursuing human rights (Human Rights Watch), or exposing corruption (Transparency International), and because they enlist citizens as funders, members, letter writers, and advocates in their work, they are not democratic. Kathryn Sikkink, sympathetic to global civil society, thus insists "NGOs and networks need to address their own asymmetries and questions of accountability and transparency, so they can enhance their internal democracy while helping to democratize international institutions."[23]

Unlike the city networks with similar purposes we will consider below (ICLEI and the C40, for example), NGOs have hierarchical organizational structures, with members acting as passive funders and supporters of self-selected leaders rather than their proactive agents or sovereign masters. That is not to say they do not or should not play a role in global governance. Joseph Nye believes, for example, that increased participation by civil society can help to correct "globalization's democracy deficit." But since NGOs are "self-selected, not democratically elected," they "deserve a voice but not a vote."[24] Thus, it may be worth considering the idea of a formal global assembly of NGOs, something already portended by the World Assembly convened annually by CIVICUS, to act as a "second chamber" to the assembly of mayors recommended in the final chapter, but only as long as its role is advisory. To do so would effectively place global civil society not just under the new parliamentary political body as a foundation but next to it as a parallel political body. It is worth noting that there are already intercity associations like CityNet (in Asia) that include NGOs in their membership.

Multinational corporations, more influential by far in an anarchic global marketplace than nongovernmental organizations, are even less democratic, although the role of shareholders in corporate governance actually gives MNCs, at least in theory, a democratic dimension missing in NGOs. However, shareholders generally "own" companies only in a technical sense, since shareholding has little to do with managing or controlling corporations or choosing or overseeing their leadership. Although they may dominate the anarchic global world today, MNCs are private and market based, and, compared with civic and clearly public NGOs, are surely more appropriately regarded as potential subjects of rather than constituent participants in democratic global governance.

As products of independent and sovereign nation-states, other traditional organizations like the international financial institutions (IFIs) and United Nations agencies reproduce the limitations of their creators. Even in the case of agencies such as UNESCO, not explicitly dependent on states, state ideologies and the member-state appropriations process sap common goals and activities and undermine the claim to true administrative autonomy (as was indicated in the discussion of UNESCO and the arts in Chapter 10). In vital security affairs, it hardly need be added, powerful nations exercise an informal veto via funding and a disabling formal veto via U.N. Security Council rules. It is noteworthy that the United Nations itself has increasingly recognized the role of nonnational actors in global affairs. Former secretary general Kofi Annan thus allowed: "The United Nations once dealt only with Governments. By now we know that peace and prosperity cannot be achieved without partnerships involving Governments, international organisations, the business community and civil society. In today's world, we depend on each other."[25] That is the meaning of interdependence.

Even when we omit these many transnational nonstate actors, there are still a host of organizations, many web based, that seek to facilitate citizen-to-citizen cooperation across borders and that compose an impressive supportive infrastructure for global civil society. They range from small inspirational strivers for specific missions, such as We The World and Light The World, to hugely successful conglomerates without fixed mandates, such as Global Citizen, a big-brand organization with powerful partners whose vague global vision and spectacular fund-raising concerts exceed its practical reach.[26] They include the Global Citizen Network, a volunteer organization that places young people in Peace Corps–style opportunities around the world (some dismiss such outfits as "voluntourism");[27] the Independent Sector, an American outfit bringing together American NGOs, nonprofits, and foundations to network and cooperate interdependently for common civic purposes (such as sparing the tax deduction for charities and NGOs from congressional budget slashers); and CIVICUS, a truly global and interdependent network of international NGOs and civic associations that is one possible model for (and rival for?) a global parliament of mayors.[28]

Pertinent, traditional governance groups of large ambition that operate globally also include the quite active Inter-Parliamentary Union and the largely symbolic old-style United World Federalists.[29] The IPU works toward communication and cooperation among national parliaments, while the World Federalists dream of true global government. The IPU is a functional organization, "the focal point for world-wide parliamentary dialogue [that] works for peace and co-operation among peoples and for the firm establishment of representative democracy." Its specific purposes are worth citing, since they suggest what a framework for a parliament of mayors might look like: In pursuing its goals, the IPU

- fosters contacts, co-ordination, and the exchange of experience among parliaments and parliamentarians of all countries;
- considers questions of international interest and concern and expresses its views on such issues in order to bring about action by parliaments and parliamentarians;
- contributes to the defense and promotion of human rights—an essential factor of parliamentary democracy and development;
- contributes to better knowledge of the working of representative institutions and to the strengthening and development of their means of action.[30]

As the IPU, working in close cooperation with the United Nations, tries to yoke the work of national parliaments to global representative democracy, a parliament of mayors might work to yoke the work of cities to global participatory democracy.

Then there are the many United Nations–related associations, of which UNESCO is perhaps the archetype, organizations that benefit enormously from their United Nations sponsorship and budgets even as they are sometimes hobbled by the United Nations' governance structures based on sovereign states. Although I have been critical of state-based international organizations like the United Nations, the success of its many agencies that manage to operate outside the daily scrutiny of interfering states in addressing global challenges from poverty and hunger to immigration and urban life (the U.N.-Habitat program, for example) can hardly be overstated. All such organizations and groups treat people as citizens of the planet and encourage them to work on behalf of global goals. One by one, they are variously influential. Even at their most impressive, the NGOs field modest organizations and budgets that limit their impact. Together, however, they represent the civic infrastructure of an interdependent planet and help lay an indispensable living foundation for intercity governance. Although I cannot give them here the attention they merit, the argument for intercity cooperation and a global mayors parliament rides the momentum these noble experiments in constructive interdependence have quietly realized.[31]

I cannot complete this very brief survey, of cross-border associations and movements that are not city based but help ground a prospective cities parliament in a robust global civil society, without a word about the Occupy movement. For less than a year between 2011 and 2012, this youth-led movement electrified the media globally by drawing attention to the radical inequalities spawned by the dominion of neoliberal ideology and its current global market practices. As the civil rights and feminist movements as well as the poor peoples' and welfare rights movements once helped to ground a new politics in social and civic protest, so Occupy Wall Street recently rekindled the ideals of urban political protest, not just within but across cities and countries. Starting in cities like New York and Oakland—fed up with predatory banks, disturbed by the irresponsibility of politicians, and daunted by a media circus wholly detached from the historical obligation of journalism to inform the citizenry—the Occupy movement was a revelation.[32] It announced two truths: that America (like the world) was deeply divided with up to 99 percent of the population dominated economically by one percent that controls a preponderance of the wealth, and that as a result democracy is in deep crisis: neither Wall Street nor Washington, D.C., is "what democracy looks like." Like the right-wing populist Tea Party in the United States, OWS channeled anger at inequality and injustice. But unlike its right-wing counterparts rooted in the politics of fear and reaction, OWS was seeking a transformative strategy to turn anger to constructive civic purposes. It distrusted the politicians' patter about democracy as one more transparent attempt (in Rousseau's phrase) to "throw garlands of flowers over our chains," and it placed the responsibility for corruption and inequality not just on government but on capitalism as well.

Perhaps most pertinent to our global concerns, Occupy quickly reached out from Zuccotti Park in Manhattan to cities across the world. It quickly became an intercity and thus a global movement with sympathizers sponsoring actions in dozens of urban capitals across the world and maintaining a loose communications network among engaged cities that allowed some degree of common planning and activity. Along with the human rights movement and the women's movement (among others), OWS has demonstrated how social movements born of urban protest can contribute to a vibrant and relevant global civil society of a kind that can give sustenance to a mayors parliament perched alone in global civic space.

To be sure, with a multihued cornucopia of perspectives reflecting their multiple origins and cultural contexts, the Occupiers have been a diverse lot. Their plural encampments embrace a panoply of causes and contain tensions and fissures the protesters themselves acknowledge and even welcome. For OWS quickly and knowingly became a vessel into which people could pour their own fears and aspirations, a strength rather than a weakness that helped the movement touch people across the planet. What its various urban incarnations shared in common was a commitment to a participatory process that was meant to signal "what democracy looks like." The consensual General Assembly approach to decision making at the core was maddeningly open and transparent, and it had to deal with the inconvenience of an inconsistent constituency, since all were welcome at the crowded assemblies that could change personnel from night to night and location to location. Moreover, decisions were ideally to be taken by proximate consensus that required patience and tolerance and could (memories of the 1960s with their marathon participatory meetings) lead to more debate and deliberation than action— which could lead to the delegation of decision making to committees.

Yet behind OWS was an ideal of urban participatory or "strong" democracy of a kind I believe is likely to be reflected in the consensual, bottom-up global parliament of mayors recommended in this book. OWS may seem naive and exasperating in its refusal to engage in ordinary politics and in its initial disdain for voting during the American presidential election of 2012. Yet the Occupiers believed there was something intrinsically wrong with how democratic nation-states do business in the age of globalization and insisted correctly that this has undermined equality and put democracy at risk. Their spirit thus helps define global democratic civil society and holds some important lessons for a democratic global parliament of mayors that aspires to be participatory as well as representative, to govern as much by consensus as by command.

Cross-Border Strong Democracy: Global Civil Society and City Networks

There are, then, myriad examples of global civic associations and citizen movements that exemplify the capacity of citizens to work across borders and prepare the ground for the novel idea of cities and their mayors acting globally and in concert around their common interests. Returning to our core concern with city-based associations, however, I want to focus on those networks that are expressly city based, drawing from the networks surveyed in Chapter 5. They include a number of truly earth-girdling organizations, some (not surprisingly) concerned with the most pressing of earth-girdling concerns, environmental sustainability. Among the most important generic networks are

- United Cities and Local Governments (UCLG), an association that mimics the name of the United Nations and is perhaps the preeminent global municipal network, certainly the most universal;
- Metropolis, an association headquartered in Barcelona (a global hive of intercity associations) representing cities with a population over a million that both works with UCLG and pursues initiatives of its own, including an annual global meeting (most recently in Guangdong, China);
- U.N. Advisory Committee on Local Authorities (UNACLA), born out of the U.N.-Habitat program on cities (it was established during Habitat II in Istanbul, in 1996/1997) but, despite (or because of?) its United Nations imprimatur, not very active;
- CityNet, an Asian cities network that is linked in globally and includes a number of non-Asian cities as well as some NGOs;
- City Protocol, the new Barcelona-based, web-centered best practices network.

Given that cities, towns, and local authorities that qualify as local governing entities number more than a million, none of these networks can be regarded as truly universal. Neither, for that matter, is a global parliament of mayors likely to be universal unless it is allowed to become an anarchic conglomerate of tens of thousands of municipalities of every size and description—hardly a recipe for civic deliberation and common action. However, the networks noted here do pursue global civic ends through effective intercity cooperation, and many are dedicated to addressing specific challenges to which states have responded badly, if at all. The Bloomberg-inspired network Mayors Against Illegal Guns, for example, combats the American scourge of gun violence, with its egregious and recurring school and mall massacres.

In a parallel effort, a number of intercity associations have taken on climate change and escalating carbon emissions, confronting an equally daunting global challenge. And at a time when foundation funding for and media interest in controlling the proliferation of nuclear weapons has waned, groups such as the Global Security Institute are more important than ever, and the work of the Mayors for Peace, if largely symbolic, seems ever more important.[33] Intercity networks have done far more to confront such threats than have posturing but procrastinating states, with their lame polemics about sovereignty.

The traditional nation-state perspective and the inter-*national* strategies it propagates have produced little more than aggravation, pessimism, and ultimately a sense of deep futility.[34] The hope with which the Conference of the Parties (COP) began back in 1994 and the promise of the U.N. Framework Convention on Climate Change (UNFCCC) associated with it have largely dissipated. In the four recent international COP conferences starting with Copenhagen in 2009 (COP 15) and Cancun, Durban, and Doha afterward, all aimed at updating the all-too-modest Kyoto Protocol on climate change, little has been achieved. Hoping to prepare the ground for a revision or new treaty, these gatherings in fact yielded neither transfer financing to developing nations nor agreement on the standards and measures to implement goals, much less consensus on how to monitor and enforce them.

As the accelerating human use of carbon resources pushes the parts per million (ppm) reading far above the 350 ppm tipping point to 400 or more and inflates the permissible number for warming from two degrees centigrade to three or more, nations continue to bluster dysfunctionally—explaining why their sovereignty and their need for economic growth preempt significant climate agreements. Nongovernmental organizations such as Greenpeace, the Sierra Club, and World Resources Institute continue to do battle, but with resources utterly incommensurate with those held by their well-heeled carbon industry adversaries. With endless funds to lobby government about carbon's supposedly indispensable role in the global economy, the carbon industry continues to dominate the process. Democratic control of the American White House has had little effect on the climate crisis to date, and even Europe seems ready to begin serious fracking on its way to a weak version of energy independence.

Intercity cooperation, however, offers an alternative strategy that does not depend on nations, the carbon industry, or international negotiation, or even on well-intentioned NGOs, to change the environmental course. 80 percent of carbon emissions are produced by cities. And cities can do more than lobby and advocate; they can directly affect carbon use within their domains through reforms in transportation, housing, parks, port facilities, and vehicles entirely under their control. More importantly, they can work through city networks such as ICLEI and the C40 to foster cooperation around common approaches and best practices that, when subjected to the multiplier effect of many cities doing the same thing, can actually lower carbon emissions. Cities do not lobby states or argue with corporations to pursue rational measures to reduce carbon use and emissions—they take direct action that reduces actual carbon use (pedestrian zones, bike-share programs, emission standards on vehicles, port cleanup measures, congestion fees, idling bans, dedicated bus and bike lanes, and green building norms, to name just a few). The capacity for real action forestalls despondency and pessimism and gives urban citizens a sense of empowerment that voters waiting for action by their elected national representatives can only envy.

There are obviously limits on just how much cities can do without the cooperation of states and international organizations, however, and intercity organizations are no less vulnerable to rivalry and politics than other political associations. The C40, an elite association of large cities with fifty-eight members and counting, and useful connections to the Clinton Foundation, has considerable clout but is viewed by some in older, more encompassing associations such as ICLEI, as a new kid on the block, stealing their thunder without realizing their agenda. Yet rivalries aside, the reality of effective city-based action locally by groups like the C40 and ICLEI, complemented by smaller organizations such as EcoCity (with its "world summit of sustainable cities"), is a game changer with respect to both democracy and climate change.

The United States has not committed to universal standards, but Los Angeles has cut carbon energy use at its massive port by up to 40 percent in just five years through its own policies. Since emissions from the port make up to two-fifths of the city's total carbon pollution, these measures have lowered urban CO_2 by 16 percent. In New York City, it is estimated that a startling 80 percent of carbon emissions come from buildings rather than vehicles, so programs such as LEED (the U.S. Green Building Council's "Leadership in Energy and Environmental Design" program) can have significant impact regardless of what happens in Albany or Washington, D.C.[35] Similarly, although China as a nation with a coal-based energy system is a massive carbon user and polluter, cities like Shanghai and Hong Kong can take meaningful ameliorative action on their own (as Beijing did at the time of the Olympics in 2010), especially given their authoritative governance structures. Meanwhile, the United Nations process aimed at updating Kyoto has initiated an endless round of good-willed but futile meetings that have resulted only in frustration and despair.

Intercity associations are, then, of a different order than NGOs and other international organizations, carrying democratic legitimacy into an arena of policy and action where change can be implemented and the real world affected in ways that hold promise for city governance globally. Their growing influence in the new interdependent world suggests the potential efficacy of dispersed and decentralized power exercised collectively but from the bottom up, through cooperation, rather than top down, by executive command. The political architecture this system of dispersed power embodies is *confederalism,* which enables decentralized cities to interact forcefully with intermediate and higher governing bodies like the state and federal government. It thus offers an inviting environment both for the autonomy of cities and for the establishment of a global parliament of mayors.

Confederalism and Municipal Authority:
Financial Autonomy and City Visas

In Chapter 6, we explored the dilemma of cities without sovereignty in a world where sovereign states, although without the capacity to work together, no longer possess the power to govern themselves alone. Intercity networks exist in this distinctive terrain of vertically divided power where rival levels of government (local, provincial, national, and interregional) vie for authority in the effort to address novel global challenges. Cities are solving problems across borders in part because the informal confederal infrastructure within which they operate allows them a certain liberty to do so. This infrastructure offers theoretical legitimacy to what cities are doing in practice. I argue here for the practicality of a global parliament of mayors. But the role of such a body in global governance can be effective only in a confederal world in which power is shared at the several levels by inter-state regions, states, provinces, and local authorities. Moreover, because in this setting cities are both local and global—"glocal" in the sense that they are civically potent at the bottom and the top—they claim a privileged normative status. They bridge the participation/power divide by affording local engagement by citizens even as they permit some access to global power through intercity collaboration and the possibility of a global mayors parliament.

The privileging of cities in the new confederal order is at least partially the consequence of the growing dysfunction of sovereign states. The concert-of-powers approach to global relations, rooted in cooperation among independent states over the last three hundred years, has grown ever more irrelevant to the challenges of an increasingly interdependent world. That is not to say that tensions between the overriding constitution-based de jure jurisdiction of traditional sovereign states and the novel de facto claims of newly cooperating cities will not persist. Two examples will serve to show how delicate and complicated the new power relations are likely to be in the setting of a not yet fully established global confederalism. The first example concerns what is perhaps the greatest challenge cities face in exercising authority in the face of traditional sovereign power: achieving sufficient financial autonomy to realize their goals. In many places, cities are being effectively strangled fiscally by higher authorities responsible for taxing urban citizens and redistributing the income. In California, where Stockton is only the best known example, city after city is facing bankruptcy. In Michigan, twenty-one "emergency managers" have been assigned to "save" cities in distress, and cities as large as Detroit face bankruptcy, while others such as Pontiac (on its third outside manager) no longer possess a shred of financial or political self-administration, having seen their basic services carved up and severed from the city—farmed out to county and state administrative bodies.[36] Even in Europe, states that have yielded some degree of their sovereign autonomy to common authority continue to dominate the European financial crisis, while cities—Europe's most successful civic bodies—bear a preponderance of the brutal consequences of the crisis. So while cities may hold the key to solving their own fiscal problems—Athens under Mayor Kaminis, we have shown (see Chapter 4), is doing better than the Greek national government in dealing with the austerity crisis—the fiscal noose remains their most difficult challenge. The second example I will discuss focuses on the challenge of immigration and the search for jobs in a global marketplace indifferent to traditional legal boundaries. This example demonstrates how new ideas such as that of "city visas" can use the confederal realities to solve questions that stymie the traditional sovereign state, a political entity that continues to confound the theoretical sovereignty it still possesses with its actual power, which is much diminished.

Urban Autarky: Meeting the Challenge of the Financial Dependence of Cities

First and foremost is the question of autarky, or the need for relative financial and administrative autonomy for cities coping with the new century's biggest problems. I will suggest below that to the degree nation states fail to secure the ends for which they are constituted (security and survival, for example), they not only become dysfunctional but lose a measure of their legitimacy and hence their authority. However, despite their diminished authority, states everywhere today continue to wield an enormous fiscal power over cities. Cities are well endowed with creativity, productivity, and other resources that make them the source of a large portion of a nation's collective wealth. They also are home to a majority of the world population. Yet the legal and fiscal jurisdiction of states over municipalities means that it is the state and not the municipality that determines how these urban resources are taxed and how revenues are distributed. Hong Kong is a leading example, with an economic and civic profile that benefits all of China, but saddled with diminished autonomy in the face of state and Party suzerainty. The city may be a primary source of state revenues, but it is not the primary decision maker with respect to their use and disbursement. Although it provides the fiscal vehicles that drive the nation, the city is hardly in the driver's seat.

Nonetheless, acting as economic engines of the nation gives cities a singular advantage in negotiating greater financial autonomy: they provide the very resources with which nations dominate them. It is a well-known irony of city and country everywhere, that the countryside complains about big government and the supposed lucre government takes from it and gives to cities (Mitt Romney's complaint about the entitled 47 percent, largely urban, supposedly on the dole forever), even as in reality it is cities around the world that pay out to national governments more than they get back. This is the irony Tom Frank explores in his fascinating study *What's the Matter with Kansas?*—the paradox of country folk who benefit little from a corporate America whose bidding they nonetheless do. The American Tea Party, like its European populist counterparts on the right, has capitalized on this critique of the supposed affinity of big government for big cities, but the fiscal reality belies the ideological claim.

In this reality can be found the potential salvation of the city. For if cities can more than care for themselves with their own resources and over the long term hold the demographic potential to be a majority (in the West, 78 percent of the population are urban citizens), then democracy and demographics alike favor the eventual fiscal self-sufficiency (if not quite autarky) of the city. The coming political struggle will be to persuade cities, once they are more empowered, to feel responsible for the planet generally and not just their own citizens. But in demanding from states that have confiscated their resources through taxation a return sufficient to get the job done, cities will have right on their side. A city should never go bankrupt in a region to which over time (if not in every fiscal year) it contributes more than it receives in creativity, productivity, and revenue. When fiscal crisis does overwhelm it, usually as a consequence of economic forces beyond its control, justice, if not power, will favor its interests and demand more, not less, autonomy. Even the fiscally conservative *Economist* magazine has suggested in the English context that "anything that boosts the economic performance of British cities is welcome. Thanks to the government's fiscal squeeze, most urban local authorities are extremely short of cash. More freedom would help them respond."[37]

This claim to autonomy is not merely a theoretical validation of the city's status: it is a premise for political action and, if necessary, a rationale for extra-political action of the kind associated with protest and rebellion—some may even call it revolution. But if provincial and national governments hold cities hostage, cities may feel constrained to entertain strategies of resistance. The government in Washington once told America's largest city, "Drop Dead, New York!" Tomorrow it may be New York shouting, "Drop Dead, Washington!" Indeed, Mayor Bloomberg has already said the same (if a little more politely) in an MIT speech where he observed that whatever Washington might think about the city's self-regarding actions, he "didn't much care" what Washington thinks (I cite his remarks in full in Chapter 1).

Such expressions are of course rhetorical, a way of amplifying urban dissatisfaction in the face of state and national government obtuseness, rather than a call to actual insurgency. New York may have one of the largest armies in the world (as Bloomberg boasted in that same speech) but the Big Apple is hardly prepared to take on the Pentagon or to even hint at the minor league treason implied in the threat. When a state court struck down Mayor Bloomberg's big-soda ban, his recourse was a court appeal, not a street demonstration, let alone NYPD enforcement of his overturned executive order. Yet Washington along other global capitals from New Delhi and Beijing to Berlin and Brasilia need to recognize that while they have the power to coerce, they no longer have either the legitimacy to ride rough-shod over cities or to act punitively against urban interests, whether in matters of taxation, immigration, or the environment.

For as a consequence of interdependence, the reality is that cities have a legitimacy they once lacked and dysfunctional states may find themselves prudently acknowledging them—if for no other reason than that cities may solve problems states cannot.

Cities, like people, when pushed against a wall, are likely to react in ways that breed trouble. In what Barry Yeoman has called "rebel towns" as small as Sugar Hill, New Hampshire, and as large as Pittsburgh, Pennsylvania, citizens irate over the behavior of energy corporations that act with arrogant indifference to both town interests and the environment have been engaging in "municipal disobedience."[38] Lawsuits are being filed to enjoin companies to cease and desist. City officials know that, as a legal strategy, their actions are often exercises in futility. As Sugar Hill's attorney acknowledges, local "governments can't override state or federal law, much less the Constitution." But it is the political aim of Thomas Linzey, the lawyer behind the Community Environmental Legal Defense Fund in Pennsylvania, to foment resistance to the power of corporations in bed with state and national government. Cities and towns need to engage in "collective nonviolent civil disobedience through municipal lawmaking," he maintains.[39] Even when the Constitution itself has to be challenged, Linzey sees such "disobedient lawmaking" as a powerful organizing tactic rather than a legal tool. He expects defeat in the courtroom but hopes to incite further civic resistance in the streets and pressure corporations and their enablers in government through the power of public opinion. Pittsburgh's City Council thus passed a unanimous rights-based antifracking ordinance in 2010 that, though nullified a year later by the state legislature, has inspired continuing litigation and ongoing political action combating climate change. More recently, in 2013, the Santa Monica City Council introduced "California's first community rights ordinance, recognizing the right to self-governance, clean air and water, sustainable food and energy systems, and the rights of nature."[40]

Critics worry that local control in defiance of state and national standards of the kind advocated by Linzey has in the past been the strategy of local governments trying to nullify civil rights and other public goods rooted in uniform national standards. But in a world where national public interests are too often subordinated to tainted private money and special corporate interests advanced by lobbying (as with the National Rifle Association's lobbying against gun control), cities nowadays are discovering that it is they that are defending public goods. They are the political bodies using lawsuits as a tactic to nullify the legislative actions of higher government authorities representing private and partial corporate interests.[41] Thus, for example, in 2011 the city council in Seattle banned plastic bags, while West Hollywood, a California city with only 36,000 residents, imposed a ban on the sale of fur garments.

Once upon a time in the great American struggle for civil rights, national courts and national law were used to defeat local authorities wedded to discrimination. Common norms and universal rights were the provenance of the whole nation not the municipalities caught up in local cultural bigotries. The cry for local autonomy concealed an antiliberal campaign to defend the past against the future. Today, when national governments are so vulnerable to money and so remote from the public interests of their citizens, municipalities have taken on the defense of public goods and the promotion of a sustainable future.

The new confederalism, and the ability of cities to cooperate across borders to pursue their common goods, is creating a new global landscape whose full implications for civil rights and public goods have yet to be revealed. In cities around the world from Nepal to Italy, and from India to New Zealand, Linzey has interacted with activists incensed by resource extraction and the carbon industry. Earlier paradigms developed in an era when it was the nation that defined the outer limits of what is "public" may no longer define those limits in an era of global interdependence. Though nations can still trump what cities do, today it is the planet that embodies the good of humankind and cities embedded in global networks rather than rival nations caught up in special interests that appear positioned to represent common human goods.

City Visas: Responding to the Challenge of Immigration
In the case of city finances, the regional and national authorities must be confronted in order to get them to loosen the purse strings. But a far more felicitous arena for the exercise of urban discretion than taxation

(where states are likely to be unflinching and the challenge to cities commensurately daunting) is the arena of policy where the state is distracted or simply indifferent. Or still better, where the state may be willing to have cities deal with controversial issues it would like to see resolved but for political reasons cannot itself resolve.

Immigration is a prime example of a problem that may leave cities some room to maneuver. From Mexico and Guatemala to Canada and the United States, from Morocco and Madrid to Hong Kong and Taiwan, the reality is that cities are brimming with immigrants whose legal (state-based) status is problematic. With or without documentation, they come in search of jobs. They are responding to the logic of the interdependent marketplace rather than the logic of independent sovereign laws, and the reality from the urban perspective is that they are there and likely to stay unless caught and forcibly evicted—something national authorities often have little motivation to undertake.

Now mayors clearly have neither the authority nor the resources to address illegality per se, but they must perforce deal with the reality of immigrants in their midst, whether they are documented or not. Will such residents have access to jobs and health care? Will their children be allowed into local schools? Is there a way to register them so they can be accounted for in city housing systems and crime control? The designation "illegal" or "undocumented" does nothing to answer such questions. Indeed, it only militates against the kinds of pragmatic steps that might be taken to ameliorate the situation. From such dilemmas arise one of the most intriguing experiments in confederalism in recent times: a novel proposal for "city visas." City visas is an idea advanced by the Urbanization Project at New York University's Stern School. In the United States, the Department of Homeland Security along with the Immigration and Naturalization Service have jurisdiction and oversight over immigration, with similar top-down arrangements in place in other nations. The INS has the formal responsibility to issue visas and will presumably insist on authorizing the visa arrangements cities might make.

A city visa program aspires to take advantage of confederalism by shifting to cities the practical responsibility for dealing with "illegals" already in residence. Cities might also use a visa program to attract new immigrants to fill vacant jobs. As described by Brandon Fuller:

> The visa could be temporary and renewable, with a path to permanent residency and eventually citizenship. Visa holders would be free to bring their immediate family members with them. Presumably, the sponsoring cities would have to adequately address some of the primary concerns of immigration opponents, ensuring that visa holders do not receive means-tested transfers from the federal government, commit crimes, or disappear into non-participating cities. A participating city could choose to sponsor undocumented immigrants, provided the city is willing to take on the responsibility of making them legal residents and eventually citizens.[42]

The innovative urbanist Richard Florida likes the idea, observing that "American cities like Baltimore, Dayton, and Detroit are eager to attract immigrants in an effort to stem population losses. . . . The potential gains from trade here are pretty huge—one has to wonder if adjustments to American immigration policy could help to realize them."[43] Some critics have suggested the idea would be feasible only if applied to skilled immigrants with proper ID, and no one has yet explored the full legal implications of a scheme where cities issued visas recognized as valid by national authorities.[44] But the crux of the idea is a system for dealing constructively and pragmatically with a bad situation—undocumented foreign workers—which is otherwise not being dealt with at all.

What is truly novel and important about the city visa idea is that it visits a kind of global citizenship/residency on immigrants, whatever their previous status, and demonstrates how cities can act in domains where the politics frightens off other actors. As the League of Nations once issued League passports to political exiles and other stateless emigrants without documentation in the 1930s and 1940s, cities might issue city visas to those left vulnerable by the collision of the logic of the marketplace with the logic of national immigration law.[45] One can imagine an ideal city visas program undertaken not by one city at a time but by a network of cities working together. Indeed, this kind of cooperation is probably a necessity if one or two brave cities inaugurating the plan are not to be overwhelmed by immigrants from all over flocking to them (as potential clients of welfare flocked to cities like New York that offered attractive welfare benefits). In time, such a program might be embraced by a global parliament of mayors and administered by a global cities secretariat that takes responsibility for local residency and employment by immigrants throughout member cities around the world. Such a collective system would stand a better chance of being recognized by nation-states in which member cities operated.

The great virtue of a confederal system that enjoys the support of both local and national authorities is that it can assist in solving problems at the municipal level that states cannot solve; or it may relieve states of having to lead on issues where they prefer to follow. For example, a well-designed city visa program could become the proving ground for those wishing to change their status from illegal to legal. Holding a city visa responsibly over, say, two years might be certified by a national government as a valid step in applying for permanent residence or even citizenship at the national level.

The Right of Cities to Act Autonomously in a Confederal World

While the examples of prospective financial autarky and the new experiment in urban visas illuminate the potential autonomy cities need to claim in order to take on global problems, they hardly prove that cities are without rivals for power and control. As I have acknowledged repeatedly, states are here to stay: their claims to jurisdiction have compelling normative and legal legitimacy, even when they fail to produce cooperative international outcomes. Nonetheless, cities are of growing consequence for global relations and it is the virtue of confederalism that it can distribute power to the advantage of those best able to exercise it—more often than not, cities. For in dispersing power vertically over local, regional, provincial, national, and international governing bodies, democratic confederalism tends to favor the local on the theory that power grows bottom up and democracy is generally constituted from local building blocks.

The successful war of independence against England by the thirteen American colonies yielded the Articles of Confederation, which then gave birth to a federal constitution and the United States of America. But confederalism's operating principle, that powers not expressly delegated to higher authorities are reserved to the original constitutive authorities at the local level, remained in the new Constitution. As the language of the Tenth Amendment puts it, "The powers not delegated to the United States by the Constitution, nor prohibited by it to the States, are reserved to the states respectively, or to the people." Translated to a global confederalism, the clause might read "the powers not delegated to provincial, national, or international powers by recognized legal documents, are reserved to the cities, and other local authorities and to their citizens." The Ninth Amendment reinforces the Tenth by insisting that "the enumeration in the Constitution of certain rights shall not be construed to deny or disparage others retained by the people." The aim is to make clear that rights do not depend on being explicitly expressed, and that all rights, express or otherwise, are retained by the people as citizens, defined in the first instance by their citizenship in the polis.

In accord with these two constitutional articles, cities may wish to claim an original right to govern and to demand the power to do so. Indeed, the appropriate global infrastructure mirrors Article II of the Articles of Confederation, which guarantees to each state "its sovereignty, freedom, and independence, and every power, jurisdiction, and right, which is not by this Confederation expressly delegated to the united states in Congress assembled." Cities belonging to intercity networks need to be bound together much the way the original thirteen states were under Article III of the Articles of Confederation: "The said states hereby severally enter into a firm league of friendship with each other, for the common defense, the security of their liberties, and their mutual and general welfare, binding themselves to assist each other against all force offered to, or attacks made upon them, or any of them, on account of religion, sovereignty, trade, or any other pretence whatever." There are worse ways to think about a parliament of mayors than, in the first instance, as a league of friendship.

The Articles of Confederation propose another idea cities might ponder: shared rights and privileges that comprise a kind of common citizenship. Substituting the word "cities" for "states," Article IV would thus read: "The better to secure and perpetuate mutual friendship and intercourse among the people of the different cities in this Union, the free inhabitants of each of these cities . . . shall be entitled to all the privileges and immunities of free citizens in the several cities, and the people of each city shall have free ingress and regress to and from any other city, and shall enjoy therein all the privileges of trade and commerce."

Of course, between the original thirteen colonies and the new confederation there existed no intermediate association demanding fealty from citizens and obedience from subsidiary governmental units. Today, the de facto confederal system is global and thus necessarily unfolds in the context of the many intermediate levels of government, with county, provincial, national, and regional authorities potentially interposing themselves between the city and a global parliament. Moreover, in the world of nations in which we live, the sovereign state remains trump: it retains the power and, by the logic of social contract, the right to jurisdiction over subsidiary units within it (including cities) and over those "higher" but hardly superior associations they choose to create (such as the International Monetary Fund or NATO or the U.N.).

It would be both foolish and futile to try to diminish the power of the states by dint of wishful thinking or tortured redefinition. My argument here is intended only to highlight and undergird the normative authority and influence of cities and urge measures to protect them from undue interference from the states to which they are legally and financially subsidiary. A new confederalism obviously must respect the legal principle of sovereignty; but it can also claim greater legitimacy for cities acting on their own behalf and on behalf of the planet—especially where states have been derelict in upholding values and pursuing goals dear to the city and its cosmopolitan citizens. After all, it is a fundamental principle of the social contract, as advocated in different forms by both Thomas Hobbes and John Locke, that the legitimacy of sovereignty depends on the power to safeguard the security, interests, and rights of the governed. This principle underwrites the logic of the Declaration of Independence.[46]

When states fail to secure the goods that justify our obeying them—as they have notably failed to do with respect to gun violence, climate change, nuclear proliferation, and immigration, to take just four urgent examples—they risk forfeiting their sovereignty. They may find themselves having to soften their absolute right to demand compliance from citizens who have other governing bodies and jurisdictions through which they can realize their goals. Sovereign power carries within it its own revolutionary teaching: that the failure of power to protect spells the end of power's legitimacy to govern. In this sense, cities can be understood as possessing a potential right to claim jurisdiction in domains where states fail to act on behalf of safety and survival. This, I will argue in the final chapter, is perhaps the chief rationale for a global parliament of mayors. Rebel town and insurgent cities can do little one by one, but in global partnership they constitute a formidable power.

Cities obviously must advance such provocative claims with extreme care—no "Declaration of Independence (from states)" for them![47]—and must proceed with the knowledge that though states may not have the power or will to solve new global problems, they retain the power to impose their ancient jurisdictional prerogatives over "inferior jurisdictions" such as cities. Vladimir Putin's resentment at Mayor Luzhkov's quasi-autonomous power in Moscow, or what he recently called the "meddling in Russian internal affairs" by global civil society organizations, are perfect examples of both the crucial role civil society can play when states fail to meet civic needs and the power states retain to punish those who intercede and act to secure their own rights—whether it is international civil society organizations or a city mayor.[48] China has shown a similar disdain for cities exercising excessive urban hubris. Even in America, the federal and state governments have shown themselves unwilling to sit still when, on the way to trying to solve their own problems, cities infringe higher jurisdictions—as the city of Washington, D.C., did when it tried to ban guns. But the gauntlet has been thrown down: nations have the power still to bully and silence cities; but unless they also deploy that power to solve the global problems that imperil citizens everywhere, the legitimacy of state power will be increasingly challenged. So the message for nations becomes this: Do the job or stand down and let cities do it.

Either way, cities will have to proceed deliberately with prudence and circumspection. But on the foundation of global civil society, global social movements, and an emerging conception of global citizens, proceed they can and proceed they will—down a path if they choose to follow it, that can lead to a global parliament of mayors.

PARK WON-SOON OF SEOUL

Like so many leaders in Asia, **PARK WON-SOON**, the youngish mayor of Seoul, is of humble origins, only a generation away from poor farmers in the village of Jangga Ri with a population of under a hundred households. Yet by the time he was thirty, Park had finished a law degree at Seoul National University and advanced studies in international law at the London School of Economics, Harvard, and Stanford. He became mayor of Seoul in October 2011, running as an independent and winning by 53 percent.

Mayor Park seems to prefer to talk not about his academic and law credentials (he spent time as a prosecutor, too) but about his experience as a human rights advocate and community organizer. His view of urban politics and democracy is rooted in bottom-up, gradualist reform rather than constitutionalism or legalism—as I learned in an hour-long Skype conversation with him broadcast on Korean television, and a recent visit to Seoul.

As a founder (in 1994) of the nonprofit watchdog NGO People's Solidarity for Participatory Democracy, he monitored government abuses of power, promoted tax reform, and sought to expand citizen participation in government and civil society. The work was concrete and resulted in dozens of new laws from anticorruption measures to welfare policies. Later, inspired by Oxfam, he established the Beautiful Foundation, aimed at cultivating voluntarism and community service in a country without a rooted tradition of philanthropy or giving. Today, the foundation raises up to $25 million a year, a considerable amount from traditional Korean business firms (chaebols) with no background in such giving.

Park's human rights commitments led to his appointment in 2005 to the Korean Truth and Reconciliation Commission, where he helped his country face up to its own record of past human rights violations.

When, in the absence of any previous political experience, Park was elected mayor of Seoul in 2011, no one was surprised that his support came from young people (two-thirds of those in their twenties, thirties, and forties voted for him) or that he made citizen engagement in governance and civil society his first priority. "Citizens are the mayor," he likes to say. To make the cliché real, he has used social media, listening workshops, a citizens' speech rostrum, a citizen as mayor-for-a-day program, a Mayor of Seoul Facebook site, and other tools.

The mayor's Twitter feed has over 600,000 followers, and Park responds directly to several hundred tweets every day. Complaints and suggestions alike are heard and responded to, many through a new Social Media Center.

Cynics will say his "citizen-centered" tenure is just politics—a pretence of interactivity that allows him to pursue his own agenda. How can ordinary neighbors really affect outcomes in what (with its suburbs) is Asia's second-largest city after Tokyo, an urban zone that includes one-fifth of Korea's population of 50 million? Yet Park's agenda reflects the concerns of Seoul's citizens rather than its traditional business interests.

In his first year, the new mayor shifted the focus from huge development projects to issues of inequality, housing for the poor, renewable energy, park space, and local agriculture. His city hall office includes an indoor urban mini-garden. His social welfare budget increased by nearly 13 percent, and he moved to underwrite education at both the primary and university level. Almost overnight he put a new eco-friendly school lunch program in place to serve 590,000 children, and then moved to offer reduced tuition and increased numbers of loans to students at the University of Seoul.

Park insists that the mayor is but an embodiment of his neighbors, thus his mantra that "citizens are the mayor." In a speech following his first year in office, he said, "Citizens are like musical instruments that make different sounds and we work together like an orchestra that produces magnificent music. I ask for your continuous participation, frank suggestions, and opinions. I will also strive to be a good conductor for this 'Seoul orchestra.'"

As his rhetoric suggests, like so many mayors from Johnson in London to Mockus in Bogotá to the late Ed Koch in New York, Park is voluble and visionary, and often enough also poetic and funny. As a result of such tendencies, like them he is assailed as a "showman"—in this case one who likens himself to an orchestra conductor and who wears his hair long and floppy. He sometimes even goes barefoot in political advertisements in order to assume a mantle of folksy humility. His critics insist he is merely playing the showman. Park's reply? "If that's so, we need more such showmen who look the people in the eye" and speak truth to the elites by listening to the people's voice. Whether such rhetoric translates to higher office is not clear—although in contradiction to global trends, two Seoul mayors have gone on to the Korean presidency.

"I've been working for 'us' my entire life," Park recalls in a recent interview; "but this year 'us' became concrete. It was 'Seoul.'" That's not quite the end of it, however. In an interdependent world, Seoul is a global city among cities and cannot isolate itself. Mayor Park has embraced intercity associations like CityNet, whose headquarters just moved from Yokohama to Seoul.

Moreover, among the dozens with whom I have talked about the idea of a mayors parliament, Park was the first to say: come to my city, let's talk; let's see what can be done. In March 2013, Park hosted the first informal meeting of a group seeking to plot a path to global democratic governance that runs through cities. This is one showman whose words mean real action and whose actions mean real change.

CHAPTER 12. A GLOBAL PARLIAMENT OF MAYORS

Bottom-up Democracy and the Road to Interdependence

> A secure world must be invented piecemeal, in multiple nations. It cannot be imagined or implemented as a unitary, preconceived plan or program.
>
> *David A. Wylie,* City, Save Thyself!

> Mayors do things. Mayors make things happen. . . . We don't have the luxury of giving speeches and making promises. . . . I don't think there's much difference in a meaningful sense, whether it's a city here or a city there . . . I was in Hanoi and Singapore . . . and they have exactly the same problems we do.
>
> *Michael Bloomberg*

> Forget Washington—Cities will win or lose the future.
>
> *Gallup CEO Jim Clifton*

Every argument offered in this book has pointed to a pressing need for global governance with both a democratic and a local face. And every description of extant and working intercity networks suggests we are already well down the road to this desired world of interconnected cities and citizens without borders. What is left to do is to take the small but critical step of convening a global parliament of mayors. The very hint of such a thing will elicit the usual cries: a bridge too far! too radical! too utopian! Yet the proposal that follows does little more than render coherent an intercity order already in the making and give formal institutional expression to the informal cooperative networks and collaborative arrangements that have for years been making a significant difference in addressing the challenges of an ever more interdependent world.

To exert influence, using soft power, not hard, a global parliament of mayors need only find a voice to announce and share best practices, need only act forcefully in connecting and extending the collaborative achievements of existing networks, need only actualize the enormous potential of what mayors are already doing. In short, a global parliament is no more than a final step down a road already well traveled, a road that has wound its way to and through such robust global intercity networks as UCLG (United Cities and Local Governments), ICLEI, Metropolis, CityNet, and City Protocol, associations we have described in earlier chapters. Such networks and dozens of other robust if little known others have already significantly influenced

- urban carbon emissions reduction,
- the United Nations campaign against nuclear proliferation,
- the global sharing of urban best practices,
- the campaign against gun violence,
- participatory budgeting across five continents,
- intercity cultural and arts cooperation.

Indeed, if there is a common complaint from mayors about the prospect for an assembly of cities, it comes from those who believe informal global urban governance is already a reality. Mayor Clover Moore of Sydney, Australia, for example, expresses skepticism about a parliament by referring to the crucial work already being done by the C40 Cities Climate Initiative.[1] Others, like Mayor Wolfgang Schuster of Stuttgart, though welcoming the idea of a parliament in theory, note that groups like UCLG (United Cities and Local Governments), of which Dr. Schuster was vice president, are already undertaking many of the tasks for which a global parliament might wish to assume responsibility. The City Protocol project initiated recently by Mayor Xavier Trias of Barcelona and Cisco Systems already envisions the convening of a City Protocol general assembly (constituted by one representative from each membership of the CPS) to represent a "City Protocol Society" (the governing body of the City Protocol) as well as a board of directors, a steering committee, and a volunteer task force, which together will be able to develop "protocol agreements" and "industry-based technological standards."[2] The global NGO association CIVICUS also holds an annual World Assembly of NGOs, while many of the intercity organizations we have described sponsor annual conferences that do some of the things a mayors parliament might do. Stuttgart's Mayor Schuster notes he already receives several invitations a week to such meetings. In a thoughtful discussion citing my argument here, Andrew Stevens and Jonas Schorr suggest that "instead of grandiose schemes like a global senate of mayors, we must concentrate on creating popular democratic demand for city networking, and on giving more power and media visibility to the knowledge exchange efforts that cities already pursue."[3]

My proposal for a parliament of mayors is no grandiose scheme, however, no mandate for top-down suzerainty by omnipotent megacities exercising executive authority over a supine world. It is rather a brief for cities to lend impetus to informal practices they already have in place; to give institutional expression and coherence to emerging cooperative relationships; to amplify their collective voice and by focusing on the bottom-up role cities already play in deliberating and deciding and voluntarily implementing policies and reforms that meet the interdependent challenges of the twenty-first century. The aim is not to add the burdensome job of governing the world to the already burdensome job of governing the city. It is only to understand that to govern their cities effectively, they may have to play some role in governing the world in which their cities fight to survive. In governing their cities cooperatively to give their pragmatism global effect, mayors need not await the cooperation of the disunited United Nations, the special interest permeated international financial institutions, private-market multinational corporations, or centuries-old dysfunctional nations. They can act now in ways that are symbolic, exemplary, and voluntary but also practical, efficient, and transformational. And they can do so in ways that directly affect more than half the world's population and indirectly serve the entire planet, without taking on massive new responsibilities. Most importantly, a global parliament of mayors will give the metropolis a megaphone and allow its voice to be heard. When the best practices by which cities define themselves can be shared and implemented in common, we can take intercity cooperation to the next level—a mayors parliament.

The truth is, as impressive as existing networks are, for all the innovative practices and experiments in intercity democracy they promote, one by one they are merely intriguing, if enormously promising. Together, however, they constitute a foundation for the establishment of an assembly of cities. Taken as an integral and associated complex—a network of networks—they are what a global parliament of mayors should be. I urge only that we raise the bar, make cooperation truly global by empowering cities to deal with and act in lieu of the sometimes obstreperous (when not altogether missing) national forces that impede the urban quest to secure justice and security for their citizens.

The call to action need not be too loud, nor the pursuit of the new institution too hasty. With cities already well down the path to informal global governance, too much attention to the next rather dramatic step could attract the censure of all those likely to be inconvenienced (or worse) by urban cosmopolitanism: proprietary international institutions, anxious NGOs, underregulated multinational corporations, and rival international financial institutions—and, most dangerously, the states under whose jurisdiction and financial suzerainty cities pushing across borders must continue to exist. There is no more lethal threat to the potential of cities for interdependence than the fiscal noose by which they dangle from superior jurisdictions. Long term, cities pay out on average (if not in every case) far more than they receive from higher authorities and thus, in theory, possess the means of their own solvency. But in practice they are often in thrall to the provinces and nations under whose legal and fiscal authority they live. So the process of convening a global parliament of mayors must proceed with patient circumspection.

At the same time, our global problems are urgent, the role of cities vital, and the opposition of states that cannot and will not act themselves, intolerable. There is perhaps no goal more crucial in establishing a mayors parliament than that of helping cities secure an autonomy of action sufficient to achieve a sustainable planet for all. Whether the issue is climate change, gun violence, nuclear security, predatory markets, or anarchic immigration, sustainable policy is the goal. In the face of nation-states pleading a sovereignty they no longer possess or an ideology of independence that our era of interdependence has superseded, cities have little choice but to act. And when obstreperously proud "higher authorities" fail to act, or interfere with and block cities ready and able to act, cities must be prepared to counter nation-state jurisdictional arrogance and ideological rigidity with problem-solving urban practicality; they must even be willing to turn urban practicality into a gentle but firm revolutionary pragmatism. The absolute necessity for action becomes a mandate for urban resistance for those who act to save themselves and their cities, and the planet that is their neighborhood. But resistance will be viable only when cities act in concert. There are many crucial reasons to convene a parliament of mayors. None is more important than establishing a proactive cosmopolis able to intervene on behalf of cities—but also on behalf of humankind and its right to collective survival at a moment when it is no longer clear nations can guarantee either survival or sustainability.

A Global Parliament of Mayors

As a starting point for giving institutional expression to the need to realize some form of constructive democratic interdependence, I propose then the convening of a global parliament of mayors—call it a World Assembly of Cities. To begin, such an assembly would represent a modest first step toward formalizing the myriad networks of cities already actively cooperating across borders around issues as mundane an express bus lanes, bike-share programs, and web-based information collection, and as momentous as climate change, nuclear security, and intelligence gathering. It turns out that in cities it is often the mundane issues that affect the momentous ones—bike-shares and express bus lanes are a way to address climate change and emissions, information sharing can be a path to collective security—which is precisely why cities can often achieve the momentous while pursuing the mundane. Perhaps it is why Las Vegas urban reformer Tony Hsieh is right to say, if rather too grandly, that "if you fix cities, you kind of fix the world."

A global assembly of cities, meeting as a parliament of mayors, offers a fresh approach to global governance because in my conception it would seek progress through voluntary actions and consensus rather than through executive or legislative mandates. The parliament I envision, operating in the absence of sovereign coercive authority, agreed-upon common law, and (initially) any means of enforcement, would not exercise executive power by command. It would of necessity rely on persuasion and consensus. For this reason, we might even wish to conceive of a parliament of mayors as a kind of "Audiament"—a chamber of listeners, where to hear is more important than to speak and where, in the absence of command, persuasion reigns; where participating cities and the people they represent act by opting into policies they agree with rather than being subject to mandates on high from which they may dissent.

In a world of concentrated but mostly illegitimate global power, we worry rightly about a global government upon which the planet's power in its abstract and awesome entirety is bestowed. The time may come when such concentrated power can be legitimated and contained—rendered democratic. But as a starting place, voluntary compliance with consensual policies makes much more practical sense. It is an inducement to cities to participate without fear of being coerced, and it also affords a partial solution to the problem of a global body that formally represents only half the world's population. For though it leaves suburbs and rural regions without formal representation, they too are free to comply or not as they wish.

Making compliance voluntary also permits mayors to see themselves, in the manner imagined by the great eighteenth-century Whig political thinker Edmund Burke, as representatives not just of their metropolises but of the common interests of the planet. This approach, where participation is bottom-up and voluntary, but actions—once consented to by cities—are universal, is the essence of "glocality." As with America's Articles of Confederation, only a very limited central authority would be conveyed, hardly enough initially to do all that needs to be done. Yet even a modest and minimal start-up would offer an alternative to the largely ineffective concert-of-nations approach that has prevailed for the last several centuries, where the will and veto of the powerful few makes decisions improbable and effective action on behalf of the many impossible.

Moreover, because the assembly-of-cities approach is focused on solving the real and common problems that give cities a natural common agenda and that invite pragmatic solutions rather than ideological diatribes, its capacity for genuine transformation is considerable, even though it would lack the executive authority we associate with transformative change. The "strong democratic" approach I have long urged for nation-states becomes far more practical in the context of cooperating cities.[4] As we have witnessed in Hong Kong, where a long-independent city government has fought hard for its autonomy and pragmatism even as it is absorbed into the greater theater of Chinese ideological politics, cities can counter or elude ideology in search of practical solutions. Michael Bloomberg, Antanas Mockus, Boris Johnson, Teddy Kollek, and most of the other mayors featured in our interchapter profiles share an aversion to ideology and an indifference to political party. During their mayoral tenure, they shed zealous party platforms and devoted themselves to problem solving. A Parliament of Mayors would embody these shared attitudes and hold out the possibility of a transition to a meaningful form of soft global governance.

The Challenge of Representation

Before trying to envision the concrete form a parliament of mayors might take, we need to address the problem of representation. As urban demographics stand today, if mayors indeed ruled the world, half the planet would not be represented. Under these skewed conditions, our proposed parliament might be realized, but seemingly at the expense rather than in the name of global democracy. Surely there can be no authentic globalization of democracy without representation. Furthermore, given that urban denizens are generally more liberal and progressive than their rural counterparts, representing cities globally could unbalance the planet's political equilibrium, giving additional voice to (in the American parlance) a "blue" (progressive) planet while further disempowering the "red" (conservative) planet. Some might argue that this would be a natural counterbalance to the tendency of rural conservatism to outweigh urban progressivism in countries like the United States, India, and China. In the United States, where the electoral system is tipped in favor of the countryside even though three-quarters of the population live in cities, urban dwellers often endure national policies dictated by a rural minority working through a gerrymandered House of Representatives and a Senate designed to thwart pure majority rule.[5] Still, whatever benefits replacing a "red" planet with a "blue" planet might bring, greater democracy would not be among them.

Are there ways, then, under a mayors parliament that the nonurban half of the world can be fairly represented and the interests of the countryside, conservative or not, are protected? Ways in which a system of accountability allows a voice or a veto to the nonurban or otherwise allows them to see mayors as quasi-legitimate spokespersons? It seems self-evident that there can be no democratic form of globalization without finding ways for cities to represent more than their own residents.

As realists, of course, we have an easy way out. We can respond to the question of how democratic city networks really are with the skeptic's counterquery, "as compared to what?" For at present such forms of globalization as can be found leave out more or less everybody, rural and urban alike. The current alternatives are utterly undemocratic and unrepresentative. Neither multinational corporations nor international banks pretend to represent anybody but themselves and (sometimes) their shareholders. Nongovernmental and nonprofit civic institutions try to look more democratic than their corporate counterparts, upholding relatively altruistic values and pursuing relatively public goods. But this hardly makes them democratic. NGO boards and leaders are pretty much self-appointed, while nonprofit identity and sometimes even nonprofit purposes tend to be opaque to the larger public in whose name NGOs operate.

State-based international organizations like the United Nations and the former Bretton Woods international financial institutions (IFIs) exhibit formal democratic structures (at least to the extent member states are democratic), but as we have seen throughout this study, they are not now and are unlikely any time soon to become effective global governing bodies. It seems as if bodies such as states and state-based international institutions, though invested with democratic legitimacy, are inefficient and ineffective as agents of interdependence, while those like multinational corporations that are more globally efficient and effective are undemocratic.

The European Union is a special case, a welcome attempt to forge a transnational democratic entity that is a genuinely democratic alternative to the nation-state. But its character to date has been more economic than political or civic. Its troubled story is unfinished and its fate remains in doubt, especially in the face of the prolonged economic recession and the Euro crisis. Some argue that even Europe has been more successful as a League of Cities than a union of states. Former mayor Schuster of Stuttgart has challenged Europe's bureaucratic affinity for hierarchy, urging greater power sharing and input from cities and regions. The aim is not just to "invite everyone to talk" and to put "a lot of opinions on the table" while "the bureaucracy decides what to do," but to develop new forms of cooperation that empower the many different "levels of responsibility and competence."[6]

These reflections on the alternatives leave city-based networks as prospective global governing mechanisms looking quite promising, both more efficient than states and a good deal more democratic than corporations. This realist argument alone is enough to justify the quest for a city-based global governance that is both quasi-legitimate and moderately efficient, even though it fails the test of full accountability and representativeness. Voltaire would be skeptical, but there is much to recommend a formula for governance in the global domain that, while not fully democratic, is nevertheless "the best of all possible democracies." Or, to paraphrase Churchill, we might agree that a global mayors parliament is the "worst form of global democratic governance in the world . . . except for all the other forms." I hope here, however, to advance arguments with more legitimacy. Fortunately, there are realistic paths to enhancing democratic legitimacy for city-based global governance that can render it more accountable to and representative of those dwelling outside cities and that can help address the complaint of a "blue" or progressive urban bias. Among these paths, the following are crucial.

Representing Commuters

Securing a representative voice for those who work in but do not reside in cities effectively incorporates suburbia and exurbia into the city. Commuters are often required to pay a city tax, with place of work trumping residence—a good reason to offer them some form of representation in a global mayors parliament. Given the benefits they receive from the city, commuters are implicitly bound to if not actually represented by the relevant decision-making bodies. To ensure this is more than rhetoric means there must be effective communication with commuters about the issues and a willingness to consider their views in proposing and disposing of policies.

Including Regions within Urban
Representative Districts

Including regions on the urban periphery within greater metropolitan areas is a way to establish a modern equivalent of the medieval notion that the burg or walled town encompassed and belonged to the regional population for purposes of safety, jurisdiction, and military protection. It may seem fanciful to appeal to the role of medieval cities in enforcing regional security as a model for modern representation. Yet it is a characteristic of cities that they are interdependent not only with one another but within the local regions and counties in which they find themselves. For purposes of shopping (malls), recreation (parks, walk lands, wetlands), security (city police patrolling county roads and state police overseeing policing in villages), and, of special importance nowadays, local agriculture, cities are embedded in their local regions in ways that tie together urban and regional interests and give rural residents a stake and interest in city policy—and vice versa. Treating cities as representative of the regions in which they find themselves will thus make a good deal of sense to regional residents. A policy demanding tariffs on local agricultural products sold within city limits, for example, would not only hurt regional agriculture but be disastrous for the city in terms of food prices. Taxing working commuters too steeply would discourage people from coming to the city and accelerate the flight of business to regions beyond the center where such taxes don't exist.

Extending the Electoral District

For purposes of representation in the global parliament, the urban electoral distinct might be extended to include the region as an urban electoral
district. Regional residents might alternatively be invited to vote on policies and issues only as they relate to votes for or in a global parliament; or
to participate in the vote for the mayor as a global representative of the
region. Of course it is one thing to say that region and city share interests.
It is quite another to actually give formal representation to those regions.
Formalizing the implicit relationship by extending voting to the region
would no doubt be viewed as radical and would be far more difficult to
achieve than some of the other ideas proposed here. At the same time, it
would go a long way toward creating a sense of regional representation in
a mayors parliament.

Guaranteeing Opt-in/Opt-out Rights

Even without possessing voting rights in the city, regional constituents
can be empowered to opt in or out of decisions made by their anchor city
or by the parliament of mayors (even in the absence of support for a given
policy by the anchor city). Because the proposed cities assembly would be
a cooperative of consenting cities rather than a top-down executive authority imposing its will, its decisions would be available for opt-in by any
local or regional authority (or nation-state, for that matter) that found
them useful. Opting in would be an option to all, even if they were not
part of the proposing process. Indeed, noncity authorities could present
ideas in the hope that the parliament might act on them. The voluntary
and consensual character of the parliament might help disarm critics
insisting they were not represented.

Establishing Direct Representation in the Global
Parliament or in a Parallel Parliament of Regions

Rather than being represented through cities in a global mayors parliament, regions might elect their own representatives to the parliament of
mayors or to a parallel body such as a parallel parliament of regions. Such
a parallel body might be a second chamber in a global bicameral parliament. Again, with decisions creating policies that are more like best

practices with which cities and regions comply voluntarily (or not), a parallel body would not necessarily compromise global governance by cities. Moreover, because the entire process recommended here is consensual, such processes are easily tried out and amended, or withdrawn, as experience dictates and protagonists choose. The ultimate safety limit on any global assembly envisioned here, whether urban or regional, is its voluntary and consensual character.

Representation as Trusteeship

Treating representation as trusteeship and representatives as trustees accords with Edmund Burke's argument that members of the British Parliament were more than mouthpieces for their constituents and had a duty to deliberate and adjudge the true national interest. They served Parliament not just as delegates of their districts but as trustees of the British nation embodying the public good. Inasmuch as they belong to a global parliament, mayors too must understand themselves as trustees of the planet—past and future as well as present. If they act in conformity, they may in fact acquire considerable authority among those who lack the right to vote for them. Representatives are by definition bound to speak on behalf of their constituents. But constituents also owe their representatives a degree of independence in judgment and leadership by conscience in reading the public good. Technically, a mayors parliament is no more than a cities parliament that at its best fails to speak for the half of the world that doesn't live in cities. But it can also be a global deliberative body whose delegates as trustees are responsible equally to their constituents and to the planetary good. Burke's admonition to the Electors of Bristol, who in 1774 elected him to Parliament, offers a prudent counsel to mayors who might sit in a global parliament.

"Parliament," wrote Burke, "is not a *congress* of ambassadors from different and hostile interests; which interests each must maintain, as an agent and advocate, against other agents and advocates; but parliament is a *deliberative* assembly of *one* nation, with *one* interest, that of the whole; where, not local purposes, not local prejudices, ought to guide, but the general good, resulting from the general reason of the whole. You choose a member indeed; but when you have chosen him, he is not member of

Bristol, but he is a member of *parliament*."[7] The very meaning of interdependence is that electoral boundaries are less consequential than the aims of elected representatives. Effective mayoral representatives in a global parliament who see themselves not merely as keepers of the interests of the city but trustees of the global public good will regard themselves not simply as mandate representatives and delegates of city dwellers but as trustees of the public interest of cities, their regions, and the world as a whole.

Indeed, Burke argued that interdependence itself is a temporal as well as a spatial good. In what is perhaps the most notable phrase in his essay on the French Revolution, Burke wrote that while society is indeed a contract, it is not "to be regarded in the same light as a commercial contract that is entered into for a limited and self-interested purpose and can be dissolved at the will of the contracting parties." Rather, "it is to be looked on with other reverence; because it is not a partnership in things subservient only to the gross animal existence of a temporary and perishable nature. It is a partnership in all science; a partnership in all art; a partnership in every virtue, and in all perfection." And "as the ends of such a partnership cannot be obtained in many generations, it becomes a partnership not only between those who are living, but between those who are living, those who are dead, and those who are to be born."[8]

None of the proposals here fully addresses the defect of a world in which global governance is undertaken by representatives of cities alone. Even Burke's notion of trusteeship, and our conviction that a deliberative assembly of mayors might take positions and recommend actions in the interests of all rather than of their urban constituents alone, fail the test of true democracy. This being said, in an imperfect political world where democracy within nations is at risk and democracy among nations nonexistent, a parliament of mayors convened by global public trustees whose decisions are voluntary and nonmandatory seems like a very good place to start.

Implementing Urban Global Governance

Representation aside, giving institutional form and political reality to a parliament of mayors involves both an inaugural process of convening interested mayors and cities to plot a way forward and the development of a working blueprint for the desired institutional arrangements. The start-up process calls for the leadership of cities on the forefront of cooperation and cross-border networking, and it might include such developed Western world cities as New York, Los Angeles, Hamburg, Amsterdam, Vienna, and London (whose mayors have long embraced outreach and global cooperation and many of whom have already spoken out on the idea of a parliament of mayors), as well as cities such as Seoul, Singapore, Hong Kong, Buenos Aires, Kinshasa, and Mumbai, whose size and influence make their participation vital and whose role in the developing world, where inequality is so prevalent, makes their participation mandatory.[9] A prudent planning process would also invite visionary and already networked mayors of smaller developed-world cities such as Stuttgart, Bogotá, Palermo, Wrocław, Gdansk, Tijuana, and others like them to the planning table, honoring the reality that to speak of cities is not just to speak of megacities, and that towns with anywhere from 50,000 to 500,000 citizens must be part of a viable global order of cities. The makeup and inclusiveness of the planning body will be critical to counter what will be a natural tendency to suspect the project is one more big-city plan to dominate lesser cities, or one more plot by the urban West to dominate the urban rest.

Taking advantage of the reality that cities already are working together informally and voluntarily around a great many global issues, and already are learning from one another and achieving practical results through voluntary cooperation, the parliament of mayors might ideally begin as a voluntary gathering, meeting perhaps three times a year in different cities, dedicated to listening and deliberation and the undertaking of voluntary actions by agreement of a majority or more of cities participating. It might even be able to piggyback on such ongoing associations as UCLG, Metropolis, and ICLEI. A city's consent to the parliament's decisions would be the only warrant needed for action in that city, although obviously action across borders would be far more effective than solitary endeavors by individual mayors. Nonetheless, action by some or even by many would impose no mandate on cities hostile to a given decision. If 500 of 900 cities, for example, decided to act on climate change by enacting mandatory recycling, common congestion fees, or limits on carbon emissions within their own jurisdictions, significant action could occur without formal legislation by any national or global sovereign body and without the need for universal consent by participating cities. Since it would exercise no metasovereignty or formal hard power, its influence would rest exclusively on global public opinion and on the force of example—the reality of voluntary cooperation by many cities opting to pursue common policies across national borders.

The parliament of mayors would also have a significant deliberative role that would contribute to its persuasive power on global public opinion. Its debates and thoroughly deliberated decisions, voluntary and rooted in listening as much as in talking, could be broadcast on television and radio and streamed on the web throughout the world. In time, technology might allow virtual participation in listening, deliberation, debate, and even voting, by cities and citizens not in attendance. Smart cities would become virtual participants. Technology would also permit, immediately, "deliberative polling" in which individuals, groups, and cities not participating in a given parliament could express (and change) their points of view through remote or virtual deliberative and voting venues in their own localities and municipalities.[10]

Because all effective action would be the result of voluntary engagement by mayors and their cities, there would be no reason for cities—represented at a given parliament or not, present or absent—not to concur in and implement any particular measures approved at a particular session of the global parliament. Indeed, cities would be free to enact policies they believed in without a majority in the global parliament concurring. Their actions could even influence the mayors parliament in subsequent sessions to change its collective mind. If New York, Seoul, Mumbai, and Hamburg, for example, took common action in a domain on which the mayors parliament had not yet reached consensus, their common action, if successful, could help generate such a consensus.

The Unique Role of Mayors

For mayors to govern the world, they must play a unique role that both reflects their role as bottom-up representatives of their local constituents and also embraces their potential as our global conscience. In order to avoid being seen as mere delegates of the special interests of particular cities (Hong Kong as a port city, London as a financial capital, Kinshasa as a land-locked African megacity), mayors convened in a global parliament must also see themselves as deliberative judges of global public goods, embodying the Burkean common spirit. Such a spirit can help them see themselves as something more than flatterers of local citizens and mouthpieces of parochial interests, and permit them to convene as members of the deliberative assembly of a single and common planet. As Burke owed his Bristol constituents his good judgment and sense of common purpose on behalf of all of England, mayors Bloomberg (New York), Johnson (London), Scholz (Hamburg), Tan (Singapore), and Park (Seoul)—or their successors—would owe their local constituents their sense of common purpose on behalf of the global good. The cities from which they come would retain their autonomous right to comply with decisions taken by the global parliament in the planet's name (or not), but members of the global parliament would have an obligation to serve a greater good. The mayor of Houston who sees himself as a surrogate Texas oil executive would be unlikely to feel comfortable calling for limits on carbon emission that would injure the local economy, but as a trustee of planet Earth may nonetheless vote for common global limits to which the city of Houston will agree to commit, even if at some injury to its immediate economic interests. The residents of Houston must breathe the air, drink the water and suffer the costs of climate change like everyone else.

Burke's idea of "a partnership in every virtue, and in all perfection" evokes a conservationist perspective in the sense of conservatism: the dead, he observes, vote through the history they have made and the legacy of traditions they leave behind, a legacy no single generation can toy with on a whim. Burke's perspective also yields a platform for a sustainable environmentalism: conserving the future in the name of the unborn, who represent humankind's destiny. Burke's contract, he avers, is but a "clause in the great primeval contract of eternal society, linking the lower with the higher natures, connecting the visible and invisible world, according to a fixed compact sanctioned by the inviolable oath which holds all physical and all moral natures, each in their appointed place."[11] The law invoked by this contract imposes an obligation on all people, including the mayors who may meet in a global parliament to discover and enact what such a law requires.

A Parliament of Mayors: Institutional Forms and Practices

Since 300 to 400 members is a rough limit on a productive deliberative body, especially if each member may represent millions of individual citizens, the parliament of mayors might be limited to 300 cities in any one session. To create a sense of continuing engagement and maximize the number of cities involved, the parliament could meet three times a year in different cities (perhaps chosen by lot from a pool of cities willing and able to host the parliament), each time with a different set of cities. Selection of participants by lot (sortition) might be considered, given that there are far more cities than seats in the parliament, even when multiplied by three sessions a year over several decades. One might also ask whether certain global megacities must be regularly represented because of their size, geography, and demographics (emulating the U.N. Security Council, on which the major post–World War II powers were seated, but without being given a veto).

To ensure that cities of every size are included in each session, the parliament could offer seats to each of three tranches of cities based on population: 50 seats to megacities over 10 million whose participation is crucial; 125 seats to cities between 500,000 and 10 million in population that stand for the great majority of cities; and 125 seats to cities under 500,000 whose participation ensures more modest towns have a stake. Cities in all categories would be chosen by lot, with none (other than the "permanent" once-a-year members) eligible for a second parliament until all cities in the category participated. Given that the objective of the parliament would be voluntary action in concert on behalf of "participating" cities whether present at a given session or not, voting in the parliament by cities regardless of their size, though hardly representative of a popular vote, would be acceptable. However, for purposes of counting citizens and of the effect on public opinion, cities might also be weighted according to population and be counted in a second supplementary accounting in weighted terms—each 500,000 citizens represented comprising one vote. The mayor of a megacity of 20 million would cast one "city vote," but also be counted in the supplementary balloting as casting 40 demographic votes worth 500,000 citizens per vote. A city of a million would cast one city vote but two demographic votes. A city of 250,000 would cast one city vote but only one-half a demographic vote.

In any case, because compliance would be voluntary and city by city, the vote count whether by city or demographic units would be exclusively for purposes of information and public opinion. Imagine a vote for a recycling mandate in which 200 of 300 participating cities agree to participate (many will have already enacted such a mandate!), but in which the popular majority represented by the weighted vote is 800 million people (against, say, 150 million). Such information, compelling and informative, is pretty powerful even in the absence of a legislative mandate, especially if these numbers are then counted along with those in cities that are not at the parliament but in agreement with the policy.

Cities would participate in opting in or out of decisions of the mayors parliament through referenda, whether or not their mayors were currently represented. Mayors would retain the responsibility for their own city's deliberative position in the parliament but also have the responsibility to gain the city's assent. Mayor Schuster offered a straightforward and pragmatic account of what they must do: "Life," he said, "is compromising. . . . So I have to find majorities and my goal is to find as large a majority as possible . . . the interest of the citizens [which] is my interest too." Merely spouting principles is not enough. "The principles are nice, but at the end of the day I have to deliver, so I am very pragmatic."[12] Putting policies passed by a majority of the parliament to a referendum to secure legitimacy and extend the sense of participation is useful to the mayor as well as to democracy. A city's compliance with a policy would require the vote of the mayor and mayor's delegation in the parliament but also a majority of citizens voting by referendum.

To summarize, one might imagine three classes of cities, based on population, eligible to be represented in the parliament by their mayors; to pursue representation, they would have to elect to join the group from which cities are chosen by lot:

1.   Megacities with populations of 10 million or more (50 seats);
2.   Cities with 500,000 to 10 million population (125 seats);
3.   Cities of 50,000 to 500,000 (125 seats).

The three-trance structure serves useful deliberative and symbolic purposes. All policies and measures remain voluntary, however, and compliance is by choice of each individual city, whether present and voting, or observing and deliberating virtually at home. Measures with a simple majority of a given parliamentary session's votes in, say, each of three annual parliaments might be given official status as a common policy. Noncomplying cities might be required, as a condition of membership, to explain their opposition and perhaps even submit all policies with such official status to a referendum of their citizens. The "three readings" requirement obliging policies to win simple majorities in three successive parliaments would mean 900 rather than 300 cities were deliberating and voting. One might even treat policies that achieve official status via three readings and votes in three successive parliaments as provisionally the common policy of all cities with membership in the global association, subject to opting out based on a referendum. Cities could obviously pursue ideas and policies they agreed with, whether or not such ideas won a majority in the parliament.

Given the voluntary and deliberative character of the parliament, mayors would be required to appear in person to represent their communities. In time, their talent and competence as global legislators and their ability to use global cooperation to further the interests of their own cities would become features of our mayors' electoral and governing portfolios. At the same time, each mayor might bring one or two citizens—perhaps also chosen by lot from a voluntary pool—to parliament as colleagues and informal advisers. Mayors would be urged to assume Burke's attitude and see themselves not merely as mouthpieces for their constituents but as deliberative representatives of broad public goods, embodying the common purposes of the city that elected them but also as representatives of the global public: humanity incarnated in the living but also in the dead and the unborn.

354

In sum, a parliament of mayors would be chosen three times annually by lot from cities in a global cities association according to three categories based on size. Compliance would be voluntary and opt-in, except in the case of policies receiving a majority in three readings in three successive parliamentary sessions; these policies would be opt-out, based on a referendum or other procedure prescribed internally by cities (with the approval of the global association).

Key principles of the parliament include the following:

Listening: Listening rather than talking is emphasized, with empathy, sharing, and attention to the other.

Deliberation: Deliberation which entails listening, changing one's mind, and seeking common ground.

Sortition: Choice of delegates and sites is by lot for fairness and true representation under conditions of too many units for all to be represented at any one time.

Glocality: Glocality is a product of integrating bottom-up and top-down approaches and eliminating the dysfunctional middle occupied by regional and national governments.

Voluntary Action: Consent is the basis for cooperation while avoiding top-down fiats.

Leading by Example: Exemplary function of alternative approach; teaching democracy.

Opt In: Policies not receiving a three-session reading and simple majority vote would require active consent.

Opt Out: The opt-out choice for adopted measures preserves freedom not to comply, yet creates momentum for cooperation.

Mayors as Global Trustees: Mayors realize their responsibility as leaders and symbols of universal goods and global cooperation.

Starting Up

A trial run for the idea of a parliament of mayors will require that several (self-selected) host cities step forward, ideally from both the developed and developing worlds, say, Seoul and New York, Singapore and Hamburg, and convene a planning assembly. The planning meeting might invite a few dozen mayors to convene and take up the procedural issues prerequisite to establishing the new institution, endorsing a provisional set of rules, and determining planning, logistical, and financial specifics for perhaps the first three years or nine sessions of the parliament. It might also establish and finance a modest secretariat overseeing the formation of a "Global Association of Cities" and participating in creating the parliament and developing a communications strategy. Indeed, the need to finance the process leading to a parliament and fund the parliament itself raises important questions. The easy solution might be tithing by participating cities, but a more creative approach could use the so-called Tobin Tax on international financial and currency exchanges (a tiny tax of circa .01 percent on each transaction). Finally, an inspirational mayor or mayors dedicated to building a new global governance edifice—elected leaders in Seoul, Stuttgart, New York, and Gdansk, for example, and others voicing interest—will be enormously important in giving real life to what is only a paper idea.

Within a decade of its heralded turning, the political mindset of our new millennium has gone from optimistic to pessimistic. With terrorism still a peril to people everywhere and climate change a taboo subject in democracies too selfishly present-minded to look to the future, democracy in its present opinion-driven form simply does not allow us to manage our future. Folded into obstreperously independent and increasingly dysfunctional nation-states and reliant on international institutions constrained by those same states and by the multinational corporate monopolies that influence them, representative government grows ever more impotent in the face of crisis.

With popular sovereignty everywhere tainted by money, reactionary fundamentalism, and the politics of fear, citizens in the old democracies are turning cynical, while those in the new democracies of the Arab Awakening, beset by instability, tribal infighting, perduring inequality and the danger of civil war, are falling into despair. If democracy turns out to mean little more than elections without citizens and anarchy in the absence of despotism, what can we expect from it? If insurgents cannot negotiate the difficult road from revolution (overthrowing tyrants) to democracy (establishing justice and the rule of law through the participation of free and competent citizens), where does hope lie? And finally, even when democracy can be made to function within nations, if democracy cannot cross borders, will it not become increasingly less relevant to the challenges of an interdependent world?

I have proposed in these pages that much of the difficulty lies with the traditional sovereign state, too large to engage local civic participation, too small to address global power, its traditional independence now an impediment to coming to terms with interdependence. I have recommended we change the subject: from states to cities, from representative to strong democracy, from top-down formal global governance as an impossible ideal to bottom-up informal global governance as an unfolding intercity reality that asks only for a stamp of approval.

Because they are inclined naturally to collaboration and interdependence, cities harbor hope. Cosmopolitan mayors have shown an ambition to write the achievements and best practices of their cities into a promissory note for the planet. The city is now our future as a demographic and economic fact. When Republican vice presidential candidate Paul Ryan suggested that President Obama was reelected mostly on the backs of urban voters, he was right, though not quite in the narrow political way he perhaps had in mind. The city is "blue"—progressive, experimental, risk-taking—and the future demands open, experimental, and progressive programs and policies. The city is thus the future guarantor of our democratic and interdependent ideals.

The urban future is not, however, without its risks and dangers. The myriad features of the city we have explored here, features that condition its origin and define its essence, make urban living seductive, productive, and perilous. They are responsible for its abrasive creativity, its generative imagination, its fractious mobility, and its discomfiting diversity. They endow it with its affinity for risk and innovation, for speed and collision, as well as its dedication to a rough civility not always as far removed from spirited barbarism as we might like to think. The city is democratic but subject to corruption and inequality. It harnesses the soft energies of citizens and civil society but lacks hard power. Our task is to embrace and exploit such traits and learn to hold their tensions in equilibrium.

In embracing the urban habitat that is our destiny, we can begin to suspend our cynicism and shed our pessimism. We are liberated to build a cosmopolitan governing edifice on the parochial foundations of the ancient city, guided by the blueprints implicit in its megasized modern successors. The Eurozone may fall apart, but its cities are coming together. The United States and China may be paralyzed by their competing sovereignties and rival ideologies and consequently may fail to address ecological interdependence, but American and Chinese cities pursue green pragmatism with a purposefulness born of realism. Gallup's CEO Jim Clifton indulges in a certain hyperbole when he urges: "Forget Washington—Cities will win or lose America."[13] Because cities are not free to simply ignore the nations by whose leave they exist as legal, fiscal, and political entities, they will have to do what they do with and not against states, with and not as alternatives to the United Nations, with and not as rivals of NGOs and multinational corporations. But in the world imagined here, they will lead rather than follow. And when necessary, when sovereign obdurateness threatens not just their right to action but the survival of our common planet, they will raise a flag of resistance.

Embracing the interdependent civic logic of the city brings us full circle. We are able finally to rediscover the polis tucked into the core of cosmopolis. We can at last recover participatory politics by securing in the anarchic world of globalization a place for the democratic neighborhood writ large. And we can even dare to offer citizens the gift of cooperation across borders in an often divided and violent world. In changing the subject to cities, we allow imagination to cut through the historical and cultural impediments to interdependent thinking in the same way a maverick Broadway cuts through Manhattan's traditional grid.

As nations grow more dysfunctional, cities *are* rising. When it comes to democracy, they command the majority. Rooted in ancient history, they still lean to the future. As we reach the limits of independence and private markets, they define interdependence and public culture. On a pluralistic planet of difference, they embrace multiculturalism. And as our times plead for innovation, they exude creativity. Reasons enough— good reasons—why mayors and their fellow citizens can and should rule the world.

APPENDIX A.
ADDITIONAL PROFILES

Dutch and Flemish Mayors

Cities in the Netherlands and in Flanders are as caught up in the ethnic and racial politics that stirs modern populist passions as almost anywhere in Europe. Yet despite the prevalence of ethnic politics and ideological controversy, the mayors of cities such as Amsterdam and Rotterdam (where mayors are appointed rather than elected) as well as Antwerp (where municipal elections are held) have been remarkably pragmatic, at least while holding city office—seeking consensus where national politicians, including some of these same mayors when they were themselves national politicians, underscore differences.

Former mayor **JOB COHEN**, a celebrated two-term mayor of Amsterdam, is perhaps typical. In earlier political incarnations, before his two mayoral terms from 2002 through 2010, Cohen was a committed Social Democrat. As mayor, he found himself presiding over a city in which more than half the residents were non-Western, mostly Muslim. When tensions came to a head in November 2004, in the wake of the murder of right-wing filmmaker Theo van Gogh by a Muslim extremist, Cohen responded with a brave embrace of inclusion and tolerance—but also a hard

approach to crime rooted in the prosecution of career felons ("*veelplegers*")—
a combination rooted more in pragmatic realism than pristine ideology.

Cohen received a *Time* magazine award as a "European hero" for his
handling of the toxic political mood of Amsterdam after van Gogh's
killing. "Islam is here to stay," he insisted; "we have to deal with Islam as
a fact, whether we like it or not." After Cohen's experiment with dialogue
and outreach, opponents belittled Amsterdam as a banana republic. But
his vision—pragmatic as well as visionary—calmed the situation and led
to his being named the runner-up for the City Mayors Foundation "2006
Mayor of the Year" award. After leaving office, Cohen returned to Social
Democratic politics, but he was perceived then as too pragmatic and
consensual in his approach, and had to resign both his leadership of the
Social Democratic Party and his parliamentary seat while his campaign
to become prime minister was thwarted.

Even more striking than Cohen's mayoralty in Amsterdam is perhaps **AHMED ABOUTALEB**'s tenure as the mayor of Rotterdam since 2009.
Aboutaleb is not only the first Muslim to serve as mayor of a large city
in the Netherlands, but also the first of immigrant descent and the
first to hold dual citizenship (in Holland and Morocco), a novelty bitterly criticized by right-wing populists such as Geert Wilders. Born in a
Berber village in Morocco, Aboutaleb began his Dutch political career
as an alderman (succeeding the scandal-ridden Rob Oudkerk) and was
appointed mayor as much for his competence and efficiency as for his
multicultural background. His mere presence in Rotterdam City Hall is
a paean to pragmatism over ideological principle and ethnic bigotry. He
governs neither as a Moroccan nor as a native-born Hollander but as a
practical manager trying to make his city work. That is simply what mayors do. It is what he did on Good Friday 2014, when he met with me and
forty civic, government, and NGO leaders in Rotterdam (I serve on
Rotterdam's International Advisory Board) to debate the role of cities in
Holland and Europe and the idea of a global mayors' parliament. This is
the very essence of cosmopolitanism.

PATRICK JANSSENS, a former mayor of Antwerp, in Flemish Belgium,
also proved adept at city governance, as I learned from his far-ranging
and astute remarks when I met him following his departure from office

in the summer of 2013. Janssens was a former chair of the Socialist Party in Belgium, and his background as a scholar included writing the National Report on Poverty. But he also had crucial experience in running the market research firm Dimarso and had held key positions in the marketing agency VVL/BBDO through 1999. With his focus on the real problems of an important port city, Janssens won election twice, the second time with a large majority. He was long-listed for the World Mayor Award in 2008.

His loss to populist candidate **BART DE WEVER** in 2012 was greeted with some apprehension on the Left—an ideologization of urban politics, some people warned—but though the verdict is hardly in, De Wever appears to be leaning a little more toward the center than expected, despite his strong Right populist inclinations. City hall often tempers officeholders with moderation and pragmatism even where they are busy trying to brand city hall with their own ideological signatures. That is what happens to mayors.

This is perhaps nowhere more evident in the tenure of Job Cohen's successor as mayor of Amsterdam, **EBERHARD VAN DER LAAN**. Van der Laan was appointed mayor of Amsterdam in 2010, following a term as a city councilor and a productive tenure as Dutch minister of Integration and Housing in the cabinet of Prime Minister Jan Peter Balkenende (with whom I met several times, before my attention shifted to mayors, to discuss the prime minister's interest in the so-called communitarian cause). Like his predecessor, Job Cohen, and most other Dutch mayors, van der Laan was a member of the Labor Party. Yet as mayor he has struck a more nonpartisan posture, one that has won him transpartisan respect both within Amsterdam and beyond Holland.

Shortly after taking office, he faced the difficult task of implementing an ordinance criminalizing squatting for which he had little sympathy; after all, he was on the board of the Dutch Resistance Museum and a leftist sensitive to the burdens of inequality. With remarkable dexterity, he managed to commit to implementing the law in principle, while making its actual realization dependent upon the "availability" of scarce police resources to clear buildings—a typical tactic using pragmatic practice to temper hard policy.

Similarly, when a crowd of thousands turned out in 2013 to protest the Russian crackdown on homosexuality (the Russian government had condemned the demonstrations in Moscow as mere "propaganda"), Mayor van der Laan joined the demonstrators in Amsterdam who were carrying signs proclaiming "love is not propaganda." In the same spirit, when the Occupy Movement came to Holland, Mayor van der Laan was one of the few politicians to meet with its angry dissidents and talk with them. As someone who had counseled the Zuccotti Square Occupy group in New York City and watched with dismay as Mayor Bloomberg condemned them, I was surprised and warmed by van der Laan's outreach.

Van der Laan does not affect, however, to pay for his encompassing sympathy for the cause of justice by baiting or disdaining markets. Amsterdam's role as a great European port city requires a careful attention to business and investment as well as to global trade. He is proud of Amsterdam's status as a center of trade and exchange, which is not incidental to its status as a cultural capital (where great theater artists like Ivo von Hove make their home). No wonder the mayor has seized on the metaphor offered by the city's thousand bridges and worked closely with the other "G-4 mayors" (Jozias van Aartsen of the Hague, Aboutaleb of Rotterdam, and Jan van Zanen of Utrecht) to build commercial and cultural bridges to Europe and the world beyond, all the way to China, as a way to give a common face to Holland's cosmopolitan heart.

Amsterdam, van der Laan says, "is built on tolerance, commerce and freedom; we now have 179 nationalities in the city and that's such a huge asset." This is especially the case in a world of interdependence, and the mayor has been willing to talk with me and others about the possible utility of a global parliament of mayors, in which urban cooperation across borders might become a reality as well as an aspiration. In September 2014, van der Laan and Aboutaleb, with the other Dutch G-4 mayors, hosted a planning meeting for the global parliament of mayors project in Amsterdam. Van der Laan's own commitment to tolerance and global cooperation has not, however, blunted his awareness of how cultural, racial, and ethnic politics can undo a city's cosmopolitan aspirations.

Dutch cities must wrestle on the ground with the nationalist and populist ideological proclivities that keep Dutch politics so volatile, just as Flemish cities in Belgium must accommodate a binational and too often dysfunctional national politics in which the French/Flemish divide is only one part of the problem. Yet in both cases, the realities of picking up garbage, cleaning the street, offering health care and education, and, yes, facilitating jobs to all residents whatever their formal citizenship status, and at the same time accommodating culture, trade, and immigration accordingly, means that mayors in the Flemish world, like mayors everywhere (whether they are socialist or conservative), must labor to make partners of private and public, must accommodate the realities of immigration, and must address the challenges of an interdependent world even when ideology might mandate a noisy partisanship or a prudent silence.

In acting in such a cosmopolitan spirit, mayors often come—if only inadvertently—to represent a potent alternative to national politics. Cities cannot permit to happen what too often happens in national capitals like Washington or Rome: you cannot allow chaos to paralyze action. You cannot permit ideological polarization to freeze policy. You cannot "close" cities the way sputtering politicians have closed the federal government in Washington. How can a mayor close New York or Amsterdam, Rio or Rotterdam, Singapore or Antwerp? For it is in such cities across the world that people live and die, learn and work, play and pray; the urban communities that define our lives must remain open and functional, whether threatened by armies laying siege to them, ideologies that deny their diversity, or posturing national politicians battering them with "high" (i.e., rigid) "principles" that thwart all compromise. In sitting down and talking with Mayor van der Laan or Mayor Janssens, or the many other mayors I have had the privilege of meeting before and after writing this book, the conversations have rarely been about abstract principles but almost always about how to make their cities function. Which is one very good reason to think that democracy might be improved and our planet better governed if mayors ruled the world.

Polish Mayors

It is easy to think "big city!" when we think "mayor," and so to focus on, say, Bertrand Delanoë of Paris or Boris Johnson of London. Or, in

Poland, on **HANNA GRONKIEWICZ-WALTZ** of Warsaw. Mayor Gronkiewicz-Waltz's short tenure in Warsaw has in fact been notable as well as controversial. It has been marked by her association with the Civic Platform Party leader and Prime Minister Donald Tusk as well as with the business of governing the capital city. But she survived a Conservative Party move to recall her as a way of discrediting her ally Prime Minister Tusk in the fall of 2013, and she is now focused on governing the capital city—so transformed in the past twenty years—in ways that offer civic leadership to Poland and to Europe beyond. Her role in EuroCities and assuring the influence of cities in Europe was highlighted by her participation in the Future of Cities conference in early 2014, where we spoke together on the same platform.

In Poland as in countries from Holland to Italy, where nations are deeply urban, the mayors who are often most important and typical are in Antwerp rather than Brussels, Nantes as well as Paris, Wrocław and Krakow rather than in Warsaw alone. Even in rural Kansas, more than half of that American cornfield countryside's population live in towns and cities, though of very modest size, and their mayors are in many ways the true "governors" of Kansas.

In surveying urban governance in Poland, then, while it is tempting to look only at the remarkable career of Mayor Gronkiewicz-Waltz (she is one of the few big-city mayors in the world who is female, although the new mayor of Paris, Anne Hidalgo, is also a woman!), there is also a great deal to be learned about how mayors govern from important middle-size cities such as Gdansk and Wrocław.

RAFAŁ DUTKIEWICZ of Wrocław embodies many of the most salient traits of city hall inhabitants around the world, the kinds of traits that persuade me that mayors may be uniquely suited to rule the world. A strong-minded political independent free of the kinds of national political allegiances that have complicated Mayor Gronkiewicz-Waltz's situation in Warsaw, Dutkiewicz entered his second term of office in 2006 with 85 percent of the votes and was reelected for his third term in 2010 with 73 percent of the votes. Presiding over the fourth-largest city in Poland (Wrocław has more than 600,000 inhabitants), Dutkiewicz is truly one of the new "interdependent" or "glocal" mayors, responsible for a town with its own complicated cross-border history: the German "East Prussian" city was called Breslau before World War II but was wholly reconstituted as the Polish city of Wrocław afterward, with radical changes in its population, its culture, and its economy. Yet at the same time, he must govern Wrocław in a world of interdependent cities and networks, where locality and globality merge in that innovative "glocality" (to which I refer often in this book!).

Given his cosmopolitan mien, it is no surprise that before becoming mayor, Dutkiewicz ran an international head-hunting firm and, having assumed office, readily accepted the appointment to the EU Committee of the Regions (in practice also a committee of the cities). His training as a logician and mathematician has served him well as a cool, analytic administrator; yet he also has the warmth and humor of a practiced politician. Humor and mathematical talent are perhaps ideal traits, however contradictory, in producing stable and prudent decision making around urban issues.

Fluent in English, German, and Russian as well as Polish, and an early member of Solidarity (he presided over the Wrocław branch in 1989), Dutkiewicz is an ardent traveler on behalf of his city, a city that is cosmopolitan by history and necessity but has become cosmopolitan by choice since the fall of the Berlin Wall. Dutkiewicz has worked hard to integrate business, education, culture, and civil society in an administration that brings together the public and private sectors in useful cooperation. Tellingly, of the four meetings I have held with Mayor Dutkiewicz, the first and last were in Berlin rather than Wrocław, because our respective global journeys happened to overlap there rather than in Wrocław.

Yet his travels are all put to the purposes of helping Wrocław grow and flourish. Three times Polish *Newsweek*'s Mayor of the Year, Dutkiewicz actually stepped aside recently and recused himself from the competition, in order to allow others to compete. His success with business—he has brought Hewlett-Packard, Whirlpool, and Siemens, among others, to Wrocław—is matched by his success with sports and culture. The film festival T-Mobile New Horizons was held in Wrocław, and the 2013 Congress of the International Society of Performing Arts also met there (I was a speaker along with the mayor at the 2013 ISPA Congress). He also brought the European Football Championships to Wrocław in 2012, drawing other large investments worth a total of $7 billion in the wake of the games.

A mayor is more than his collected competences and noteworthy achievements, however. In a world where cities are so vital, Rafał Dutkiewicz is a crucial face of urban citizenship and a driver of urban democracy in Poland and Europe. He has occupied these roles with audacity and spirit. Yet successful as he has been, Mayor Dutkiewicz is by no means nonpareil. Indeed, it is my argument here that such talents are in many ways inherent in what it means to govern cities today, and that a great many mayors bring similar capacities to bear or learn them once in office. For that is what it takes to govern the municipalities that define our lives.

Hence, north of Wrocław on the southern tip of the Baltic where the Vistula and Motława rivers empty into the sea, there is another border city between old Prussia and new Poland: Gdansk (once Danzig). And it, too, is governed by an extraordinary mayor, **PAWEŁ ADAMOWICZ**. Since 1998, when he was just thirty-three years old, Adamowicz has presided over the city whose shipyard gave birth to the Solidarity Movement in the early 1980s and is hence associated with the astonishing events of 1989 and the fall of the Wall between East and West.

Like Dutkiewicz, Adamowicz is an ordinary citizen who governs both with and over his neighbors with extraordinary facility—perhaps because he is more like his neighbors than he is different from them. The mayor and I walked down Long Market not so long ago through Gdansk's painstakingly reconstructed "Old Town" (painstaking because it was almost totally destroyed during the war and then had to be rebuilt not as the German Empire city of Danzig but as the pre-nineteenth-century and hence pre-German Pomeranian and Polish city of Gdansk). We had just attended a ceremony in which Solidarity cofounder, former Polish president, and Gdansk native Lech Wałesa had bestowed the Wałesa prize on former Brazilian President Luiz Lula da Silva, a typically global happening in a seemingly modest town.

To be sure, Mayor Adamowicz struck me as a modest and welcoming local host rather than the overachieving mayor of Polish Pomerania's largest city (with nearly a half million citizens, Gdansk is Poland's sixth-largest city) and one of Northern Europe's greatest historical towns. As a leading member of the medieval Hansa League (renewed in a modern form not long ago) and Poland's largest seaport, Gdansk in fact plays its local fiddle in a global orchestra of which Adamowicz is the energetic director, even as Gdansk's sphere of influence grows. In a close relationship with neighboring Sopot, a well-known international spa town on the Baltic, and other suburbs, the Gdansk "tri-city" conurbation now encompasses three quarters of a million people.

Gdansk is as diverse and various in its history as Europe itself: at one time or another, in addition to being governed by the medieval and modern kingdoms (and then successive republics) of Poland, it was ruled by the Duchy of Pomerania, the Teutonic Order, the Polish-Lithuanian Commonwealth, Prussia, the German Empire, and Weimar Germany. For a brief period in the interwar era before the Nazis occupied it, it was simply the Free City of Danzig—though just how free it could really be as a German-majority town with a great many Nazi sympathizers, yet dependent under its League of Nations Mandate on Polish foreign policy during the rise of the Nazi regime, was another matter.

Yet it was not history but current politics that occupied our conversations that day in the Long Market and in subsequent conversations: the mayor would remark on President Barack Obama's reputation in Europe, Gdansk native Donald Tusk's challenges as Polish prime minister, and Lech Wałesa's durability, which, despite the ebbs and flows in his popularity, has made him a Nobel Prize–winning icon of courageous resistance. With his remarks, Mayor Adamowicz was not engaging in pleasantries or gossip. As the mayor of a great North European Hansa port city engaged in a felicitous rivalry with other Hansa cities along the northern European coast and with Poland's other key cities like Krakow, Lublin, Wrocław, and Katowice (their rivalry is a race to the top, not a race to the bottom!), he was surveying the political and economic landscape of Europe (and the North Atlantic and Asia as well) to consider how best to draw corporate and national investors to Gdansk and to secure a fair portion of global business and trade for the local economy. As a port and petrochemical center, Gdansk's fortunes were fairly certain, but diversification is essential to modern economies, and the mayor knows it. As in Wrocław and Krakow, the information economy and the knowledge society are never too far from the mayor's consciousness, with new IT firms, food-processing businesses, and pharmaceutical companies opening for business in the shadow of the city's still-robust shipbuilding industry.

The city could look back and revel in its enduring reputation as a Hansa trading port and celebrate the resistance Solidarity offered to Communism and which the city continues to memorialize in the Lech Wałesa Center and the presence of Wałesa himself (which also draws tourists), but it had also to look forward. Its virtues and economic attributes could not just stand as a finished edifice embodying local pride but must also become a foundation for economic and cultural development in a global-market world.

Moreover, as Adamowicz told me, Gdansk has to become a world market port and trading center without sacrificing its commitment to social welfare and equal opportunity. Although Poland has certainly taken that cold shower of capitalism that social democrats worry can undermine the social state, under its new mayor, Gdansk is unlikely to become a "tale of two cities" (as the new mayor, Bill de Blasio, described New York's income divide). Adamowicz's evenhanded zeal for development and justice may be one of the reasons why he was awarded the Pro Ecclesia et Pontifice medal by Pope Jean Paul II as well as the Cross of Merit by the Polish president.

Yet when interviewed by the *European Times* in 2013, Mayor Adamowicz spoke like the modest pragmatist and problem solver he is: no high-minded rhetoric about interdependence (though he is keen on the concept and a contributor to the dialogue about a global mayors' parliament in which I have been engaged) but a straightforward portrait of a city which, in his words, "has undergone a major transformation from socialism to capitalism. After Poland joined the EU, there was a huge infrastructure and cultural gap between Polish cities and other cities in Europe, and we have been closing that gap through significant investments. Gdansk has modernized its housing, sewage and water systems, roads and bridges and more . . . the process continues . . . and the quality of life here has greatly improved."

Leave it to a mayor, when asked about his most spectacular achievements, to talk about "housing, water and sewage systems." That is the true meaning of efficient government and, more important, of democracy in action. And that is why I argue throughout this book that we might all be better off if mayors ruled the world.

APPENDIX B.
INTRODUCTION TO THE CHINESE EDITION

This is a book about mayors around the world, and about the crucial role cities are playing in our interdependent twenty-first century. The first lesson of the book is a commonplace of comparative studies: cities are everywhere different. We can generalize about them as I do in here. But they vary from culture to culture, country to country, place to place. China is a unique culture with a distinctive history, politics, and civilization. Everything I write here must be filtered through that culture.

In China (as in France, for example), mayors are not for the most part elected but are appointed as part of a national political party system. In other cultures, including the United States and the United Kingdom, city managers may play a principal role. There are "strong mayor" systems that give mayors a powerful potential to shape their municipalities, and there are "weak mayor" systems where the power is mostly ceremonial (Belfast or Dublin, for example) or, as in China, subsidiary to national power. Port cities like Shanghai or Hamburg have different challenges than do inland cities like Beijing or Berlin—which are also capital cities, different from other cities in their special relationship to central government. Large megacities such as Mexico City or Chongqing, with thirty million people, are hard to compare with smaller cities like Guadalajara or Suzhou, with four million, while towns of under fifty thousand people scarcely seem cities at all.

Thus, although I make some important general claims for urban living and mayoral rule that really do apply right across the world, my arguments must be read through this cultural filter. In China this means appreciating a number of significant factors that can shape urban realities, including these:

- In China, one of the oldest civilizations in the world, great cities are as ancient as the nation, and the Chinese metropolis is deeply embedded in that history and less easily understood as merely another level of jurisdiction.
- Yet as a country that for centuries has been dominated by its rural villages rather than its coastal or near-coastal cities, its urbanism is relatively new. Until just a few decades ago, a great majority of Chinese citizens—more than a billion—lived in small towns and villages, and although cities were economically dominant, they were demographically recessive.
- Thus, despite the ancient character of many of its municipalities, China has also witnessed an unprecedented growth in "new cities" that only ten or fifteen years ago were suburbs or small towns, yet are now home to more than a million people. McKinsey estimates that within ten years as many as one hundred of the world's cities with the largest GDP will be Chinese.
- That said, in China, as elsewhere, what counts as a "city" depends on a unique national political infrastructure. The Chinese system establishes five distinctive levels of governance: provincial, prefectural, county, town, and village. More important, "cities" can be counted as occupying a number of these levels. For example, there are four centrally administered megacities at the provincial level, each in charge of strategic economic planning: Beijing, Tianjin, Shanghai, and Chongqing. Moreover, their powerful mayors also belong to the central government's State Council. Another 284 large cities exist at the prefectural level, where—as with the provinces—the

cities encompass the expansive suburban and countryside regions around them (Chongqing "city" is larger than Hainan Province!). Then there are over 1,200 county-level "cities," and 41,000 townships. And while the village population is migrating to larger cities, there are still 644,000 villages in China.

- Although mayors of Chinese cities possess less intrinsic local power than mayors elsewhere in the world, the mayors of the four great provincial cities are not only members of the State Council but frequently become powerful national figures. Both Jiang Zemin and Zhu Rongji served as mayors of Shanghai during the 1980s before they became national leaders, while Deng Xiaoping and Li Peng as national leaders remained focused on Shanghai's economic development. Finally, Hong Kong and Macau are special administrative districts with special histories that give them greater autonomy and their mayors greater discretion.

- The relative subservience of Chinese cities to the national government reflects China's highly centralized political system, rooted not only in the historical one-party rule of the Communist Party, but in strong national government all the way back to the Han dynasty. An ancient historical imperative has been to hold together a vast land encompassing three disparate kingdoms and to fend off local "fiefdoms" that might risk national dissolution.

- Centralization means that while cities may be large and economically dominant, their mayors remain relatively weak and subject to higher jurisdictions not just as a matter of organization but as an objective of policy. Cities are in every sense "inferior jurisdictions" with respect to provincial and sovereign national governments. As a consequence, the power of the central state in China leaves less room for strong, independent mayors, even where they are successful locally.

- The hold of central government over local government, and the inclination of political officials to use municipal governing experience as a stepping stone to higher office means that (as in France) mayors are part of a political process that often elevates them quite quickly to higher status. Promising talent is rapidly siphoned off to higher office, and many mayors serve less than two years. Frequent turnover can mean little trust and inconsequential achievement and thus no real mayoral "legacy." The China Mayors Association found in a study that 67 percent of mayors did not even complete their tenure. As Tao Siliang, vice-chair of the association, has said, this often means spending "too much effort climbing up the ladder," which in turn tends to "fuel short-sighted activities and sloppy projects." In the United States, in contrast to China, no major city mayor has ever become president, and mayors tend to remain local, however successful they are.

• Unlike other parts of the world, where mayors are often trusted more than other political leaders, local corruption in Chinese cities and the absence of autonomy or longevity for mayors can breed lower trust levels in local political officials than in national political figures. The case of Bo Xilai, brought down on charges of corruption after a seemingly too successful stint in the megacity (and region) of Chongqing, is instructional in this regard. A key question for China is whether regional party officials will continue to be the real wielders of power in cities, or whether mayors can come to play leadership roles reflective of their cities' prominence.

Once we appreciate these many distinguishing features of the Chinese political system and how they can shape the particular evolution of cities in China, we can assess the applicability of my book's more general arguments to the Chinese situation. The issues of municipal autonomy and mayoral capacity are perhaps most pressing, especially with respect to creativity and innovation: the lack of trust in local governance and the weak position of mayors may inhibit these virtues and rob both Chinese cities and the Chinese nation of their benefits. By the same token, to the extent the Chinese national government since the Deng era has given greater economic autonomy to both regions and local municipalities, a certain flexibility and freedom have appeared in local governance that have facilitated urban creativity and growth, though they have been largely limited to the economic domain.

China is certainly not alone in its centralized governance system. France, the United Kingdom, and Japan are just a few of the many systems that have preferred not to devolve power through a strongly articulated federal system. Yet though China has offered a good deal of space for economic and entrepreneurial creativity and technocratic innovation in its cities, its fierce central control over the political system has both risks and costs. The central government may worry that treating cities as laboratories of creativity and innovation risks making them "cradles of democracy" or even of resistance. Yet greater municipal autonomy is inevitable in this era of global free markets, and granting Chinese cities greater autonomy will increasingly be a condition for the continued expansion of the Chinese economy and Chinese power. For in an interdependent world where progress and success depend on intercity cooperation, international trade, cultural exchange, and common global policy making to combat climate change, terrorism, and pandemic disease, and where both technology and markets know no borders, cooperation is essential. And it is cities that are the key to making cross-border cooperation work.

A good example of where greater autonomy for China's cities could serve China well is in the domain of carbon emissions and pollution, where many of China's cities face dire conditions. In Beijing and Tianjin, air-quality standards are met on fewer than half of the days of the year. Cities such as Haikou, Zhoushan, and Lhasa, on the other hand, fully meet national standards—but largely because of their felicitous location. Yet cities with similar smog and emission problems—(nearly 80 percent of greenhouse gases are generated in cities!)—such as Bogotá, New York, and Los Angeles, have proven that municipal government can address the challenge when they have the authority to put in green and efficient public transportation systems, impose higher insulation or emission standards, or green up a port. Through participation in global city networks committed to a green planet such as ICLEI and the C40, China's cities can both share in and catalyze green development and sustainable urban living.

The bottom line for China is that internal cohesion and national unity, crucial concerns to be sure, will not serve China well if they are purchased at the cost of insularity, obstructionism, and resistance to the realities of interdependence. Cities can play a leading role as centers of pragmatism, problem solving, cooperation, and cultural and economic exchange. As China is able to empower its cities and its urban citizens, it is likely to be able to play a global role fully appropriate to its extraordinary history and unparalleled capacities and resources—a role that will benefit China no less than the planet.

NOTES

Chapter I. If Mayors Ruled the World

1. Eric Corijn asks that precise question, "Can the city save the world," in a work on rescaling the planet and remodeling the city. Eric Corijn, "Can the City Save the World," in *The Future of the Past: Reflections on History, Urbanity and Museums,* ed. M. Nauwelaerets, Antwerp: Koning Boudewijn Stichting, 1999, pp. 263–280.

2. Edward Glaeser, *Triumph of the City: How Our Greatest Invention Makes Us Richer, Smarter, Greener, Healthier, and Happier,* New York: Penguin Books, 2011, p. 15.

3. The United Nations Population Fund reports that for 2008, 3.3 billion people, more than half of the world's population, lived in cities, with 5 billion projected to do so in 2030. In the developed world, the percentage is much higher, approaching 70 percent. Compare these numbers with figures from the Population Reference Bureau: 3 percent of the population, lived in cities in 1800, and 30 percent in 1950. Today 90 percent of urbanization is occurring in developing nations, much of it in midsize towns and cities rather than just in megacities. There is, to be sure, some controversy over these figures because what counts as urban varies from region to region and can include people living in suburbs and towns with populations of as little as 50,000—in communities that may not feature many of the characteristics associated with the city as an essentialist construct. However, if the precise number is contested, the direction of the arrow—from country and town to urban and metropolitan—is unquestioned, and for the purposes of this book that is enough. The "representation" question must in any case be addressed, whether 50 percent, 25 percent, or 10 percent live outside of urban areas.

4. John Dewey, *The Public and Its Problems*, New York: Henry Holt, 1927, p. 142.

5. Ibid., p. 184.

6. Mayor Bloomberg, Speech at MIT, November 29, 2011.

7. Press Release of ICLEI (Local Governments for Sustainability), December 12, 2011.

8. See www.cityprotocol.org.

9. Jean-Jacques Rousseau, *Emile*, New York: Everyman edition, 1993, p. 433.

10. Alderman Colón cited in Jay Walljasper, "How Cities Can Get Drivers Biking," *Yes Magazine*, July 27, 2012, http://www.yesmagazine.org/planet/how-cities-can -make-biking-safer.

11. As with Mayor Schuster here and throughout the book, I will cite interviews and "surveys" completed with mayors. These materials, including the complete survey results, can be found on the book website at www.ifmayorsruledtheworld .org. The comment in the text here is from the interview with Mayor Schuster, July 2012. The mayor of Stuttgart for two eight-year terms, who left office in 2013, has focused on building city networks and is former vice president of ICLEI. His work is proof again that Europe lives democratically in its cities. As he says, "step by step we develop our society from the citizens [up], first at the city level and then up to other levels, civil society and [the] culture of local democracy, which is missing in so many countries."

12. Saskia Sassen, *The Global City: New York, London, Tokyo*, Princeton, NJ: Princeton University Press, 2001, p. 9.

13. See Benjamin R. Barber, on the Mailer campaign, "Birthday Party Politics," *Dissent*, Summer 1973.

14. Richard Florida, "It's Up to the Cities to Bring America Back," BusinessInsider .com, February 3, 2012, http://www.businessinsider.com/richard-florida-its-up- to-the-cities-to-bring-america-back-2012-2.

15. Edward Glaeser, *Triumph of the City*, New York: Penguin, 2011, p. 15.

16. Max Weber, *The City*, Glencoe, IL: Free Press, 1985, p. 25.

17. Edward C. Banfield, *The Moral Basis of a Backward Society*, New York: Free Press, 1958.

18. Pelu Awofeso, "One Out of Every Two Nigerians Now Lives in a City," *World Policy Journal*, Winter 2010–2011, p. 68.

19. Richard Dobbs, Sven Smit, Jaana Remes, James Manyika, Charles Roxburgh, and Alejandra Restrepo, *Urban World: Mapping the Economic Power of Cities*, McKinsey Global Institute, March, 2011, http://www.mckinsey.com/insights /urbanization/urban_world.

20. Part of this relates to time zones in servicing, say, stock markets, but beyond "the times zones, there is an operational aspect that suggests a distinct trans- territorial economy for a specific set of functions." Sassen, *The Global City*, p. 327.

21. Constantinos Doxiadis, *Ekistics*, Oxford: Oxford University Press, 1966.

22. There are a number of visionary science fiction works on the city, for example by Clifford D Simak (*The City*, 1952) and William Gibson (*Neurumancer*, 1984).

23. James Lovelock, *Gaia: A New Look at Life on Earth, 1979*, 3rd ed., Oxford: Oxford University Press, 2000, p. 1. See also James Lovelock, *The Revenge of Gaia: Earth's Climate Crisis and the Fate of Humanity*, New York: Basic Books, 2007.

24. Barcelona in Catalonia (Spain) is among the most visionary cities, the home not only of the IAAC, but of the new City Protocol project described in Chapters 5, 9, and 12. See IAAC (Barcelona), *Third Advanced Architectural Contest: Self Sufficient City (Envisioning the Habitat of the Future)*, 2010.

25. Masao Miyoshi, "A Borderless World? From Colonialism to Transnationalism and the Decline of the Nation State," *Critical Inquiry*, Vol. 19, No. 4 (Summer 1993), pp. 726–751.

26. David A. Wylie, *City, Save Thyself!* Boston: Trueblood Publishing, 2009, p. 131.

27. Ibid., p. 201.

28. Bill Clinton's Democratic Convention Speech, September 5, 2012, http://abcnews.go.com/Politics/OTUS/transcript-bill-clintons-democratic-convention-speech/story?id=17164662.

29. Matthew Taylor, "Inter-city Thoughts," Matthew Taylor's Blog, October 16 2012, http://www.matthewtaylorsblog.com/uncategorized/inter-city-thoughts/.

30. Peter Laslett's moving account of the withering of village life in England, *The World We Have Lost*, New York: Methuen, 1965.

Profile I. Michael Bloomberg of New York

1. Gabriel Sherman, "The Mayor of Mayors," *New York Magazine*, June 11, 2012.

2. Sridhar Pappu, "What's Next for Michael Bloomberg," Fastcompany, August 8, 2011, http://www.fastcompany.com/1769004/whats-next-michael-bloomberg.

Chapter 2. The Land of Lost Content

1. Ralph Waldo Emerson, *Nature* [1836], in *Nature/Walking*, ed. John Elder, Boston: Beacon Press, 1994, p. 6.

2. Michael Lesy, *Wisconsin Death Trip*, New York: Pantheon Books, 1973.

3. In novels like *Far from the Madding Crowd* and *Jude the Obscure*, Thomas Hardy could be both endearing and caustic about rural life in England, but writers like Laurie Lee (*Cider with Rosie*) and John Betjeman captured the romance of the English countryside without ambivalence in their poetry. Peter Laslett gave a philosophical turn to the love of village life in his touching account of "face to face" living in early England under the tellingly nostalgic title *The World We Have Lost*. There is an extensive literature on the virtues and attractions of village life, including Laurence Wylie's *Village in the Vaucluse* and Robert Putnam's *Making Democracy Work: Civic Traditions in Modern Italy*. Putnam traces the later social capital of northern Italy to nineteenth-century rural society and the choirs that typified village life.

4. Johannes Ewald, printed in the Raetian journal *Der Sammler*, Chur, Switzerland, 1780, No. 51 (my translation).

5. Tom Perrotta, "Entirely Personal: Selected Letters of Willa Cather," Sunday Book Review, *New York Times*, April 25, 2013.

6. Raymond Williams, *The Country and the City*, Oxford: Oxford University Press, 1973, p. 1.

7. Hank Williams Jr., "A Country Boy Can Survive," 1982.

8. Jean-Jacques Rousseau, *Emile*, New York: Everyman Edition, p. 26.

9. For details see Benjamin R. Barber, "How Swiss Is Rousseau?," *Political Theory*, Vol. 13, No. 4, 1985.

10. Rousseau, *Letter to D'Alembert*, where he also argues that the vices of theater are in effect referred pain associated with the corruption of the city. In his *First Discourse on the Arts and Science*, Rousseau had challenged the Enlightenment conception of history as progressive, insisting instead that "every step in individual progress was a step toward species decline." For more, see Benjamin R. Barber, "Rousseau for Our Time, Paradoxes of the Dramatic *Imagination*," *Daedalus*, Summer 1978.

11. Jean-Jacques Rousseau, *Constitutional Project for Corsica*, part I. "Projet de constitution pour la corse, 1765," in C. E. Vaughan, *The Political Writings of Rousseau*, Vol. 2, New York: John Wiley & Sons, 1962, pp. 306–307 ff.

12. Ebenezer Howard, *Garden Cities of Tomorrow*, New York: Classic Books International, 2010, p. 2.

13. Jefferson, Letter to James Madison, December 20, 1787, Jefferson, *Political Writings*, edited by Joyce Appleby and Terrence Ball, Cambridge: Cambridge University Press, 1999, pp. 360–364.

14. Thomas Jefferson, *Notes on the State of Virginia*, Query XXII, in Merrill D. Peterson, ed. *Jefferson*, Library of America Edition, New York: Viking, 1984, p. 301. The classic of rural republicanism and the "new American man" was Crevecoeur's *Letters from an American Farmer*, penned in 1782.

15. Thomas Bender, *Towards an Urban Vision: Ideas and Institutions in Nineteenth Century America*, Baltimore: Johns Hopkins Press, 1975, p. 3. Bender's book offers a deeply dialectical portrait of attitudes about the city and rural life in nineteenth-century America, where writers like Walt Whitman thought they could achieve "a symbolic reconciliation of these opposites (city and country) in the poet's imagination" (p. 15).

16. Tom Stoppard, *Arcadia*, London: Faber and Faber, 1993, p. 27. Stoppard's play features the collision of the rational French Enlightenment garden with the "natural" English gardens of the nineteenth century which recreated nature with agonizing artifice.

17. Howard, *Garden* Cities, p. 7.

18. Ibid.

19. Robert S. and Helen M. Lynd, *Middletown: A Study in American Culture*, New York: Harcourt, Brace and World, Inc., 1929.

20. Lewis Mumford, *The City in History*, New York: Harcourt, Brace and World, Inc., 1961.

21. *Metropolis* was among the most famous silent films, certainly the most expensive, ever shot. Its dystopic take on the city makes an interesting comparison with G. B. Shaw's Garden City view of both humane capitalism and the utopic industrial town at the end of his play *Major Barbara*. In both *Metropolis* and *Major Barbara*, capitalism's fate is linked to that of the city, with a happy outcome for Shaw and an unhappy outcome for Lang. Along with Thomas Bender (*Towards an Urban Vision*), cultural historian Leo Marx offers a brilliantly concrete portrait of the conflict over industrialism and the American Garden of Eden in his *The Machine in the Garden: Technology and the Pastoral Ideal in America*, Oxford: Oxford University Press, 1964/2000.

22. Edward Banfield, *The Moral Basis of a Backward Society*, New York: Free Press, 1958.

23. Michael Lesy, *Wisconsin Death Trip*, New York: Pantheon Books, p. 250. A "dark" version of the Rodgers and Hammerstein musical *Carousel*, produced at Lincoln Center a few years ago, turned a country romance into a rural tragedy.

24. George Crabbe, *The Village*, 1783 (cited in Williams, *The Country and the City*, p. 10).

25. Carlo Levi, *Christ Stopped at Eboli*, New York: Farrar, Straus, 1947, p. 12.

26. Ibid., p. 11.

27. Lesy, *Wisconsin*, p. 250.

28. See Richard Florida, *The Rise of the Creative Class*, New York: Basic Books, 2004.

29. Williams, *The Country and the City*, p. 1.

30. Henry David Thoreau, *Walking*, in *Nature/Walking*, ed. John Elder, Boston: Beacon Press, 1992, p. 80.

31. From his description of a crowd at the Lord Mayor's Show of 1879, cited by Williams, *The Country and the City*, p. 216.

32. Thoreau, *Walking*, pp. 80–81. Rousseau similarly happens upon a mountain manufacturing site in the high Alps on a walk and notes how it destroys his peace. *Reveries of a Solitary Walker*, New York: Oxford University Press, 2011; originally published posthumously as *Les Rêveries du promeneur solitaire*, and written in the last years of Rousseau's life between 1776 and 1778.

33. Perrotta, "Entirely Personal," op. cit.

34. Williams, *The Country and the City*, p. 1. See also Max Weber's account in *The City*, Glencoe, IL: Free Press, 1985; first published in 1921 after Weber's death. There, Weber's rich typology is also defined by the city's many differences as cities evolve over time.

35. Franklin, in Bender, *Urban Vision*, p. 6.

36. Emerson, *Nature*, p. 4.

37. Walt Whitman, "Song of the Open Road," Sections 1 and 5.

38. Bender, *Urban Vision*, p. 17, citing Mumford's perspective in *The Golden Day* and *The Brown Decades*.

39. Cited by Bender, *Urban Vision*, p. 13.

40. Frederick Law Olmsted, *Civilizing American Cities: Writings on City Landscapes*, ed. S. B. Sutton, New York: De Capo Press, 1997, p. 75.

41. Jane Jacobs, *The Death and Life of Great American Cities*, New York: Vintage Press, 1992, p. 61.

42. For a riveting account of this history with revealing maps, see Hilary Ballon, ed., *The Greatest Grid: The Master Plan of Manhattan 1811–2011*, New York: Museum of the City of New York and Columbia University Press, 2012.

43. Cited in Ballon, ed., *Greatest Grid*, p. 103.

44. Olmsted, cited in Ballon, ed., *The Greatest Grid*, p. 120.

45. In his masterwork, *The Idea of Fraternity in America*, Wilson Carey McWilliams attributes Olmsted's "crusade for parks and recreation areas" to the latter's hope that "citizens might be able to overcome isolation and suspicion." Wilson Carey McWilliams, *The Idea of Fraternity in America*, Berkeley: University of California Press, 1974, pp. 3, 4.

46. Bruce Mau, "Urbanity, Revised," *World Policy Journal*, Winter 2010–2011, p. 20. Mau also wants to imagine cities without museums yet as places of beauty, cities without traffic yet with silent, clean, and "sexy" cars, and cities that (re) imagine luxury and sustainability so that seeking "pleasure, wealth, beauty and delight" are compatible with a new sustainability "more beautiful, more thrilling, more luxurious than anything we have ever experienced." This is perhaps thinking so far outside the box that the reality of the box goes missing. Mau still manages to remind us that cities are and must be about "massive change."

47. Olmsted, *Civilizing American Cities*, p. 75.

48. John Muir, *Meditations of John Muir: Nature's Temple*, comp. and ed. Chris Highland, Berkeley: Wilderness Press, 2001, p. 113.

Chapter 3. The City and Democracy

1. Walt Whitman, *Democratic Vistas*, in *The Complete Poetry and Prose of Walt Whitman*, New York: Garden City Books, 1948, pp. 229–230.

2. Figures are all from McKinsey Global Institute, *Urban World: Mapping the Economic Power of Cities*, March 2011.

3. McKinsey, Executive Summary, p. 2.

4. Eric Corijn points to a connection between Fordist mass production, the automobile, and American suburbanization that has given many American cities a different look than the "specific European form with town halls, towers and belfries and civic clocks and bourgeois freedoms." Eric Corijn, "Urbanity as a Political Project: Towards Post-national European Cities," in *Creative*

Economies, Creative Cities: Asian-European Perspectives, ed. Lily Kong and Justin O'Connor, New York: Springer Publishing, 2009, p. 199.

5. Daniel Brook, *A History of Future Cities*, New York: W. W. Norton, 2013. Brook's study of new cities like St. Petersburg and Dubai, roughly modeled on an image of old cities like Amsterdam and Las Vegas, offers a fascinating look at where past and future collide in contemporary urban space.

6. In his *Mutual Aid: A Factor in Revolution*, London: William Heinemann, 1902, Prince Kropotkin offers a vision of natural cooperation and reciprocal assistance in place of the Darwinist struggle of all against all. Like Stirner (see *The Ego and Its Own: The Case of the Individual Against Authority*, London: Rebel Press, 1993) or Nietzsche, Ayn Rand espouses a radical individualism hostile to community altogether, whether central or local.

7. Max Weber, *The City*, Glencoe, IL: Free Press, 1985; Lewis Mumford, *The City in History*, New York: Harcourt, Brace and World, Inc., 1961; Jane Jacobs, *The Death and Life of Great American Cities*, New York: Vintage Press, 1992; Peter Marcuse and Ronald van Kemper, eds., *Globalizing Cities: A New Spatial Order*, Oxford: Blackwell Publishing, 2000; Saskia Sassen, *The Global City: New York, London, Tokyo*; and Eric Corijn, "Urbanity as a Political Project."

8. See, for example, Berthold Brecht's play *In the Jungle of Cities*.

9. For his classic statement, see Le Corbusier, *The Radiant City*, 1935. In Paris, Le Corbusier proposed to level a large swath of traditional boulevards and low-rises to build modernist towers in the park, signature high-rise monoliths set down in a sea of green. James C. Scott offers a provocative critique of Le Corbusier in his own overstated takedown of top-down planning, *Seeing Like a State: How Certain Schemes to Improve the Human Condition Have Failed*, New Haven: Yale University Press, 1998. In a chapter titled "The High-Modernist City," he accuses Le Corbusier of bombastically seeking "total city planning" through "a lyrical marriage between Cartesian pure forms and the implacable requirements of the machine," p. 107. But Scott misses entirely Le Corbusier's parallel decentrist inclinations that aspire to purchase open green space in the city with high-rise towers.

10. Jane Jacobs, *The Death and Life of Great American Cities*, p. 65.

11. Jane Jacobs is anxious to distinguish the city (or "great city") from entities that, while like it, are distinctly not it! "Towns, suburbs and even little cities," she writes, "are totally different organisms from great cities . . . to try to understand town in terms of big cities will only compound confusion." *The Death and Life of Great Cities*, p. 22.

12. Richard Florida, *The Rise of the Creative Class*, New York: Basic Books, 2004.

13. Natural men, pre-moral, were innocent rather than bad, as Thomas Jefferson acknowledges in his *Notes on the State of Virginia*, in Merrill D. Peterson, ed., *Jefferson*, Library of America Edition, New York: Viking, 1984, and J.-J. Rousseau acknowledges in Rousseau, *Discourse on Arts and Sciences* as well as in *Discourse on the Origin of Inequality*, Indianapolis: Hackett Publishing, 1987 (Part Two).

14. Don Martindale, Introduction to Max Weber's *The City*, Glencoe, IL: Free Press, 1985, p. 13.

15. Jane Jacobs writes: "Nations are political and military entities, and so are blocs of nations. But it doesn't necessarily follow from this that they are also the basic salient entities of economic life or that they are particularly useful for probing the mysteries of economic structure, the reasons for the rise and decline of wealth." *Cities and the Wealth of Nations: Principles of Economic Life*, New York: Random House, 1984, p. 31.

16. Saskia Sassen, *The Global City: New York, London, Tokyo*, Princeton, NJ: Princeton University Press, 2001, pp. 3–4.

17. Carlo Levi, *Christ Stopped at Eboli: The Story of a Year*, New York: Farrar, Straus and Giroux, 2006, p. 28. Indeed, whether the land is poor or not may depend on whether legal systems allow for inheritance by a single son or enforce partibility that divides land bequests generation after generation, until only untenable fragments remain, enhancing rather than diminishing poverty. This is not a feature of country life, however, but a product of legal codes.

18. Robert Putnam, *Making Democracy Work: Civic Traditions in Modern Italy*, Princeton, NJ: Princeton University Press, 1994.

19. Levi, *Christ Stopped at Eboli*, p. 30.

20. Sharon Zukin, *The Culture of Cities*, London: Blackwell, 1995, p. 259.

21. Ibid., p. 294.

22. Robert William Fogel and Stanley L. Engerman, *Time on the Cross: The Economics of American Negro Slavery*, Boston: Little, Brown, 1974. More attention was given to its seeming exoneration of slavery, at least from an economic perspective, but its intention was more to underscore the powerful inequalities of urban capitalism.

23. For more on the "Southern Mystique," see Howard Zinn, *The Southern Mystique*, Cambridge, MA: South End Press, 2002.

24. C. V. Wedgwood, ed., *The Trial of Charles I*, London: Folio Press: J. M. Dent, 1974, pp. 88–91.

Profile 3. Boris Johnson of London

1. John F. Burns, "Athletes Arrive in London, and Run into a Dead End," *New York Times*, July 14, 2012.

2. "105 Minutes with Boris Johnson," interview with Carl Swanson, *New York Magazine*, June 17, 2012.

3. Ibid.

Chapter 4. Mayors Rule!

Epigraph: Lyndon Johnson quote from "Troubled Cities—and Their Mayors," *Newsweek*, March 13, 1967.

1. Paul Maslin, "Cities: The Last Remaining Redoubt of Public Confidence," Remarks by Paul Maslin, 2011, U.S. Conference of Mayors in Los Angeles

at http://www.usmayors.org/laleadership. Polls from July 2011 show that nationally, about 27–28 percent of people say the country is moving in the right direction. Presidential approval rating is at about 47–48 percent. Congress has a 19 percent approval rating. A poll of a dozen big cities since around 2008 shows 47 percent of their citizens say their cities are moving in the right direction, and 64 percent of urbanites give their mayors high approval ratings. http://www.usmayors.org/laleadership.

2. Wolfgang Schuster, *Nachhaltige Staedte—Lebensraeume der Zukunft*, Munich: Oekom Verlag, 2013, p.13.

3. Maslin, "Cities," op. cit.

4. Jay Walljasper, "Mayors Are Taking Over the World," *Odewire*, October 2006, http://odewire.com/52440/mayors-are-taking-over-the-world.html.

5. Cited in Richard Flanagan, *Mayors and the Challenge of Urban Leadership*, Lanham, MD: University Press of America, 2004, p. 3. Flanagan wants to "bring mayors back in" to the political debate and depict the features that afford them strong leadership.

6. These include the London School Economics, LSE Cities, http://www2.lse.ac.uk/LSECities/home.aspx; City University of New York, Center for Urban Research, http://www.urbanresearch.org/; New York University, Center for Urban Science and Progress, http://www.nyu.edu/about/; and the Globalization and World Cities research network (GaWC), http://www.iboro.ac.uk/gawc/.

7. "105 Minutes with Boris Johnson," interview with Carl Swanson, *New York Magazine*, June 17, 2012.

8. Sarah Lyall, "London Journal," *New York Times*, April 23, 2012. Livingstone, a former mayor, faced Johnson, the current mayor and "more recognizable than anyone in British politics, including Prime Minister David Cameron" in 2012 in a battle not so much of political parties as of personalities.

9. Although he is an unprecedented three-term mayor, Mockus was a nonstarter in two presidential campaigns in 1998 and 2006, suggesting again that mayors and presidents may have noncommensurable virtues that do not translate well.

10. Quoted in RT online, http://rt.com/politics/luzhkov-mayor-united-russia-317/, February 2, 2012. United Russia was a merger of the Fatherland Party, led by Luzhkov in the 1990s, and the Unity Party, whose "bulk" ultimately absorbed Fatherland's "intellect," according to Luzhkov.

11. See Leoluca Orlando, *Fighting the Mafia and Renewing Sicilian Culture*, San Francisco: Encounter Books, 2001.

12. Mayor Michael Nutter, in an interview with other mayors on *Charlie Rose*, May 22, 2011.

13. It was also noted at Koch's funeral in February 2013 that the most Jewish of New York mayors was being buried at the most Episcopal of New York cemeteries in what has become the most Dominican of New York neighborhoods—a perfect emblem of not just his city, but cities everywhere.

14. In the rhetoric of NRA executive vice president Wayne LaPierre in "Mayors Against Your Rights" in the NRA magazine *America's First Freedom*, May 2012, p. 8.

15. This was an ad lib in Clinton's formal speech, one of the spontaneous additions that added about a third more time to his justly celebrated but lengthy peroration in Charlotte.

16. "Jerusalem is a city that aspires to fanaticism. . . . A city of pilgrims and dreams . . . where Jesus walked, or King David. And then along comes Teddy [Mayor Kollek] and says 'Look, I'll fix your sewers if you knock off the sermons.'" Thomas Friedman, "Teddy Kollek's Jerusalem," *New York Times*, August 4, 1985.

17. Teddy Kollek, "Jerusalem", July 1977, *Foreign Affairs*, http://www.foreignaffairs .com/articles/27888/teddy-kollek/jerusalem.

18. The language is from a report of the Israeli government's Agency for the Coordination of Government Activities in the Territories. Some critics have written off the model as a PR job—see Jodi Rudoren's reporting in the *New York Times*, and Jonathan S. Tobin, "Palestinian Politics Jenin Style," *Commentary*, May 5, 2012, but there is no question that the late governor (who died of a heart attack after an assassination attempt in 2012) was committed to a politics far more pragmatic than that of most Palestinian radicals and ideologues.

19. See Zecharya Tagar, "Municipal Cooperation Across Conflict Divides: A Preliminary Study," London: Chatham House, 2007, http://www.chatham house.org/publications/papers/view/108621.

20. From our interview with Mayor Dutkiewicz, June 2012 (full transcript online at www.ifmayorsruledtheworld.org).

21. Mayor Michael Nutter on *Charlie Rose*, May 22, 2012.

22. Cited in Flanagan, *Mayors and the Challenge*, p. 171.

23. "Decentralization and Local Democracy in the World," *First Global Report by United Cities and Local Government*, World Bank, 2009, p. 229.

24. *Time Magazine*, May 2005; *Time*'s list included, along with Hickenlooper, Chicago's Richard Daley, Atlanta's Shirley Franklin, Baltimore's Martin O'Malley, and New York's Michael Bloomberg.

25. Inaugural Address, 2011, cited in the official website of Governor Hickenlooper, http://www.colorado.gov/governor/.

26. Mayor Paes in a TED talk, February 2012, http://www.ted.com/talks/eduardo _paes_the_4_commandments_of_cities.html.

27. Christopher Dickey, *Securing the City: Inside America's Best Counterterror Force—the NYPD*, New York: Simon and Schuster, 2009, p. 2.

28. Boris Johnson, *Johnson's Life of London*, London: Harper Press, p. 1.

29. Mayor Bill White in an interview with Charlie Rose, April 16, 2012.

30. See Jennifer Medina, "Building Ties to a Neighbor on the Border," *The New York Times*, May 13, 2013.

31. Richard C. Schragger, "Can Strong Mayors Empower Weak Cities?" *Yale Law Journal*, Vol. 115, 2006, p. 2542.

32. Robert Dahl, *Who Governs? Democracy and Power in the American City,* New Haven, CT: Yale University Press, September 1963, p. 204.

33. Mayor Michael Nutter, interview, *Charlie Rose,* May 22, 2011.

34. Schragger, "Strong Mayors," p. 2569.

35. Ed Koch, *Mayor,* New York: Simon and Schuster, 1984, p. 55.

36. Maia de la Baume, "France's President-Elect Has Fans Aplenty at Home," *New York Times,* May 7, 2012.

37. Kathy Hayes and Semoon Chang, "The Relative Efficiency of City Manager and Mayor-Council Forms of Government," *Southern Economic Journal,* Vol. 57, No. 1, 1990, p. 176.

38. Elisabeth R. Gerber and Daniel J. Hopkins, "When Mayors Matter: Estimating the Impact of Mayoral Partisanship on City Policy," *American Journal of Political Science,* Vol. 55, No. 2, 2011, pp. 326–339. The authors attribute the lack of impact of ideology on the limited affect mayors have on national policy, but whatever the reasons, the results are a less ideological local political policy-making process.

39. Eugene T. Lowe, "Voters Still Have Confidence in Mayors Running Cities," http://www.usmayors.org/usmayornewspaper/documents/08_01_11/pg8_voters.asp.

40. Data from Ulrik Kjaer, "The Mayor's Political Career," in Henery Back, Hubert Heinelt, and Annick Magnier, eds., *The European Mayor: Political Leaders in the Changing Context of Local Democracy,* Wiesbaden: Vs Verlag, 2006, p. 90.

41. Andrew Cuomo, as secretary of Housing and Urban Development, in 1997. J. Philip Thompson III, *Double Trouble: Black Mayors, Black Communities, and the Call for a Deep Democracy,* New York: Oxford University Press, 2006, p. 6.

42. Eugene T. Lowe, "Voters Still Have Confidence in Mayors Running Cities," http://www.usmayors.org/usmayornewspaper/documents/08_01_11/pg8_voters.asp.

Profile 4. Wolfgang Schuster of Stuttgart

1. "Listening to Local Leadership in Stuttgart: Lord Mayor Wolfgang Schuster," Cities of Migration, February 16 2012, http://citiesofmigration.ca/ezine_stories/listening-to-local-leadership-in-stuttgart-lord-mayor-wolfgang-schuster/.

2. Wolfgang Schuster, from interview on website www.ifmayorsruledtheworld.org.

Chapter 5. Interdependent Cities

1. Wolfgang Schmidt, Hamburg's current foreign minister, recounts the story, noting the one exception: a visit by Queen Elizabeth in 1965, when then mayor Paul Nevermann took a few steps down toward her Majesty—not, it was said, because Elizabeth was a queen but only because she was a lady. In another tribute to the city's freedom, a mural hangs in Hamburg's old Festival Hall in which the artist meant to portray a bishop under Carl the Great blessing a young man from Hamburg. The Senate refused to accept the painting or the idea that freeman

were in need of imperially inspired blessings until the artist Robert Vogel blanked out the freeman, leaving the king's bishop foolishly blessing empty air!

2. For a more detailed account of the early Swiss and Raetian Leagues, see my early work, Benjamin Barber, *The Death of Communal Liberty: The History of Freedom in a Swiss Mountain Canton*; Princeton, NJ: Princeton University Press, 1974.

3. Cisco.com, The Network (Cisco news site), news release, August 20, 2011, http://newsroom.cisco.com/press-release-content?articleId=680179, March 1, 2012. Also see www.CityProtocol.org. The City Protocol was formally presented at the SmartCity Expo in Barcelona, November 13–15, 2012.

4. Eric Corijn, "Urbanity as a Political Project: Towards Post-National European Cities, in *Creative Economies, Creative Cities: Asian-European Perspectives*, ed. Lily Kong and Justin O'Connor, New York: Springer Publishing, 2009, p. 199.

5. Sociologists distinguish the resources, assets, and attitudes that hold together communities internally (bonding capital) from those that open communities to outreach, trade, and cross-border cooperation (bridging capital). See, for example, Robert Putnam, *Bowling Alone: The Collapse and Revival of American Community*, New York: Simon and Schuster, 2001.

6. Manuel Castells, *The Information Age: Economy, Society and Culture*, Vol. 1: *The Rise of the Networked Society*, London, Blackwell, 1996, p. 386. Castells's study is the seminal work on cities, globalization, information, and society. For a fuller account see Benjamin Barber, "Brave New World," *Los Angeles Times*, http://articles.latimes.com/1999/may/23/books/bk-39970.

7. Saskia Sassen, ed., *Global Networks: Linked Cities*, London: Routledge, 2002, pp. 2–3.

8. Kathleen McCarthy, interview, January 19, 2013; see website for full quote, www.ifmayorsruledtheworld.org. "The lack of cities limited the growth of philanthropy in the antebellum South. Philanthropy was also more governed by the state: it was harder for many groups (especially African Americans) to get charters, and the most heavily capitalized institutions—the biggest universities—tended to have public, vs. private charters and state-appointed trustees, which meant that they were run by prominent slaveholders and those who served them. This also meant that there were fewer independent pots of money for investment (both in terms of endowments, and excess funds from dues or donations), and fewer opportunities for groups like women and African Americans to play financial roles in their communities, including having the capital to lend for mortgages and small businesses development. So there were economic consequences as well."

9. Kathleen McCarthy, *American Creed: Philanthropy and the Rise of Civil Society 1700–1865*, Chicago: University of Chicago Press, 2003, p. 96.

10. The project was implemented by the United Nations Economic and Social Commission for Asia and the Pacific (UNESCAP) in collaboration with the

United Nations Development Fund for Women (UNIFEM), the Network of Local Government Training and Research Institutes in Asia and the Pacific (LOGOTRI), and the Regional Network of Local Authorities for the Management of Human Settlements (CITYNET).

11. David A. Wylie, *City, Save Thyself! Nuclear Terror and the Urban Ballot*, Boston: Trueblood Publishing, 2009.

12. Christopher Dickey, *Securing the City: Inside America's Best Counterterror Force—The NYPD*, New York: Simon and Shuster, 2010, p. 36.

13. Craig Horowitz, "The NYPD's War on Terror," *New York Magazine*, February 3, 2003, http://nymag.com/nymetro/news/features/n_8286/.

14. Dickey, *Securing the City*, p. 169.

15. Ibid., p. 255.

16. The congressional investigation of these fusion centers is described by James Risen, "Criticism of Centers in Fight on Terror," *New York Times*, October 3, 2012.

17. Mathieu Deflem and Lindsay C. Maybin, "Interpol and the Policing of International Terrorism: Developments and Dynamics since September 11," in *Terrorism: Research, Readings, & Realities*, ed. Lynne L. Snowden and Brad Whitsel, Upper Saddle River, NJ: Pearson Prentice Hall, 2005, pp. 175–191. The Fujimori case has a curious background; as Deflem and Maybin write: "An Interpol notice for Fujimori, who is now living in self-exile in Japan, was placed by Peruvian authorities in 2001. But Japanese police and justice authorities have not sought extradition for Fujimori because he has in the meantime become a Japanese citizen."

18. The 2013 Conference Executive Committee includes the mayors of Hiroshima and Nagasaki, and Akron, Belgrade, Brussels, Florence, Granollers, Halabja (Iraq!), Hannover, Malakoff, Manchester, Muntinlupa, Volgograd, Ypres, Fongo-Tongo (Cameroon), Montreal, Mexico City, Montevideo, and Frogn.

19. Fourteen nations possess nuclear weapons, but another thirty generate atomic energy, and eighteen more are building reactors. All are potential nuclear weapons powers in the coming years.

20. ICLEI website, www.iclei.org.

21. Ibid.

22. From the C40 Cities website, http://www.c40cities.org/about/.

23. See Benjamin Barber, *The Death of Communal Liberty*, Princeton, NJ: Princeton University Press, 1974, pp. 245–246, 249.

24. Official website of France's National Commission for Decentralized Cooperation, http://www.cncd.fr/frontoffice/bdd-monde.asp.

Chapter 6. Cities without Sovereignty

1. President Ford never actually used the phrase, and eventually helped bail out the struggling city with federal loans that were in time fully repaid. After all, Ford's vice president was New York's Nelson Rockefeller. But the headline

captured the mistrust that often characterizes the big-city relationship to Washington. It also presaged the animus of Tea Party conservatives against urban progressives, as the *New York Times*, on October 7, 2012, mimicked the *New York Post* in a headline reading, "REPUBLICANS TO CITIES: DROP DEAD." Vice presidential candidate Paul Ryan famously blamed cities for Governor Mitt Romney's loss to President Obama in the 2012 presidential race.

2. John M. Broder, "Bigger Toolkit Needed to Manage Climate Change," *New York Times*, December 11, 2011.

3. This is not an argument about decline and does not address the arguments advanced by the antideclinists such as Dani Rodrik, who call the idea that globalization had "condemned the nation-state to irrelevance" as a "foundational myth" of the era. See Dani Rodrik, "The Nation-State Reborn," Project Syndicate, 2012, http://www.project-syndicate.org/commentary/the-nation-state -reborn, and his *The Globalization Paradox: Democracy and the Future of the World Economy*, New York: W. W. Norton, 2012.

4. Wayne LaPierre, "Mayors Against Your Rights," *America's First Freedom, Journal of the NRA*, January 2012. Though there is a new climate in the United States, it is not clear that cities will prevail in the struggle against a less popular but still powerful national gun lobby.

5. Sabrina Tavernise, "As Gas Drilling Spreads, Towns Stand Ground over Control," *New York Times*, December 15, 2011.

6. "60% in City Oppose Mayor's Soda Ban, Poll Finds," *New York Times*, August 22, 2012.

7. The influence of private wealth on public decision making is perfectly reflected in the work of the American Legislative Exchange Council, a powerful national lobby masquerading as a nonpartisan tax-deductible charity. ALEC has several thousand state legislators as members and represents more than forty corporations, including Wal-Mart, Coca-Cola, Kraft, Amazon, Johnson & Johnson, and General Motors. Over more than thirty years, ALEC has offered hundreds of "model bills" on policy decisions of interest to them and on the dockets of state legislatures. Many of these bills become legislation with hardly a comma being moved. Today, through campaigns being waged by the Center for Media and Democracy and Common Cause, ALEC is being challenged, its tax status is in peril, and its corporate members are in flight, although some fear the IRS scandal (involving the targeting of Tea Party NGOs applying for 501c4 tax status) in the spring of 2013 may blunt the attack on ALEC's suspect tax status. On ALEC, see Bill Moyers, Schumann Media Center, *The United States of ALEC*, a documentary film, 2012.

8. Bruce Katz and Jennifer Bradley, *The Metropolitan Revolution: How Cities Are Fixing Our Broken Politics and Fragile Economy*, Washington, D.C.: Brookings, 2013. David Brooks is fascinated by what he calls an inversion of national and local politics in his discussion of the Katz/Bradley book in his "The Power Inversion," *New York Times* (op-ed), June 7, 2013.

9. Carlo Levi, *Christ Stopped at Eboli: The Story of a Year*, New York: Farrar, Straus and Giroux, 1947, p. 78.

10. Bloomberg, Speech at MIT, November 29, 2011.

11. See Michael Kammen, *Mystic Chords of Memory: The Transformation of Tradition in American Culture*, New York: Vintage, 1993.

12. See Graham Robb, *The Discovery of France: A Historical Geography*, New York: W. W. Norton, 2008. Robb's account of the discovery of France is also an account of the invention of France and French character, and it offers a personal as well as a historical take on the formation of the French nation.

13. This happened in Libya with the NATO intervention in 2011. The protection of civilians and regime change were good causes, but what transpired was the violation of Libyan sovereignty with many untoward consequences, including the murder of an American ambassador, the unleashing of forces of chaos, militia rule, and revanchist terrorism in Libya, Mali, Algeria, and elsewhere in the Sahel that good-willed democratic forces were unable to control. See "The West Must Be Honest about Its Role in Libya's Violent Chaos," *The Guardian*, September 16, 2012.

14. R. Burdett and D. Sudjic, eds., *Living in the Endless City*, London: Phaidon, 2011.

15. Leslie Kaufman and Kate Zernike, "Activists Fight Green Projects, Seeing U.N. Plot," *New York Times*, February 3, 2012. The paranoia about smart meters is ironic in light of the newly revealed global surveillance by the U.S. National Security Agency.

16. Charlie Savage, "Order on Interpol Work Inside U.S. Irks Conservatives," *New York Times*, December 31, 2009.

17. Jean-Jacque Rousseau, *The Social Contract*, Book I, Chapter 8; ed. and trans. Victor Gourevitch, in *The Social Contract and Later Political Writings*, Cambridge: Cambridge University Press, 1997, pp. 53–54.

18. Cities are not all on the same trajectory. Charles Correa argues that Mumbai sixty years ago was far more pluralistic and welcoming than it is today. "Because of narrow parochialism and religious bigotry, our politicians today are rapidly destroying this pluralism. . . . For a city is a network of people, goods and services. Demolish those networks and you destroy the city." Once a world city, Correa concludes, Mumbai "has actually diminished since then into a monstrous provincial town." See Correa, "The Long View," in R. Burdett and D. Sudjic, eds., *Living in the Endless City*, p. 121.

19. D. A. Bell and A. de-Shalit, *The Spirit of Cities: Why the Identity of a City Matters in a Global Age*, Princeton, NJ: Princeton University Press, 2011.

20. The exception is "America the Beautiful," surely more a paean to grace and place than a typical national anthem; but then of course it isn't the American anthem, an honor reserved for the war-embossed "Star-Spangled Banner."

21. The Regional Network of Local Authorities for the Management of Human Settlements, Yokohama, Japan, 2009, http://www.citynet-ap.org/docs/medium -term-plan.pdf.

22. For a forceful if rather exaggerated expression of this viewpoint, see Eric A. Posner and Adrian Vermeule, *The Executive Unbound: After the Madisonian Republic*, New York: Oxford University Press, 2012.

23. Robert Kagan, "The Myth of American Decline," *New Republic*, February 2, 2012. "Has America lost its advantages? The answer is no. . . . In economic terms . . . America's position in the world has not changed. Its share of the world's GDP has held remarkably steady. Its share of GDP has been roughly 25% since the 1970's." See also his *The World America Made*, New York: Knopf, 2012.

24. Paul Kennedy, *The Rise and Fall of the Great Powers*, New York: Random House, 1987. At a time when Japan was dominating the electronics and automobile industries and Rockefeller Center in New York had been purchased by Japanese investors, it was easy to think Japan was the next superpower. Kagan uses the lesson of Japan to remind us that China is no more likely to succeed the United States than Japan was. But he insists the story is still about number one, whether any state can surpass the United States, while the brute realities of interdependence and their impact on sovereignty go unremarked.

25. Benjamin Barber, *Jihad vs. McWorld*, New York: Ballantine Books, 2nd ed., 2001, pp. 12–13.

26. Rodrik, "The Nation-State Reborn." See also his *The Globalization Paradox*.

27. K. C. Sivaramakrishnan, "Democracy and Self-Interest," in Burdett and Sudjic, eds., *Living in the Endless City*, p. 93. Comprehending the dialectic, he adds that "similarly, even the largest city, with all its resources, cannot superimpose itself as a substitute for the state."

28. Mayors Surveys on book website, www.ifmayorsruledtheworld.org.

29. Ibid.

30. Gerald Frug, "Democracy and Governance," in Burdett and Sudjic, eds., *Living in the Endless City*, p. 355. Frug notes that fostering the growth of global cities can be an important part of a national agenda, which means that states will take a lively interest in urban policy.

Profile 6. Yury Luzhkov of Moscow

1. Paul Abelsky, "Still Highly Popular after 14 Years, Moscow Mayor Looks to the Future," *City Mayors*, http://www.citymayors.com/politics/moscow_mayor.html.

Chapter 7. "Planet of Slums"

1. Paul Collier calls them "the Bottom Billion," those living in "trapped countries," who are "clearly heading toward what might be described as a black hole." See Paul Collier, *The Bottom Billion: Why the Poorest Countries Are Failing and What Can Be Done about It*, New York: Oxford University Press, 2007.

2. David Harvey, *Spaces of Hope*, Berkeley: University of California Press, 2000, p. 9. The urban poor, writes Harvey, "seem caught, helplessly passive, imprisoned, and fragmented within the web of urban life being constructed by agents of power that seem far away." He may overstate their passivity, however.

3. Mike Davis, *Planet of Slums*, London: Verso, 2006, p. 17. A more optimistic treatment of the impact of immigration from the rural to the urban planet can be found in Doug Saunders, *Arrival City*, New York: Vintage, 2011.

4. Richard Florida, *The Rise of the Creative Class Revisited*, New York: Basic Books (Perseus), 2012, p. 380.

5. Davis, *Planet of Slums*, p. 23.

6. Rahul Mehrotra, "The Static and the Kinetic," in R. Burdett and D. Sudjic, eds., *Living in the Endless City*, London: Phaidon, 2011, p. 108.

7. Suketu Mehta, "Looking for the Bird of Gold," in Burdett and Sudjic, eds., *Living in the Endless City*, p. 105. Mehta writes that "modern slum rehabilitation is the war of the individual against the communal, of anomie against community."

8. The 2003 U.N.-Habitat Report, cited by Davis, *Planet of Slums*, p. 24.

9. Nicholas D. Kristof, "For Obama's New Term, Start Here," *New York Times*, January 24, 2013.

10. According to Davis's figures, a composite from different sources, in 1950 Mumbai had a population of about 3 million and in 2004 it was over 19 million; Manila in 1950 was 1.5 million and in 2004 it had grown to 14.3 million. Cairo went from 2.4 million to 15.1 million, Lagos from less than .33 million to nearly 14 million, Istanbul from 1 to 11 million, Bogótá from less than a million to 8 million, Kinshasa/Brazzaville from 200,000 people to nine million. Now factor in the percentage of people in these burgeoning megacities living in slums, and it becomes apparent that Davis's Planet of Slums is really a third-world planet.

11. The Kerner Commission, *Report of the National Advisory Commission on Civil Disorders*, Washington, D.C.: U.S. Government Printing Office, 1968.

12. A lead editorial signed by Matthew Continetti in the *Weekly Standard*, November 14, 2011.

13. "The financial crisis unleashed a new realization that our economic system was not only inefficient and unstable but also fundamentally unfair," offending not only equality but the possibility of equal opportunity. Joseph E. Stiglitz, *The Price of Inequality: How Today's Divided Society Endangers the Future*, New York: W. W. Norton, 2012, pp. xiv–xv.

14. For a review of the changed circumstances that have impacted traditional liberalism, see Benjamin Barber, "Towards a Fighting Liberalism," *The Nation*, November 7, 2011.

15. Heather Timmons, "Trial in Rape Defies Delays," *New York Times*, January 24, 2013. There is a connection to governance, of course. The United Nations reported that, based on 2008 data from sixty-five nations, India ranked the fourth-lowest in judges per million people (fourteen), just ahead of Guatemala, Nicaragua, and Kenya. A powerful new film from director Richard Robbins, *Girl Rising*, explores the impact of education on the prospects for women in a still-skewed world of gender discrimination.

16. Harvey, *Spaces of Hope*, p. 9.

17. Davis uses this as an epigraph for his *Planet of Slums*; he cites Geddes from Lewis Mumford, *The City in History*, New York: Harcourt, Brace, 1961, p. 464.

18. Davis, *Planet of Slums*, p. 26. Davis notes that while cities like Rio de Janeiro have had slums for a long time (the first favela there was established in the 1880s), most of today's megaslums are new excrescences of emerging megacities.

19. Jeremy Seabrook, *Cities of the South: Scenes from a Developing World*, New York: Verso, 1996.

20. Davis, *Planet of Slums*, p. 138.

21. Katherine Boo, *Behind the Beautiful Forevers: Life, Death, and Hope in a Mumbai Undercity*, New York: Random House, 2012, p. 8.

22. Ban Ki-Moon, cited in U.N. News Centre, "Global Partnership Key to Achieving Millennium Development Goals by 2015—UN report," July 2, 2012, http://www.un.org/apps/news/story.asp?NewsID=42372#.UaZQAqytbD4.

23. Abraham Lincoln, November 21, 1864, Letter to Colonel William F. Elkins, in *The Lincoln Encyclopedia*, Archer H. Shaw ed., New York: Macmillan, 1950.

24. The *New York Herald*, May 3, 1837. Similarly, from the *New York Post*, May 1, 1837, "The present commercial revulsion is without a parallel in our history. The distress pervades all classes—the prudent and the foolhardy, the regular merchant and the speculator, the manufacturer, tradesman, laborer, banker— all are involved in one general calamity."

25. The editors, "The Gilded City," (cover story), *The Nation*, May 6, 2013, p. 11.

26. James K. Galbraith, *Inequality and Instability: A Study of the World Economy Just Before the Great Crisis*, New York: Oxford University Press, 2012, p. 254.

27. Ibid., p. 249. Timothy Noah likewise acknowledges that "changes in the global economy are making incomes less equal in many countries outside the United States." But he also argues that "the income-inequality trend of the past three decades has been unusually fierce here in the world's richest nation," turning the phrase "American exceptionalism" into a slur rather than a compliment. Timothy Noah, *The Great Divergence: America's Growing Inequality Crisis and What We Can Do about It*, New York: Bloomsbury Press, 2012, p. 5.

28. Kerner Commission, *Report of the National Advisory Commission on Civil Disorders*, op. cit.

29. Fred R. Harris and Lynn A. Curtis, eds., *Locked in the Poorhouse: Crisis, Race, and Poverty in the United States*, Lanham, MD: Rowman & Littlefield Publishers Inc., 1998. The two Eisenhower Foundation Reports were *The Millennium Breach* and *Locked in the Poorhouse*, 1998.

30. *Tracking American Poverty and Policy* was introduced at a Demos national bipartisan conference in July 2012, cohosted with the Center on Budget and Policy Priorities, the Georgetown Center on Poverty, Inequality and Public Policy, and *The American Prospect* magazine.

31. The Correctional Association is an NGO focused on the criminalization of youth behavior. Its work includes a partnership with the National Black Theater

in presenting Bryonn Bain's play *Lyrics from Lockdown* in 2013, typical of the integration of art and politics in the city (see Chapter 10).

32. The so-called LIBOR or London Interbank Offered Rate is a global benchmark for many other rates used by banks, municipalities, and others around the world. Cities do "rate swaps" as part of their financing at an interest pegged to LIBOR. By illegally manipulating the rate during the fiscal crisis, banks prevented cities like Baltimore from getting the full interest due them on their swaps. Baltimore and other affected cities initiated an expensive suit. For details of the lawsuit, see Nathaniel Popper, "Rate Scandal Stirs Scramble for Damages," *New York Times*, July 11, 2012.

33. Full story in Danny Hakim, "Syracuse's Democratic Mayor Gets under Governor's Skin," *New York Times*, January 24, 2013.

34. From Jean-Jacques Rousseau, *Constitutional Project for Corsica*, part I. "Projet de constitution pour la corse, 1765," in C. E. Vaughan, *The Political Writings of Rousseau*, Vol. 2, New York: John Wiley & Sons, 1962, pp. 306–307 ff.

35. Angela Glover Blackwell, ""Progress, Paradox, and the Path Ahead: A Roundtable," *American Prospect*, July-August 2012, p. 51. Blackwell is a former Rockefeller Foundation vice president and the CEO of Policy Link, a research institute focused on advancing social and economic equity. Meanwhile, using Michael Harrington's figure of 22 percent of Americans in poverty back in 1962 (from his *The Other America*, op. cit.), that figure is down to under 12 percent, though nearly half (44 percent) of those are in "deep poverty," living at less than half the poverty level (according to Peter Edelman, in the same *American Prospect* Roundtable.)

36. David Harvey, "Possible Urban Worlds" in Steef Buijs, Wendy Tan, and Devisari Tunas eds., *Megacities: Exploring a Sustainable Future*, Rotterdam: 010 Publishers, 2010, p. 168.

37. Boo, *Behind the Beautiful Forevers*, Preface, p. xx.

38. Ibid., p. 12.

39. Carl H. Nightingale, "Segregation as a Tool of Power," May 22, 2012. *Global Segregation*, http://globalsegregation.com/segregation-and-power/.

40. Alan Ehrenhalt portrays the "inversion" process in his *The Great Inversion and the Future of the American City*, New York: Alfred A. Knopf, 2012. Joel Kotkin has also been a critic of downtown rehabilitation.

41. Carl H. Nightingale, *Segregation: A Global History of Divided Cities*, Chicago: University of Chicago Press, p. 10.

42. Ibid.

43. Gary, Indiana, for example, was founded in 1906 by the U.S. Steel Company and quickly became an industrial-age powerhouse with over 170,000 population and, as in historian S. Paul O'Hara's book title, "the most American of all American cities (see *Gary: The Most American of All American Cities*, Bloomington: Indiana University Press, 2011). Yet with the exporting of the steel industry, today its population is under 80,000, it has closed its public library, and it can maintain only six of its fifty-seven public parks. The chief source of revenue for

the town's ailing budget ($60 million with a projected 2012 deficit of $15 million) is two riverboat casinos. See Don Terry, "Where Work Disappears and Dreams Die," *American Prospect*, July-August 2012, pp. 58–61.

44. See John Daniel Davidson's lively travel reports on Beziers, one of France's oldest cities, or Marseille, its greatest multicultural capital, for excellent reportage on France's own rustbelt crisis, at http://bygonebureau.com/2012/04/25/the-rust-belt-of-france-montpellier/, April 25, 2012.

45. Edward Glaeser and Jacob Vigdor, *The End of the Segregated Century: Racial Separation in America's Neighborhoods, 1890–2010*, Civic Report No. 66, The Manhattan Institute for Policy Research, January 2012. Glaeser and Vigdor write that "All-white neighborhoods are effectively extinct. A half-century ago, one-fifth of America's urban neighborhoods had exactly zero black residents. Today, African-American residents can be found in 199 out of every 200 neighborhoods nationwide. The remaining neighborhoods are mostly in remote rural areas or in cities with very little black population." They add that "gentrification and immigration have made a dent in segregation. While these phenomena are clearly important in some areas, the rise of black suburbanization explains much more of the decline in segregation." http://www.manhattan-institute.org/html/cr_66.htm.

46. Harvey, *Spaces of Hope*, p. 45.

47. James K. Galbraith sees speculative markets as a cause of inequality, but not just in cities, and more often than not, elsewhere than in cities. Galbraith, *Inequality and Instability*, p. 83.

48. Sako Musterd, "Segregation, Urban Space and the Resurgent City," *Urban Studies*, Vol. 43, No. 8, July 2006, p. 1332.

49. Rice's Pulitzer Prize–winning drama, played out entirely on an urban stoop and the street in front of it, became a successful musical (with score by Kurt Weil and lyrics by urban poet Langston Hughes) and, like the Gershwins' *Porgy and Bess*, incarnated the energy and drama of real urban life—edgy and dangerous in the manner of real human life rather than as defined by criminality and urban rapaciousness.

50. In the words of L.A.'s Mayor Villaraigosa, "Beverly Hills has a history of opposition to the subway. . . . They say they want it, but they don't want it there." Cited in Adam Nagourney, "Subway Line Meets an Obstruction," *New York Times*, July 16, 2012. The *Times* cites old charges (that Beverly Hills defenders dispute) that "the community synonymous with wealth and privilege, does not want to open its border to mass transit and the not-so-prosperous people who ride it."

51. Helia Nacif Xavier and Fernanda Magalhães are responsible for the estimate of the three-hour average work commute by bus from the favelas. Helia Nacif Xavier and Fernanda Magalhães, *The Case of Rio de Janeiro*, 2003, p. 19, http://terra-geog.lemig2.umontreal.ca/donnees/Projet%20Bresil/urbanisation/slums%20orio%202003.pdf.

52. According to Xavier and Magalhães, such a household spends circa 220 reals on transportation, 225 for a month's rent, and 100 for food.

53. Nightingale, *Segregation*, p. 12.

54. Similar complaints have been made about odd/even license plate plans that bar autos from downtown on odd and even days. The wealthy simply have two cars, one with an odd plate, one with an even.

55. Judith N. Shklar, *On Citizenship: The Quest for Inclusion*, London: Cambridge University Press, 1998, pp. 100–101.

56. See William Julius Wilson, *When Work Disappears: The World of the New Urban Poor*, New York: Random House, 1997, and *The Truly Disadvantaged: The Inner City, the Underclass, and Public Policy*, Chicago: University of Chicago Press, 1990.

57. Michael Cooper, "Few Cities Have Regained Jobs They Lost," *New York Times*, Wednesday, January 18, 2012.

58. Report from the National Employment Law Project, *New York Times*, August 31, 2012, cited in an article by Catherine Rampell, "Majority of New Jobs Pay Low Wages, Study Finds," August 30, 2012, http://www.nytimes.com/2012/08 /31/business/majority-of-new-jobs-pay-low-wages-study-finds.html?_r=0.

59. Figures for London, Office for National Statistics, November 18, 2011; for Johannesburg, Official Website Johannesburg, 2006; for Delhi, Department of Urban Development, Government of Delhi, 2006; for Rio de Janeiro, www.ibge .gov.br; for New York, http://www.nyc.gov/html/sbs/wib/downloads/pdf/civil _service_july2006.pdf; in 2006, 15.4 percent of New York wage/salary jobs were in the federal, state, and local government sector, employing about 550,000 people.

60. Groups like Judicial Watch and Transparency International are useful sources in tracking urban corruption. The list in the text is a mere drop is a depressingly large bucket.

61. Boo, *Behind the Beautiful Forevers*, p. 28. Working inside a corrupt system, even obedience to rules can become a form of gaming the system, as happens when unions take a rigid "work to rule" approach to a factory line in which obeying the letter of the law undermines productivity.

62. The great German-American political theorist Carl J. Friedrich, who helped write the postwar German constitution, once suggested that corruption, like arsenic, though deadly, could actually be an aid to civic health in trace amounts.

63. Katherine Boo, interviewed by Leonard Lopate on WNYC, December 21, 2012, made the point underlined in Note 61 on the air once again.

64. Boo, *Behind the Beautiful Forevers*, p. 28.

65. Monica Davey, "Rate of Killings Rises 38% in Chicago in '12," *New York Times*, June 26, 2012.

66. In 2012, Mexico's former top antidrug prosecutor was arrested on suspicion of accepting $450,000 in bribes in Sinaloa. In 2009, ten mayors and twenty other officials were detailed in a drug investigation. According to the Center for Research and Higher Education in Mexico City, "organized crime (in Mexico) has not just penetrated police bodies but government spaces at all levels." Sara Miller Llana,

"Mexico Drug War Worsened by Organized Crime's Tight Grip on Politics," *Christian Science Monitor,* November 5, 2010, http://www.csmonitor.com/World /Americas/2010/1105/Mexico-drug-war-worsened-by-organized-crime-s-tight -grip-on-politics. Recently, mayors and mayoral candidates are being murdered.

67. R. Buettner and W. Glaberson, "Courts Putting Stop-and-Frisk Policy on Trial," *New York Times,* July 11, 2012.

68. Eric Goode, "Philadelphia Defends Policy on Frisking, with Limits," *New York Times,* July 12, 2012. Having to honor "constitutional concerns" at the price of more homicides or cut crime by endangering rights is not a choice cities should have to make.

69. "India Rape Victims See Police as Part of Problem," *New York Times,* January 23, 2013. Police pay in India is less than $100 a month, there are fewer officers per 100,000 people (130) than in all but four third-world countries, and there are very few female constables. Things are little different for crime generally in states such as Mexico, Afghanistan, or the Congo. Even in American ghettos, citizens wonder if the police are friends or enemies of neighborhood safety. Unreasonable traffic stop and search tactics by police are still labeled as DWB or "driving while black" among drivers of color.

70. Vandana Shiva, *Water Wars: Privatization, Pollution, and Profit,* Cambridge, MA: South End Press, 2002, and Maude Barlow, *Blue Covenant: The Global Water Crisis and the Coming Battle for the Right to Water,* New York: New Press, 2009.

71. See Eric Jaffe's articles at the *Atlantic On-Line,* "How Urban Parks Enhance Your Brain," July 16, 2012, and "Can Trees Actually Deter Crime," May 25, 2012—both at http://www.theatlanticcities.com/arts-and-lifestyle/2012/07/how-urban-parks -enhance-your-brain/2586/, http://www.theatlanticcities.com/neighbor- hoods/2012/05/can-trees-actually-deter-crime/2107/. What might appear as frivolous opinion pieces are in fact rooted in research at the University of Vermont and elsewhere, though the connections are not—writes Jaffe—"purely causal."

72. Paul M. Scherer, *The Benefits of Parks: Why America Needs More City Parks and Open Space,* San Francisco: Trust for Public Land, 2003, p. 21. Scherer estimates that a full tree cover can remove up to 15 percent of the ozone, 14 percent of the sulfur dioxide, 13 percent of particulate matter, and 8 percent of nitrogen dioxide.

73. Richard Mitchell and Frank Popham, "Effect of Exposure to Natural Environ- ment on Health Inequalities," *Lancet,* November 8, 2008. See also "Community Green: Using Local Spaces to Tackle Inequality and Improve Health," CABE Space, London, 2010.

74. Jennifer Wolch, John P. Wilson, and Jed Fehrenback, "Parks and Park Funding in Los Angeles: An Equity Mapping Analysis," Sustainable Cities Program: GIS Research Lab oratory, USC, http://biodiversity.ca.gov/Meetings/archive/ej /USC.pdf.

75. Khaled El-Khishin, "Cairo's Al-Azhar Park: Millennium Development Goals Etched in Green," *Journal of the Malaysian Institute of Planners,* Vol. 4, 2006, pp. 23–30.

76. The Trust for Public Land, "City Parks Facts for 2012," Washington, D.C., 2012.

77. See Nicholas Lemann, *The Promised Land: The Great Black Migration and How It Changed America*, New York: Vintage, 1992.

78. The Levitt Foundation, established by Liz Levitt Hirsch, has established pavilions in a dozen American parks, including MacArthur Park in Los Angeles, that feature free summer concerts for residents and that have helped create safe community nature spaces in dense city neighborhoods.

Profile 7. Ayodele Adewale of Lagos

1. "Nigerian Constitution Does Not Regard the Youths—Comrade Ayodele Adewale," September 4, 2012, Global Excellence, http://globalexcellenceonline.com /nigerian-constitution-does-not-regard-the-youths-comrade-ayodele-adewale/.

2. Dr. Keziah A., a resident of Amuwo Odofin, "Testimonials for Ayodele Adebowale Adewale," City Mayors, http://www.worldmayor.com/contest_2012/ comments-amuwo-odofin.html.

Chapter 8. City, Cure Thyself!

1. Richard Florida, *The Rise of the Creative Class*, New York: Basic Books, 2004, p. 285.

2. Although economist James K. Galbraith is concerned with universals such as the relationship between inequality and stability, he observes that, for example, "the experience of economic inequality in [Brazil and Argentina] is marked by differences rooted in their divergent social histories and economic structure"— Brazil historically unequal as a result of the plantation economy and slavery, Argentina historically more egalitarian due to the European legacy and a strong labor movement. If culture is important, global trends can trump culture. In Brazil and Argentina, many of the differences were eroded by global forces, narrowing the inequality gap between the two nations in recent decades (negatively). See Galbraith, *Inequality and Instability: A Study of the World Economy Just Before the Great Crisis*, New York: Oxford University Press, 2012, p. 254.

3. Michael Harrington, Conclusion, *The Other America*, New York: Touchstone, 1962.

4. Patrick Sharkey, "The Urban Fire Next Time," *New York Times*, op ed page, April 29, 2013.

5. Timothy Noah, *The Great Divergence: America's Growing Inequality Crisis and What We Can Do about It*, New York: Bloomsbury Press, 2012, pp. 179–195.

6. Charles Murray, "Why Capitalism Has an Image Problem," *Wall Street Journal*, July 30, 2012.

7. James Boswell, *London Journal*, cited in Danny Heitman, "Love Letter to London," *Wall Street Journal*, July 28, 2012.

8. Denis Diderot, *Rameau's Nephew*, 1769 (although not published in Diderot's lifetime).

9. Jane Jacobs, *Cities and the Wealth of Nations: Principles of Economic Life*, New York: Random House, 1984, p. 31.

10. Ibid., p. 110.

11. Florida, *Rise of the Creative Class*, 2004 ed., p. 285.

12. Richard Florida, "For Creative Cities, the Sky Has Its Limits," *Wall Street Journal*, July 28, 2012. The American Planning Association published a paper called "Growing Cities Sustainably" that debated the benefits and costs of the so-called "Compact City" model. Density is by itself not necessarily an urban virtue. On the Sustainable Cities Collective website, see Aafrin Kidwai, "For Cities: To Be Dense or Not to Be Dense, That is (not) the Question," Sustainable Cities Collective, August 8, 2012, http://sustainablecitiescollective.com /sustainable-cities/55401/cities-be-dense-or-not-be-dense-not-question.

13. Julianne Pepitone@CNNMoneyTech, tweet, February 25, 2013.

14. Richard Florida, *The Rise of the Creative Class, Revisited,* new introduction, New York: Basic Books, 2012, p. xi.

15. James M. Quane, William Julius Wilson, and Jackelyn Hwang, "The Urban Jobs Crisis: Paths toward Employment for Low-Income Blacks and Latinos," *Harvard Magazine*, May–June, 2013.

16. Richard Florida offers a provocative picture of inequality in American cities for which his arguments try to provide an explanation, in his *Rise of the Creative Class*, p. xvi. His list of "regions with the highest levels of inequality" include Raleigh-Durham, San Francisco, Washington-Baltimore, Austin, Houston, New York, West Palm Beach, San Diego, Los Angeles, and Boston, while those with the lowest levels of inequality are Milwaukee, Portland, St. Louis, Memphis, Salt Lake City, Oklahoma City, Buffalo, Louisville, Indianapolis, Grand Rapids, and Las Vegas. Pay for jobs turns out to be critical.

17. There are truly new cities: not just new towns like Celebration, Florida, built by Disney, or planned and "garden cities" growing out of the new urbanism movement such as Radburn, New Jersey, before World War II, or Greenbelt, Maryland, after, but cities like Las Vegas that, as Robert Venturi quips, "was built in a day" and "not superimposed on an older pattern" (Robert Venturi et al, *Learning from Las Vegas,* rev. ed., Cambridge: MIT Press, 1977, p. 18). Brazil built a new capital in the middle of nowhere (Brasilia), England has experimented with new towns, and of course China is seeing dozens of cities springing up where there were only village exurbs. But none of this changes the reality that, once established, towns and cities are living habitats, and they are the first and most immediate level of government and public service that citizens experience.

18. David Harvey, "Possible Urban Worlds," in *Megacities: Exploring a Sustainable Future*, ed. Steef Buijs, Wendy Tan, and Devisari Tunas, Rotterdam: 010 Publishers, 2010, p. 278.

19. Harrington, *The Other America*, conclusion.

20. Harvey, "Possible Urban Worlds," p. 52.

21. Frances Fox Piven and Richard Cloward, *Poor People's Movements: How they Succeed, How they Fail*, New York: Vintage, 1978.

22. Ibid., p. 91 ("turbulence"), p. 34 ("reform").

23. I do so in my essay "Occupy Wall Street: We Are What Democracy Looks Like!" *Huffington Post*, November 7, 2011. It is worth noting that in the very early days of OWS, young activists in New York talked to a number of older movement activists, including Frances Fox Piven as well as with the author.

24. I have offered an extended account of market fundamentalism's impact on liberal politics and thought in Benjamin Barber, "Towards a Fighting Liberalism," *The Nation*, November 7, 2011, pp. 20–23.

25. A Pew poll from April 10, 2010, put overall trust in government at only 22 percent. The numbers on trust in various levels of government and the 67 percent for state and national government are from a Gallup poll, October 2, 2011. For more see http://politicalticker.blogs.cnn.com/2011/10/03/poll-americans-trust-local-government-more-than-federal/. Even in cities there are some discouraging signs of civic ennui. In recent 2013 mayoral elections in San Antonio, Texas, Julian Castro won a third term with only 7 percent of the electorate voting, and in Los Angeles a contested election that allowed Eric Garcetti (the first Jewish mayor of L.A.) to defeat Wendy Gruel, only 18 percent voted. Where nationally, citizens vote for leaders without trusting them, urban dwellers in the United States seem to trust their leaders without actually feeling the need to vote for them! See http://www.citymayors.com/news/metrones-Americas.html, May 28, 2013.

26. *The Nation* devoted a special issue to the question "Can We Trust Government Again," April 9, 2012, answering: not so much that we do or can, but that we must!

27. Joseph E. Stiglitz, *The Price of Inequality*, New York: W. W. Norton, 2012, p. 267.

28. Hernando de Soto, cited in Alan Budd, "A Mystery Solved," *Times Literary Supplement*, December 15, 2000.

29. De Soto, *The Mystery of Capital: Why Capitalism Triumphs in the West and Fails Everywhere Else,* New York: Basic Books, 2000, p. 46.

30. I have offered criticism in depth of de Soto as well as of C. K. Prahalad and Muhammad Yunus (below) in Benjamin Barber, *Consumed: How Markets Corrupt Children, Infantilize Adults, and Swallow Citizens Whole*, New York: W. W. Norton, 2007, pp. 323–326. De Soto has acknowledged the issues and observed that a considerable number of those who have been supposed beneficiaries of legalizing capital have expressed a preference for going back to the old invisible system.

31. C. K. Prahalad, *The Fortune at the Bottom of the Pyramid: Eradicating Poverty Through Profits*, Upper Saddle River, NJ: Wharton School Publishing, 2004, pp. xi–xii.

32. For a useful, if dated, narrative depicting Grameen's beginnings and its founding vision, see David Bornstein, *The Price of a Dream: The Story of the Grameen Bank and the Idea That Is Helping the Poor to Change Their Lives*, Chicago: University of Chicago Press, 1997. Recent scandals surrounding the

Bank and Yunus have undermined Yunus's reputation and damaged the idea of microfinance, though the charges have yet to be made credible. Susan F. Feiner and Drucilla K. Barker, "A Critique of Microcredit: Microfinance and Women's Poverty," http://imow.org/economica/stories/viewStory?storyId=3693. Sudhirendar Sharma, "Microcredit: Globalisation Unlimited," *The Hindu,* January 5, 2002. My own view, however, is that innovative ideas, especially those impacting "normal market capitalism" are almost always assailed over time, often through personal libels involving their authors. Global finance has yet to receive anything like the scrutiny unleashed on Yunus, and it does not pretend to serve the poor. This is not to say there are not valid criticisms to be made of microfinance.

33. See "The Defamation of Muhammad Yunus." *Philanthrocapitalism*, http://forumblog.org/2011/01/the-defamation-of-muhammad-yunus/, January 7, 2011. The charges of corruption and misuse of funds have not been judicially validated. This is not to say there are not valid criticisms to be made of strategies rooted in the invisible economy or the wealth at the bottom of the pyramid or microfinance, and I have offered some myself in a previous work (*Consumed*). This is not the place to reargue the critique; only to propose that these ideas are worthy of serious attention as part of a mitigation strategy that is uniquely urban.

34. Karen E. Klein, "Microfinance Goes Where Banks Fear to Tread," *Bloomberg Business Weekly*, June 24, 2010.

35. The 2005 film *Man Push Cart* tells the story of Ahmad, a Pakistani immigrant who tries to make a living dragging a heavy cart along the streets of New York to sell its goods. Directed by Ramin Bahrani, starring Charles Daniel Sandoval.

36. Jesse Katz, "The Geography of Getting By," *American Prospect*, July–August 2012, p. 15

37. The following discussion of street vending is from Katz, ibid., pp. 14–25.

38. Lee Kuan Yew, *From Third World to First: The Singapore Story, 1965–2000,* Singapore: Times Media, 2000, p. 116. Singapore followed a slow and paternalistic road to democracy, and it still suffers from a degree of intolerance for free media and multiparty democracy. On the other hand, unlike many developing democracies, it has created an enormously fair and productive society, without an overweening welfare state; and unlike China, it has promoted the gradual emergence of real democratic politics. My personal experience in Singapore, and discussions with new leaders like President Tony Tan and the environmental minister, Vivian Balakrishnan, persuade me that cities across the planet have a great deal to learn from Singapore, especially as they seek greater global cooperation.

39. I have taken up these issues in much more depth in Benjamin Barber, *An Aristocracy of Everyone: The Politics of Education and the Future of America*, New York: Oxford University Press, 1994, and *A Place for Us: How to Make Society Civil and Democracy Strong*, New York: Hill and Wang, 1998.

Profile 8. Sheila Dikshit of Delhi

1. Shirish Sankhe, "Creating a Modern Indian City: An Interview with Delhi's Chief Minister," McKinsey Quarterly, October 2007, http://unpan1.un.org/intradoc/groups/public/documents/APCITY/UNPAN029044.pdf.

Chapter 9. Smart Cities in a Virtual World

1. Eric Schmidt and Jared Cohen, *The New Digital Age: Reshaping the Future of People, Nations and Business*, New York: Alfred A. Knopf, 2013. The Google authors are not naive techno-zealots, and open their book warning that "the Internet is among the few things humans have built that they don't truly understand," and noting that it is "the largest experiment involving anarchy in history" (p. 3). But they quickly fall into claims like "soon everyone on Earth will be connected . . . (and) everyone will benefit from connectivity" though, they acknowledge, not equally (p. 13). By the end of the book, though still cautioning that "technology alone is no panacea," they make very large claims for how it will dominate the world (pp. 254–255).

2. The idea of e-government, inclusive of e-voting, has been around since the 1980s and was a fashionable subject for political debate throughout the 1990s when the European Community held numerous conferences on the subject.

3. Cited by Gavin Newsom, former mayor of San Francisco, in his own quite zealous book on digital government called *Citizenville: How to Take the Town Square Digital and Reinvent Government*, New York: Penguin Press, 2013, p. 8. As mayor, Newsom introduced what he liked to call Web 2.0 into government—which, he argues, functions right now "on the cutting edge—of 1973." He contrasts its bureaucratic opacity and top-down governing mechanisms with digital technology's "bottom-up, two-way, nonhierarchical structures," which are "completely antithetical to the way government currently runs" (p. xvi). Participatory democrats like Newsom see the promise of the web's horizontal, interactive architecture, but are not always attuned to the downside.

4. See P. J. Taylor, "World City Networks: Measurement, Social Organization, Global Governance, and Structural Change," http://www.lboro.ac.uk/gawc/rb/rb333.html, 2011.

5. Rick Robinson, "Open Urbanism: Why the Information Economy Will Lead to Sustainable Cities," Sustainable Cities Collective, October 11, 2012, http://sustainablecitiescollective.com/rickrobinson/72436/open-urbanism-why-information-economy-will-lead-sustainable-cities.

6. Cities include Amsterdam, Barcelona, Boston, Buenos Aires, Busan, Copenhagen, Derby, Dublin, Genova, Helsinki, Hyderabad, Istanbul, Lima, Livorno, Lyon, Maputo, Medellin, Milan, Moscow, Nairobi, New York, Nice, Paris, Quito, Rome, San Francisco, Seoul, Taipei, Torino, Uppsala, Venice, Vienna, and Yokohama. Key business partners are Abertis, Accebtyrem Agbar, Accenture, Capgemini, Cisco, CItit, Fujitsu, GdF Suez, GrupoEtra, HP, IBM,

Indra, Italtel, Microsoft, Opentext, Oracle, Philiops, Ros Roca, SAP, Schneider-televent, Siemens, and Telefonica. Universities include the Argonne National Laboratory, the London School of Economics, the University of Chicago, the University of Sydney, the University of Virginia, Universitat Politechnica de Catalunya, and Yonsei University.

7. Cisco.com, The Network (Cisco news site), news release, August 20, 2012, http://newsroom.cisco.com/press-release-content?articleId=998539&type =webcontent. Also see www.CityProtocol.org. The City Protocol was formally presented at the SmartCity Expo in Barcelona, November 13–15, 2012.

8. The Intelligent Community Forum is a think tank that explores how cities adapt to broadband and digital technology. Since 1999, the Forum has given annual Visionary awards, including a Visionary City Award that has gone, starting in 1999, to Singapore, LaGrange (Georgia, USA), New York City, Calgary (Alberta, Canada), Seoul, Glasgow, Mitaka (Japan), Taipei, Waterloo (Ontario, Canada), Gangnam-Gu (South Korea), Stockholm, Suwon (South Korea), Eindhoven (Netherlands), and (the last award in 2012) Taichung (Taiwan).

9. Our Barcelona Mayor Survey on our website, www.ifmayorsruledtheworld.org.

10. Nicos Komninos suggests, for example, that while cyber cities emphasize "digital networking, human-machine communications, sensors, intelligent agents, and other [processing] technologies," intelligent communities treat "intelligent cities to be a combination of human innovativeness, collective and digital intelligence." Nicos Komninos, *Intelligent Cities and Globalisation of Innovation Networks*, London: Routledge, 2008, p. 248.

11. "IBM Extends Smarter Cities Initiative through Acquisition of Cúram Software," IBM Press Release, http://www-03.ibm.com/press/us/en/pressrelease /36134.wss.

12. Rick Robinson discusses these and many other smart urban apps in his article in the *Sustainable Cities Blog*, "Open Urbanism: Why the Information Economy Will Lead to Sustainable Cities," October 11, 2012.

13. From www.smartcitiescouncil.com. The council's executive leaders are Electric- ite de France, General Electric, IBM, and Itron. Registration is free, but anything more, including "Premium Content," requires fees.

14. Nigel Jacob said: "A lot of people ask us if this [smart city initiative] is about efficiency. In a lot of ways it isn't about efficiency, it's really about rebuilding trust with the public. A lot of the challenges we face as a society are increasingly problems of engagement, where people aren't spending enough time getting to know each other, and we see this as the gateway drug for civic engagement. This is an easy way that people can start caring about and considering the life of the city. So we think this has huge potential." From the documentary film *Thinking Cities, Networked Society*, February 2012, viewable online at http://www.youtube .com/watch?v=6ctxP6Dp8Bk. As we have seen, former San Francisco Mayor Gavin Newsom (currently California's lieutenant governor) has championed the participatory uses of Web 2.0.

15. Ibid.

16. Boyd Cohen, *Top Ten Smart Cities*, http://www.fastcoexist.com/1679127/the-top -10-smart-cities-on-the-planet.

17. Scrolling ads and commercial links are the primary means, but they have not yet brought the returns once garnered on print media. Moreover, as television once stole advertising from print, and desktop computers cut into television revenue, so today mobiles are taking advertising from desktops and laptops. The successful financial exploitation of digital technologies, despite their devotion to commerce and their inflated stock market values, has yet to be realized. This might be taken as an argument for more nonprofit experimentation but instead has driven companies and users alike to seek to solve the puzzle of profits even more zealously.

18. Rick Robinson, "Can Digital Platforms Transform Our Cities?" Sustainable Cities Collective, June 22, 2012, http://sustainablecitiescollective.com/rickrobin son/43545/digital-platforms-smarter-city-market-making.

19. Benjamin R. Barber, *Strong Democracy: Participatory Politics for a New Age*, Princeton, NJ: Princeton University Press, 1984, p. 274.

20. Herbert Hoover, cited in Langdon Winner, "The Internet and Dreams of Democratic Renewal," in *The Civic Web: Online Politics and Democratic Values*, ed. David M. Anderson and Michael Cornfield. Oxford: Rowman and Littlefield, 2003, p. 168.

21. Eli Pariser, *The Filter Bubble: How the New Personalized Web Is Changing What We Read and How We Think*, New York: Penguin Books, 2012. William F. Baker, former president of WNET, thus speaks of "Google's Internet grab," and suggests the issue is monopoly in this "dominant new information medium." "Google's Internet Grab," *The Nation*, February 11, 2013.

22. Nicholas Kulish, "Twitter Entering New Ground, Blocks Germans' Access to Neo-Nazi Account," *New York Times*, October 19, 2012.

23. Cass Sunstein's prescient book *Republic.com* focused on the web's tendency to separate and isolate rather than bring us together. See Sunstein, *Republic.com*, Princeton, NJ: Princeton University Press, 2009.

24. An important aside: the "cloud" sells itself as a miraculous and invisible nonspace to its users, but for its owners and providers it is an electronic network of linked servers no less real than the personal devices on which it is accessed by ordinary users.

25. Google bought Blogger in 2003, and in 2006 bought YouTube for $1.65 billion.

26. Jason Lanier, *You Are Not a Gadget: A Manifesto*, New York: Vintage Books, 2010.

27. Foucault's study of the history of prisons opens with an appalling portrait of a prisoner being torn apart on the rack but goes on to argue that far worse is the capacity for violence to the psyche of prisons in which a central guard cell can watch prisoners in a circular building where universal surveillance is possible. See Michel Foucault, *Discipline and Punish: The Birth of the Prison*, 2nd ed., New York: Vintage, 1995.

28. From the website of Fishkin's Center on Deliberative Polling at Stanford University, http://cdd.stanford.edu/polls/docs/summary/. James Fishkin is the creative innovator behind deliberative polling, which aims to modify public opinion and encourage public judgment through guided public debate by sample representatives of a population, which can be local or national. See Fishkin's seminal volume *Democracy and Deliberation: New Directions for Democratic Reform*, New Haven, CT: Yale University Press, 1991, as well as his collaboration with constitutional law scholar Bruce Ackerman, *Deliberation Day,* New Haven, CT: Yale University Press, 2004, and his recent book *When the People Speak: Deliberative Democracy and Public Consultation*, New York: Oxford University Press, 2009. Fishkin currently is trying to reform the California initiative and referendum process so that rather than merely canvassing votes it improves the voters' deliberative judgment.

29. Though in many cases, as my mother, Doris Frankel, demonstrated, authors simply moved to the new medium, as she moved from writing drama and comedies for Broadway (such as *Love Me Long* with Shelley Winters) to writing them for radio (*Ma Perkins*) to writing them for television (*All My Children*, *The Brighter Day*, *General Hospital*).

30. Try following the thread of "discussion" that accompanies thoughtful blogs on reputable news and opinion sites and ask whether the public is being informed and educated by such debates.

31. Jeff Jarvis, *Public Parts: How Sharing in the Digital Age Improves the Way We Work and Live,* New York: Simon and Schuster, 2012.

32. See Lori Anderson, *I Know Who You Are and I Saw What You Did: Social Networks and the Death of Privacy*, New York: Free Press, 2012. Anderson proposes a Social Network Constitution as a "touchstone, an expression of fundamental values, that we should use to judge the activities of social networks and their citizens."

33. Evgeny Morozov, "The Internet Intellectual," review of Jarvis, *New Republic*, November 2, 2011. For Mozorov's wittily skeptical views see his *The Net Delusion: The Dark Side of Internet Freedom*, New York: PublicAffairs Press, 2012; and *To Save Everything, Click Here: The Folly of Technological Solutionism*, New York: Public Affairs, 2013.

34. Friedman's preoccupation with globalization and technology can be a welcome riposte to American parochialism and its tendencies to the Luddite; but he is far too often a fan without discretion, as when he writes about the "tightening merger between globalization and the latest information technology revolution." He rhapsodizes, "The more information and trends you are able to mine and analyze, and the more talented human capital, bandwidth and computing power you apply to data, the more innovation you'll get." See "So Much Fun, So Irrelevant," *New York Times*, January 4, 2012.

35. The stark dualism of views about new cyber technology is reflected in the titles of the many books that have appeared about it. Put *The Civic Web: Online Politics*

and Democratic Values next to Jaron Lanier's *You Are Not a Gadget: A Manifesto*; or contrast the celebratory *Democracy.com: Governance in a Networked World* with Lee Segal's dour *Against the Machine: How the Web Is Undermining Culture and Destroying Our Civilization;* or try to align Beth Noveck's *Wiki Government: How Technology Can Make Government Better, Democracy Stronger, and Citizens More Powerful,* with *The Myth of Digital Democracy.*

36. A touching case in point is Aaron Swartz, the gifted young computer genius who committed suicide in 2012 after his arrest for hacking. In his "Guerilla Open Access Manifesto," Swartz wrote: "Providing scientific articles to those at elite universities in the First World, but not to children in the Global South? It's outrageous and unacceptable. . . . We need to fight for Guerilla Open Access." Cited by Noam Scheiber in "The Internet Will Never Save You: The Tragic Tale of Aaron Swartz," *New Republic*, March 12, 2013.

37. Newsom, *Citizenville*, p. 10.

38. The Editors of *The New Atlantis*, "Online Democracy," *The New Atlantis*, Number 4, Winter 2004, pp. 103–104. Hacking is the omnipresent problem, an issue even for those notorious Diebold voting machines.

39. As with so many other games and apps, traffic patterns on *Second Life* suggest that civic and educational goals, even when addressed by designers, are mostly ignored by users. A fundamental flaw of market approaches to politics, education, and culture is that they rely on the very market choices that politics, education, and culture are intended to modify—if consumer choices were not subjected to the markets they are trying to alter.

40. Rick Robinson, "Five Roads to a Smarter City," Sustainable Cities Collective, August 7, 2012. Robinson observes that there may be an impetus to act in new-build cities such as Masdar, or in cities regimented from the outside like Guangzhou in China, or in cities such as Rio facing challenges like preparing for the Olympics, where radical measures are needed but can provoke social unrest and civic protest as they have in Rio. The *Second Life* venue called Democracy Island was a creation of the same person, Beth Noveck, who worked with President Obama and then Prime Minister Cameron to incorporate notions of the civic web into their administrations. See note 51 below.

41. Jay G. Blumler and Stephen Coleman, *Realizing Democracy Online: A Civic Commons in Cybersapce*, Institute for Public Policy Research, 2001.

42. The London project lasted four years, but is now over.

43. From its website, http://wegf.org/: "Le World e.gov Forum est un espace de débat inédit pour les décideurs publics, élus, acteurs privés et membres de la société civile qui souhaitent échanger sur l'avenir de l'administration électronique et de l'e-démocratie. Les lauréats des trophées de l'e-démocratie et de l'e-administration ont été dévoilés le 13 octobre [2010] lors d'une cérémonie au ministère des Affaires étrangères et européennes."

44. Other sponsors and partners are the University of Toronto, IDRC (International Development Research Center), OECD (The Organization for Economic

Co-Operation and Development), UNEP (United Nations Environment Program), and Cities Alliance. See www.cityindicators.org.

45. Lee Siegel, *Against the Machine,* New York: Spiegel and Grau, 2008, p. 147.

46. Ibid., p.122.

47. Yves Sintomer, Carsten Herzberg, and Anja Roeke, "Participatory Budgeting in Europe: Potentials and Challenges," *International Journal of Urban and Regional Research*, Vol. 32, No. 1, March 2008, p. 166.

48. James Crabtree, "Civic Hacking: A New Agenda for e-Democracy," http://openDemocracy.net, June 1, 2007.

49. Newsom, *Citizenville*, p. xii.

50. So-called Groupware now offers a means toward supporting collaborative environments where human ICT-mediated interaction is the objective.

51. Beth Noveck, *Wiki Government: How Technology Can Make Government Better, Democracy Stronger, and Citizens More Powerful*, Brooking Institution Press, 2009. Noveck established one of the democratic "islands" on *Second Life* and worked in the Obama administration to contribute to the effort to realize some of the promise of the new technology as practice. In the 1990s, she worked with me on an online deliberative democracy application we called Unchat, which secured a patent.

52. Irving Wladawsky-Berger, cited by Noveck, *Wiki Government*, p. 145.

Profile 9. Teddy Kollek and Qadoura Moussa

1. Roger Friedland and Richard Hecht, *To Rule Jerusalem*, Berkeley: University of California Press, 2000, p. 2.

2. Thomas Friedman, "Teddy Kollek's Jerusalem," citing philosopher and rabbi David Harman, *New York Times*, August 4, 1985.

Chapter 10. Cultural Cities in a Multicultural World

1. Yo-Yo Ma, interview with Benjamin Barber on Interdependence, on the book website at www.ifmyaorsruledtheworld.org.

2. See, for example, the studies of the economic benefits of cities from France: Rafael Boix et al., "The Geography of Creative Industries in Europe: Comparing France, Great Britain, Italy and Spain," European Congress of the Regional Science Association International, 2010. Additional data can be found on London: *Creative Industries: The Essential Next Step for Your Business*, London and Partners, http://d2mns3z2df8ldk.cloudfront.net/l-and-p/assets/business/creative_industries_brochure.pdf; for Singapore, "Economic Contributions of Singapore's Creative Industries," Toh Mun Heng, Adrian Choo, Terence Ho, 2003, http://portal.unesco.org/pv_obj_cache/pv_obj_id_31D85D8BA91100FC3C1AE5DCB267E20D958F0200/filename/MICA+-+Economic+Contribution+Singapore+2003.pdf; for China, "Understanding the Creative Economy in China," http://martinprosperity.org/media/CreativeChina_EnglishVersion.pdf; more generally, see R. J. Phillips, "Arts Entrepreneurship and Economic

Development: Can Every City Be 'Austintatious'?" *Foundations and Trends in Entrepreneurship*, Vol. 6, No. 4, 2010, pp. 239–313.

3. Scott Timberg, "How Raw Capitalism Is Devouring American Culture," *Alternet*, November 10, 2012, www.alternet.org. Digital publishing and book buying are the obvious immediate culprits here, but the tyranny of profit drives corporations to monopoly and sits in the background.

4. Sharon Zukin, *The Culture of Cities*, Oxford: Blackwell, 1995, p. 294.

5. Dan Chiasson, *The New York Review of Books*, January 13, 2011.

6. For a full critical account see Benjamin R. Barber, *Consumed: How Markets Corrupt Children, Infantilize Adults and Swallow Citizens Whole*, New York: W. W. Norton, 2008.

7. A few artists like Grayson Perry manage to subvert for real—as he does in a medallion he struck recently called "Born to Shop," carrying the portrait of a haloed child and the words "Easy, Fast and Simple" (taken from my book *Consumed*, where I contrast these commercial ideals with "hard, slow and complex") in order to capture the paradoxical essence of the consumerist mentality that he also embroiders into wall hangings and paints onto his exquisite vases.

8. Benjamin Barber, International Society for the Performing Arts Keynote Lecture, New York, NY, January 2011.

9. BAM (Brooklyn Academy of Music) is America's oldest performing arts center: in its own self-description, it is a "multi-arts center located in Brooklyn, New York. For more than 150 years, BAM has been the home for adventurous artists, audiences, and ideas—engaging both global and local communities. With world-renowned programming in theater, dance, music, opera, film, and much more, BAM showcases the work of emerging artists and innovative modern masters."

10. Carey Perloff, "The Perloff Years: Part 1," *American Theater*, January 13, 2013.

11. Tachelas in Berlin, now something of a graffiti-strewn wreck and as much a tourist as an artistic center, is giving way to developers, as is an analogous community arts center (qua squat) in Paris called La Miroiterie, founded in 1999. Its story is told by Elvire Camus, "For Enclave of Rebel Artists, Much in Life Was Free, but Not Real Estate," *New York Times*, March 14, 2013. As artists themselves agree, such communities have a natural life and then vanish and reappear in new venues.

12. Perloff, "The Perloff Years."

13. Lionel Trilling, *The Liberal Imagination*, Oxford: Oxford University Press, 1982.

14. Walt Whitman, *By Blue Ontario's Shore, The Complete Poetry and Prose of Walt Whitman* (Deathbed Edition), Two volumes in one, ed. Malcolm Cowley, New York: Garden City Books, 1954, pp. 318–319.

15. In her *In a Different Voice*, Harvard University Press, 1982, Carol Gilligan challenges the manly and aggressive moral schemata set forth by traditionalist moralists such as Lawrence Kohlberg's *Stages of Moral Development*, New York: Harper & Row, 1984. Virginia Held offers an alternative to the

ethics of consequentialism in her *Ethics of Care*, New York: Oxford University Press, 2006.

16. Carol Gilligan, "Learning to See in the Dark: The Roots of Ethical Resistance," Lecture at M.I.T., July 24, 2009.

17. From an interview I conducted with Yo-Yo Ma at Tanglewood prior to the Fourth Interdependence Day in Casablanca, September 2006. The interview is on the book website.

18. A prize-winning 2010 German documentary, *Kinshasa Symphony*, chronicles the making of the orchestra.

19. From the ISPA website, www.ispa.org.

20. The Distinguished Artist award has gone to artists such as Martha Graham, Joseph Papp, Jerome Robbins, Helen Hayes, Rudolf Serkin, Robert Joffrey, Mikhail Baryshnikov, Benny Goodman, Arthur Mitchell, Dave Brubeck, Suzanne Farrell, Robert Brustein, Philip Glass, Anna Sokolow, Marcel Marceau, Pierre Boulez, Lukas Foss, Merce Cunningham, Eliot Carter, Twyla Tharpe, Max Roach, Mark Morris, Byungki Hwang, Akram Kahn, Michael Lewis, Eliza Gerner, Nicholas Hytner, Anna Deavere Smith, Grupo Corpo, the Emerson String Quartet, Lin Hwai-min, Gilberto Gil, Audra McDonald, Ravi Shankar, Van Cliburn, Tan Dun, Laurie Anderson, and Pina Bausch. I list some of them here as reminders of how global the reach, diverse the backgrounds, and unique the talents of artists are.

21. From an interview with David Baile, November 2012, on the book website. It is not an accident that David Baile serves on the executive committee of the Interdependence Movement, along with Rachel Cooper of the Asia Society and Jackie Davis of the Lincoln Center Library of Performing Arts.

22. From the website, http://ifacca.org/.

23. These organizations include, for example, CREATE, Collective Resources for the Arts and Talents Enrichment; Collective Resources; CINARS, International Exchange for the Performing Arts; MASA, Marche des Arts du Spectacle Africain; UK Arts International; Kulturkontakt Nord, Nordic Culture Point; International Federation of Musicians; Centre International des Civilisations Bantu; Fonds Soziokulture; Asia/Pacific Cultural Centre for UNESCO; AfricanColours; Africinfo.org; Arts in Africa; Portal Iberoamericaino de Gestion Cultural; Corporation of Yaddo; Creative Culture; Development Gateway; Festrival Media Corporation; and International Child Art Foundation.

24. The language is from UNESCO's online site summarizing the policies and declarations defining its cultural mission. Preservation of cultural heritage is another key goal.

25. The projects include the Slave Route project—Resistance, Liberty and Heritage; the Silk Road project; the intersectoral initiative (Rabindranath Tagore, Pablo Neruda, and Aimé Césaire) for a Reconciled Universal; the Arabia Plan; and the Roads to Independence—the African Liberation Heritage project.

26. A Center for Islamic Education was also established in Mecca Al-Mukarramah in the Kingdom of Saudi Arabia.

Profile IO. Antanas Mockus of Bogotá

1. Mockus on himself in Sondra Meyers, ed., *The Democracy Reader*, New York: International Debate Education Association, 2002, p. 79.

Chapter II. Citizens without Borders

1. Sara M. Evans and Harry C. Boyte, *Free Spaces: The Sources of Democratic Change in America*, Chicago: University of Chicago Press, 1992.

2. Seyla Benhabib, "Claiming Rights across Borders," *American Political Science Review*, November 2009, p. 2.

3. David Held et al., *Global Transformations: Politics, Economics and Culture*, Cambridge: Polity Press, 1999, p. 444. Also see David Held, *Democracy and the Global Order*, Cambridge: Polity Press, 1995.

4. In Benjamin Barber, *Strong Democracy: Participatory Politics for a New Age* (Princeton, NJ: Princeton University Press, 1984), I explored the potential for greater participation in an evolving American political system increasingly shaped by citizen movements and new digital media. My benchmark for enhanced participation in America's representative system was relative: citizens participating in some public affairs at least some of the time. By this standard, urban politics is rather more susceptible to strong democracy than national politics.

5. The Service Learning movement at Rutgers University in the 1990s, which I helped found, became one source for President Clinton's Corporation for National and Community Service for which I served President Clinton as an adviser.

6. For an early and enthusiastic account of the Porto Alegre experience, see Boaventura de Sousa Santos, "Participatory Budgeting in Porto Alegre: Toward a Redistributive Democracy," *Politics and Society*, Vol. 26, No. 4, December 1998, pp. 461–510. But though the Porto Alegre "founding" is widely heralded, we need to keep in mind that "the standard of living there is above the average of other Brazilian cities." Nonetheless, participatory budgeting "has contributed to this circumstance" and "provided for a reversal of priorities" in which, for the first time, primary health care for the poor, schools and nursery schools for the poor, and street asphalting and enhanced water supplies in poor neighborhoods have all received unprecedented budget support. See also Yves Sintomer, Carsten Herzberg, and Anja Rocke, "Participatory Budgeting in Europe: Potentials and Challenges," *International Journal of Urban and Regional Research*, Vol. 32, No. 1, March 2008, p. 166.

7. Participatory design invites citizens in the urban design process up front and gives them a stake in what might otherwise be the radical ideas of experts or politicians. A participatory design approach to the greening of New York City

intersections like Times Square and Herald Square might have made critics more tolerant and citizens more accepting of radical changes to the city's pedestrian and traffic patterns. For a critical discussion see Molly Sauter, "Participatory Design," MIT Center for Civic Media, Website, November 15, 2011; and Finn Kensing and Jeanette Bloomberg, Participatory Design: Issues and Concerns, *Computer Supported Cooperative Work*, Vol. 7, 1998, pp. 167–185.

8. Benjamin Goldfrank, "Lessons from Latin American Experience in Participatory Budgeting," presented at the Latin American Studies Association Meeting, San Juan, Puerto Rico, March 2006. In Portuguese, the process is called *orcaqmento participativo,* and it originated in Porto Alegre in 1990 as part of that city's experiments in democracy, including its role as a site of the antiglobalization conferences of the World Social Forum.

9. Sintomer, Herzberg, and Rocke, "Participatory Budgeting," p. 167.

10. De Sousa Santos, "Participatory Budgeting," p. 461.

11. Goldfrank, "Lessons," p. 2.

12. For a sympathetic compendium on the social forums, see Jackie Smith et al., *Global Democracy and the World Social Forums*, London: Paradigm Publishers, 2004.

13. See Elizabeth Whitman, "Participatory Budgeting Hits New York City," *The Nation*, April 16, 2012.

14. In Los Angeles these miniscule grants are given to district councils, which then engage citizens directly in the local budget allocation process. They also engage citizens in policy decision through town meetings and consultation.

15. From an author interview with Mayor Antonio Villaraigosa, November 8, 2012.

16. See James Fishkin's Deliberative Polling project referenced above.

17. Among the thousands of towns and cities now experimenting with participatory budgeting are, in Brazil, Porto Alegre and Belo Horizonte; in Germany, Berlin-Lichtenberg, Bergheim, Cologne, Hamburg, Leipzig, and Freiburg; in Italy, Modena, Rome, Bergamo, and Reggio Emilia; in Spain, Getafe, Cordoba, Albacete, Jun, Pereta Malaga, and Jerez; in Portugal, Lisbon; in Peru, Miraflores; in Korea, district Buk-Gu; in India, Pune; experiments are also under way in Africa, North America (Los Angeles, Chicago, and New York), Canada, Japan, and Australia. See http://democracyspot.tumblr.com/post/30115472781/participatory-budgeting-technology-innovation-in; and Sintomer, Herzberg, and Rocke, "Participatory Budgeting, Democracy Spot, September 2012."

18. Tiago Peixoto, "Beyond Theory: e-Participatory Budgeting and Its Promises for eParticipation," *European Journal of ePractice*, No. 7, March 2009, http://www.epractice.eu/files/7.5.pdf. PB Unit, "The role of new technology in participatory budgeting," Manchester: Participatory Budget Unit, 2007.

19. Peixoto, "Beyond Theory."

20. Jennifer Shkabatur, "Participatory Budgeting in Berlin-Lichtenberg," *Participedia.net*, January 7, 2010, http://participedia.net/en/cases/participatory-budgeting-berlin-lichtenberg.

21. I have had personal experience with Focolare, a Catholic movement active today in more than eighty countries. Focolare became an early and zealous supporter of the Interdependence Movement ten years ago, when its founder Chiara Lubich was still alive, and remains active with us today. Its monthly journal *Living City* offers a remarkable vision of world fellowship, religious tolerance, and global peace and justice that reflect its living practices as a community of interfaith fellowship.

22. See, for example, Sanjeev Khagram, James V. Rikasr, and Kathryn Sikkink, eds., *Restructuring World Politics: Transnational Social Movements, Networks, and Norms*, Minneapolis: University of Minnesota Press, 2004; Jackie Smith, *Social Movements for Global Democracy*, Baltimore: Johns Hopkins University Press, 2008; and Andrew Kuper, *Democracy Beyond Borders: Justice and Representation in Global Institutions*, Oxford: Oxford University Press, 2004. Peter Singer's *One World: The Ethics of Globalization*, New Haven: Yale University Press, 2002, offers the classic account of the ethics of a cosmopolitan world, while John Rawls offers the classic liberal account of a law-based international order in his *The Law of Peoples*, Cambridge: Harvard University Press, 1999. It is important to make clear that these are complementary rather than rival approaches to the notion of global governance advanced here. A global democratic system rooted in norms, social movements, NGOs, and law can only help ground and render effective an intercity governance system with a global mayors parliament capstone.

23. Khagram et al., *Restructuring World Politics*, p. 301.

24. Joseph Nye, "Globalisation's Democratic Deficit: How to Make International Institutions More Accountable," *Foreign Affairs*, Vol. 80, No. 4, July–August, 2001.

25. Kofi Annan's address to the World Economic Forum, Davos, Switzerland, January 1999, cited by the BBC World Service, "What Is Civil Society?" http://www.bbc.co.uk/worldservice/people/highlights/010705_civil.shtml.

26. Global Citizen portrays itself on its website (http://www.globalcitizen.org/) as "a tool to amplify and unite a generation's call for justice. It's a place for you to learn, and act, to bring an end to extreme poverty." But rather than offering citizen-to-citizen interaction and collaborations, which is difficult and time consuming, it focuses on big-name celebrity events, such as the concert in Central Park in the fall of 2012 that attracted tens of thousands of fans of Neil Young and Foo Fighters to what Global Citizen boasted was the "largest syndicated charity concern in online and broadcast history." As often happens, many of the young people drawn to the concert had little idea of the aims of its sponsors or about funds being raised for the underlying "Global Poverty Project." Global Citizen is powered by the Global Poverty Project, whose aims are worthy and global—addressing such issues as hunger, disease, and poverty ("we're a not-for-profit organization whose vision is much like yours: to live in a world without extreme poverty," it proclaims.)

27. According to its website, www.globalcitizens.org, the Global Citizen Network exists to promote "peace, justice and respect through cross-cultural understanding and global cooperation . . . while preserving indigenous cultures, traditions and ecologies." In practice it promotes community development projects in developing countries in which volunteers participate by building relationships with "members of our indigenous partner communities in the U.S. and abroad." It appears to charge fees and airfare to "volunteers," who are not required to have any specific skills (they can be families with children!), and thus gives the impression online of being a tour organization focused on "life-changing" learning experience for volunteers rather than a development NGO devoted to the solution of problems. Such groups specializing in what cynics call "volunteer vacations" are dismissed as exercises in "voluntourism" of a kind more likely to be featured in *Oprah Magazine* or *Budget Travel* than in reports of the United Nations Development Programme. I do not wish to be too skeptical here, other than in refusing to admit Citizens of Humanity (a brand name for Nordstrom blue jeans) or Benetton into the civic pantheon.

28. There are far more web-based than actual global citizen groups—many have a one-time entry, years old with no updates at all, indicating that they have come and gone without effect. A vice of the web is the ease with which a virtual organization can be "created" with no real-world correlate.

29. The United World Federalists organization was founded in 1947 in Asheville, North Carolina, by global idealists worried that the new United Nations would be no more effective than the defunct League of Nations. It brought together five existing world government groups: Americans United for World Government; World Federalists, U.S.A.; Student Federalists; Georgia World Citizens Committee; and the Massachusetts Committee for World Federation. In the mid-1970s it adopted its present name of World Federalist Association. But constituted by individuals rather than groups, government bodies, or nations, it obviously lacks impact, though it remains a powerful depository of ideals.

30. From the IPU Mission Statement, http://www.ipu.org/conf-e/124/strategy.pdf.

31. Another far more modest cross-border association is the Interdependence Movement, a campaign I founded, trying to advance an agenda of citizens without borders by challenging parochialism and changing how people think about globalization and the interconnectivity of the planet. See www.Interdependence Movement.org. The movement, sponsored by the NGO CivWorld, was from the outset an intercity organization that featured annual celebrations and forums in world cities including Rome, Paris, Casablanca, Mexico City, Brussels, Istanbul, Berlin, New York, Melbourne, and Los Angeles.

32. Benjamin Barber, "Occupy Wall Street—We Are What Democracy Looks Like!" *Huffington* Post, November 7, 2011, http://www.huffingtonpost.com

/benjamin-r-barber/occupy-wall-street-we-a_b_1079723.html?view=print&
comm_ref=false.

33. Despite the new START Treaty enhancing cooperation between the United
States and the Russian Federation on limiting Cold War nuclear weapons,
proliferation is off the radar of the nations that can do something about
it—except when it comes to supposedly rogue state adversaries like Iran and
North Korea. The Ford Foundation has closed its Peace and Security funding
department and the MacArthur Foundation no longer offers support for the
abolition of nuclear weapons.

34. Not every political thinker sees nations as inimical to democracy. Anxious
about the fate of Europe, and wedded to the role of sovereign states in
nurturing popular government, the French political theorist Pierre Manent
offers a robust critique of reducing politics to individual rights embodied in
"universal" transnational institutions. Pierre Manent, *Democracy without
Nations? The Fate of Self-Government in Europe*, Wilmington, DE: ISI Books,
2007.

35. Mireya Navarro, "City's Law Tracking Energy Use Yields Some Surprises,"
New York Times, December 25, 2012. Fewer than 2 percent of the city's buildings
account for as much as 45 percent of the energy expended by the entire building
stock of the city, suggesting how efficiently a cleanup plan focused on just a
handful of buildings might operate.

36. For details concerning Detroit and Pontiac, Michigan, see Steven Vaccino,
"Lessons for Detroit in a City's Takeover," *New York Times*, March 14, 2013.

37. "Freedom at Last: English Cities," *The Economist*, February 2, 2013.

38. Barry Yeoman, "Rebel Towns," *The Nation*, February 4, 2013.

39. Ibid. In 2011 a suit was filed by young people in San Francisco accusing the
American government of failing to protect the earth for generations unborn,
rooted in a doctrine of "public trust" going back to Roman times. Again, the
intent of the case seems political rather than legal. See Felicity Barringer, "Suit
Accuses U.S. Government of Failing to Protect Earth for Generations Unborn,"
New York Times, May 5, 2011.

40. See the Community Environmental Legal Defense Fund website, http://
www.celdf.org/, for details. For the Santa Monica ordinance, see http://
therightsofnature.org/general/rights-of-nature-on-the-santa-monica-city
-council-agenda/.

41. Wayne LaPierre, the NRA's executive vice president, regularly argues that the
sovereignty of the Constitution (his reading of the Fourth Amendment) trumps
the right of states and cities to resist. Indeed, he suggests it is "bizarre to see
Mayor Bloomberg make virtually the same argument that Eugene 'Bull'
Connor used to enforce segregation laws in Birmingham 50 year ago." See
"Mayors Against Your Rights," *America's 1st Freedom* [the NRA magazine],
January 2012.

42. Reihan Salam, "Brandon Fuller on City-Based Visas," *National Review Online*, August 16, 2012, http://www.nationalreview.com/agenda/314256/brandon-fuller-city-based-visas-reihan-salam.

43. Richard Florida, "The Case for City-Based Visa," September 4, 2012, http://www.theatlanticcities.com/jobs-and-economy/2012/09/case-city-based-visas/2946/.

44. I suspect the issue of facilitating visas for immigrants with skills is more easily solved inside the framework of national laws.

45. In this spirit, the state of North Carolina is planning to give some young immigrants driver's licenses, although its intention to mark such license with a pink stripe appears to some as a kind of Scarlet Letter that taints the intentions of the plan and risks "humiliating" the 15,000 who have applied. See Kim Severson, "North Carolina to Give Some Immigrants Driver's Licenses, With a Pink Stripe," *New York Times*, March 6, 2013.

46. The Declaration affirms that "whenever any Form of Government becomes destructive of these ends ["Life, Liberty and the Pursuit of Happiness," but also "Safety"], it is the Right of the People to alter or to abolish it, and to institute new Government."

47. Even the Declaration cautions that "Governments long established should not be changed for light and transient causes" and goes on to enumerate a "long train of abuses and usurpations," pointing to "absolute Despotism" that alone justifies rebellion. Democratic states extracting taxes from cities under their jurisdiction and neglecting sustainable environmental policies wished for by urban citizens hardly meets this high standard!

48. In Profile 6, I note above how Yury Luzhkov, Moscow's long-term mayor, was finally ousted from office by an irritated President Medvedev, ostensibly because he (and/or his wife) was corrupt and seemed to favor Putin over him, but also because Luzhkov represented an alternative seat of authority with which the Kremlin preferred not to have to deal (Putin did nothing to reverse the mayor's dismissal upon regaining the Russian presidency). Clifford J. Levy, "Mayor's Fall Doesn't Settle Who Rules in Russia," *New York Times*, September 28, 2010.

Chapter 12. A Global Parliament of Mayors

1. Some mayors worry that the intercity responsibilities they already shoulder, along with the discretionary business of governing globally, may distract them from the vital business of governing locally in the name of which they were elected. Clover Moore, the mayor of Sydney, Australia, warns that given that "the primary responsibility of mayors is governing their cities; it would be difficult and impractical for them to devote the time and commitment that a global parliament of mayors would require," and other mayors like Naheed Nenshi of Calgary have expressed similar concerns. Yet as Moore acknowl-

edges, when we review the networks, alliances, partnerships, and informal linkages highlighted in Chapter 5—networks Sydney and other cities have already forged—it is apparent how far we have come. And how inviting taking the next step is. For defined by their problems and challenges, as Mayor Bloomberg has observed, "there's not much difference, whether it's a city here or a city there. . . . Hanoi or Singapore . . . they have the same problems." See our Mayors Survey on the website for more.

2. See www.cityprotocol.com.
3. Andrew Stevens and Jonas Schorr, "Reforming the World's Cities Networks," April 18, 2012, http://globalurbanist.com/2012/04/18/city-networks-2.
4. See Benjamin Barber, *Strong Democracy: Participatory Politics for a New Age*, 20th anniversary edition, Princeton, NJ: Princeton University Press, 2004.
5. Roughly 20 percent of Americans, mostly rural, can outvote the other 80 percent of the country, largely urban, in a Senate where rural votes are weighted by the two senators per state regardless of population, and where the additional skewing effect of the filibuster (Senate Rule 22) allows only forty-one senators to effectively overturn a majority's vote, often paralyzing action by the majority.
6. Mayors Survey. See also Wolfgang Schuster, Working Paper, *Governing in Partnership*, 2012, and his study of development and sustainability in Stuttgart, *Nachhaltige Staedte—Lebensraume der Zukunft*, Munich: Oekum Verlag, 2013.
7. Edmund Burke, Speech to the Electors of Bristol, 1774. (The formula is wise, but flies in the face of the more popular and "democratic" mandate notion of representation, in which a chosen member is but a delegate and mouthpiece for the views of his constituents, and parliament is—American style—a congeries of conflicted interests. By the by, Burke was not reelected!) My own view is that Burke is a democrat, if measured by a greater representation across generations.
8. Edmund Burke, *Reflections on the Revolution in France*, London: J. Dodsley, 1791, pp. 133–134.
9. Mayor Won-soon Park of Seoul convened a small preliminary meeting of several individual and urban representatives in early 2013 to speak concretely about a possible planning path that could lead to a convening of a mayors parliament. Further meetings are scheduled in New York and Hamburg.
10. See the work of James S. Fishkin on deliberative voting. As described by the Center on Deliberative Polling, "Deliberative Polling is a technique which combines deliberation in small group discussions with scientific random sampling to provide public consultation for public policy and for electoral issues. A number of Deliberative Polls have been conducted in various countries around the world, including China, Japan, Britain, Australia, Denmark, and in the US, some national and some local."

11. Burke, *Reflections*, pp. 133–134.

12. Stuttgart, Mayors Survey.

13. Jim Clifton, "Forget Washington—Cities Will Win or Lose America," *The Chairman's Blog*, November 14, 2012. http://thechairmansblog.gallup.com/2012/11/forget-washington-cities-will-win-or.html.

INDEX